Liberties Lost

Caribbean Indigenous Societies and Slave Systems

Hilary McD. Beckles

Verene A. Shepherd

CAMBRIDGE
UNIVERSITY PRESS

CAMBRIDGE
UNIVERSITY PRESS

Shaftesbury Road, Cambridge CB2 8EA, United Kingdom

One Liberty Plaza, 20th Floor, New York, NY 10006, USA

477 Williamstown Road, Port Melbourne, VIC 3207, Australia

314–321, 3rd Floor, Plot 3, Splendor Forum, Jasola District Centre, New Delhi – 110025, India

103 Penang Road, #05–06/07, Visioncrest Commercial, Singapore 238467

Cambridge University Press is part of the University of Cambridge.

It furthers the University's mission by disseminating knowledge in the pursuit of education, learning and research at the highest international levels of excellence.

www.cambridge.org
Information on this title: www.cambridge.org/9780521435444

© Cambridge University Press & Assessment 2004

First published 2004

20 19 18 17

Printed in Great Britain by CPI Group (UK) Ltd, Croydon CR0 4YY

A catalogue record for this publication is available from the British Library

ISBN 978-0-521-43544-4 Paperback

Dedication

This book is dedicated to Norma Joy Lazarus (d. 1982)
and to
The people of Haiti on the occasion of the bicentenary of Haitian independence
(1804–2004)

Contents

Map of the Caribbean

Introduction

'If you know your history, then you would know where you're coming from; then you wouldn't have to ask me: who the hell do you think I am.'
(Bob Marley)

The audience for this book

This book, like its companion volume, *Freedoms Won*, aims to help teachers and students in their journeys through the Caribbean history syllabus offered by the Caribbean Examinations Council (CXC). The two books accommodate the entire CXC history programme, including the new syllabus in Caribbean/Atlantic history known as CAPE (Caribbean Advanced Proficiency Examinations).

Both volumes will be of value to students and teachers engaged in the Cambridge 'A' level syllabus on the post-slavery history of the Caribbean. They should also be of use to college/university students participating in foundation courses in Caribbean history, as well as to the general reader seeking basic information on the history of the region.

The focus of this book

The indigenous Caribbean people

We begin with a focus on the indigenous Caribbean societies, and move on to the slave systems that were built by European colonisers. The first Caribbean people created societies that were complex in culture. Some of these societies shared common beliefs and practices. The development of these societies was undermined when the Europeans arrived in the Caribbean, beginning with Christopher Columbus's mission of 1492. After this, six European nations fought the indigenous people and won control of territory in the region.

Europe's Caribbean project

Spain, France, England, Holland and Denmark had the greatest impact upon Caribbean societies. Sweden was a minor coloniser and did much less to reshape the region. These imperial powers established and developed large- and small-scale settlements and trade networks. They succeeded despite protest and violent opposition from the indigenous people who tried to protect their lands, liberty and lives by all the means available to them. In general, the resistance of indigenous people was not as effective as intended; the result was the overthrow and reorganisation of the traditional Caribbean world.

European settlement and rivalry

An important outcome of the European settlement was that it militarily defeated, enslaved, and mass murdered the indigenous people. A few communities survived this genocide. They are now scattered mostly within the interior areas of Guiana and Suriname, in parts of Central America, and in the Eastern Lesser Antilles. They are still an oppressed and marginalised people, who still seek respect for their cultural identity and independence.

The rapid destruction of indigenous communities in the Greater Antilles and their continued armed struggle in the Lesser Antilles, meant that the European settlers did not have the quantity of servile labour force they desired. So, the European settlers used two main systems of labour bondage – they imported indentured servants from the 'old world' of Europe and they used Africans as chattel enslaved.

The transatlantic trade in enslaved Africans

By the end of the 17th century, European indentured workers were no longer so important. Now the Europeans mainly used enslaved Africans as the labour system with which they exploited the Caribbean. Over 12 million Africans were imported into colonial 'America 'to achieve this end.

The mass enslavement of Africans in the East Atlantic islands happened before Columbus' voyage to the Caribbean in the West Atlantic. The mass enslavement was a westward movement. It began in the mid-15th century with the establishment of large-scale chattel slavery in Madeira, an island in the East Atlantic. Here, Europeans built sugar plantations that became a model for the rest of the Caribbean. So the Madeira model was a launch pad for the wealth generating, life destroying machine - the Caribbean plantation.

Sugar and slavery

By the end of the 18th century, sugar plantations and African enslavement dominated the social and economic life of the Caribbean. The main driving force was the search for profits. In most places, the mining, coffee, cotton, cattle and tobacco industries were secondary to the main export staple, sugar.

The enslaved African population carried out many different tasks and experienced slavery in different ways. Many were artisans, fisherfolk, sailors, overseers, domestics, vendors, sugar technologists (boilers and distillers), soldiers, lumberjacks, builders, and entertainers. The vast majority, however, worked on sugar, cotton and coffee plantations, cattle and timber farms, and mines.

The type of work they did influenced the life of the enslaved populations in important ways, for example, their general health, life expectancy and social life. The enslaved were overworked, malnourished and physically and mentally brutalised. Poor health, physical exhaustion and psychological trauma contributed to the fact that more African people died than were born. So for most of the period of slavery, the enslaved population could not increase naturally.

Enslaved workers were constantly badly affected by a range of nutritionally related diseases. The major killers were fevers and dysentery. Poor nutrition meant that they could not easily defend themselves from these diseases. As a result the death rate of the African communities was far higher than the death rate of the White communities.

African culture and community life

Slavery did not stop Africans from surviving. They tried to survive by creating an independent social and economic life of their own. They demanded the 'free' use of leisure time, which they filled with activities that ranged from entertainment to selling goods, to family engagements. These activities came to symbolise the spirit of freedom that shaped their day-to-day resistance to slavery.

The work of enslaved Africans produced money and profits for their enslavers. The Caribbean economy included world trade and investment networks, and it generated a lot of money for colonisers. Much of this wealth was exported capital and it contributed greatly to the funding of industrial growth in Western Europe.

However the transatlantic trade in enslaved Africans and the wealth it produced in the Caribbean for colonisers led to the long-term economic decline of Western Africa. For over 300 years the Caribbean world was the centre of Europe's global empires, the centre of a system of trade, finance and production.

Revolt and resistance

But life in the Caribbean was very insecure and unstable. Europeans fought each other for the largest share of loot, trade, power and status. The region was a theatre of war, both on land and at sea. It was known for its violence and turmoil. Africans fought for their freedom and so added to the violence that shaped social life everywhere. They were determined to uproot slavery and this meant that there was constant conflict between Africans and Europeans.

Between 1791 and 1793 the enslaved people in the French colony of St Domingue won their freedom after a bloody civil war. Once they had won their social freedom they demanded political freedom from France. In 1804 they declared national independence and renamed the colony Haiti – the indigenous name for the island on which the nation emerged. Boukman Dutty, from Jamaica, and then Toussaint L'Ouverture and others led this freedom revolution. But it was Jean Jacques Dessalines who emerged as the country's first president. Haiti became the second independent republic in the 'New world', following the United States of America. So Haiti was the first Caribbean nation.

The impact of Haiti on slavery everywhere was profound. It affected both the pro-slavery interests and the anti-slavery campaign. Slavery was deeply weakened. Black people all over the region tried to follow the example of armed self-liberation. The region became more unstable than ever as the number of rebellions increased.

After Haiti the rebellions of enslaved workers were more effectively planned and organised than those before. The rebellions were expressions of the growing desire for freedom among women and men, skilled and unskilled, old and young. The women especially forged links across generations, between those who worked in the fields and in the planters' households. They used culture and religion to strengthen unity and to raise consciousness.

In the end, the slave system was brought down by a combination of anti-slavery rebellion in the Caribbean, the economic decline of the region's sugar industry, and the increasing effectiveness of European parliamentary and public anti-slavery politics.

Caribbean emancipation

It took nearly 100 years to complete the process of general emancipation. It began with the self-liberation of Africans in Haiti in 1793 and ended with the abolition of slavery in the Spanish colonies in the 1880s. The process of emancipation was a major political and social undertaking by Africans, Europeans, and people of mixed racial origins. They all had a stake in uprooting the horrid slave system from modern life.

So, this book tries to summarise, and in some places narrate and illuminate, the literature on these aspects of Caribbean history. It relies upon the work of many historians whose published research informs our understanding of the subject. We have not always given the names of all these colleagues but we would like to think that what is presented here is in part a celebration of their efforts.

We have kept references and quotations to a minimum to facilitate easy reading. However, we take full responsibility for any shortcomings that have resulted. Finally, we hope that this text will serve to stimulate some students to follow the historian's craft or at least become historians in spirit.

Acknowledgements

Several debts were accumulated during the researching and writing of this book. We would like to acknowledge our research assistants, all of them graduates of the University of the West Indies: Jaset Anderson, Dalea Bean, Symone Betton, Eldon Birthwright, Henderson Carter, Cavell Francis, Shanette Geohagen, Karen Graham, Tannya Guerra, Georgia Hamilton, Natalie McCarthy, Kerry Ann Morris, Nicole Plummer, Coral Purvil, Ahmed Reid, Mitzie Reid, Michelle Salmon, Pedro Welch and Vernon White.

We would also like to thank our students at UWI who read Caribbean history courses. They debated in seminar many issues raised in the text and provided valuable and stimulating feedback. Teachers and students who attended the Trinidad and Tobago History Teachers Association Workshop at the University of the West Indies, St. Augustine Campus, in November 1998, also debated the content of several draft chapters. Their criticism helped to shape the final text, and for this assistance we are appreciative.

Reviewers of the manuscript made many important observations and offered valuable suggestions for the overall improvement of the work. Their comments and criticisms were essential in helping us to craft the final text.

Carol Thompson, Grace Franklin and Grace Jutan were very kind and patiently assisted with the preparation of the various drafts of the manuscript. We thank them most sincerely.

Finally, we thank our families for their support in the completion of this project

H.McD.B./V.A.S.

The publisher and authors are also grateful to the following for permission to reproduce images:

Courtesy of the National Library of Jamaica: 5 (top left and right), 6 (top and bottom), 7, 8, 9, 10, 11, 12, 13, 14 (left and top right), 15, 19, 34, 35, 37, 39, 40, 41, 42, 47, 48, 54, 59, 61, 62, 76, 78, 80, 83, 84, 85, 87, 91, 92 (top), 103, 104, 105, 106, 114, 115, 116, 122, 123, 126, 128, 129 (top and bottom), 130, 139 (left), 140, 141, 143, 145, 146, 147, 151, 156 (left and top right), 158, 159, 160, 162, 163, 171 (top), 174, 175, 177, 178, 179, 186, 187, 194, 197 (top and bottom), 198, 199, 201, 208, 213; Archivo Oronoz: 90; www.gettyimages/Gallo Images: 31, 187, 222, 223; DDB Stock Photography: 81, 93; 2003 Mark van Aardt/Fotozone: 10; Photo Access: 10, 18; INPRA: 22 (bottom right), 23, 45, 131, 170, 206, 207 (top and bottom right), 214 (bottom left and right); DASPHOTO: 20, 46, 132, 165, 216; Werner Forman Archive: 21 (top left, National Museum of Anthropology and right, NJ Saunders), 22 (NJ Saunders), 24 (top left, Museum für Volkerkunde, Berlin), 25 (top left, NJ Saunders and bottom right, Museum für Volkerkunde, Berlin), 29, 30, 70, 71 (National Museum, Lagos), 72 (British Museum), 73, 86, 92 (bottom); Dennis Ranston: 203; courtesy of the John Carter Brown Library at Brown University: 26, 27, 95, 111, 112, 119, 139 (right), 171 (bottom), 173, 188; Verene Shepherd: 109; Carl DeC. Branch: 191

Maps on the following pages by Maré Liebenberg: vi, 2, 3, 4, 7, 16, 32, 33, 34, 38, 44, 52, 58, 72, 85, 176, 181, 191, 196

Lyrics of songs:
For the songlines that preface chapters 3 to 13, we gratefully acknowledge permission from the Bob Marley Foundation.

Cover image: Sale of slave woman and her children. Benoit. Courtesy of the John Carter Brown Library at Brown University.

Every attempt has been made to locate copyright holders for all material in this book. The publishers would be glad to hear from anyone whose copyright has been unwittingly infringed.

Chapter 1

The indigenous Caribbean people

'Fighting on arrival, fighting for survival ...'
(Bob Marley)

Three thousand years before the Christian era a distinct Caribbean civilisation was established. These civilisations had a strong influence on the peoples of the ancient world. They, together with other communities, helped shape the way society was organised, how work, money and the economy were planned, and how human culture was created and developed. Together with their continental cousins in Mexico, Guatemala, Peru and elsewhere, the ancient Caribbean communities engaged with and used their environment in dynamic and creative ways. The Caribbean, then, was home to an old and ancient cultural civilisation that continues to shape and inform our present-day understanding and identity.

> In this chapter we will learn about:
> 1. The culture of indigenous Caribbean people
> 2. The Ciboney
> 3. The Taino
> 4. The Kalinago
> 5. Continental cousins: Maya, Aztec, and Inca

1

1 The culture of indigenous Caribbean people

It has taken over 7,000 years for a Caribbean civilisation and culture to evolve. Throughout its history different groups of people like the Taino, Kalinago and Maya brought a range of beliefs, practices and traditions to create the foundations of the rich Caribbean culture that still exists today.

Researchers generally agree that before 1492 the populations of the Caribbean region were very large. They say that the islands were home to between 5 and 13 million people with a range of cultures. When the Europeans arrived in the Caribbean, they caused the devastation and decline of these cultures.

Once the Spanish-funded explorer, Christopher Columbus from Genoa in Italy, crossed the Atlantic Ocean in 1492, he linked the Caribbean and the Americas, Europe and Africa. He triggered what is now known as the wider Atlantic civilisation. The East and West Atlantic came together as one bigger and broader community. In the East Atlantic were the so-called 'Old Worlds' of Europe, Africa and the islands off its coast. In the West Atlantic was the so-called 'New World'.

The Columbus journey ensured that indigenous Caribbean cultures were systematically linked with African and European cultures. Over the next 200 years, from 1492 to 1692, one effect of this was that the indigenous Caribbean people were almost wiped out. Hundreds of thousands of people died because of war, disease, social problems and poverty. Within 20 years of the Spanish arrival, for example, the Taino population of the island of Hispaniola was reduced from about 3-4 million people to about 60,000.

The arrival of the earliest inhabitants

Who were the ancient ancestors of Caribbean civilisation? This question is the subject of lively archaeological research in the Caribbean. Since the 16th century historians have assumed that the indigenous people of what is now called the American continent, entered this huge land from elsewhere. Two arguments are given for why people migrated or moved to the American continent. Both arguments are based on the belief that a mass of Asian people crossed either a landbridge or an icebridge.

a. The first argument is that 25,000 years ago, what we now call the Bering Straits was above sea level and formed the Beringia landbridge. Then 25,000 years ago, during the Ice Age people from the area now known as Mongolia in northeastern Asia, crossed the Beringia landbridge from Siberia into the American landmass at Alaska. It is believed that they were either fleeing the icy conditions or they were chasing the migratory herds of deer on which they survived.

b. The second argument is that there was no landbridge 25,000 years ago but that there was an icebridge between Siberia and Alaska. This argument says that the Asians crossed this bridge and then followed the corridor between the Alaskan and Canadian mountains into the Canadian plains, pushing south to the very end of the continent.

Now however, biological scientists say that most of the major groups who

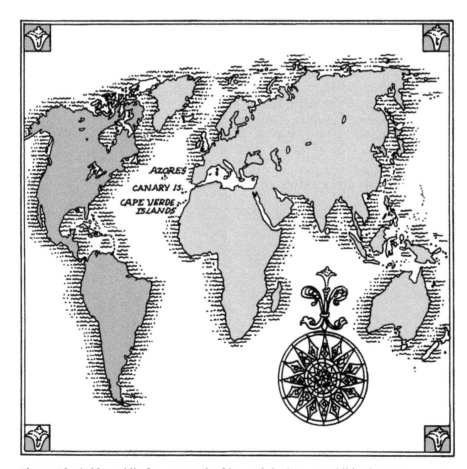

Fig 1.1 The 'Old World' of Europe and Africa and the 'New World' in the West

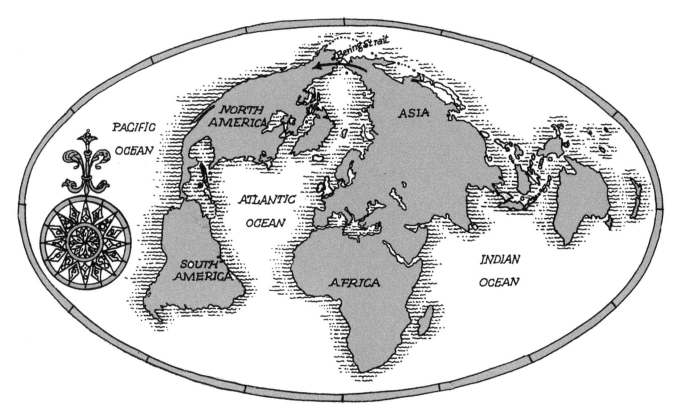

Fig.1. 2 The movement of people from Asia across the Bering Strait to the American landmass

came to occupy the American continent are genetically related and are indeed very similar. However they classify the Eskimos in the north as a separate group related more to the people of western China.

So, the Beringia landbridge/icebridge arguments suggest that there was an Asian migration 25,000 years ago. This rules out the possibility of prehistoric human settlement on the continent before this time. This is now a very debatable argument and has recently been shaken by archaeological excavation in South America that suggests that prehistoric human development did exist on the American continent long before this migration.

This recent research shows that people settled in the American continent possibly millions of years ago, rather than simply 25,000 years ago. Scientists are, however, still not sure whether one million years ago the continents of South America and Africa were joined – allowing for prehistoric humans to migrate across continents.

Prehistoric human development in the Caribbean

Significant research has been done, and much is ongoing, that seeks to identify the origins of Caribbean habitation. An archaeological excavation in southwest Trinidad has suggested that people settled in the areas as far back as 5000-3000 BC to 7,000 years ago. Archaeological evidence shows that these first inhabitants ate shellfish and made bone and stone tools.

Archaeologists in Cuba have found similar types of evidence that show human settlement in about 2050 BC. There is evidence too from sites in Santo Domingo that suggests community development as far back as 5000 BC.

It is likely that these people entered the islands from Central America, as the evidence is very similar to that found in Nicaragua.

In about 1000 BC the earliest inhabitants of the Caribbean were joined by another major group of migrants who travelled north from the Venezuelan mainland in South America, and entered the Caribbean Sea at Trinidad. Researchers describe this group of people as meso-Indians. They had a more advanced social structure than previous groups and they used advanced agricultural technologies.

They travelled through the islands and reached the northern Caribbean where they established large settlements. There is no doubt that they were skilled navigators, great explorers of new lands and open seas, and builders of large communities.

The archaeological evidence at the sites of these early Caribbean communities shows that they did not use

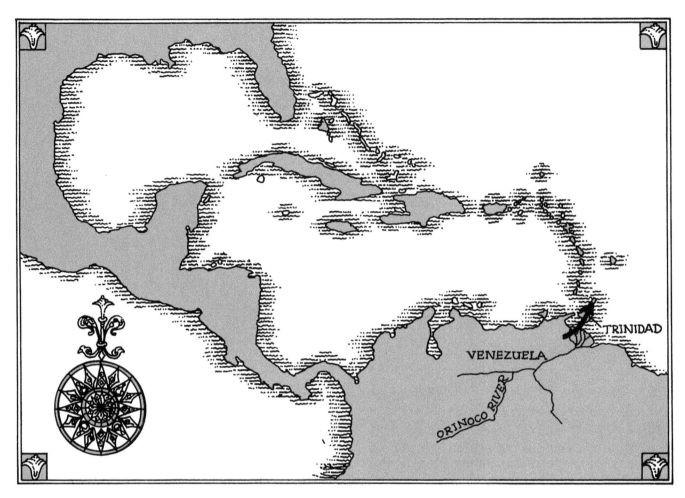

Fig 1.3 Migration from the Venezuelan mainland into the Caribbean

agriculture or farming to survive. Rather, they relied upon hunting animals like the manatee; fishing for turtles, crustaceans and a range of reef fish; and gathering wild vegetables. Their tools were made of bone, wood, shells, and stone. They knew the art and science of pottery-making and their ceramic work that was found in the Dominican Republic resembles work found at a site in Colombia.

Historians have named these people the Ciboney. The name was used in the mid-16th century by the Spanish priest Las Casas, who came across them in Cuba and Hispaniola. The Ciboney, the Guanahacabibe, lived as nomadic hunter-gatherers, dwelled in caves and gullies and used the sea for food more than they used the land.

However despite the research of archaeologists, we still do not have a clear picture of the cultural identities, social relations and belief systems of these first inhabitants. We know that they built walls, assembled large stones for cultural purposes, and developed irrigation systems, but we still do not fully understand exactly for which purpose these structures were used. Nonetheless, there is enough

evidence to show that they made up the foundation societies of the Caribbean world and that the Caribbean had an ancient culture long before the Christian era.

So we have seen that the cultural pillars of Caribbean civilisation date back to the times of other known ancient cultures such as those of Pharaonic Egypt and that of the classical Greek world of Europe. In 1492 Columbus and subsequent colonisers, established the contact between Europeans and the indigenous Caribbean settlers.

The European explorers met the Ciboney or Guanahacabibe, whom they said were wild and 'as fleet as deer'. They also met the three major Caribbean groups whom they labelled Arawaks, Caribs and Maya, although these groups had their own names to define and identify themselves. Historians now believe, for example, that the people called Arawaks and Caribs were the Taino and Kalinago respectively. In recent times, the term 'Taino' was used to define the Arawakan speaking group, and now appears widespread in the literature.

chapter 1 | *The indigenous Caribbean people*

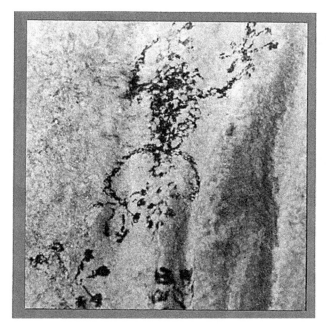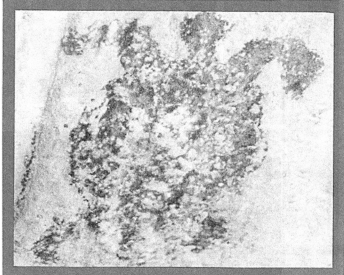

Fig 1.4 Pre-Columbian cave art found in Mountain River Cave, St Catherine, Jamaica

2 The Ciboney

The earliest and smallest known group of Caribbean inhabitants was the Ciboney, who were nomad hunter-gatherers. They used the Caribbean space in creative ways, taking from it only what they required to survive, and making only minimum changes to it. They did not store, distribute or trade any extra or surplus food.

Origins

Initially, archaeologists suggested that the Ciboney in Cuba and the Bahamas migrated from the south via the Lesser Antilles. However no matching sites were found in these places. Later on archaeologists suggested that the Ciboney entered the Caribbean through the Florida peninsula. However, insufficient evidence remained to support this theory. The most popular view now is that the Ciboney were from pre-farming cultures that entered the Antilles from South America, not as one ethnic group, but as waves of different migrants over a very long period of time.

Technology

Their technological development was not advanced. They did not make textiles for clothing, or ceramics for domestic or ritualistic religious purposes. The Ciboney went naked and did not use any complex domestic utensils. They did not make weapons and had no military organisation or army. Their simple political organisation was expressed in nomadic bands, and there is no evidence of any enforced social hierarchy. In other words, people did not have different status in the group.

As hunter-gatherers, the Ciboney did not live in a village and use agriculture and industrial technologies. They did not even cultivate cassava, upon which all the ethnic groups in the Caribbean, Central and South America relied heavily for survival. When they first came across the Taino and Kalinago groups they recognised them as newcomers to their world. However they could not defend themselves against these groups.

European sources from the time of Columbus suggested that the numerous and technologically developed Taino dominated the Ciboney. In battle, the Ciboney threw stones and used wooden clubs. This shows that their society was not organised for modern military activity. In all the islands they occupied they were outnumbered and marginalised by the Taino – in Jamaica, Hispaniola, Bahamas, and Puerto Rico.

3 The Taino

The material culture of the Taino and Kalinago was broadly similar. However, they came from two language groups: those who spoke Arawakan and those who spoke Cariban. Both language groups were widespread throughout the Caribbean and in the northern South America. They were a highly developed agricultural people. Their industrial technology in textiles and

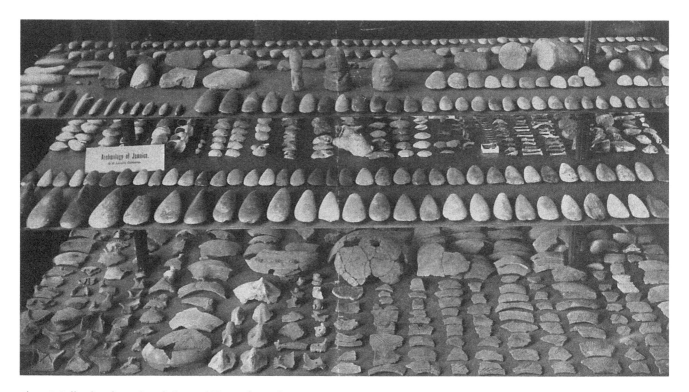

Fig 1.5 Collection from the Kitchen Middens of Jamaica:
Upper shelf – stone pendants, stone gods, spindle shape celts, stone axes
Middle shelf – celts (axes), shells and bones of fish and coney
Lower shelf – fragments of pottery. At rear are baking slabs used for baking cassava bread

ceramics was of the same standard as that of the rural communities of Asia and Europe.

Origins

Archaeologists have traced the cultural origins of the Taino back to the lower Orinoco. They arrived in the Caribbean through the Venezuela-Trinidad gateway in about 300 BC. After that several waves of the Taino groups entered the Caribbean. They were expert seafarers, and quickly navigated their way up the island chain until they reached the Greater Antilles where they formed the largest communities in about 250 AD.

Between 250 AD and about 1000 AD many different Taino groups entered the Greater Antilles and established themselves as large communities. They soon took over from the Ciboney as the main cultural force within the evolving Caribbean civilisation. In time the Ciboney were completely displaced, marginalised and weakened in Cuba, Hispaniola, Puerto Rico and, to a lesser extent, the Bahamas.

Culture and identity

Archaeologists have identified two separate Taino groups by analysing their ceramic techniques and styles. They have classified the first Taino to arrive in the Caribbean

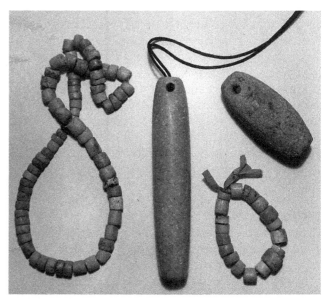

Fig 1.6 Examples of Saladoid and Barrancoid ceramics

chapter 1 | The indigenous Caribbean people

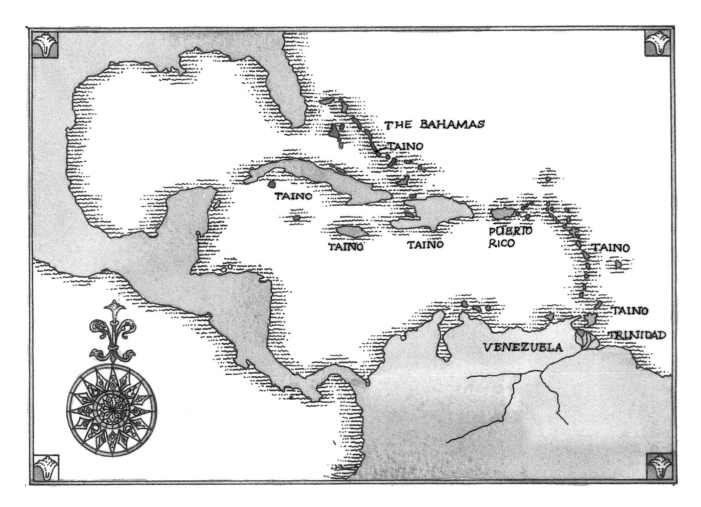

Fig 1.7 Areas of Taino settlement

around 300 BC as the Saladoid culture group. They were
known for their common use of white-on-red artistic
pottery decorations. Archaeologists have classified the
second Taino to arrive as the Barrancoid culture group.
Their pottery styles were more varied and less distinctive,
and they were more widespread throughout the Lesser
and Greater Antilles than Saladoid pottery.

Since the 1980s more and more has been written about
Taino society and economy. The archaeological work of
Irving Rouse, and the ecological and geographical work of
David Watts, added considerably to our knowledge. We
now know that the Taino constructed their settlements
throughout the Caribbean in a range of different
environments: rainforests, mountain valleys, dry, open
plateaux and to a lesser extent, on the savanna
grasslands.

Taino culture was similar across the region. Whether
communities lived in the Lesser Antilles or the Greater
Antilles, they shared a common language, had similar
social and hierarchical systems in their groups, and used

Fig 1.8 Taino loading a canoe

the same technologies in agriculture, canoe building, ceramics, house construction, and in the fine arts, especially to produce gold ornaments. The Europeans of Columbus' times were genuinely impressed and fascinated by their sophisticated industrial technology in textiles, ceramics and, of course, the gold craft.

Taino economic planning and production

David Watts has shown that the Taino economy consisted of three main ways of producing enough food for their survival: conuco cultivation, house gardens and fishing, hunting and gathering.

Conuco cultivation

Conuco cultivation was an organised system of large-scale agriculture that produced starch-based foods and foods rich in sugar. This cultivation was based on the planting of roots, seeds and vegetables. The Taino rotated their crops to make sure that staple foods were available through all the seasons.

Watts explains that under this system it was normal for each family to have a conuco, or small farm plot, which was close to the village, usually a few miles away. Family members cleared the land by felling trees and burning bushes and prepared for the tilling and planting process.

A family would cultivate a conuco intensively for 2-3 years. When the soil was no longer fertile and production levels fell, the family would move on to a new, fresh plot. The old conuco would be left uncultivated for about the same length of time (2-3 years) before it was brought back into production. It was only later that the Taino developed the technology of fertilising soils with animal and vegetable manure. Shortly before the European arrival, fertilisers were widely used. Before this, traditionally the Taino believed that heavily used soils became infertile and unproductive because of some magic or religious forces at work.

The main crop that Taino farmers produced on their conucos was manioc, or cassava as it was known. Throughout the Caribbean this crop dominated agricultural activity. It grew well on most Caribbean soils, whether acidic or alkaline, and yields were high in both dry and wet conditions. Each year the farmers harvested two cassava crops.

There were two main varieties of the cassava plant; one was called the sweet cassava, and the other the 'poison' or 'bitter' cassava. It was called this because it was bitter in taste and contained cyanic acid, which was highly poisonous. The sweet cassava plant was not as high in yield as the 'bitter' plant. Its tubers were much softer and

sweeter but both could be harvested between 5-8 months after planting.

Taino women knew how to process the tubers of the 'bitter' cassava and to remove the acid and much of the bitterness. They grated the tubers, then repeatedly washed and packed them together until the poison acids were strained out. They then dried the grated substance and ground it into flour.

Fig 1.9 *Mealing stones used by Taino to grind maize and cassava*

The Taino women also made various types of bread with cassava flour, some unleavened, some sweetened. Cassava breads and cakes were the staples of Taino people. They generally did not use the sweet cassava to make flour. Rather, because of its sweetness and softness they boiled and ate it with fish. Sometimes they roasted it on an open fire and ate it with various types of meat.

The Taino adopted the cassava plant as a staple food because it was high in nutritional content, it was suitable to different soils and climate, and it sprung from minor roots when the major tubers were harvested. In favourable conditions, the calorie yield of the cassava flour is three times that of maize flour. No other Caribbean crop was more productive in starch content, and it could be stored for a much longer time in humid conditions.

Taino farmers set aside some conuco space for the cultivation of the sweet potato, a secondary staple within their food system. The yield of sweet potato was not as high as the bitter cassava. However, it had a shorter planting-harvesting cycle of 2-4 months and it was ideally suited to the moisture and conditions in conucos in rain forest and mountain valleys. The high sugar content of the sweet potato allowed the Taino to use it to make cakes and puddings, although it was mainly eaten boiled or roasted.

The sweet potato, like the cassava, could be found throughout the Caribbean, as well as in Taino conucos in Central and South America. Two, sometimes three crops, could be harvested per year. This made the potato an attractive crop particularly in communities with fast growing populations.

Taino farmers also grew a South American variety of yam, tania, protein-rich peanuts, arrowroot, maize, peppers and beans as supplements to both cassava and sweet potatoes. These other foods were less starchy, which gave balance and nutritional richness to the people's diet.

We can see that the Taino used a sophisticated agricultural system. It was based on an advanced understanding of the nutritional value of different food types, a co-ordinated planting and harvesting system, and an appreciation of the importance of soils and climate.

Gender roles: the division of labour

To be effective, conuco planning and management required skillful decision-making and the recruitment of organised labour. Within the family men and women were assigned different roles, indicating developed ideas about gender and production. Young men did infrastructural work on the conuco. They felled trees, cleared the hand-dug drains, heaped the soil and planted the crops. Women took day-to-day care of the crops, the clearing of weeds, and the watering of planted seeds and roots. Children helped with clearing the crops of pest, weeding to clear crops of parasitic vines, and chasing away birds.

Taino women would leave their villages at dawn so that they could complete a day's labour by midday and avoid the afternoon sun and heat. So the management role of women in agriculture was very important. Women made important management decisions that influenced the yield or output of the conuco. They needed to have an in-depth understanding of the relationship between crops and soil, and how different plants related to each other within the same field.

Watts notes that, 'The intermixture of crop plant species meant that demand for any one nutrient within the environment complex never became excessive and this in turn helped to preserve soil fertility for as long as possible.' So women needed both scientific understanding as well as management intelligence to make sure that the yield of conuco was at the most favourable level. In summary, Watts suggests that, 'Conuco agriculture seems to have provided an exceptionally ecologically well-balanced and protective form of land use.'

Women also made harvesting arrangements, but they did not participate in or take responsibility for the transportation of crops from the conuco to the village. It was common for different families to pool labour and to carry out the harvesting process together. This indicates the spirit of collective community life that was a part of Taino culture.

Domestic economy: house gardens, domestic birds and animals

Taino women developed a culture of supplementing or adding to their food by building gardens around the houses and keeping birds and animals within the yards. Taino ancestors cultivated many of the fruits that are common in the Caribbean today. In fact, much of the knowledge we have today about the planting of fruit trees, about cultivating and consuming fruits comes from the indigenous civilisation of the Taino. In their garden plots, Taino women planted fruit trees such as the guava, hog plum, sweet sop, sour sop, mammey apple, cashews and the paw-paw. They also planted different types of pineapples. From Trinidad in the south to Hispaniola in the north, one could find these fruit trees around the houses in Taino villages. Children were encouraged to eat as much fruit as possible, leaving the starchy cassava foods for adults.

The Taino had domesticated a few animals and kept them in their yards. They kept pigs for eating, and Europeans wrote that the Taino also reared a small animal that looked like a dog but did not bark. Their animal protein came from these sources, although Taino men were expert hunters and they caught a wide range of wild animals, birds and reptiles for eating. In Trinidad, the small brocket deer was a speciality, so too was the agouti. In Cuba, Jamaica, and Hispaniola, people ate various types of wild pigeons, doves, iguanas, and snakes.

Fig 1.10 Taino hunting party

Their hunting technology was simple but effective; it comprised spears, darts, slings, nets and traps. The Taino did not use the bow and arrow for hunting or for military purposes as did First Nation peoples on the North American mainland.

They caught pigeons, doves and parrots, kept them in cages and bred them on a small scale for eating. They tried to capture and keep many wild birds and animals within their household economy, but the Taino were not very keen on this as a way of supplying food.

Fisherfolk

The Taino could not rely solely on their conuco and hunting expeditions as sources of protein and fats. The dry seasons took their toll on agriculture, and hunting was not always sufficiently reliable to keep large villages fed, especially those located on the high plateaus and open grasslands. So, fishing in rivers and in the sea was a major part of the Taino food culture. In fact, fishing in the rivers and sea was a core feature of the region's cultural heritage. The sea was the preferred fishing area. Not all territories had rivers that were big enough to sustain an adequate supply of fish. Often the mud and silt that coloured the more turbulent rivers meant that they were an ineffective source of fish supply. The sea, however, offered a wide variety of food types, and there was always an abundance of fish. However, the Taino could not always get enough fish because of their own limited fishing technologies – mainly spears, hooks and lines, and small nets.

The staple food within the Taino diet throughout the Caribbean was the green turtle. The Taino developed an advanced scientific knowledge about the turtle's behaviour in the sea, particularly their feeding and

Fig 1.12 Cat fish, used to supplement the staple diet

hatching habits. They knew the places where these turtles congregated in herds and when they did this. All Taino fishermen knew that the green turtle grazed for food near the surface of the sea, in the clear shallow places, and that the use of nets and spears were the best way to catch them. The Taino mapped the turtle's hatching sites so that they could collect eggs on an ongoing basis. They ate most of the turtle and spared very little: organs were enjoyed as delicacies prepared with cassava. Indeed a large turtle that could weigh up to half a ton would feed several households for many days.

The Taino supplemented turtle meat with a range of reef fish: the catfish were favourites, but mullets and eels were also common. Many varieties of shellfish were also part of the dietary culture especially conch and oysters. The manatee was difficult to catch because of its water speed and sensitivity to noise and movement. They were a

Fig 1.11 The green turtle, the staple food of the Taino

Fig 1.13 Duho, Taino chief's ceremonial seat

chapter 1 | The indigenous Caribbean people

challenge to even the most effective fishermen who relied upon nets to catch them in much the same way they caught the green turtle.

So, the evidence suggests that the Taino developed an eating and cooking tradition that used a wide variety of meats, fruits and vegetables. Their systems of farming, hunting, and fishing could keep large populations well-fed and nourished. Their diets were rich in starch, proteins, sugars and fats, and this helped them to avoid malnutrition and other diseases associated with bad diet. Depending on where they were located and what the weather conditions were like, the Taino either concentrated on conuco cultivation, hunting or fishing. The high calorie level of cassava, and the easy availability of protein from animal meats, fish and some plants ensured that they could survive effectively within the different environments of the region.

Technology and household manufacturing

The Taino developed a range of goods that they produced on a small as well as large scale. Artisans used home-made instruments for their crafts and arts. They also used technology to produce more goods for storage or to trade any extras or surpluses. Some goods were used for agricultural production but most were created and used in the household or in industry.

Our knowledge about goods from agricultural production is more reliable than our knowledge about goods from industrial creations. We know about the manufacture of goods such as tobacco, cotton, dyes and powders and some medicines and poisons. People in Barbados, the Leeward Islands, in Jamaica, Cuba and Hispaniola, collected the cotton plant where it grew wild, or they also cultivated it on the conuco.

Taino women were sophisticated weavers of cotton. They made fibres that were then used to make nets for fishing, nets for protection against insects, hammocks and strainers. Throughout the Caribbean, Europeans noted the fine quality of Taino cotton fabric and noted that the women were very skillful in weaving quickly and accurately. The Europeans also referred to the strength of fabrics designed for the making of hammocks, and noted that cotton fibre was meshed with other string materials to ensure this strength.

Equally common throughout the Taino Caribbean was their sophisticated basket weaving, which was related to the cotton weaving technology. Taino baskets came in many styles and shapes, which showed the artistic creativity of the weavers, who were both males and females. These baskets were used for many different purposes. The most common material used for basket weaving was the palm leaf, which was used both in the green and dried form. In some societies various types of grass were used as well, but the palm leaf was the main material, as it was known for its durability, strength and ability to absorb indigo-based dyes.

Fig 1.14 Examples of Taino pottery

Fig 1. 15 Taino preparing for a journey

The Taino tobacco culture was not based on smoking. Rather, Taino grew the plant and dried the leaves, which they chewed and sucked. They also made a powder from the tobacco leaf, which is now called snuff. There is no evidence that they produced alcohol though, interestingly, people in parts of the Orinoco basin did know how to produce it. They cultivated a lot of indigo and used it as a dye in body painting, fabric colouring, and to decorate ceramics. The European writers of the time spoke about the common red, blue and black dyes which were used in clothing, pottery and body art.

The different Caribbean Taino shared a ceramic culture that brought them together as one civilisation. Ceramics were not made by using a wheel, but rather by using the coil method. The clay was prepared, rolled into finger-like coils, and used to build objects from a solid base. Many different objects were made in most societies – bowls, pots and ornaments. Many of these survived and are on exhibition in many Caribbean galleries.

Taino hard material technologies ranged from the use of stone to gold working. They were not great stone workers in the way that the Maya, Aztec and Inca were. There is no evidence of great stone monuments, though they built large walls – we still have no clear explanations for why they did this. They worked stone into tools and weapons. Stone tools allowed them to use logs in the building of houses, bridges, canoes and utensils.

However, the Taino were known for excellence in canoe production. It was no easy task to convert tree trunks into dug-out canoes that showed balance, and were designed for speed and easy steering. The canoes had to be light enough to facilitate speed, long enough to carry up to 50 persons and effectively balanced to negotiate turbulent waters. Their favourite building material was the silk wood tree, though cedar and mahogany were also used in different parts of the Caribbean.

The Taino (mainly the men) cut the tree trunk into shape as follows: they first burnt certain parts of the trunk and then they could easily hack these parts with stone tools. They needed skill in carpentry for this, as well as considerable strength. They built the canoes to last, and used mainly porous or waterproof woods. In Trinidad, and other places where pitch or tar was available, it was used to coat the canoes as a water-resistant seal.

The Taino were creative workers of gold, but did not mine the metal as an industry. They probably did not have the technology for gold mining. The gold they used in Cuba, Trinidad, Hispaniola and elsewhere was collected in riverbeds and worked on by their goldsmiths. They had no metal tools, so they used stone instruments to hammer the nuggets of gold into thin plates.

Fig 1.16 *The Bird Man, one of the most important Taino carvings found in a cave in Jamaica*

They then stripped, shaped and designed these plates into many kinds of jewelry. Both men and women wore gold nose rings and earrings and necklaces. They also made masks of gold and used them in entertainment and religious rituals. Some household ornaments were also made of gold, and the amount of gold that an individual had was an indication of social status or rank.

Trinidad and Hispaniola were centres of Taino goldsmith technology because the metal was available on these islands. Archaeologists have excavated gold ornaments that have been dated around 1500 AD, including a pendant in Cuba. This suggests that this island may very well have been a major goldsmith site as well.

The Taino were traders who travelled through the archipelago. They were connected to the cultures of Central America, and those in their ancestral Venezuelan hinterland. However, there is no evidence to suggest that gold trading was a core economic activity for them. They did place a high value on gold, and this is reflected in the use of it to demonstrate social rank in the group. But the value of gold as a form of buying power did not drive activity within Taino society.

Gold was the only metal with which they worked. So it is rather puzzling that Columbus mentions a silver ornament worn by a Taino in Cuba. This may have come from earlier trade between the Taino and a Central American community. There were several communications routes linking communities on the islands with the mainland. These routes were used by people for trade purposes – in food, pottery, textiles and gold – as well as for migration purposes.

The Taino were a highly mobile people who saw the region as a space for community interaction. Island trekking by canoe was an important part of their culture. It was done for recreation as well as for food distribution, trade and resettlement of communities. The sea was no barrier to effective communication. They travelled the Caribbean Sea with an ease that spoke of familiarity. They knew the islands and the relationship of one island to another. Each island played a part in their wider survival strategies.

Taino religion

So far we have seen that the Taino were a developed civilisation with broadly similar cultural features, though with some language differences. Their societies were based on the principle of respecting their environment, and their politics promoted peaceful co-existence, rather than hostile wars. They were a very religious people and they had very distinctive theological ideas. They expressed their religious beliefs through complex rituals and ceremonies. At the core of their religious beliefs was the recognition of a spirit world in which both humans and gods were classified and ranked.

They called their religious spirits or gods, Zemis. They displayed these gods in the shape of images made from gold, wood, stone and bones. Each person had his or her own highly personal way of worshipping Zemis, and Zemi images reflected the thinking of the individual worshipper. Each person, then, had his or her own Zemi images, and sometimes several were carried around the necks.

Many of the Zemi images have survived, and we can see that they were designed to show the supernatural powers of the gods. For example, some Zemi images were carved with prominent sexual organs to show the fertility power of a god; others had large focused eyes to show that this god dealt with the powers of vision and perception. These designs show how the individual worshipper believed that a god had given him or her certain capabilities as a social being.

However, the Caribbean Taino world did not develop religious rituals as extensive and complicated as their counterparts on the mainland, particularly the Maya, Aztec and Inca. The exact theological relationship between chiefs who ruled the villages, gods and the community remains unclear. However we do know that the chiefs had considerable political and social power and this was based on the belief that they had been empowered by a divine spirit.

Fig 1.17 Taino carving found in Jamaica

Society and community

Village communities also worshiped Zemis together in open ceremonies. Each village was designed to facilitate public functions and community life. The houses were designed as places for sleeping and resting, not places of recreation.

People did not just build their houses in the village in an arbitrary way. Houses were built around the community square and the living space. Villages interacted as a community in this open space. The Taino were keen ball players and the ball courts were located in this space. Public ball courts found in villages in Cuba and Hispaniola show that in most civilisations throughout pre-Columbian America ball games were part of the popular culture.

Fig 1.18 Replica of interior of a Taino hut with hammock, displayed in Arawak Museum, White Marl, Jamaica

At the time that Columbus invaded Hispaniola there were village communities all over the island. They ranged in size from district to district. It was normal for a town to have up to 3, 000 residents. They lived in multi-family households. This meant that the extended family was grouped together in a cluster of adjoining houses. The extended family unit was the basis on which the farming on conuco was done and people lived in a collective way.

Village communities and small towns were established in forest clearings or in mountain valleys. The Taino tried to avoid coastal sites and were not too keen on the open savannah. The main factors in community development were the availability of fresh water, fertile land for conuco, and ease of travel across the territory. Houses were called bohios and were built of hardwood where available, mahogany being a favourite. The evidence from the Bahamas, for example, shows extensive use of this wood in housing construction. In some places, particularly in the heavy rainfall zones, people used mud to case the outer sides of the houses to keep out water and moisture.

The roofs of houses were thatched in an intricate way with palm branches and wood rafters, which were tightly woven with string. The house of the chief was made differently from the others, indicating special status and need for distinctiveness. It generally had a rectangular shape with a gabled roof, while those of villagers were circular in design with conical roofs. All the houses were located around the central square. The arrangement reflected an orderly approach to planning with an emphasis on communal activities and outdoor living.

Politics

As in all civilisations, the Taino political system varied from place to place. The size of communities was clearly an important determining factor in politics. The small settlements in the Lesser Antilles were organised in a similar way with minor variations, in comparison with the large settlements in the Greater Antilles.

All communities were ruled by a chief or *cacique*, no matter their size. The chief was usually male and was not a military person but a civic leader with responsibility for judicial or legal, cultural, political and religious functions. The *cacique* was generally a hereditary status, passed on through the female line of the family. The Taino practised the system of matrilineal inheritance, in other words, the ruling lineage passed through the female line of the family. If the male *cacique* had no heir within the female side of his family, or if such person was considered inadequate for the tasks, then the community elected a leader from among a family outside the ruling lineage.

A *cacique* led communities that consisted of a small cluster of families, or large settlements of thousands of inhabitants. In 1500 Hispaniola was divided into six chiefdoms. Each *cacique* had authority over his or her area of control. The Taino population of the island at this time was estimated at 500,000. Puerto Rico, on the other hand at the same time was divided into 18 chiefdoms, but had an estimated population of only 45,000.

The Taino custom was to grant the *cacique* significant social status and cultural authority, but no real political power or military leadership. His or her role was largely ceremonial, though he or she was expected to settle disputes within the village and between villages. At all cultural events and in ceremonial rituals *caciques* were expected to lead activities and then preside as the dominant spirit representative. In return for these duties they were presented with specially prepared gold Zemis and foods, a larger house and canoe with the insignia of leadership, and the most elaborate dress and body decorations.

Apart from these benefits, *caciques* did not impose special taxes or demand tributes that would allow them to become wealthy. Their leadership status was not based on wealth, military prowess, or the power of personality. They were not expected to pass any formal leadership test and did not receive special education. They were community leaders whose authority rested on popular consent and support within a civilisation where peaceful co-existence was a priority. The *cacique* was generally a male but there is evidence of the rise to power of female *caciques*. An example comes from Hispaniola where Aracoana, the cacique Coinabo's principal wife, took the chieftainship of Xaragua when her brother Behecio died.

4 The Kalinago

When the Europeans, led by Christopher Columbus, invaded the Caribbean in 1492, they encountered the Taino as well as another indigenous cultural group who called themselves the Kalinago. The Europeans soon described them as 'Caribs'.

Culture and identity

The Kalinago ethnic origins are with a parent culture group in the Amazon basin. They found their way into the Caribbean through much the same routes as the Taino. Since about 900 AD the Kalinago used the Venezuelan coastal plain to migrate in waves into Trinidad and Tobago and the Lesser Antilles. They established communities also in Barbados, St Lucia, Grenada, St Vincent, and Dominica in the Windwards group, then moving up the archipelago to the Leeward Islands.

When the Europeans arrived in the Caribbean, Kalinago were still arriving from the mainland. Those in the Lesser Antilles had pushed north, deep into the heartland of Taino civilisation. This led to considerable conflict throughout the Caribbean between the settled, more numerous Taino communities and the small bands of mobile Kalinago warriors who wanted to establish their Caribbean ethnic supremacy.

It is important to understand that despite the ethnic conflict that developed between them, Taino and Kalinago had a close cultural link. So the differences between them were of degree rather than kind. As they had only recently arrived, the Kalinago had little time in which to establish fully their culture in terms of social, economic, political, and religious organisation.

Also they were arriving in the Caribbean with many more males than females, so their one objective was to integrate Taino women into their communities. The influence of Taino women on Kalinago culture can be found in areas such as agriculture, language, artisan technology and religion. They also helped to shape the inter-cultural identity that developed. Cultural similarities already existed between the two groups and so the cross-cultural fertilisation was not a complex social process.

So, the Kalinago push into the Caribbean was associated with two very different processes:

a. The Kalinago dominated, expelled and conquered the Taino in the Lesser Antilles. This process led to their integrating Taino women and some children into Kalinago communities as wives and unfree workers. There is archaeological evidence that suggests that this gender aspect of Kalinago settlements happened in places like Barbados, Trinidad, Grenada, Martinique and Antigua.

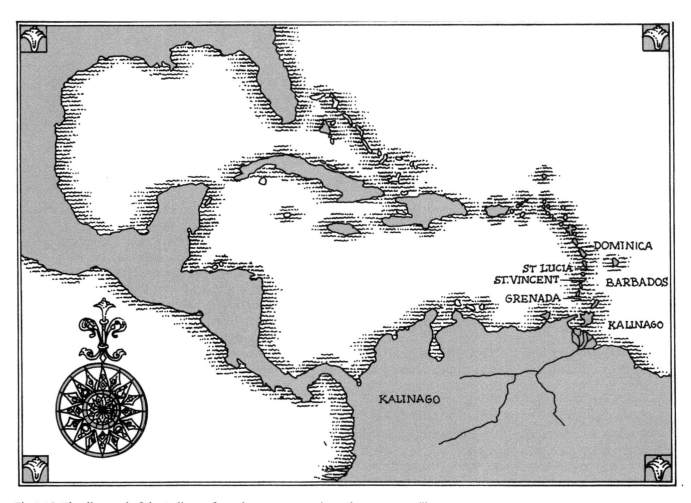

Fig 1.19 *The dispersal of the Kalinago from the Amazon Basin to the Lesser Antilles*

b. The Kalinago eventually clashed with the Europeans whose aims were similar to their own, namely to conquer the Taino, secure unfree labour, acquire material gains and assert a different kind of cultural leadership.

European attitudes

When Columbus and later Europeans wrote about the Kalinago in the Greater Antilles, they showed them as aggressive, militant and inhumane. The reason for this was that the Kalinago refused to accept European domination of the spaces in which they had settled. At first the Kalinago retreated from contact with the Europeans. They had already come across the Spanish and did not know fully what their intentions were. The Europeans recorded this first response. They spoke about the Kalinago fleeing into the forested interior and mountain recesses so that they could observe and understand who these new people were and what they wanted.

After this initial reaction and once the Kalinago had had enough time to examine the Europeans, they began to defend their lands, liberty and labour. At first the Europeans could not differentiate between Taino and Kalinago, but they soon acquired the ability, largely with the assistance of the doubly oppressed Taino. In situations where one group is oppressed, more often than not they will try to manipulate new arrivals to assist them in their political struggles.

Columbus tells us that Taino *caciques* tried to get the Spanish to support them in their resistance against Kalinago. To do this, they presented themselves to the Spanish as cooperative and non-violent. They presented Kalinagos and the other groups based in the smaller Lesser Antilles islands as militant, anti-social and hostile to their community independence.

In this Taino-Spanish discussion, the Kalinago were described by Europeans as cruel warriors who sometimes ate the hearts of other brave warriors. They were called uncivilised and therefore European invaders believed they deserved a large-scale military attack against their settlements. Hernando Colón, Columbus's son, wrote that on 26 December 1492, while shipwrecked off the coast of

Hispaniola, his father was invited on shore by a Taino *cacique*. According to Hernando, Columbus was offered by the *cacique*:

> A feast of sweet potatoes and yucca (cassava), which are the principal foods, and given some masks with eyes and large ears of gold and other beautiful objects which they wore around their necks. He then complained about the Caribs, who captured his people and took them away. He was greatly cheered when the Admiral comforted him by showing him our weapons and promising to defend him with them.

The Spanish then wrote that they were conscripted into the Caribbean civil war as defenders of the Taino against Kalinago, even though their objective was to rob, enslave and suppress them both.

The Taino had good reasons to adopt this political strategy. They had been virtually forced out of the Eastern Caribbean by the Kalinago who were aggressively seeking space for their own community development as a migrant frontier people. The Kalinago decision to use Taino women to build their population and to acquire more advanced agricultural and industrial technologies, gave them an intelligence base with which to assault Taino settlements. Taino felt not only very vulnerable but also incapable of effectively defending themselves against the Kalinago.

The tragedy of the European arrival in the Northern Caribbean was that it took place at a time when the indigenous Taino were already severely weakened by conflict with Kalinago over space. Weakened, fractured and retreating, the Taino could not offer any sustained or ongoing resistance against the European robbers and enslavers.

It is also important to understand that although the Taino tried to enlist the Spanish in their resistance against Kalinago, they understood that the Spanish wanted to enslave and conquer them. The Kalinago understood this too. So, on several occasions in different places, the Taino and the Kalinago united to mobilise military offensives against Spanish armies and settlements. In Cuba, Puerto Rico, St Croix and other places, Taino-Kalinago leaders led these collective struggles to protect themselves as indigenous peoples against the common enemy.

To plan and then implement joint military actions against the Spanish shows that the Taino and Kalinago realised that there was a threat to their independence and identity. They drew upon the cultural similarities that could bind them. Some Taino women facilitated this process, as they possessed both cultural identities – Taino and Kalinago. As mothers of children with Kalinago fathers they understood and could be loyal to both cultures.

Community economic planning and production

The Taino had a more advanced socio-political organisation and economy than the Kalinago. This might have been because the Taino had a longer history as a settled agricultural civilisation, and the Kalinago still had a highly mobile, nomadic, semi-military organisational culture. Both groups built their subsistence economy around conuco farming and produced cassava and sweet potatoes. However, the Kalinago mass produced arrowroot, which was a starch based crop. The Taino did not really know this plant and were possibly just becoming aware of it around the time of the European encounter.

There are many other plants that we now find in the Caribbean that may have been introduced by the Kalinago during their migrations. Watts has noted that among these are the coconut, the sugar cane and the plantain, although these plants might not have reached all the islands. The Kalinago could have introduced the coconut into some islands, as it certainly existed on the Pacific coast of Central America before 1492.

It is uncertain when the plantain was introduced in the Caribbean. The Kalinago grew it in St Kitts, Martinique, Guadeloupe and possibly some other islands in the 1620s, before the European settlement. In the 1620s the Kalinago in the Lesser Antilles also cultivated a plant that seems similar to sugar cane, particularly in St Vincent, St Kitts, Martinique, Guadeloupe and possibly Barbados. It is understood that the Kalinago might have introduced the plant from South America where natives grew it extensively.

Kalinago communities were small and highly mobile, and so hopping from island to island was the norm. They liked to hunt for food and fish and they used conuco farming as a back-up. When communities decided to settle on an island for longer periods then often the Taino women played the lead role in developing the conuco cultivation.

In both the Taino and Kalinago cultures women were the skilled agriculturalists, who took responsibility for crop mixing and selection, and for overall production levels. St Kitts was an example of their long-term planning. There they produced large amounts of cassava on the conuco. The women were so impressed with the rich soils on the island, that they called it 'Liamuiga', the fertile island.

Like the Taino the Kalinago also kept a few domestic animals, but unlike them they reared the muscovy duck as an important meat supplement. In addition, they hunted lizards, crabs and the agouti, which were cooked with sweet potatoes, yams, beans and peppers. So in Kalinago culture there were effective food production levels and people ate a well-balanced diet. Widespread disease was not part of their history in the Caribbean.

Fig 1.20 The muscovy duck, reared as a meat supplement

Kalinago technology

Kalinago industrial technology was very similar to that of the Taino. In some areas their products seemed more refined and in others less so. Both men and women participated in basket weaving, pottery, canoe-making and cotton-weaving. A recent inclusion in their production system was beer-brewing which was not widespread among the Taino. The pottery evidence left behind by the Kalinago shows that they were not as sophisticated in ceramics as the Taino. However, their cotton textiles technology was more advanced. They were well-known for their woven cloths, especially that found on Guadeloupe.

Their hunting technology was also more advanced than that of the Taino. This is not surprising because they were more equipped for living on the frontier as a new migrant culture. They were very skilled with the use of bow and arrow, which was not a Taino technology. Their skill with the bow and arrow was demonstrated in food hunting as well as in warfare. Also their canoes were of better design and quality than those of the Taino. The Kalinago impressed both Taino and Europeans with the speed and sophistication of their war canoes, known as piraguas. They could carry over 100 soldiers with great manoeuvrability.

In some places Taino quickly acquired the military technologies of the Kalinago and used them in their resistance against both Kalinago warriors and Spanish conquistadors. The process of cultural interaction between Kalinago and Taino was ongoing. There is evidence of Taino bowmen defying the Spanish in Cuba, Puerto Rico and Jamaica during the 15th century. This suggests that this cultural interaction between the two groups helped bring about change.

Politics and society

In the design and layout of their villages, the Kalinago betrayed the fact that they were a mobile frontier people who had not yet settled in an organised system of community development. There were no grand squares or plazas at the centre of their villages. Rather at the centre of the village they used a communal fireplace. They had no ball courts and their ceremonial activities were minor affairs.

Their houses were smaller than those built by the Taino, although they also used wooden frames with oval or rectangular shaped thatched roofs. We do not know as much about the details of Kalinago culture as we know about Taino culture. This is mainly because European writers did not become as familiar with it because they were in constant violent conflict with each other. It is believed that their land was owned communally as property. But other properties, such as canoes and ornaments could be privately-owned. We also know that they produced tobacco, which was also used as a form of money in commercial exchange.

Like the Taino, the Kalinago lived in a housing cluster that included the extended family. They too practised polygamy, that is, husbands had many wives. Usually, the village chief was the head of the largest family. He was responsible for economic, political and military leadership, particularly the raids upon the Taino and later European settlements. His most important job was military leadership, whereas other civil aspects came second. This was because of their recent immigrant status in a Caribbean world that was dominated by Tainos and later Europeans.

Religion and spiritual beliefs

The Kalinago did not have spirit gods called Zemis. Their religion was entirely centred on the individual relationship with the spiritual self. Each person had a personal spirit, deity or god, which took many physical forms. They offered material goods, such as water and food, to their personal deity.

They believed that the world was divided into good and evil spirits that fought each other for supremacy and that the individual mind was the battlefield of this struggle. In their society, they supported persons who functioned as priests or shamans. It was their duty to help the different spirits reach reconciliation. In other words, the priest's

chapter 1 | The indigenous Caribbean people

Fig 1.21 Chatoyer, powerful Kalinago chief in St Vincent, Brunias, 1773

task was to settle conflict between people and maintain harmony within the community.

So the Kalinago did not have hereditary ruling families from which a cacique was selected. Their society was much less hierarchical than that of the Taino and leadership could come from any family. This method of creating military and spiritual leadership suited their nomadic culture and was consistent with their military objectives.

5 Continental cousins: Maya, Aztec and Inca

In terms of economic development ancient Caribbean civilisation was steadily advancing when the Europeans arrived. There was widespread conuco farming that led to agricultural self-sufficiency in which people cultivated more and more plants and domesticated animals. Alongside intensive, organised farming goes large-scale community development.

When the Spanish arrived not all indigenous groups on the continent were practising organised agriculture. Many of them were still dependent on hunting and gathering for food. We have already seen that in this respect Caribbean civilisation was more advanced than other civilisations on the continent as throughout the islands there were well-established villages based on crop cultivation.

On the other hand there were other ethnic groups on the continent that were more advanced than Caribbean civilisation. These groups developed farming to very advanced levels, producing a wide range of crops such as potatoes (white and sweet varieties), avocados, tomatoes, pumpkins, beans, tobacco, as well as coconuts and sugar-cane. They used the hoe technology in cultivation, although they did not use the plough, as we know it today. They could produce more crops than they needed for immediate survival or subsistence. In other words, they could create an agricultural surplus and feed more people than their own immediate family. This helped them form large towns and cities.

They used stone tools, and also developed advanced building technologies that helped them build their large cities and splendidly constructed pyramids, which were beautifully decorated with massive sculptures. They also developed more complex systems of social organisation, political governance, and cultural and intellectual expression.

Three groups were particularly sophisticated in these areas and are recognised as representing the peak of achievement in Native American development. These groups are the Maya and Aztec of Central America and Mexico, and the Inca of the Andean region in South America.

Maya

Before the Maya made their significant strides as a developing culture, there was an earlier group of people called the Olmec who had established Central America as a place of historically significant civilisation. It is said that Olmec culture flourished in about 1000 BC. They invented systems of writing and mathematics, which were later modernised and improved by the Maya and later by the Aztec.

After about 300 AD the Maya emerged with a system of mathematics that we can understand today. Even experts find the Olmec writing almost impossible to decipher, although they can understand their number system. Even by today's standards, Maya mathematics was sophisticated and intellectually challenging. The Maya used the concept of zero as well as the idea of place value. Their mathematics found expression in the beautiful stone buildings they constructed, but also in the invention of lunar calendars.

Fig 1.22 Maya stone buildings

chapter 1 | *The indigenous Caribbean people*

Fig 1.23 *Old Mayan calendar: the symbols record an exact date and event*

Some of these calendars are more refined than others. The one that has had a significant impact on the wider world is the one that conceived 365 days grouped together in classes of 20-day sessions; the remaining five days were added to complete the 365-day cycle, and were interpreted by priests as unlucky days. Experts say that this was the most scientifically advanced calendar in the world at the time.

The Maya developed a highly structured society, in which a significant amount of power was consolidated in the hands of a king and royal family. Within their society there were several groups who occupied higher social positions based on their occupation and family. But the whole social system rested upon a massive class of workers who were farmers and artisans, many of whom were enslaved.

The king had a council that gave him advice and was responsible for the day-to-day political management of the society. They had built a considerable empire over much of Central America, and so the ruling elite had to devise systems of control, methods of getting revenue for the government, and ways of maintaining the respect for law and legal decisions, and for the regulation of trade.

This political management was supported by a large army whose leaders were nobles selected by the king. The rank and file soldiers were conscripted from the peasantry. The army also included paid mercenaries who carried out military tasks not expected of the regular army. The political and military power of Maya kings allowed them to build large cities throughout Central America and to manage them effectively for about 1,000 years.

They built most cities with the initial intention that they could be independent political, social and economic units. However, kings soon found it important to enforce a system of confederation within which these units were centrally administered.

From about 1150 to the end of the 14th century, the splendid City of Mayapán was the capital of the confederate empire. At its height Mayapán and the surrounding cities were places that maintained an intellectual elite of priests, astronomers, mathematicians, engineers and teachers. There was a huge market economy in which merchants engaged in local and long-distance trade in goods varying from cotton textiles, ceramics, foodstuffs and gold. The Maya believed in the beauty of the decorated body and both men and women wore necklaces of gold and jade, bracelets, ear and nose rings made of precious metals. These goods were extensively traded throughout the region.

However, as in all empires, there were political movements in the confederation who were calling for the release from central authority. After a series of revolutions Mayapán was destroyed and the confederation disintegrated. Internal political turmoil continued and eventually led to the decline of the Maya civilisation. By the time of the European arrival, Maya civilisation had collapsed into smaller disjointed settlements.

Fig 1.24 *The ceremonial centre of Uxmal*

Aztec

The fall of Mayapán and the disintegration of the Maya empire coincided with the emergence of the Aztec as the principal power in Mexico. In fact the decline of the Maya empire was partly a consequence of the rise of the Aztecs. Maya civilisation had influenced the political and social development of most ethnicities in the northern territories, particularly the Tolmec.

Fig 1.25 The Plaza of the Moon and the Pyramid of the Sun in Teotihuacán.

The Tolmec borrowed from Maya science and technology to rebuild the pyramids of the sun and moon, and the very large shrines and temples in the city of Teotihuacán, the cultural capital of Mexico. The Aztec, however, by force of superior military and political organisation managed to displace the Tolmec and establish effective control over Mexico. They built their capital city by linking many small towns on adjoining islands. Today these towns comprise Mexico City.

The military leaders were responsible for political administration. For this reason some people have seen it as a military state, in which civic life was less important than the objectives of imperial conquest. It is true that Aztec leaders possessed absolute authority. However, they ruled with the assistance of many senior officials who had the responsibility for public governance in the main areas of civil life. There was an official whose job was to administer justice and manage legal affairs throughout the many regions.

These types of officials had considerable power and the ordinary people understood them to be the voice of the leader. There were also state officials who were responsible for trade and marketing and for religious and spiritual matters. So these officials had to achieve effective local governance, and they also had the task of promoting the regional expansion of Aztec influence and conquest. They played critical roles in the spread of Aztec influence throughout Central America and beyond. Wherever small groups were conquered, you would find the presence of Aztec officials, merchants, priests and spies.

The capital was Tenochtitlán. It was a densely populated city that was inhabited by some 300,000 people. It ranked as one of the largest cities in the world at that time. A city of this magnitude could exist because of three factors:

a. It had an effective agricultural economy that produced a massive surplus of food for the urban population.
b. It had a complex network of trading and marketing that assisted with the distribution of this food.
c. It had a reliable system of raising taxes and revenues to finance the operations of public governance.

The Aztec were highly efficient in all of these operations.

Agricultural economy and distribution of food

For management purposes, Tenochtitlán was divided into 20 districts. Each district had its own local leadership of clans, who built and maintained their own schools, churches and armies. In addition, each district allocated lands for farming on a communal basis and took responsibility for the cultivation, harvesting and marketing of produce.

Fig 1.26 Aztec calender

System for raising revenues

The Aztec leadership raised revenues to maintain the elite and the state bureaucracy. It did this by forcing conquered groups on the edge of the empire to contribute substantial tribute in the form of taxes paid in food, gold, silver, textiles and other commodities. These commodities were also given to people who were to be publicly sacrificed to the gods as a way of receiving their blessings and soothing their anger.

So, Aztec civilisation developed with the imperial ruling of neighbouring peoples. For this reason it was very unstable because there were constant revolts and resistance from the oppressed. Every day there were attempts to overthrow Aztec rule by people whose lives were gripped by its awesome military, political and economic power. As Aztec civilisation grew in size and influence so did the determination of those it oppressed to free themselves. More and more the oppressed learned how to exploit the organisational weaknesses of the state and to weaken its authority.

Inca

When the Europeans followed Columbus to the Americas after 1492, Caribbean civilisation was still in the process of developing. However, other civilisations in the Andean sub-regions of South America had already achieved considerable development in the areas of economic activity, social organisation and political governance.

Starting in the vicinity of Peru, many indigenous peoples had made major advances in agriculture, trade, urban expansion and government. But it was the Inca who stood out as the most highly organised cultural force. From about 1000 AD the Inca laid the foundations for the construction of a powerful empire throughout the Andes sub-regions. This has been recognised throughout the world as an outstanding management achievement.

The Incas believed in the power of planning and of organisation to achieve their objectives. They left little of importance to evolve without central planning and monitoring. All aspects of life were subject to scrutiny, policy attention, and coordinated strategic action.

For centuries the Quechua-speaking people had lived in the Cuzco valley, which lies at 12,500 feet between the central and eastern ranges of the high Cordilleina. In the early 14th century they actively began to conquer and suppress their neighbours in the valley and beyond. By the end of the century they had established effective control over communities in Ecuador in the north and in Chile to the south.

The entire coastal plain of Peru, from Chimu in the north to Ica in the south became the base from which Quechua-speaking people launched their expansionist programme. In the 1460s, the Inca armies had seized control of the Chimu kingdom, and 30 years later the Inca were subdued. J H Parry has described this process of military success in the most unsupportive territory as 'a breath-taking story both of arms and organisation'. All around, in the mountain and along the valleys separate communities fell under Inca control.

The Inca established the most highly structured political system in the Americas, much more sophisticated than that of the Maya and Aztec. They built an empire that had a clear political structure with distinct lines of authority and communication that led back to the king, the Sapa Inca. His power was absolute, unquestioned and his decisions were non-negotiable. His power and authority was said to come from the Sun God.

The Sapa Inca was a hereditary king. He ruled through a group of royal and noble families whose position in society was also hereditary. They knew the law and custom very well. From his headquarters in Cuzco, the Sapa Inca allowed this group to rule as an imperial elite backed by a fearsome military force. Together, monarch and aristocracy became an imperial dynasty that was unmatched in its strength and power anywhere in the Americas and in many places in Europe, Africa or Asia.

The power of the Sapa Inca at home and beyond was based in the Inca religion of the Sun God, which said that the Sapa Inca was the Sun God's earthly manifestation. The Sapa Inca held the empire in place by the strategic development of garrisons, a complex road and

Fig 1.27 Inca wooden figure

Fig 1.28 Inca gold female figurine

communications network, the persuasion of priests, and the use of social welfare policies to distribute goods and services to all, especially the aged, sick and infirm.

Historians have described Inca civilisation as militaristic and monolithic because of the highly centralised nature of Inca state power. There were, however, many sub-divisions within the state; these have been classified as tribal districts, or village clans known as the allyu. An Inca chief ruled in each allyu. The imperial officials from the ruling elite supervised him. Each allyu had to be self-sufficient and self-contained with regard to food production, industrial output and decision-making in the areas of trade, religion and general infrastructures.

Each allyu had its own capital city, and its inhabitants had to wear a distinctive form of dress so that the imperial overlords could differentiate between one group and another. The imperial overlords closely supervised trade, as well as all forms of contact between the various allyus. The allyus were also expected to supply soldiers for the imperial army, but all top ranking officers were drawn only from the Inca group and not from subordinated clans.

At 15, all Inca boys outside the nobility were conscripted into the imperial army. They served in the army until the age of 20 and were catered for as a special group. They received superior food and clothing and if they gave outstanding service there were opportunities for them to secure important employment in government.

The Sapa Inca richly rewarded loyalty and bravery, while all forms of disrespect for the state and its officials, or revolt and disloyalty to the Sapa Inca, were punished by mutilation and death. The penalty of imprisonment was applied only to the nobility. The need for absolute discipline and loyalty was emphasised by the state in all areas of life and was enforced without exception.

All persons in the Empire had a role and place assigned to them to which they were tied. Even the Sapa Inca and his nobility were not allowed to marry outside their group so as to assure that the elite remained totally exclusive. The Sapa Inca himself had to marry within his own family. All gold and silver mined within the Empire belonged to the Sapa Inca, and each allyu was expected to pay tribute taxes to him. These were calculated on their ability to pay. Any rebellion towards authority was not tolerated.

The Sapa Inca had a monopoly or full control over the gold and silver mines. This monopoly together with the imposition of taxes were designed to enrich the monarchy and aristocracy; and also to support the massive army and imperial state bureaucracy; to finance the extensive public works (roads, bridges, irrigation projects, state houses, temples and shrines); to finance an advanced system of social welfare. The state kept stores for feeding and clothing the elderly, and offered material rewards to young people to marry and have children. The policy of focusing upon the young and the elderly was to ensure their discipline and loyalty, and also to effectively promote the god-given wisdom of the Sapa Inca.

However, the Inca Empire is not known for its political, military and economic achievements. It was a civilisation that placed a lot of emphasis upon spiritual development, intellectual creativity in the arts and science, as well as in technological advancement. Their temples and religious shrines fell short in comparison with the architectural sophistication shown by the Maya and Aztec. But the physical durability and the spiritual and aesthetic beauty of their stonemasonry were unparalleled.

The Inca did not develop astronomical calendars or recognisable writing systems like the Maya. But an intellectual creativity informed their public stone constructions. Their numbering system was relatively crude. It consisted of a series of knotted strings called a quipu, which was used with an abacus for keeping records and making calculations.

Fig 1.29 Inca temples and shrines at Machu Picchu

Inca pottery was the most sophisticated of all produced in the Americas. Also, the beauty of their jewelry made from gold, silver, bronze and copper was unchallenged at this time. According to John Parry, their 'weaving was developed to a point perhaps unequaled by man in the whole course of human history'. Inca women were the technologists in both the wool and the cotton textile crafts. The beauty of patterns and colour, and the fine finish of the products, indicated artistic and technical qualities that took centuries to perfect.

So, the continental cousins of the Taino and Kalinago made significantly greater advances with respect to economic development, social organisation, political governance and cultural sophistication. But each group responded to their environments in creative and self-sustaining ways. Caribbean civilisation was ecologically balanced and well-developed within its physical context; it was not static but was continuously evolving in its own way and pace.

Resistance: Aztec, Maya and Inca

The Spanish launched their military expedition against the Aztec Empire from the Caribbean. It was organised by Diego Velázquez, governor of Cuba. But it was led by Hernando Cortés, his administrative assistant and business partner.

Cortés left Cuba in 1519 for the mainland with 600 volunteers whom he had recruited mostly in the Spanish Caribbean colonies. He landed on the Mexican coast at Tabasco, and immediately encountered the resistance of neighbouring communities. Seeking to defend their territory and liberties these communities fought against the colonisers. An observer described this initial resistance as a 'serious battle'. Cortés emerged victorious, and prepared for further military encounters.

News of the defeat at Tabasco soon spread further along the coast and inland. Cortés advanced closer to Aztec settlements, and established military headquarters near what is now Vera Cruz for four months. What happened there will help us understand the effectiveness of native resistance to Spanish aggression in the future.

Coastal communities that resisted Spanish conquest were defeated by the superior military capability of Cortés and his local alliances. He won over as allies many local communities. They believed that it was in their strategic interest to support the Spanish against the dominant Aztec. In the end, this divide and rule approach to the natives proved a successful strategy for the Spanish.

Cortés effectively used soldiers from one community against others, a tactic that allowed the Spanish to confront the Aztec with a powerful military force. These supportive groups were drawn mostly from communities dominated by Aztec overlords, and forced to pay tribute. They resented Aztec rule, and as they could not overthrow it, they saw an opportunity in the Spanish presence to create an anti-Aztec alliance.

Aztec resistance to the Spanish colonisers took many forms. Also the objectives of the resistance changed over time. We can see an example of this in the political responses of the Tlaxcalans and Totonacs to the presence and proposals of Cortés. Cortés encountered these two groups on his way through the rain forest of the Vera Cruz

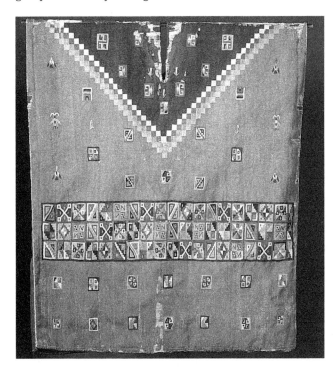

Fig 1.30 An Inca woven poncho

hinterland, up to the high plateau of Central Mexico, the heartland of Aztec civilisation. Both were under the control of Aztec military rule. The Totonacs sought assistance from Cortés to free their capital, Cempoala, from Aztec officials who ruled over it from the Aztec capital of Tenóchtitlan.

The Cempoalans in return promised to assist Cortés with food supplies, contracted and paid labour, and military information about the Aztec Empire. They also advised Cortés to assist the Tlaxcalans who had been at war with the Aztecs for three decades. Cortés approached the Tlaxcalans with the political intention of establishing friendly and supportive relations, at least until he was better prepared for war.

The Tlaxcalans were suspicious of Cortés' proposal for peace and an alliance against the Aztec. They chose to go to war against the Spanish intruders. For several days, they fought the Spanish and their Totonac allies. Battles were bloody with heavy losses on both sides. In the first Tlaxcalan victory, some 3,000 soldiers ambushed the Spanish and made them flee in fear. But after regrouping, the Spanish repelled them with the greater fire-power of gun-powder cannon artillery.

The intensity of Tlaxcalan resistance caused Cortés to reconsider his strategies. The Tlaxcalans were skilled, professional soldiers. On 2 September 1519, some 6,000 of them marched against Cortés. He was forced to give in to their request, which was to release prisoners who had been captured earlier.

Although Cortés did release the prisoners, the Tlaxcalans intensified their attacks upon the Spanish. They did so with a barrage of arrows, sling stones and darts, and then engaged in hand-to-hand combat. Superior firepower saved the Spanish. The Tlaxcalans were charging into guns and cannons. Even when 10,000 of them, led by their military chief, Xicotencatl, attacked much smaller Spanish contingents, many more Tlaxcalans than Spanish died.

Ultimately the Spanish defeated the Tlaxcalans. The leaders made peace arrangements with Cortés that included their promise of support for his march into Aztec territory. Cortés wanted to secure their full backing in the event that he was to engage the army of Montezuma.

With the support of the Tlaxcalans secured, Cortés entered Tenóchtitlan. He did not encounter any organised resistance from the Aztec at this stage. In fact, he managed to establish a power-sharing arrangement with Montezuma that suited his interest.

But the peace settlement was fragile because the Aztec resented the Spanish military presence. The Aztecs soon removed Montezuma because he was subservient to the Spanish, they stoned him to death, and elected a new

Fig 1.31 *Montezuma*

leader who declared war upon the Spanish. The rise of the Aztecs was formidable and Cortés chose to pull his troops out of Tenóchtitlan.

When Cortés attempted to flee the city, he lost a third of his troops. Once their military chief was on the run, the Tlaxcalans saved him and his men. They enabled the Spanish to regroup for the successful counter-attack that ultimately brought down the Aztec empire in 1521.

The Maya also offered solid resistance to Spanish invaders. Starting in 1522 and continuing into 1524, the Spanish organised expeditions against the Maya. The Maya resisted the 1524 expedition led by Pedro de Alvarado through Tehuántepec into Maya cities in Guatemala. The Maya also resisted another expedition that year by Cristobal de Olid into the communities near the Bay of Honduras.

Although Maya resistance caused considerable loss of Spanish life, Maya fatalities were greater. The Spanish already had a technological advantage with respect to warfare. As with the Aztec there were also divisions between Mayan communities. This enabled the Spanish to weaken and undermine the possibility of effective collective Maya resistance.

At the time of the Spanish invasion, two main Maya groups, the Cakchiquel and Quiche, were deepening their mutual hostility. The Spanish facilitated this conflict. They ultimately defeated both groups and attempted to push them back to the coast.

Inca resistance

The nature of Inca resistance to Spanish military invasion indicates similar trends and patterns to Maya resistance. When Francisco Pizarro departed Panama for Peru in 1530, accompanied by 180 men and 26 horses, his intention was to conquer the Inca Empire. He expected the kind of resistance Cortés had experienced from the Tlaxcalan in Mexico. On arrival, though, he found political circumstances similar to those in Maya territory. The divisions in Inca communities weakened their capacity to defend themselves. So Pizarro used these divisions to his advantage.

Fig 1.32 Inca Royal Family

When Pizarro arrived at Tumbez, on the northern coast of Peru, he witnessed the civil war that was coming to an end between warriors loyal to the ruling Inca, Huáscar, and his half brother Atahualpa. Huáscar was defeated and this meant that Atahualpa's new regime would try to establish itself from the conflict that remained.

Pizarro attacked the troops of the victor, Atahualpa, killed most of his inner-guard and took him prisoner. This development crippled the people's capacity to immediately resist the Spanish. By November 1533 the Spanish had fully established their authority.

However, Inca peasants and soldiers soon regrouped and reorganised themselves under a new leader, Manco Inca. He was a successor to Huáscar who Pizarro had tried to subdue with patronage and friendly gestures. The Manco rebellion was widespread and threatened to end Spanish rule.

The ranks of Manco's army grew large. But at the same time this large army placed considerable pressure on food supplies. This development in turn weakened their ability to stay in the field. For three months, however, Manco's army kept Spanish forces confined to the garrison. It was only with the arrival of additional troops under the leadership of Diego de Almagro that the Spanish were able to counter-attack.

The clash between Manco's soldiers and Almagro's troops resulted in the defeat of the Inca rebellion. Manco fled to the mountains with a loyal band of soldiers and continued a guerrilla struggle against the Spanish until his death in 1551.

While they were in exile the various factions of the Inca political elite fought each other. The War of Chupas, for example, broke out between the followers of the dead Atahualpa and Huáscar. This war undermined all real hopes of an effective resistance to the Spanish, whether led by Manco or any other Inca.

So armed resistance by natives was a feature of the Spanish conquest. The Aztec, Maya and Inca organised considerable opposition to the invaders. However, internal conflict and warfare between rival native communities weakened the effectiveness of this resistance. These rivalries also helped the Spanish who already had superior weaponry.

To sum up

Long before the arrival of the Europeans and the Africans, Caribbean civilisation was complex, rapidly evolving, and characterised by considerable economic and social growth, as well as by political conflict. It was a changing world that was expanding along lines broadly similar to other civilisations and it had cultures dating back to antiquity. It was an old world, this Caribbean civilisation. It expressed both the features of ancient traditions and the transforming energies of the approaching modernity.

Revision exercises

1   a   How and when did Caribbean civilisations develop?
    b   State two recent archaeological conclusions about the early settlement of the Caribbean region.

2   a   Explain how the Ciboney came to settle in the Caribbean region.
    b   State two reasons why Ciboney technology was regarded as 'undeveloped'.
    c   State two cultural differences between the Ciboney and the Taino.

3   a   State two reasons why the Europeans insisted on categorising the Kalinago as 'cannibals'.
    b   State two reasons for the conflicts between Kalinago and Europeans.
    c   State two reasons why, in contrast to the Taino, Kalinago resistance against the Europeans was more successful.

4   What evidence exists of interaction among the various Caribbean indigenes?

Chapter 2

The European–Caribbean project

'Is there a place, for the hopeless sinner, who has hurt all mankind, just to save his soul?'
(Bob Marley)

The Caribbean was the first site of the historic encounter between Europe, Africa and the Americas. However, this was not the first European journey to Africa or the Americas. The Europeans had for many years been successfully navigating the world, and they had a long history of important developments in the fields of science, politics and economic activities. It was against this background that Columbus' journey of 1492 took place.

The indigenous peoples in the Caribbean were completely unprepared for the encounter with the Europeans. The strength and might of the European military was aimed directly at them and they did not have the same military strength with which to respond. Their contact with the Europeans brought them sudden disaster from which they could not escape. Their cousins in other parts of the hemisphere did only a little better in terms of surviving in greater numbers from the genocidal European colonialism.

In this chapter we will learn about:
1. The first 'American' journeys before Columbus
2. Asia and the Crusades
3. Portuguese in West Africa
4. Colonising the islands in the East Atlantic
5. The Columbus Project

1 The first 'American' journeys before Columbus

There were many important steps that were taken by the Europeans, which eventually led to the 'Columbus project'.

The Norse, or the Viking from Norway, Sweden and Denmark, were probably the first Europeans to set foot in America, but their visit had no major impact on either side of the Atlantic. Eric the Red, the legendary Norse explorer, arrived at a mass of land in the middle of the 10th century. By the end of that century, Norse people were living in Greenland. Eric's son, Leif, had also stated that he encountered lands even further west of Greenland that he called the 'Flatland', the 'Timberland' and the 'Vinland'.

It is very possible that these lands were Baffin Island, Labrador, and Newfoundland, which were inhabited by people he described as 'swarthy', 'broad of cheek', and with 'heavy hair' on their heads. The indigenous people violently resisted the Vikings and pushed them back into Greenland. By the middle of the 11th century, this first European project of settling in the west was literally put on ice for another four and a half centuries.

Recently, the Guyanese scholar, Ivan van Sertima, has argued that the north-western Africans made the transatlantic journey into the heartland of American civilisation long before Columbus. He argues that for centuries before Columbus, African mariners had travelled the African coast from the north to the west and that for a long time they had the technical know-how for crossing the Atlantic. In Africa, the Egyptians, Tuaregs and Moors further to the north-west, were ancient sailors who knew the East Atlantic Ocean very well. It was only logical that they would journey deeper into the ocean in search of new lands like the Norse did later on. Van Sertima suggests also that Columbus learned how to cross the Atlantic when he was travelling in Africa in the mid-15th century where he met Portuguese sailors who interacted with Africans.

Van Sertima further argues that the people of the central American regions have many African cultural characteristics, especially the Olmec, Tolmec, Maya and Aztec. In his judgment, this confirms that African explorers travelled to central America. He says that the Egyptian influence was especially strong and can be seen in these groups' building technologies and their religions based on the worship of the sun. African facial features, he argues, can be seen in their fine arts and crafts. He insists that the famous Olmec heads, which are carved from basalt, were symbols to celebrate the arrival of black people from Africa. This African arrival helped local culture to grow. The local people in turn, focused on the new immigrants and produced large African images to mark the importance of the contact with them.

Fig 2.1 Famous Olmec head said to celebrate arrival of black people from Africa

According to van Sertima, many material objects or artifacts show this early contact with African explorers. However, there is no written evidence of it and so these journeys have been hidden from public knowledge. Maybe in this way, the Africans and Norse have been written out of their proper place in American and, therefore, Caribbean history. In time, archaeological and other forms of research will unearth more evidence and it is important that scholars remain open to new and challenging interpretations.

2 Asia and the Crusades

In the 15th century, Europeans had no real interest in exploring the West Atlantic. Their main focus was on taking the Holy Land from the Muslims by force. They had a burning desire to secure Christianity throughout the world, and it was from this desire that the crusades were created. The crusades were a huge movement in Europe.

It is ironic that they probably had a greater impact upon world development because they failed, at this time, to secure Christianity throughout the world rather than because they succeeded.

European monarchs, the landed elite, professional soldiers and educated professionals travelled long distances to challenge the Muslims and to drive them out of southern Europe where they had settled. In this journey these Europeans came into contact with a higher level of scientific knowledge and intellectual discussion, which they did not have in European society. The Muslim and Byzantine imperial civilisations had a developed scientific and artistic knowledge from classical ancient times. So, the crusaders were intellectually challenged and uplifted by their encounter with the Muslims. They came across books and learned much about medicine, mathematics, philosophy, astronomy, geography, history and the arts.

Fig 2.2 *Reverse view of the Caird astrolabe used for calculating latitude*

The European intellect and imagination were awakened and stimulated when they came across the science of the compass, the power of gunpowder and the possibilities of the astrolabe. Muslim navigators used the compass and had probably come by the compass technology from the Chinese. They had also probably learned about gunpowder from the Chinese who had invented it. Europeans eagerly learned about the compass and immediately saw the potential of gunpowder in the making of military weapons. They also learned how to use the astrolabe, a brilliant technology that allowed sailors to measure latitude by measuring the height of the sun at noon.

By the early 15th century the effects of this intellectual and scientific encounter were changing the European maritime culture. Ships were longer, leaner and faster; they could be more easily manoeuvred in different wind conditions because they used many sails. This gave sailors greater flexibility and confidence on the high seas. Their map making was completely revolutionised. They restudied the geographical work of Ptolemy, a second century scientist, who showed that the world was round. The educated elite had not entirely dismissed Ptolemy's idea, but now more and more ordinary people rediscovered this powerful fact. What was now to be discovered were the true geometric dimensions of the earth.

The Europeans had already established a colonial settlement on the islands in the East Atlantic: the Canaries, Madeira and the Azores. These islands would now be the starting point for the grand journey westward into what was expected to be the East – Japan, China and India. The Europeans had everything – maritime technology, scientific understanding, and the spirit of exploration. The East attracted them, with its trade, wealth and precious riches.

By the mid-15th century the Europeans believed it was possible to sail west to the Orient. They had to find a quicker and cheaper way to reach India and China other than the caravan routes across Asia. They thought that this land voyage was uncomfortable, a financial burden and politically uninspiring.

Europeans had made this land journey as early as 1241. The first European to cross Asia was John of Plano Carpini, the Franciscan monk and ambassador of Pope Innocent IV to Ghengis Khan. William de Rubruquis, also a Franciscan, was sponsored by King Louis IX of France to make the trip in 1253. Both men paved the way for Marco Polo, the Venetian trader, who travelled the Orient between 1274 and 1295. Marco Polo's descriptive writings of Asia now acquired a very special meaning. The route he had taken along the Atlantic coast of Africa was exactly what European explorers were interested in; his book with details of his journeys through Asia was published in 1477 and was very widely read. Columbus kept a copy as his inspiration.

Asia was real and reachable. It was no longer a place of the imagination. Merchants, monarchs, and mariners all believed that soon all the silks, satins, velvets, spices, rugs, gems, china, perfumes, dyes and countless other rare and expensive Asian goods would be flooding the European world and creating wealth and grandeur that had never been seen before. When anyone said the word 'Asia' women and men thought of a world of money and would sit up and pay attention. Everyone believed that oriental goods would become affordable to the many and lifestyles would be changed. But first the sea passage to India had to be found.

Another forum in which the 'passage to India' was discussed was in politics, particularly in Spain and Portugal. All monarchs could think about was being the first to reach Asia, possess its wealth, and colonise its land and people. Christian nations searched fiercely and competitively to take the political, military and economic lead. The Catholic Church claimed that it wanted to convert non-Christians to Christianity and so it too wanted to journey into Asia too in search of souls. Riches came first, souls and other goals came second.

In 1479 Spain united and the new order committed itself to expanding the Spanish empire and to military exploits. The Catholic Church joined in this passion to conquer and control foreign things and people, and blessed the royal policies of the Crown. According to John Parry, who is an authority on the Spanish New World Empire, the unity of Spain created a particular 'state of mind'. People developed very strong nationalist feelings and became Christian militants once again. In the early 15th century, the African Muslims (Moors) had conquered the Spanish kingdom of Granada. The African conquerors brought Islam into southern Europe and Christian militancy had declined. The Muslims intended to capture most of Western Europe and spread Islam.

However, the unification of Spain led to the organising of men and resources for the greatest crusade of all, one that would drive the African conquerors out of Spain. By 1492 Granada, the last of the African Muslim strongholds in Western Europe, had collapsed. This was seen as a great victory for Christianity. However, the Spanish were not prepared to stop at this. Conquest brought them glory and power. By the time Columbus was ready to sail across the Atlantic in 1492, Spain was politically and psychologically prepared for waging war and establishing political control over peoples and lands beyond its shores.

Spain could fight effectively against the African Muslim conquerors because they had brought together a large alliance of soldiers, farmers, churchmen, intellectuals, politicians and workers. These people were also now thirsty for conquest of non-European lands and people. A lot of racial hostility had surfaced in the war against the African Muslims. This racial hostility remained a feature of Spanish expansionism. The African Muslims were superior to Europeans in culture and had brought much intellectual activity to Spain. It was now Spain's chance to regard others as inferior beings worthy of being civilised.

Navigational developments

At the beginning of the 15th century, European navigators did not have a reliable way of locating their position on the ocean, once they had lost sight of a known landmark. This was extremely frightening and was an 'almost paralysing discouragement' for ocean adventures.

Both Europeans and Arabs saw the Atlantic as the 'green sea of darkness'. Even the best available literary works on geography and cosmology were useless to the practical sailor in the early 15th century. Sailors therefore sailed known routes and clung fearfully to the coastline. They could not plot their latitude once they could not see a landmass. Only astronomers had ways of making this calculation using a complicated process of stargazing. However the average navigator did not know about this process.

By 1484 these problems had been solved. A group of astronomers, working under King John II of Portugal, realised that latitude could be accurately calculated by plotting the sun's destination and location at midday. This scientific breakthrough was simplified and made available to navigators in Europe. By the 1490s, navigators no longer had to cling to the coastline. They could now plot their latitude, location and direction. The fears and mysteries were taken out of ocean navigation. All that was now needed were skillful and fearless sailors. Columbus' journey into the Atlantic Ocean was, more than any other thing, a tribute to accurate navigation.

Fig 2.3 Instruments of navigation from the 1490s – compass and magnifying glass

The crusading tradition against African Muslims

In the 15th century the economies of Western Europe did not expand rapidly. Things were only now returning to normal after the 'Black Death', which had killed at least one-third of European people in the 14th century. Christianity too was not expanding; in fact, fewer people were converting to Christianity. Probably the most powerful and expansive civilisation at that time was that of the Chinese, ruled by Tartar dynasties. The Chinese had taken Mongolia, Turkestan and parts of Russia. In Europe, the Turks were expanding, taking most of the Mediterranean and spreading Islam. In the early 15th century, Islam, under the Turks and Berbers of North and Northwest Africa, was the most powerful and expanding force.

The Crusades were wars fought against Islam and were led by Christian kings. They were fighting both the religious and cultural aspects of Islam. The Catholic anti-Islamic Crusaders had a thirst for looting, trade, glory and adventure. Most European Christians wanted to go on the Crusades. The Christian merchants, clerics and soldiers went hand in hand. In other words, trade, religion and power could not be separated.

The Spanish desire for slaves, gold, silver, spices, textiles and other commodities was just as strong as their desire to drive the Muslims out of Europe. Their long-term aim was to find a way to the East, so that they could get access to oriental trade and wealth. At the same time they could convert some Muslims and Hindus to Christianity.

So, by the late 15th century the quest of most Spanish and Portuguese merchants, sailors, soldiers and clerics was to find a route to the East. There was so much literature and rumours about oriental wealth and how it enriched the Arabs. The Christians believed that their exclusion from this wealth was an act of hostility. They had driven the African Muslims out of Europe. Now their aim was to take the war right into Islam's camp. However, they could only do this if they found an eastern sea route. Columbus was convinced that he could find an eastern sea route by sailing west across the Atlantic.

3 The Portuguese in West Africa

In the mid-15th century Portugal had the most developed merchant or trading class in Europe. The Portuguese knew the European Atlantic coastline well, because their trading in spices, gold, fish and other goods led to the growth of many coastal towns. The Portuguese began their Crusade against Islam by attacking Muslim trade routes and bases along the Atlantic coast. This time they attacked along the African Atlantic coast to the far south.

The first major Portuguese strike was as early as 1415. It was against the Muslim town of Ceuta in northwest Africa. The attack was successful and represented the first conquest by a European state of Islamic territory outside Europe. Although this attack was a real crusade, its objective was also to gain control of the port of entry into

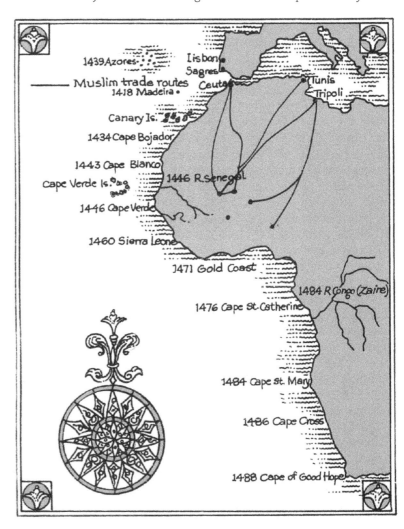

Fig 2.4 Muslim trade routes and the extent of Portuguese exploration on the west coast of Africa

the Mediterranean. For the first time, a Christian state had taken a colony outside Europe.

In the mid-15th century the Portuguese continued to press further south, establishing trade bases along the coast of West Africa. From the African merchants they obtained enslaved African workers, gold, ivory, spices and silks in exchange for European goods. By the end of the 15th century, they had established their political and commercial power in West Africa and had gone around the Cape. All of this happened before Columbus sailed for the New World.

4 Colonising the islands in the East Atlantic

Long before Columbus' New World project was thought about, the Portuguese were the first to lead the way in seafaring and colonising activities in 15th century Europe. The four groups of Atlantic islands off the southwestern coast of Portugal came under their domination. They were Cape Verde, Madeira, the Azores and the Canaries. Later Spain was in control of the Canaries, which it claimed by virtue of a papal bull of 1344.

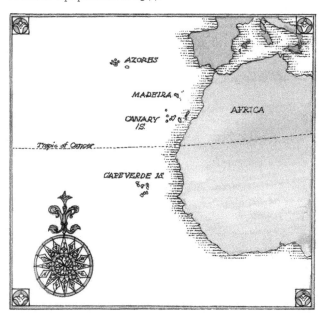

Fig 2.5 Map of East Atlantic islands

These island colonies were valuable to the Portuguese. They could get subtropical commodities from them. Also, these islands became stopping points for the imperial mission into western and southern Africa. Indigenous people had not settled permanently on these Portuguese-controlled islands, except for the Spanish Canaries. Here a

people who were known as the Guanches had settled. They violently resisted Spanish settlers into the late 16th century. They were an agricultural and hunting people, and so they used spears and other throwing devices in battle. They had no gunpowder, which the Europeans did have and which gave them the critical military advantage. In the Canaries the Spanish established a settlement in Grand Canary and developed sugar plantations, using enslaved Guanche labour. The islands were profitable for Spain, and gave them their first taste of colonisation. By 1492 Spain had established settlements on all the Canary Islands.

The Canary Islands are very important in understanding Spain's New World experience and Columbus's vision. On these islands the Catholic Church had its first experience of converting indigenous people to Christianity. Merchants had their first experience of trading in colonial produce. So by the time Columbus sailed to the Caribbean, Spain was an experienced colonial nation. For the Spanish, the Caribbean was not the beginning of their colonising mission, but rather an extension of it. For them the Caribbean islands were merely islands further out to sea.

5 The Columbus project

Columbus planned to arrive in the East by sailing westward across the Atlantic. This journey was the logical outcome of Spain and Portugal's colonisation of Atlantic islands and of their African expeditions. In this respect Columbus was just another European voyager caught up in the 'discovery mania', which had taken over maritime life in Spain and Portugal in the 15th century. In fact, although Columbus came before Vasco da Gama, Da Gama's activities and plans seemed more practical and more fascinating to people at that time. Da Gama was making a genuine search for a passage to India by sailing around Africa; while Columbus was looking for the long-lost world of Marco Polo. Da Gama was building upon the tradition of African missions, while Columbus was proposing something completely new by sailing west to the farthest point of the Atlantic.

Everyone at the time accepted that the world was round and not flat. So to Columbus there seemed no reason why he could not arrive in the East if he kept sailing westward across the Atlantic. He believed that this was the shortest and easiest route to Asia.

Most learned people and many kings of Europe rejected his idea and refused to give him financial support for this journey. He sent his brother Bartholomeu to France and England to ask the royalty there for financial support.

Fig 2.6 Christopher Columbus

However, Bartholomeu did not succeed and Christopher too did not make any progress with the king of Portugal. People did not believe his theory. Everyone knew that he was a sailor with years of experience in the East Atlantic coast, that he had visited Africa several times and that he knew the winds and the maritime community there. They knew that he was a skilful and knowledgeable sailor. The Portuguese who were the most experienced navigators of all, found his project incredible and thought that Columbus' navigational science was inadequate. It was only after a series of events that Queen Isabella agreed tentatively to support Columbus.

On 17 April 1492 she drew up a contract with Columbus. He was to sail west to 'discover and acquire islands and mainland in the Ocean Sea'. The islands were the mythical islands in the Atlantic and the mainland was Cipangu and Cathay – the names Marco Polo gave Japan and China. On 3 August 1492, the Columbus expedition left Palos. It sailed to the Spanish settlements in the Canaries, and then departed across the Atlantic on 9 September. On the night of 12 October, they sighted land. The Spanish had made contact with the Caribbean.

News of the Columbus voyage greatly disturbed the Portuguese. This was because Da Gama was planning to reach Asia by sailing around the African continent, and his project had not yet reached maturity. The Portuguese had spent close to 70 years pushing farther south along the African coast. They considered themselves far ahead of any other European country in the race to reach Asia. In 1479 Portugal and Spain had signed the Treaty of Alcaçovas. In this treaty Spain had agreed to accept Portugal's sole rights to colonise lands off the African coast. Now Portugal saw the Columbus voyage as Spain breaking the treaty and illegally trespassing on their territory – Africa.

Spain argued that Colombus was trying to find the outer, western zones of the Atlantic – this was land beyond the boundaries mentioned in the 1479 treaty. The dispute continued. The Pope was brought into the conflict to negotiate a settlement. He negotiated the Treaty of Tordesillas in 1494. By this time Columbus had gone west and returned. Under the Treaty of Tordesillas, the so-called non-Christianised world was divided into two parts: all lands 1,100 miles west of the Cape Verde Islands went to Spain, and lands to the east went to Portugal. The Pope approved the arrangement and gave it the Catholic Church's approval.

The Portuguese were still convinced that they and not the Spanish were on the right track in trying to get to Asia. In 1488, Bartholomeu Dias had reached the Cape of Good Hope. In 1497 Vasco da Gama reached India by sailing around the Cape and returned to Portugal to tell the tale. It was, of course, a greater tale than that told by Columbus who had certainly not reached India.

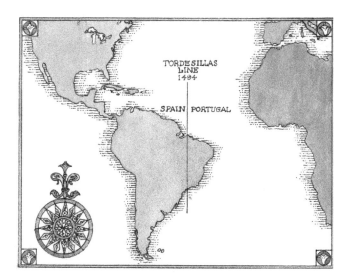

Fig 2.7 Tordesillas line

To sum up

The Columbus project that led to the Spanish arrival in the Caribbean was long in the making. The idea was to reach Asia by penetrating deep into the West Atlantic. The search for a route to Asia was the principal maritime objective of the 15th century, and Columbus was a part of the craze to trade or plunder the riches of Asia.

Lost in the Caribbean Sea, he was found by the indigenous peoples of the Bahamas whose gesture of welcome ushered a new global era. The Atlantic, east and west, would be forever linked as the space where the Europeans began a massive colonial and imperial enterprise.

Revision questions

1 a Name two countries from which early explorers to the Americas originated before the Spanish conquest of the region.
   b State two reasons why van Sertima argues that Africans were in the Caribbean before the arrival of Columbus.

2 a State two reasons why overseas expansion was important to Europeans in the 15th century.
   b Name three technological developments that facilitated European voyages of conquest .
   c Name three explorers who undertook expeditions to the Americas before Columbus.
   d Give three reasons why Columbus got lost on his journey to the East in the 1490s.

3 a What impact did the European invasion have on the Caribbean in the 15th century?
   b State three ways in which the European invaders' actions in the Caribbean differed from those they carried out in Asia and Africa.

Chapter 3

Spanish settlement and indigenous resistance

'See them fighting for power, but them don't know the hour.'
(Bob Marley)

Spain's imperial policy to build up its Empire through acquiring colonies, led to a war of conquest in the Caribbean. The military assault on Caribbean society by Columbus and those who came with and after him led to widespread devastation, slavery and mass murder of the indigenous population. The Tainos resisted the best they could, but the might of the Spanish overwhelmed them. The new colonised space needed to be administered properly and so did the exploitation of enslaved labour. This required the Spanish to set up complex systems of governance and economic organisation. Spain tried to be efficient and effective in achieving these objectives.

In this chapter we will learn about:
1. Lost in the Caribbean
2. Spanish colonial policy and settlement patterns
3. The oppression and enslavement of the Taino
4. Taino resistance
5. Spanish political and economic systems in the Caribbean

1 Lost in the Caribbean

Fig 3.1 Representation of an initial meeting between Columbus and the Taino.

In the early morning of 12 or 13 October 1492, the Taino found a lost and desperate Columbus and his party. Columbus was drifting along the coast of Guanahani, one of the islands in the Bahamas. From a distance the Taino watched in silence and then welcomed Columbus and his party ashore.

Columbus believed that he had arrived on the outer islands of the Asian continent. He eagerly asserted his right to be there, because of his support from the royalty of Spain and the Pope. Columbus was surprised by the welcome from the Taino and he took their hospitality as a sign of docility and that they were weak and unprepared for battle. Each group used its own values to weigh up the other.

The welcoming *cacique* (chief) found it very difficult to explain to his people how the Spanish had arrived at Guanahani. Columbus seemed impatient. He wanted to know where he was. He was lost and he had no knowledge of the unfamiliar civilisation that faced him. The Taino could not help him with answers. He was in their world. They did not know where he had come from or where he thought he had arrived.

Columbus wanted to know where Japan, China and India were and where was all the gold and riches of their civilisations. The Taino did their best to help him, but Columbus became more impatient. He was disappointed with their simple clothing and their simple lifestyle and circumstances. They did not wear fine, elaborate fabrics and only some of them were decorated in gold jewelry.

Columbus kept asking them where the route from Guanahani to the mainland was. But the answers the Taino gave him seemed unclear and not very helpful. Despite this, the Taino celebrated the arrival of the Spanish, exchanged gifts with them and fed them. It was a Caribbean greeting that Columbus appreciated but found unsatisfactory and sadly unrewarding. He thought of what he wanted and began to examine the Taino closely. His journal tells us about some of his first observations, 'They seemed to be a very poor and deprived people, and those I could see were young, none of them apparently more than about 30 years old'. He wrote about their technological development, 'They had no proper weapons; no metal objects, and used pikes without metal tips; sometimes they decorated the ends with fish bones.'

Columbus' experience of Africa and the Canary Islands influenced his opinions of the Taino. The Spanish saw colonisation as a way of obtaining cheap slave labour and as an opportunity to convert people to Christianity. He wrote of the Taino, 'They ought to make good servants, and they have lively minds, for I believe they immediately repeated what I said to them. I think it would be easy to convert them, as they do not seem to me to belong to any religion.'

Columbus wrote this last thought after his very brief encounter with the Taino. A few days later, he left Guanahani because he wanted to look at the neighbouring islands. On 25 October, he arrived in Cuba. Columbus was still convinced that he was near China and Japan, but he encountered more Taino, similar to those he had met on Guanahani. After a few weeks of surveying the northern Caribbean Columbus headed back to Spain. He arrived there on Friday, 15 March 1493. He docked at Palos, the same port from which he had departed on 3 August the previous year. He brought with him from the Caribbean, from Cuba and Hispaniola, a small quantity of gold, some coconuts and from Guanahani, a few Taino. He left behind at Hispaniola the crew of the wrecked *Santa Maria*, one of his three ships. They were to build a fort there.

Columbus was determined to return and to intensify the search for the Asian mainland. He promised to do as much in his report to his royal sponsors. In future voyages, he wrote, 'I will procure as much gold as they need, as well as a range of exotic goods, particularly spices, drugs, cotton and silks'. In this way he stimulated the royal sponsors' appetite and even though they were disappointed with what he had brought back from his voyage, they eagerly sponsored his return voyage. Before the end of the year, with a fleet of 17 ships, he headed back to the Caribbean. In his first voyage Columbus had surveyed the northern Caribbean and reported back to his Queen. He was still convinced that he was on the outskirts of the Asian mainland. But now, in this age of colonisation, it was more important for Spain to understand more

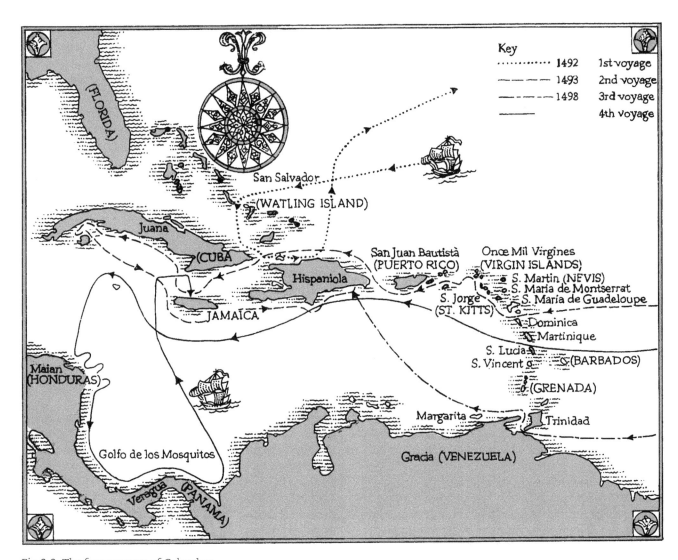

Key
.... 1492   1st voyage
— — — — 1493   2nd voyage
— - — - — 1498   3rd voyage
————   4th voyage

Fig 3.2 The four voyages of Columbus

about the Caribbean and to colonise it before their rivals, Portugal stepped in.

We saw in Chapter 2 that in 1479, by a papal bull, Spain and Portugal had already divided up the non-Christian world between themselves (see page 34). Portugal wanted to protect her African settlements and so claimed everything south and east of the Canaries. Spain claimed all lands west of the Canaries. According to this division the Caribbean was allocated to Spain. In 1494, the Treaty of Tordesillas confirmed this allocation. Today it is hard for us to understand how the Pope could be so arrogant and just allocate communities, lands and people to Christian kingdoms. However at that time the Catholic Church believed that this was its duty.

Unlike the first voyage, Columbus' second voyage concentrated on the Lesser Antilles. He passed along the coastline of Dominica, Guadeloupe, Montserrat, Antigua,

Santa Cruz (St Croix), Nevis, St Kitts, Saba, and the Virgin Islands in the middle of Kalinago territory. He began his colonisation during this voyage, starting on the island which he renamed Hispaniola. His main aim at Hispaniola was to use native labour to search for precious metals, and if possible to establish plantations. He described the soils as being extremely fertile. This colonisation was very much the same as the Canary Islands process.

Columbus was obsessed with finding the Asian mainland, and the settlers on his second voyage were obsessed with finding gold. The deposits of gold in the Canary Islands were now all finished and to attract settlers to the Indies, Columbus used the story of 'endless Caribbean gold'.

So, colonisation began at Santo Domingo (Hispaniola) in early 1494. The Spanish settlements were small, temporary and scattered because the Spanish were

          chapter 3 | *Spanish settlement and indigenous resistance*

constantly moving in their search for gold. They raided Taino villages, located far into the interior of the island. They frantically searched for gold, food and women. But the settlers found very little gold and soon they became more desperate. By March 1494, the first party, under Antonio de Torres, arrived in Spain with some 30,000 Caribbean gold ducats. This was the beginning of the ruthless subjection of the Taino by the Spanish.

In the meantime, although Columbus was searching the Atlantic, he could not find Asia, or any of the things he imagined Asia possessed. On his second voyage, he settled a colonial priest at Hispaniola, and then moved on to explore the Taino civilisation in Jamaica and Puerto Rico. He also journeyed south into the northern Lesser Antilles where he encountered larger communities of Kalinago. He returned to Spain in 1496.

He undertook altogether four voyages. The third voyage took place between 1498 and 1500, along the South American coastline. The final voyage took place between 1502 and 1504 and was an exploration of the central American coast. Columbus died in 1506, still convinced that he was correct in saying that Asia was somewhere 'around the corner'. Many historians have commented that he died with rich experiences of the Caribbean world, but without possession of its wealth. It is believed that he is buried in the Dominican Republic, the old Hispaniola.

2 Spanish colonial policy and settlement patterns

For the first ten years of colonisation, Hispaniola was the only colony in the Caribbean where the Spanish settled. In the 16th century Hispaniola was the centre of the Spanish colonial system in the Caribbean. Columbus was satisfied with the agricultural development in the colony, but he thought that Hispaniola was particularly important because he believed there was gold.

For its Caribbean exploits Spain set up a structure that looked like a commercial company that was run by Columbus to look after the Crown's interests and monopoly. The people who went with Columbus on his voyage were not colonists but employees of 'the company'. By 1510 the Spanish had mined most of the gold in the Caribbean and the Spanish population had increased from a few hundred in 1494 to several thousands. By 1515 there were at least 18 new towns in the northern Caribbean with Santo Domingo as the centre.

In the second half of the 16th century, the gold mines in Hispaniola were totally depleted. So the settlers began migrating to Cuba, Puerto Rico and Jamaica, looking for new mines and more Taino labour. By 1519 Hernan Cortés

had brought together a huge army of Spanish settlers for his Mexican voyage for he believed that there was a great abundance of gold and silver in Mexico. By 1530 the gold in the Greater Antilles was practically finished. Spaniards began to abandon these settlements and go to the Central American mainland. Only Santo Domingo remained, but it was also decaying fast. It was at this time that the Spanish colonisation of the Caribbean mainland took place. The Spanish settled along the Tierra Firme coast, from Cumaná to Panama, just as they had earlier settled in Jamaica, Cuba and Puerto Rico.

Fig 3.3 Taino panning gold for the Spaniards.

The early Spanish history of Jamaica, Cuba and Puerto Rico is similar to that of Hispaniola. The Spanish frantically searched for gold, they fought, defended and quickly wiped out the Taino, abandoned their settlements, and migrated to the mainland. By the 1540s there were undeveloped Spanish settlements all along the Caribbean coastline of Central and South America.

The Spanish explored the coast of Tierra Firme between 1500 and 1508. In 1509 Alfonso de Ojeda and Diego de Nicuesa left Hispaniola and established settlements in Central America. These settlements were disasters until Vasco Nunes de Balboa established a permanent colony in the Gulf of Darien. From this colony the Spanish established colonies along the Isthmus of Panama, including Costa Rica.

It was from these settlements that the Spanish attacked Nicaragua and Honduras, where they discovered the silver mines. At the centre of the silver boom was the city of Panama, and it attracted Spanish settlers from the islands. The indigenous peoples of Honduras and Nicaragua fought back and were only fully defeated in the 1540s. The Maya of the Yucatán peninsula also resisted the Spanish colonisers, but they were finally massacred in 1546.

The settlements on the Caribbean Central American mainland were poor and very bare. From the beginning, the Yucatán was a distant place and the Spanish did not worry about it too much. It had no gold and few indigenous people to fight with. In the 1560s, the settlements at Mérida and Campeche in the Gulf of Mexico held more Spaniards than these Central American colonies, because the Central American colonies were swampy valleys, full of disease which took a heavy toll on Spanish life. The settler population of Costa Rica was virtually wiped out by disease in the late 1570s. In 1580 the number of Spanish deaths in this region was much higher than in the islands. These settlements did not really develop in the 16th century, even though there were a few silver mines that attracted many settlers from the Caribbean islands.

3 The oppression and enslavement of the Taino

Columbus forced the Taino to pay the Spanish tribute to satisfy both the Crown's and the settlers' greed for gold, and to obtain food for his settlements. The Taino's agricultural system produced enough food for themselves but it could not also support the Spanish. In addition, the Taino could not spare their labour power to go off into the hills searching for gold, as people were needed to farm. The Taino economy began to collapse. The same experience was repeated in Cuba. The Cubans' friendly acceptance of the Spanish was now suddenly turning into a nightmare. People tried to resist but by 1495, civil war had broken out between the Cuban Taino and the Spanish. By 1497, people in Hispaniola were starving and living in terror. Columbus brought in a colonial regime in the Caribbean, and its most obvious feature was death and destruction. In creating a Spanish empire in the Caribbean, Columbus began the undoing of Taino society and economy.

Enslavement was another factor that contributed to the hardships of the colonised indigenous people. Remember that in Columbus' time the aim of owning colonies was that they should bring profits to the colonising country. But after a decade of Caribbean colonisation, Spain was still not satisfied with the financial rewards. The 'gold rush' was short-lived and the

Fig 3.4 *Thousands of Taino committed suicide rather than suffer the effects of slavery. Parents killed their children rather than let them grow up and become enslaved.*

wealth they got from it was not huge. So, at this stage, Columbus thought that a trade in indigenous enslaved Caribbean peoples could bring him and the Crown rewards. He had seen how the sale of enslaved Africans in Europe had brought Portugal wealth. So why should Spain not sell its non-Christian people? Columbus had already commented on what good servants they would make, and had taken a 'sample' of them home after his first voyage.

In 1493 Columbus spoke to Queen Isabella about a Caribbean slave trade, but she was not impressed and rejected the proposal. He placed it before her once again in 1494, this time with a difference. He argued that as the Taino were considered to be under the protection of the Crown, they could not be sold as captives, but why not enslave and sell the Kalinago? They had been waging a war of resistance upon Spanish rule and so were enemies of the Crown.

At this stage, the Spanish merchants analysed Columbus' proposal and rejected it for three reasons. First, they said that too many naked enslaved Caribbean people would die when the ship crossed the cold northern Atlantic Ocean. This would make the voyage and the trade uneconomical. Second, the farming sector of Spain was not suffering from a labour shortage. So imported enslaved Caribbean labour would be too expensive and the demand for it would be too low. Third, the Queen, while longing for gold and profits, was taking her role as the moral and spiritual protector of the Caribbean peoples a little more seriously than the settlers had expected and wished. She would not approve of a lively trade in enslaved Caribbean people. No one was against the enslavement and exploitation of the indigenous people in the colony, but they did object to shipping people to Europe and selling them there.

However, in the winter of 1495 there was some attempt to trade in enslaved Taino. On 24 February, a fleet of ships under the command of Antonio de Torres took a 'cargo' of some 650 enslaved Taino for sale in Spain. Half of the Taino died of cold on deck long before reaching Cadiz. The experiment was not repeated as it proved unprofitable. So the Portuguese kept their monopoly of selling non-Christian enslaved peoples on the European market.

Encomienda enslavement

Between 1498 and 1509, the colonial relationship between Ciboney, Taino and Kalinago on the one hand, and the Spanish on the other, was settled. This was done by an arrangement called the *repartimiento* system (a system of allocating enslaved labour to Spanish settlers by Crown officials), which was later modified and called the *encomienda*. This system detailed a way of making the change from war conditions to a colonial society and it was a way of controlling and enslaving indigenous people. How did this system come about? When Columbus arrived in Hispaniola in 1498, during the third voyage, he found Spanish settlers subverting the authority of his brother Bartholomeu whom he had left in charge. The Taino were also in rebellion. Those who were loyal to the Columbus project could not meet the demands for food, women and gold that the Spanish were making.

To pacify the Spanish settlers, Columbus used the same slave system that was used in the Canaries. The Queen's 'natives' were shared out amongst the settlers as enslaved estate labourers. They had to work for their new enslavers and pay tribute to them. This was the *repartimiento* system and it signalled the beginning of the organised enslavement of the first nation Caribbeans. In return for the slaves, the Spanish settlers who benefited from this system were expected to be loyal to both the Columbus regime and the Crown.

However, Columbus could not control the labour system he had started. In late 1498 Francisco de Bobadilla replaced him as governor. But it was only in 1502 that a lasting system for enslaved labour and race relations was established, when Nicolás de Ovando was appointed as governor of Hispaniola. It was Ovando's duty to organise the enslaved labour in the colony for productive work. The first thing he did was to develop fully the Columbus labour strategy. He started an organised system which forced the enslaved Taino to pay money and a commodity tribute and to provide involuntary labour to the settlers.

In 1509, a Spanish group led by Juan de Esquivel captured Jamaica. Then in 1511 Diego de Velázquez colonised Cuba. They imposed the *repartimiento* system on the defeated Taino in these two islands. By 1525 this system was found in almost every region under Spanish control in the Caribbean.

In some cases the system of slavery allowed Taino to be allocated to one person in a specific area. In this area he collected money and commodity tribute from the Taino and had rights over their enslaved labour. This was called an *encomienda* grant. The owners of these *encomienda* grants to enslaved Taino were called *encomenderos*. *Encomenderos* had to enforce the Christianisation of the Taino by keeping a priest among them. Thus *encomenderos* became an elite who eventually exercised great power over the future of Caribbean civilisation.

Fig 3.5 *Diego Velázquez.*

The encomienda and the Laws of Burgos

The *encomienda* system provided the framework within which the destruction of the Taino took place. The Spanish moved Taino families from place to place so that families were broken up under the system. The conuco crop production was devastated. The Spanish ruthlessly exploited females sexually. All this led to Taino families being unable to support themselves, an increase in the death rate, and at the same time a decrease in the Taino birth rate. In addition, all the wars of resistance and suicides contributed to the Taino's catastrophe.

The priests and clergy of Hispaniola did nothing to prevent this catastrophe because they identified with the interests of the *encomendero* class. The Franciscan missionaries who arrived with Ovando in 1502 did not campaign against the enslavement of the Taino. They did not report to the Crown how quickly the Taino population was declining. In 1510, a group of Dominican friars arrived on the island, and were immediately shocked by the situation. They reported to the Crown that the Taino were being enslaved, overworked, ill-fed, and were generally in the most terrible condition. Most of all, they reported that the Taino could not increase their population naturally. This was the beginning of a strong humanitarian protest against the *encomienda* system. In 1512-1513, the friars succeeded in making King Ferdinand pass laws to protect the Taino. These laws were called the Laws of Burgos.

The laws tried to improve the condition of the Taino by limiting their hours of labour, keeping children under 14 out of the mines, keeping families together and making the *encomendero* responsible for looking after their social welfare. However, the laws also stated that the basic relationship of racial domination between Spaniards and Taino was not to be changed. In the introduction to the laws it stated that the Taino were by nature inclined to be lazy, vicious and not interested in Christian learning. It also justified racism by stating that the Taino would only improve if they were under the control of Christians. The friars were most disappointed with these laws, which achieved little. In fact the laws endorsed the system. The condition of the Taino, both material and spiritual, continued to worsen. These laws are a classic example of how ineffective Spanish colonial legislation was.

Las Casas and the New Laws

In the 1520s the *encomenderos* did not obey the Laws of Burgos when they conflicted with their own interests. They also condemned the Dominican friars because they were interfering in their business. The *encomenderos* continued to enslave the Taino, and they were not particularly disturbed that there were less than 2,000 of them left on the island of Hispaniola by 1530. The leader of the Dominicans, Pedro de Córdoba, kept up the humanitarian movement. However his powers of persuasion with the Crown grew less and less, while the *encomenderos'* power grew more and more. It was only Bartholomé de las Casas who supported Córdoba in his grand effort to protect the remaining Taino.

Las Casas had lived in both Hispaniola and Cuba from 1502 to 1512. He was an *encomendero* in Cuba, and so knew this class well. He became a reformer in the days after the Laws of Burgos. In the 1520s and 1530s he emerged as the leader and champion of the Taino cause. On behalf of the Taino and the church, he appealed to the Council of Indies (*Consejo de las Indias*), the body through which the Crown ruled the colonies. He had seen how Córdoba had failed, and he knew that moral argument alone would not destroy the *encomienda* system. Instead, he informed the Crown and the Council of the Indies, that unless the system was destroyed two things were likely to happen. Firstly, the Taino would be wiped out. Secondly, the *encomendero* class would become so strong that it would eventually resist the rule of the Crown. This second argument, more than the first, was probably the reason why the Crown responded to Las Casas' petitions.

Fig 3.6 Bartolomé de las Casas

In 1542 the Crown passed a body of legal provisions, known as the New Laws. These laws forbade the enslavement of the Taino in the way that Africans were enslaved as property. They also did not allow new *encomiendas* to be granted. The Crown ordered church

chapter 3 | *Spanish settlement and indigenous resistance*

members and royal officials to give up their *encomiendas*. They hoped that within 20 years the system would be destroyed. These laws were supposedly humanitarian. However, the Crown's real aim was to control and subdue the *encomendero* class as it was beginning to show signs of being a colonial elite, putting its own interest before that of the Crown.

The *encomenderos* resisted the New Laws. In Peru they killed a viceroy and in Mexico the royal representative did not publish them. In 1545-46, the Crown was forced to cancel the laws and allow the *encomenderos* the right to leave *encomienda* grants to their sons and daughters as an inheritance. This inheritance became known as a *vida*. The *vida* system increased the powers of the *encomenderos*, and by the late 1590s the Taino were virtually extinct.

In 1548 the famous Spanish historian, Fernandez de Oveido, noted that the population of the four large islands of the Greater Antilles had been reduced from over one million to a few thousands. By 1560, an estimated 500 Taino remained on Hispaniola; and by 1600, the remaining 'pure' indigenous people could scarcely make up a village. In this part of the world, an estimated 1,000,000 native Americans had been reduced to only a fraction of their numbers as a result of the impact of the European invasion.

4 Taino resistance

Indigenous people did resist and fight back. G K Lewis, the acclaimed historian of Caribbean culture, says that the Taino and Kalinago had built a civilisation and a homeland, which they were prepared to defend in a spirit of defiant 'patriotism', just like the Aztec, Maya and Inca. They wished that the 'Europeans had never set foot in their country'. From the beginning, however, European colonial forces were technologically more prepared for a violent struggle for space. Columbus' mission was not just about maritime courage and determination. It was also about imperialist or colonial aims which they would defend by mobilising a huge amount of money and by using the science and technology they had. At this time European nations competed with one another for ethnic superiority in the world. They did this through invading and taking over the space of others, and by seeing themselves as culturally superior to the conquered.

At first European colonisation did not focus upon the complete destruction of indigenous societies. The colonisers preferred to absorb and integrate local people and resources into the imperial economic order. In the Greater Antilles, the Spanish succeeded in imposing settler institutions upon Taino communities so that they would be productive for the settlers. This action took its toll on Taino lives.

But the idea that the Taino were passive in the face of Spanish aggression is a myth. There is considerable evidence to show that the Taino fought costly, long wars of resistance, even though they had limited technical capabilities. Although they had initially welcomed Columbus and the early Spanish arrivants, once they saw that the Spanish wanted to take their land, life and liberty, they defended themselves. It was not easy for them to change from their community-minded, agricultural mentalities into the military mode. But they did manage to mobilise a large number of people to try to drive the Spanish out. Many of these wars of resistance ended in the Taino's defeat and their massacre by Spanish soldiers. Las Casas estimated that at least 10,000 Taino rebels died in a single day, on 24 March 1495.

Some of the rebels hid in the caves and mountains, and tried to establish more favourable terms of resistance and revolt. In fact, the Taino first established the Jamaican Maroon heritage, when they launched a long, guerilla-style war against Spanish settlers. There was no easy time for the *encomenderos*. There was constant tension and the *encomenderos* had deep fears because the Taino continually resisted their enslavement.

Many Taino communities in Cuba, Jamaica, Puerto Rico, and the Bahamas used different tactics to subvert and drive out the Spanish. They destroyed crops, refused to work, poisoned water supplies and burnt stores to try to starve the Spanish out. These actions forced the Spanish into the hills and forests in search of wild meat. Here Taino Maroons ambushed them. These battles continued throughout the 16th century until the Spanish finally crushed the Taino's resistance. But the Spanish also suffered huge losses in terms of life and property. The resistance also meant that the interior of the large islands were not settled as quickly as the Spanish had expected because Taino soldiers made it unsafe for the Spanish to inhabit those areas.

So in the Greater Antilles, Taino offered a spirited military resistance to the Spanish. In some places they were supported by a group known as the Karifuna, the offspring of mostly Maroon Africans and Kalinago and Taino. The mixed race Karifuna were engaged in the anti-slavery struggle as well as the war against European occupation. In the early struggles for Puerto Rico, Karifuna from neighbouring St Croix came to the Taino's assistance. In 1494, when Columbus led 400 men into the interior of Hispaniola in search of food, gold and Taino for enslavement, several *caciques* (chiefs) mobilised their armies in resistance. Guacanagari, a leading *cacique*, had tried previously to negotiate a settlement with military

Fig 3.7 *The southern islands inhabited by the Kalinago*

commander Aloso de Ojeba. Now he marched with a few thousand men upon the Spanish. He was unsuccessful. In 1503, another 40 *caciques* were captured at Hispaniola and burnt alive by Governor Ovando's troops. Anacaona, the main *cacique*, was publicly hanged in Santo Domingo. A state of civil war existed in the Greater Antilles because of Taino wars of resistance. But with Kalinago support, the Taino were even more determined to fight the Spanish to death.

In Puerto Rico, Taino soldiers frequently attacked the Spanish settlement party led by Ponce de León. Many Spanish settlers were killed; however, many more Taino and Kalinago were defeated and crushed in the counter-assault. In 1511 resistance in Cuba, led by *cacique* Hatuey, was put down. The Spanish captured Hatuey and burnt him alive. The Spanish crushed another revolt in 1529. In these struggles, thousands of Taino were killed in battle. Also the Spanish publicly executed many of them in an attempt to break the spirit of collective resistance. Some soldiers fled to the mountains and forests where they expanded Maroon settlements and continued the war against the Spanish.

Many authors have commented on the growing death rate among Taino on Hispaniola, caused by disease, violence and famine. Spanish slavers raided the indigenous populations of neighbouring islands, usually from Jamaica and Puerto Rico. In addition, they brought an estimated 40,000 enslaved Taino from the Lucayas (Bahamas) to work the mines of Hispaniola in the first decade of the 16th century. In 1511 they went as far south as Trinidad into Kalinago territory to capture persons for

enslavement. Here slave practices eventually led to similar famine and human population decline.

By the middle of the 16th century the Spanish had successfully crushed Taino and Kalinago resistance in the Greater Antilles. Community structures were smashed, and their members reduced to various forms of enslavement in Spanish agricultural and mining enterprises.

According to Carl Sauer, 'As the labour supply from Espanola declined, attention turned to the southern islands'. These southern islands, from St Croix and neighbouring Puerto Rico to the Guianas, were inhabited by the Kalinago. A Spanish royal declaration dated 7 November 1508 and 3 July 1512, authorised settlers to capture and enslave Kalinago on 'the island of Los Barbudos (Barbados), Dominica, Matinino (Martinique), Santa Lucia, San Vincente, La Asunción (Grenada), and Tavaco (Tobago)', because of their 'resistance to Christians'.

By the end of the 16th century, however, the Spanish had decided to adopt a 'hands off policy' in the Lesser Antilles. They accepted that there was no gold in the Lesser Antilles and that they would lose many people at the hands of Kalinago soldiers. So they turned their attention to the Greater Antilles. As a result, the Greater and Lesser Antilles became politically separated at this time by what Troy Floyd described as a 'poison arrow curtain'.

5 Spanish political and economic systems in the Caribbean

By the end of 1493, it was clear to the indigenous people of the Caribbean that the Spanish were not leaving. Their stay would be permanent. Remember that in this age of colonisation, Spain needed to legalise the Caribbean as a Spanish colony, before her competitor, Portugal, could challenge this. Remember that these two nations had already arrogantly divided the non-Christian world between themselves in 1479. According to this division Spain was allocated the Caribbean and in 1494 the Treaty of Tordesillas tried to confirm this allocation.

Portugal was not the only competitor that Spain feared. Europe was completely taken with Da Gama's successful voyage to India, much more so than with Columbus' voyage to an unknown place. While Columbus was still insisting that he had reached Asia, Da Gama had proven it beyond doubt. This was how it was at first, but over the next 20 years people changed their minds. But Portugal was the European nation that began to reap the rewards of the Asian trades. The Portuguese did not end their project with Da Gama's India success. They also wished to know where Columbus had actually gone. They were convinced that it was not Asia, but they also wanted to be

chapter 3 | *Spanish settlement and indigenous resistance*

Fig 3.8 *Americus Vespucius, whose name was given to the continents in the West Atlantic*

a part of this unknown world about which Columbus had spoken. In 1500, Pedro Cabral, a Portuguese sailor who worked the African coast, sailed west across the south Atlantic and came upon the land we now call Brazil. Portugal claimed this land under the Treaty of Tordesillas.

There was a strange twist in the Cabral voyage which wrote him out of the centre pages of Atlantic history. In 1500 on board his vessel there was a merchant from Florence called Americus Vespucius. After the voyage of 1500 he presented evidence to the European courts that he had made the voyage three years earlier, in 1497. He claimed that the Cabral voyage was a copy of what he had already accomplished.

The evidence that Americus presented to prove his case was used in the first major geography book about the West Atlantic which was published in 1507. The volume editor was a well-known printer called Martin Maldsee-Muller. He described the continent in the West Atlantic as 'America's land'. Other books published after this book simply accepted this language and gradually more and

more people recognised it. This was how 'America' was invented and not discovered; it was a process of claiming by 'renaming' rather than 'discovering'.

This was a time in which the English, French and Dutch were cast in the role of followers, trailing behind the Portuguese and Spanish. In the late 15th century, they had followed the Portuguese and Spanish along the African coast and now in the beginning of the 16th century they were again following them westward, hunting for Asia. They did not yet have the military might and political confidence to defend themselves against Spanish power. So they moved carefully and quietly around the edges, not wishing to arouse the anger of the Iberian giants. But the English, French and Dutch were persistent and they did contribute to the European story of Atlantic voyaging.

In 1497 there was another sailor from Columbus' town, Genoa in Italy. He was called John Cabot, although his real name was Giovanni Cobato. The English King Henry VII financed him to sail across the north Atlantic in search of Asia. Just like the Norse, the Viking sailors 500 years earlier, John Cabot came upon 'Newfoundland'. Now the English had a reason to make their claim to the 'new' lands of the Atlantic.

In 1524 the King of France financed another Italian sailor, Giovanni de Verrazano, to make a French claim upon West Atlantic lands. He sailed along the eastern coastline of North America between the areas now known as Maine and the Carolinas. However, when he returned to France he reported that he couldn't find the Asia wealth or trading empire. Ten years later, the French tried again. This time they used their own sailor, Jacques Cartier. He travelled into present-day Canada, exploring the grand St Lawrence River. Again, he reported there was no gold, silver, spices, or exotic goods for the French elite.

It all seemed rather uninteresting until 1519 when the Spanish, led by Hernando Cortés, arrived in Mexico. In 1521 they marched into the Aztec capital, Tenóchtitlan, defeated the army of King Montezuma, and looted and destroyed the ancient kingdom. They stole all the riches of the Aztec Empire. Remember that the Portuguese had ridiculed Spain for a long time because Spain kept searching for a sea-route to Asia, which the Portuguese had already found. Now Spain was back at the centre of attention as far as colonising the Atlantic world was concerned.

From looting the Aztec wealth, ridiculing King Montezuma and destroying the ancient empire, Spain became the wealthiest country known until that time in the history of the European world. Wealth in the form of gold and silver poured into Spain by the royal shiploads. The Spanish monarchy, who had grown tired of the fruitless Columbus Caribbean project, had finally fulfilled its dream.

However, the Spanish did not stop their process of stealing the wealth of indigenous civilisations, razing cities to the ground and enslaving inhabitants. Destroying the Aztecs of Mexico was just the beginning. In 1532, Francisco Pizarro arrived in Peru. He marched into Cuzco – the heart of the Inca Empire – with an army of 164 men and 62 horses and began to dismantle the rule of the Inca. They looted Inca riches by raiding temples, cities, stores and households. In 1572, the Spanish toppled the last Sapa Inca. This signalled the political defeat of one of the greatest civilisations of the Atlantic.

The wealth that the Spanish took from the Inca was far more than what they had taken from the Aztec. And while their wealth was stripped from their land, the Inca and other ethnic groups died in thousands from European diseases and swords, just as the Mexicans had. In the meantime the Spanish were no longer that interested in precious metals. They were now beginning to think of a

different kind of project – accumulating wealth through the production and trade of agricultural products.

Administering the Caribbean Empire

In the late 15th century, Spain used a system of monopolies to manage economic and political life. This meant that a few individuals, in this case the royalty of Spain, had exclusive control over trade and politics. It is therefore not surprising that Spain used this same system to manage her colonies. From Columbus' days in the 15th century to the mid-18th century, Spain's grand aim was for the royalty to have a monopoly over the colonies. They saw the Caribbean as the 'possession' of Spain, or more precisely, the Spanish Crown. All foreigners were seen as intruders. This system of monopolies was based on the idea that the wealth of a country depended upon its

Fig 3.9 *Customs house in Cadiz, Spain*

chapter 3 | *Spanish settlement and indigenous resistance*

balance of trade, in other words, the balance between what the nation imports and exports. There should be more exports than imports because then money and wealth flowed into the country. Spain was determined to have sole or exclusive trading with the Caribbean, so that no other nation could get the wealth of the Caribbean. The Caribbean was a ready market for Spain's exports and Spain was the only country that would be able to get the Caribbean's precious metals.

The system of monopoly was also applied to political life. The Crown had the sole authority to dictate policy, pass laws and appoint colonial officials. So the way the colonies were managed, economically and politically, showed this royal monopoly and absolute power.

The Crown had to make sure that Spain kept its monopoly over trade in the Caribbean. So in 1494 the Crown ordered that all trade with the colonies had to pass through one port – Cadiz. Here a customs house monitored all 'ins and outs' of the colonies and kept a royal official record of them. In 1495 the Crown opened trade with the colonies to all Castillians, but Cadiz remained the single port. The Crown claimed one-tenth of every tonnage to and from the colonies but did not impose any freight charges.

The House of Trade

In 1503 Seville replaced Cadiz as the main port. In Seville the House of Trade (*Casa de Contratración*) regulated and controlled the colonial trade. An agent of the House of Trade was based in each Caribbean colony. It was the agent's duty to represent the Crown by making sure that duties were paid and trade controlled. In 1717 Cadiz once again became the main port, and the House of Trade was moved there. In 1789 the Crown declared 'free trade'. This meant that all Spanish ports and not only Cadiz were allowed to trade with the Caribbean.

Remember that the aim of the monopoly was to prevent foreigners from trading with the Caribbean and getting their precious metals. This influenced the way in which trade was conducted in the Caribbean. For example, the colonies were only allowed to import foodstuffs and other goods from only Spain and not from other Europeans, even if Spain could not supply them. This meant that the colonists in the Caribbean had to start developing their own industries and supplying their own goods. Many different kinds of small-scale businesses and large-scale agriculture developed as a result. The economy of the Caribbean quickly broadened and expanded. At this time Spain was not a rapidly industrialising country like England and the Netherlands. So there were many goods which the colonists needed but which Spain could not produce. For example, Spain had few sugar refineries, shipyards and tanneries.

So the colonies had to develop their own industries. In the 1580s all of these new industries were developing in Cuba, Jamaica and Hispaniola. The Crown also gave the colonists permission to make wine and so the wine industry developed in most islands, as did tobacco blending. In 1584 the Crown passed laws to encourage the colonists to develop their own manufacturing industry to take economic pressure off the Spanish economy. By 1600 Cuba was more advanced than Hispaniola, and Havana became the commercial centre of the Caribbean.

The Council of the Indies

The Council of the Indies operated in the area of administration in the same way as the House of Trade functioned in commerce. The Council was established in 1511 but it was only constituted as a separate body in 1524. It was a council of experts and officials that were nominated by the Crown. Their aim was to protect royal and Spanish control of the colonies. The Council prepared all laws, assessed all the officials of the colonial government and was the highest legal body in the colony. It had control over the royal bureaucratic system and the military system.

Remember that at that time, the church played a very important role in Spanish politics. So the Council was made up of the church and the state or government, who ruled together. The state-appointed governors were all-powerful, although the church also had many powers. But the governors had some control over the church. The official from the royal treasury was independent of the governor; he was a 'royal official' or a royal governor of the Crown.

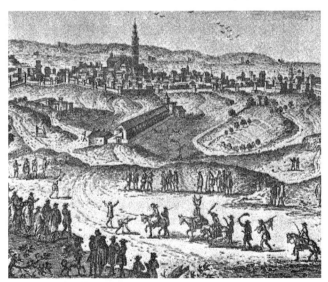

Fig 3.10 Seville, which replaced Cadiz as the main Spanish trading port in the 16th century

From the Spanish point of view, Ovando was the first effective royal governor in the Caribbean. When he returned to Spain in 1509, the Crown appointed an independent body to replace him. The purpose of this body was to hear all appeals against the decisions of governors and magistrates. This tribunal became known as the *audencia*. It was a Court of Appeal made up of lawyers, judges and administrators. It was controlled by the governors. One of its jobs was to watch the activities of royal officials.

Cabildos

Most settlers and *encomenderos* lived in towns, and enjoyed a very high quality of life. A municipal council called the *cabildo* administered the towns. For example, in 1507 some towns of Hispaniola were incorporated, and *cabildos* had municipal control over them and the immediate surrounding countryside. The members of the *cabildos* were called *regidores*. At first they were appointed by the governors from among the *encomendero* class. They, in turn, would nominate their own replacements. In some towns, like in Havana up until 1570, the people elected the *regidores* from among the heads of households. However, the Crown did not encourage popular elections and

democracy. It was more concerned with absolute power and monopoly. So the Crown soon got rid of this system in Havana. By 1550, some *regidores* were appointed for life and could sell their post or leave it to someone when they died if the royal governor approved. This system guaranteed that the Crown kept its control over the towns.

Economic policy and activities

Mining industry

We have seen that the economy of the Spanish Caribbean was first established with a 'gold rush'. So at first economic activity and the way people settled in places were based upon the mining industry. This was the same in Jamaica, Hispaniola, Cuba and Puerto Rico. In the European Middle Ages, mines were usually owned and controlled by the Crown and the Spanish Crown, therefore, quickly established its exclusive rights over the mines in the Caribbean. This only applied to gold and silver mines, and did not apply to the copper mines exploited by colonists in Cuba in the 16th century.

In 1504 Spanish settlers had to register their mines with the Colonial authorities and bring all ore to the royal

Fig 3.11 *Marketplace, Havana*

chapter 3 | *Spanish settlement and indigenous resistance*

smelters for tax assessment and to be stamped. These restrictions were only completely removed in 1584. The settlers had to pay a portion of the gold mined to the Crown. By 1580 this royal portion was lowered from a half to one-fifth. Eric Williams has estimated that in 1503 the royal income from Caribbean mines amounted to 8,000 ducats; in 1509 to 59,000 ducats; and about 120,000 ducats in 1518. According to Williams, '… during the period 1503-90, a total income from the Indies amounted to over 5 to 8 million ducats.'

Sugar cane industry

The sugar cane industry replaced mining as the main economic activity in the islands in the mid-16th century. After his second voyage Columbus had developed sugar cane farming. Hispaniola became the centre of the first Caribbean sugar industry. Gonzalo de Vedosa established the first sugar mill there in 1516. He used an animal-powered mill called the *trapiche*. In the 1520s the numbers of these increased. Later the water mill, or *ingenio*, was introduced. In the 1530s the sugar industry was expanded into the other islands.

Ovando, writing from the Spanish colonies in the 16th century, stated that profits were occasionally good but generally average. It cost about 10,000 gold ducats to establish each ingenio. This meant that only the rich could afford to produce sugar. In 1523 there were 30 *ingenios* in Jamaica and ten in Puerto Rico by 1533. Most of the sugar produced was sold in the Caribbean, but small amounts were exported to the mainland colonies and to Spain. Spain was already producing enough sugar at home so the market for Caribbean sugar was small and limited.

Cattle ranching and leather industry

Another important part of the formal Spanish Caribbean economy was cattle ranching. It continued to play an important role in the economy in the period when sugar was the main export crop. On the open plains of Jamaica, Cuba and Hispaniola the cattle of the *encomenderos* roamed. From cattle ranching came the leather industry. Leather was in demand in Europe and Caribbean hides were sold in England, France and other European countries. By the 1550s the Spanish settlers had solved their food problem. Now most settlements were self-sufficient in beef.

Tobacco and farming industries

The Spanish also grew tobacco for export. Caribbean tobacco soon dominated the European market, and to this day Cuban tobacco is still rated among the best in the world. The settlers learnt much from the Taino about farming, and

expanded maize and cassava output during the second half of the 16th century. By the end of the 16th century, the Taino were a people of the past, the export base of the islands was not strong, but the *encomendero* class were eating well and in full control of the colonial economies.

The African as enslaved labour

The Spanish Caribbean economy had a variety of industries that needed a substantial amount of labour. The sugar plantations and the mines generally employed large numbers of women, children and men. But by the mid-16th century the indigenous Taino could no longer meet these labour demands. The settlers thought about bringing in free labour from Europe, but these labourers could not be forced to work under the conditions demanded by the *encomenderos*. So between 1520 and 1530, the church suggested that enslaved Africans, whom the Portuguese were selling in Europe, should be imported into the Caribbean to replace the fast-dying Taino.

The church helped develop the racist argument that the Africans were not 'native' subjects of the Crown, but were subjects of the so-called 'barbaric' and 'heathen' kings. So neither the church nor the Crown saw any moral or ethical reason why Africans should not be imported and enslaved in the Caribbean. The Portuguese had already organised the trade in enslaved Africans in Brazil from the early 1530s. In addition enslaved Africans were already used in Spanish society, so this system could very easily be extended to the Caribbean. All that was needed were the right economic conditions. These presented themselves in the mid-16th century, when the sugar and tobacco industries and cattle ranching expanded and needed more labour to continue growing.

The Portuguese settlers in Brazil had often argued that they could force one enslaved African to produce more in a year than five indigenous persons. This became a useful economic justification for introducing enslaved Africans. In 1523, the King of Spain ordered that provision be made for the importation of 4,000 enslaved Africans into the Caribbean. Of these, 1,500 would go to Hispaniola, 500 to Puerto Rico, 300 to Jamaica and Cuba, and the rest to the mainland colonies.

Las Casas noted that by 1540 some 30,000 enslaved Africans had been imported into Hispaniola. By the 1570s the Spanish imported them into the island at a rate of 2,000 per year. These were the official figures, but contraband traders imported many more enslaved Africans illegally. By the end of the 16th century, the enslavement of Africans was fully established, and the well-known relationship of 'sugar and Black slavery' was deep-rooted in Caribbean society.

To sum up

After the establishment of settlements in the wake of the Columbus Project, the Spanish unleashed a reign of terror upon the Caribbean world. This resulted in the virtual elimination of the native communities, large-scale enslavement of Africans, and the declaration of an imperial policy of exclusive rights to the wealth of the region. To give effect to this policy, the Spanish imposed a system of labour organisation, political administration, and economic regulation upon the Caribbean. The native community resisted Spanish settlers the best it could, and some Spanish settlers in turn resisted royal and imperial authority. The frantic search for wealth, while at the same time trying to lessen the social disaster of Spanish policies, was contradictory. As a way of dealing with the crisis, African enslavement was imposed upon the ruins of the native community. The crisis of imperial rule deepened as the wealth the settlers got from looting increased.

Revision questions

1 a Name the Treaty by which the Catholic Church claimed to divide the world between Spain and Portugal.
  b State three reasons why other European powers were opposed to the Treaty.
  c State three ways in which other European powers demonstrated their opposition to Spanish monopoly in the Caribbean.
  d State two ways in which Spain defended its interests from attackers.

2 a How did Spain govern its American empire in the 15th and 16th centuries?
  b State four economic benefits that Spain derived from its Caribbean colonies.

Chapter 4

Other European settlement and rivalry

'So you think you have found the solution, but it's just another illusion.'
(Bob Marley)

Within a half century of the Columbus project, the Caribbean had become important to European states, to an extent that had never been seen before in the westward imperial drive. The East Atlantic Islands and West Africa did not excite the European imagination in the way the Caribbean did. All European nations pledged their commitment to securing a share of the Caribbean wealth, whether by looting, farming or trading. The Spanish tried to keep them all out by stating that it had monopoly rights and by backing up this claim with military power and legal authority. The northwest European nations, England, France, Holland and Denmark especially, challenged Spain by attacking its ships, raiding settlements, and conquering territory. These efforts increased in intensity over time and became more effective. By the early 17th century the other European nations were not so fearful of Spanish power and by mid-century they had broken Spanish effective monopoly power. These rival powers formed alliances against the Spanish, the common enemy, although they also fought each other for an advantage in the Caribbean. The indigenous communities also participated in these rivalries. They sought to take back territory and protect their liberty. The Caribbean became a theatre for imperial war and resistance to colonialism.

In this chapter we will learn about:
1. The challenge to Spanish monopoly by other European nations
2. The ways in which European nations challenged the Spanish monopoly
3. The Spanish counter-attack
4. The resistance of the Kalinago in the Eastern Caribbean

1 Challenge to Spanish monopoly by other European nations

European politics was greatly affected by the Spanish control of the Caribbean in the 16th century. Spaniards wrote books, reports and other literature about the Caribbean and these were translated into English, Dutch and French. Most Europeans therefore knew about the Spanish colonisation of the Caribbean. These Europeans were not prepared to allow the Spanish to have exclusive rights to New World wealth. They objected to all papal bulls that allowed Spanish control. They also realised that if the Spanish were not stopped, in time Spain might become the most fearsome force in Europe.

Consequently, the other European countries, mainly through the activities of male adventurers, pirates and colonisers, began to attack the Spanish monopoly in the Caribbean. This came in three broad phases. First, from the time the Spanish made contact with the Caribbean to the mid-16th century, the northern European powers were not yet aware of the full significance of the New World. Their protest against Spain's exclusive rights to the Caribbean was mainly vocal. They did not act to stop Spanish control. Second, from 1555 to about 1640, the English, French and Dutch consistently attacked Spanish trade and settlements. In the earlier part of this period these attacks came mainly from privateers and interlopers. But in the second decade of the 17th century, the attacks were mainly from settlers, organised merchant companies and states. Third, after the mid-17th century to the War of Jenkins' Ear in 1739, Spain was forced to make trade concessions. When the Seven Years' War ended in 1763 they gave up the Windward Islands to Britain and opened up some Caribbean ports, particularly those in Cuba, to British merchants.

By the mid-17th century, Spain was dubbed the 'sick man in the Caribbean'. English and French colonies had overtaken the Spanish colonies in trade, wealth and population. Spain's monopoly existed in theory only; the world that Columbus had created for Spain had long been destroyed.

European nations competed with each other for positions in the Caribbean. In the 16th century, the Caribbean was a frontier or border. Here war was the normal way used to settle differences. The Dutch, French and English formed an alliance against the Spanish, and secured their own share of the Caribbean. Then they started fighting among themselves for 'the' dominant position. Between 1655 when the English captured Jamaica and the Seven Years' War in 1756, the four nations fought each other to become 'ruler of the Caribbean'. The Kalinago strongly resisted all European intrusions upon

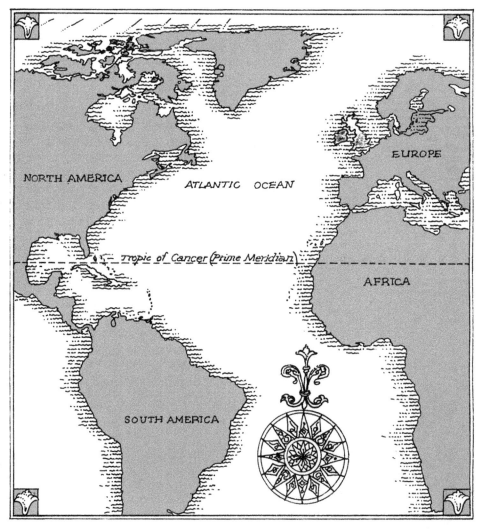

Fig 4.1 The prime meridian beyond which governments no longer protected the adventurer

chapter 4 | *Other European settlement and rivalry*

the Lesser Antilles where they were still dominant. War and trade went together in the same way that war and politics seem inseparable. In the late 18th century the English emerged as the most successful Caribbean colonists and Spain was forced to remove its policy of Caribbean exclusiveness.

In the mid-16th century, the Caribbean lay beyond the line or outside territorial limits set down by European treaties. European laws had no effect in the Caribbean; here law and power were seen simply as 'effective occupation'. In 1559, the French and Spanish politicians would not give up their claims to the New World. They worked out this policy of 'no peace beyond the line' – beyond the territorial limits set down by European treaties there would be no peace agreements. The Spanish refused to give up their 'right' to not allow 'foreigners' into the Caribbean. The French refused to give up their 'right' to go there. The parties agreed to disagree in the Caribbean, but to keep peace at home. Anyone who went beyond the prime meridian in the mid-Atlantic or south of the Tropic of Cancer was on his own; the governments could no longer represent or protect the adventurer.

In the late 16th century, this policy regulated European rivalry. English, Dutch and French pirates and merchants operated in the New World, but they could not claim to be representing any government. When the Spanish authorities caught English adventurers beyond the line, Queen Elizabeth I of England denied knowledge of them and their activities.

In addition, when Spanish and English politicians got together in 1604 and 1609 to draw up peace treaties, they used the same principle. According to these peace treaties, the English were free to settle in unoccupied lands, or land not occupied by any Christian prince, and the Spanish government was free to kill these settlers and keep its policy of Caribbean exclusiveness. As the Caribbean lay between Spain and its silver empire in Peru and Mexico, the Spaniards were very concerned about all 'enemy' settlements in the region.

Anyone living beyond the line was stateless, was not represented by any government and was in danger. Much blood was spilt in the Caribbean as a result of this policy. It is difficult to find another area in the world where Europeans destroyed the native population and then started killing each other with such speed.

Privateers and interlopers

Up to the 1530s Spain's settlements in the Caribbean did not bring it any real material wealth so the Caribbean remained largely unattractive to other Europeans. However, the northern Europeans began to show a new interest in the region after the rise of the sugar industry in the 1530s, and the settlement of Mexico in 1519 and Peru in 1531.

This new interest led to direct interference in the colonial business of the Spanish by the northern Europeans. We can place this direct interference into two categories. First, the operation of contraband trade by northern European merchants. They exchanged enslaved peoples, wine, textiles and other goods with Spanish colonists for gold, silver, tobacco, hides, sugar and other colonial produce. Second, the northern Europeans raided settlements and convoys carrying produce back to Spain. Looting was big business and the Spanish empire, scattered in the central zones of the Americas, seemed vulnerable.

The looting was probably more damaging to the Crown than the contraband trade but it was not easy for the Spanish imperial government to control either activity. On the other hand, the settlers were more opposed to raids upon their towns than upon ships on the high seas. They generally encouraged the contraband trade, in spite of governors' protests. The material needs of the settlers were far stronger than their loyalty towards the Crown or to Spain. In any case, they felt that they were being suppressed by an authoritarian Crown which did not understand the nature of their everyday difficulties.

Between 1530 and 1575 the most valuable commodity traded by non-Spaniards in the Caribbean were enslaved Africans. At this time the Portuguese were the primary suppliers. After the 1580s the Dutch were the main suppliers. In the 1530s the Portuguese were the first to obtain an *asiento* (a contract to sell human cargo in Spanish colonies). But after 1560 the English began to sell enslaved Africans illegally in the Caribbean. In Cuba, Hispaniola and the Bahamas smuggling of Africans was common. From these smugglers, encomenderos and others obtained Africans at lower prices than those offered by the legal *asiento* suppliers.

In the 1540s the French began to make their presence felt in the Caribbean. After they had failed to settle in Brazil in the 1530s, the French started a programme of illegal trade and looting in the Spanish Caribbean. Looting became more profitable than trading, and also more attractive. This form of activity dominated French relations with the Spanish empire. The French made a successful series of small raids on Spanish shipping in 1536. They then encouraged Jean Ango, a French shipping magnate, to organise a more systematic programme of looting. The French captured many Spanish ships and took a number of small towns in Hispaniola, including Yaguana (present-day Port-au-Prince).

From the 1540s, all fleets from the Caribbean to Spain were protected by convoys and had secret sailing directions. All towns were heavily protected. In 1553,

François Le Clerc of France, with a fleet of ten ships, ransacked Spanish towns in the Greater Antilles. He took Santiago in Cuba. The following year his lieutenant, Jacques Sores, took Havana and destroyed it. The French showed up the weaknesses in the Spanish Caribbean colonial system, and exposed to ridicule its monopoly and exclusiveness policy. The French easily took Havana and after this it was easier to take other colonies.

At this stage the Spanish imperial government realised that only a well-coordinated sea and land defence could save its Caribbean interests from this form of attack. In 1560, Pedro Menéndez de Avilés was given a mission by the Spanish government to plan the sea and land defence. However, Menéndez' arrival was just a little late because the English had already joined the French in Caribbean piracy and looting.

Between 1552-68 the pioneer of English activity in the region, John Hawkins, made four voyages. His plan was to trade as much as possible, and loot when necessary. He wanted to secure a licence to trade enslaved Africans with Spanish settlements, but pressure from both the imperial government and Portuguese merchants designated him as just another smuggler. In 1568 a Spanish patrol caught up with him and he was chased out of the region. His party was damaged and he just made it back to England.

Fig 4.2 Sir Francis Drake

Menéndez did effective work. He kept Spanish shipping and settlements quite safe until the English started attacking again under the now famous pirate, Francis

Drake. Drake had had some experience as a pirate while serving with Hawkins, but he did not begin his first voyage until 1572. This voyage was his well-known seizure of a mule train at the isthmus of Panama, which was carrying silver from Peru.

In 1585 Francis Drake reorganised his attack and subsequent voyages looked like well-planned naval operations rather than raids. His aim was to completely cut off Spain's communication with the colonies. However, he was not very successful because of the strength of Spanish naval defences. In 1596 the English, French and Dutch formed an alliance against the Spanish. They destroyed a Spanish fleet and broke up communication between Cadiz and the colony for two years.

In 1604 a peace treaty was signed and a new development took place in the nature of Caribbean rivalry. England agreed to respect the exclusive rights of Spain in areas where Spain had effective settlements. At the same time all areas where there were no settlements were open to competition. This policy was set out in the 1609 Truce of Antwerp. Spain did not disagree or agree with this policy so its silence was seen as agreement. By this time England had established an effective settlement in Virginia and the Spanish did not contest this. The days of privateering were coming to an end, and agricultural settlements were becoming more common.

English, French and Dutch settlements

After the English settled in Virginia in the present USA in 1609, privateers and interlopers renewed their hostilities against Spanish Caribbean interests. In 1612 the governor of Cuba reported to the Spanish imperial authorities that there were so many pirates and contraband traders on the coastlines of the colony that the settlers accepted them as a normal part of life. In 1615 Hispaniola was also reported to be hiding hundreds of contraband traders. There was nothing the Santo Domingo authority could do. The imperial government ordered the governors to bring into being an anti-contraband policy. This policy had little effect. For example, when it was applied against the tobacco smugglers at Cumána, off the coast of Venezuela it merely forced smuggling into Trinidad where the French and Dutch developed a profitable trade. In the early 1620s the Spanish could no longer control the trading activities of the Dutch, French and English in the Caribbean.

Europeans made many efforts to settle in the Guianas, and many were also persistent in their search for El Dorado (the city of gold). For these reasons many Europeans came to the southern Caribbean. By 1620 the northern Europeans concentrated their colonial efforts in the southern and eastern Caribbean. Their aims were now to settle on the land, to farm and and make a living by trading produce. These aims became the main feature of non-Spanish colonisation in the Caribbean.

At this time 'rebel' activities happened mainly in the Lesser Antilles – the smaller islands of the eastern Caribbean in which Spain seemed to have no settlement interest. Neither the English nor the Dutch were prepared for a full-scale war with Spain, and so were prepared to take the 'crumbs' of the Spanish Caribbean Empire. The Kalinago settled these islands and from the beginning unleashed a full-scale war upon the European intruders. The Kalinago had seen the earlier destruction of the Taino and were not prepared to enter into any friendly relations with Europeans. The French, Dutch, and English, on the other hand, were not inexperienced; they had had success in earlier adventures and were firmly committed to colonisation.

The English made their first serious attempts at settlements in the Caribbean in Guiana. Guiana was located between the Orinoco River, which was held by Spain, and the Amazon, which was held by Portugal. In the rear were resisting Kalinago. The English were not very successful. They tried to settle on the South American mainland in 1604, 1609, 1620, 1629 and 1643. In the 1620s they successfully settled on the islands of the Lesser Antilles.

In 1621 the Dutch West India Company was formed. The company and its policies were supported by the Dutch state. It was in fact the parent of non-Spanish colonisation in the Caribbean. The objectives of the company were bold; to attack Spanish settlements and to establish Dutch commerce at all cost. This was typical of the confidence of the northern Europeans in forcing Spain to liberalise its colonial policy.

The English: from Guiana to the Caribbean Islands

In 1624, the Dutch West India Company launched an attack upon Brazil. When the Crowns of Portugal and Spain had been joined by marriage in 1580, Spain assumed authority over Brazil. In 1624 Spain was forced to defend Brazil. While this was happening the French and English took the opportunity to settle as many islands in the Lesser Antilles as possible. This colonisation drive was directed and financed by a new colonial agent – the merchant adventurer. Prominent among them in the 1620s were Sir William Courteen, Robert Rich (later the Earl of Warwick), Ralph Merrifield and Marmaduke Rawden.

St Christopher

In 1623 Robert North's settlement efforts in Guiana failed. Then in 1624, Thomas Warner sailed into the eastern Caribbean and established the colony of St Christopher (later St Kitts). Warner found that the colony was well-suited for agriculture. It was outside the Spanish zone of direct interest, and he felt that with a good army the Kalinago could be thrown on the defensive. Here on the island of St Christopher the English began their first permanent Caribbean settlement.

The English settlement programme was financed by a London merchant company headed by Ralph Merrifield. The king of England had given Warner a commission to settle the island, as it was not yet colonised by any 'Christian Prince'. The London merchant company financed the land clearance, sent tools and servants to the colony, and organised the shipping. These kinds of merchant companies played the leading role in English and French colonisation in the Caribbean.

By 1624 the 3,000 English settlers at St Christopher were exporting tobacco, indigo and dyewood. The tobacco was not as good as that exported by the Spanish of the Virginias, but it paid for some of the cost of settlement, and established the colony as a permanent Caribbean feature.

Barbados

Sir William Courteen, an English merchant of Dutch background, arranged for a merchant company to finance the settlement of Barbados in 1627. In the colony Captain Henry Powell represented the company. Courteen Associates began what was to become in the 17th century the richest island colony in the world. Between 1627 and 1629 the company invested £10,000 in Barbados. Just like in St Christopher, tobacco was immediately planted for exportation and the early settlers were not colonists but employees of the Courteen Company. The company paid wages, brought tools, seeds and other implements, collected the crop and did the marketing in London.

Labour

Initially, in both St Christopher and in Barbados, labour was supplied under the system of indentured labour. Unlike the Spanish, the English found no natives who could be reduced to slavery. So the tobacco and cotton plantations were worked – not by indigenous people or Africans – but by European indentured labour. In England from the 13th century onwards, the Enclosure Movement had been forcing the poor off the land. By the early 17th century a class of landless workers existed in England. They moved to wherever they could find work and were ready to be exploited by the merchant-planter class. In 1652 in Barbados it was reported that there were some 12,000 English and Irish labourers working in the plantations, and some 4,000 worked in the French islands. Many also worked in St Christopher. Indentured labourers were oppressed and ill-treated, but they were not enslaved. Legally they were free persons under contractual obligations. They worked in gangs from 6 a.m. to 6 p.m., and like enslaved Africans, were generally fed on potatoes, salted meat and water.

Planters and their managers established complex systems of authority to control and discipline indentured servants. If these systems failed, a planter could ask for help from the parish constables, the provost marshal, or, as a last resort, the parish militia. In the 17th century, the full weight of the law was used to discipline servants, whom some thought were as great a threat to peace as the enslaved Africans. Some overseers drove the servants as hard as they did enslaved Africans. Servants could not leave the plantations without the planter's permission, and the planters sold their contracts to other planters, like goods to raise cash, to settle debts and to pay taxes. The contracts were also used as capital or money to back mortgage agreements. In every market sense they were seen and used as property. On the other hand, they did have legal rights to petition magistrates for maltreatment. However, the magistrates rarely made decisions against the planters. Visitors to the islands frequently referred to the indentured labourers as 'White slaves'.

By way of comparison, in the French islands, the situation was not much different. Here, the servants *engagés* worked shorter contracts. The planters could not attract as many of these *engagés* as the English, and this held back the pace of their early economic development. France was a peasant country where the rural poor held strong attachments to the land.

Nevis
From St Christopher the English settled the neighbouring islands of Nevis, Antigua and Montserrat. The Nevis settlement was financed by a London merchant company organised by Thomas Littleton. Anthony Hilton represented this company in the colony. Thomas Warner in St Christopher had encouraged Hilton to organise the settlement and gave him much assistance in the early days. The two men had hoped to cooperate in tobacco planting and, in time, compete fiercely with their Virginia cousins. The settlement was greatly assisted by 150 seasoned settlers from St Christopher in 1628, and tobacco and cotton planting quickly got off the ground. By the mid 1630s Nevis was a well-entrenched colony.

Montserrat
Montserrat and Antigua were colonised in 1632, but it was not until 1636 that they became developed agriculturally. Montserrat stood out as an English colony in the Caribbean because it was predominantly settled by the Irish. Captain Anthony Briskett, who later became governor, attracted many Irish indentured labourers and peasants. In effect, the island became a Catholic colony amongst other English colonies dominated largely by Puritans. As in St Christopher and Nevis, tobacco and cotton were planted, along with many different types of ground provisions.

Antigua
The settlement of Antigua was a direct development of the St Christopher experience. It is now generally accepted that the first English settlers to this island came from Warner's party. Edward, the son of Thomas Warner, became its first governor. The colony got off to a moderate start in the mid-1630s. It trailed behind Barbados in terms of volume of trade, population expansion and political development.

Santa Cataline, San Andreas, Tortuga
In 1630 the Providence Company was founded. It had a royal charter and was operated by Puritan politicians in England. The company settled three small islands in the western Caribbean: Providence (Santa Catalina), Henretta (San Andreas) off the coast of Nicaragua, and Tortuga at the entrance to the windward passage between Hispaniola and Cuba. The early settlers were farmers. They planted and sold corn, tobacco and cotton and occasionally raided the Spanish. The Puritans soon found looting more rewarding than planting, and became buccaneers instead of farmers. Tortuga became their headquarters and it was the most famous pirate base in the early 17th century. However, the Spanish recaptured Tortuga in 1635 and Providence in 1641. The efforts of the Providence Company were short-lived compared to the settlements at Barbados and the Leeward Islands.

The French and Dutch
St Christopher
The English outpaced the French in the colonisation of the Caribbean. In the 1530s the French were trying to establish a settlement in Brazil and also on the Florida peninsula. The beginning of their Caribbean settlement process was unplanned. In 1625 a party of French privateers under the leadership of d'Esnambuc made an unsuccessful attack upon a Spanish vessel. Their ship was terribly damaged and so they sailed to St Christopher for repairs. After discussions with Thomas Warner, they were invited to share the colony. The English needed their help in defending themselves against the Kalinago and Spanish.

Warner was convinced that the days of privateering were limited, and that the future lay with farming and legal trade. So the French stayed on, and began their colonisation of the Caribbean with a portion of a small island, St Christopher. From here, the French moved on to settle in Martinique and Guadeloupe in 1635.

Martinique and Guadeloupe

The French government was not that enthusiastic about colonisation and the French settlements remained lightly populated until the late 17th century. In relation to the English settlements, the French colonies were undeveloped. In 1635 the settlement of Martinique and Guadeloupe came under the authority of the French Company of the Islands of America (*Compagnie des Iles d'Amérique*). The company was given the right to grant land, build forts and raise the militia. It was also supposed to supply to the colonies some 4,000 French Catholic settlers within 20 years. Tobacco and cotton were planted, and proved to be moderately rewarding crops. Indigo was also raised for exports along with dyewood.

The Dutch traders

The English were more successful as colonists in the Caribbean in the 17th century than the French, but the Dutch were the traders and financiers of excellence. They were more committed to attacking Spanish trade convoys, and trading in Spanish ports than the English and French were, and were consistent in implementing it. Their main aim was to take control of the salt mines in the south. The Dutch got their salt, which was used as a meat preservative and in the fishing industry, from the islands they settled, Aruba, Curaçao and Bonaire.

The Dutch also succeeded where everyone else had failed – they established permanent settlements in the Guiana region – in Essequibo in 1616 and Berbice in 1624. Establishing the Dutch West India Company in 1621 strengthened their colonial effort. In the first half of the 17th century almost every French and English settlement became dependent on Dutch shipping and finance. They were the true 'parents' of early Anglo-French settlers.

The Dutch were also interested in agricultural colonies. Between 1630 and 1640 they settled Saba, Curaçao, St Martin and St Eustatius. Although these islands were small and rocky and did not have much potential for farming, the Dutch made them into trading posts along the Caribbean trading network. It cannot therefore be argued that the Dutch were interested only in trade and not settlement.

From the beginning of French and English settlements in the Lesser Antilles and the rise of the Dutch trading network, the Caribbean took on a new level of economic importance in the world economy. Under Spanish control the Caribbean economy did not grow at all. But with the development of the colonies in the Leeward Islands and Barbados, the Caribbean became an area where Europeans invested heavily and where there was expansive trade. This was the beginning of dynamic capitalism in the region. Agriculture and trade, more than mining, launched the Caribbean into this prominent position.

Tobacco farming

The French settlers had an open tobacco market at home and did well. In the French colonies there was a rapid increase in population and a high level of trade – these showed that the economy was growing in this region. The English settlers made moderate profits, even though they did not succeed in driving the Virginians out of the London tobacco market. The English found that their domestic tobacco market was divided along class lines. The upper classes continued to smoke the expensive imported Spanish tobacco, while the lower classes chose between the Virginian and West Indian brands. In the first 15 years of tobacco production in the Caribbean the English had a few, moderate rewards which were enough to help them expand the infrastructure of the colonies.

Cotton plantations

The first five years of cotton production led to increased economic activity – more and more plantations developed. The planters in Antigua, St Christopher, Martinique and Guadeloupe followed those of Barbados. By the early 1640s there were more cotton plantations than tobacco plantations. However, cotton suffered a similar fate to tobacco. Too much cotton was produced and this led to a drop in prices, which threatened profitability. Traditional historians argue that these early years were generally unprofitable. However, recent evidence shows that before the sugar era, between 1625 and 1645, the economies of the Lesser Antilles islands expanded and the build-up of money and profits was at levels acceptable to both merchants and planters.

The minor powers, the Danes and Swedes, did not develop as extensive an empire in the Caribbean as their neighbours. The Danes settled the islands which now form the United States Virgin Islands, St Jan, St Croix and St Thomas. In 1783, St Barthelemy fell under the control of Sweden but was later given back to the French.

African enslavement

By the 17th century sugar plantations surrounded most of the islands of the Lesser Antilles. The greatest growth of these plantations took place between 1645 and 1670, and at the time money was produced at a level that had never been seen before. For example, the 1650 crop of Barbados was valued at over 3 million pounds. Barbados had replaced Hispaniola as the 'sugar centre' of the Caribbean. The French islands were behind the English, but their production of sugar rose steadily over the century. In 1674 their production level was 5,350 tons, it rose to 7,140 tons in 1682, and 13,375 tons in 1698.

For the Europeans, sugar meant turning away from the use of indentured labourers. In the Lesser Antilles, as in

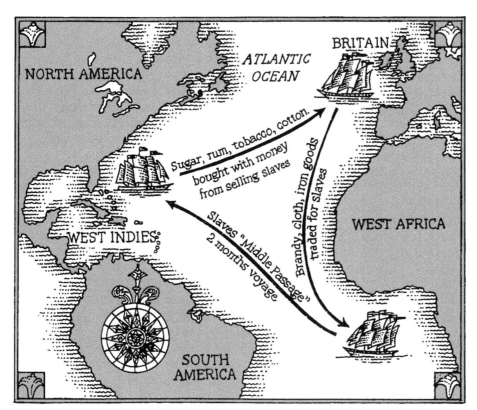

Map labels:
NORTH AMERICA
BRITAIN
ATLANTIC OCEAN
Sugar, rum, tobacco, cotton, bought with money from selling slaves
Brandy, cloth, iron goods traded for slaves
WEST INDIES
Slaves "Middle Passage" 2 months voyage
WEST AFRICA
SOUTH AMERICA

Fig 4.3 The triangular trade in enslaved Africans

Hispaniola and Brazil, sugar meant large-scale adoption of enslaved Africans. By 1650 the buying and selling of enslaved African captives was seen as the 'life-line' of the Caribbean economy. In 1645, two years after the beginning of sugar production, Barbados had only 5,680 enslaved Africans. By 1698 one observer estimated that 42,000 enslaved were used there. Jamaica was captured from the Spanish by the English in 1655 and followed Barbados into sugar and slavery. In 1656 Jamaica had only 1,410 enslaved Africans, but in 1698 it had over 41,000.

The death or mortality rate of the enslaved Africans was high. Overwork, malnutrition, resistance – all contributed to this. Every year the planters needed fresh captives to keep up their stock of Africans. In 1688 it was estimated that Jamaica needed 10,000 fresh enslaved Africans, the Leewards 6,000 and Barbados 4,000 to keep up the existing stocks. The Caribbean now depended on a dual economy – the sugar trade and the trade in enslaved Africans. One side of the triangle was this: ships left Europe loaded with goods, mainly cheap manufactured goods. They exchanged these goods for captive Africans in West Africa. The second side of the triangle: ships sailed from West Africa for the Caribbean where the Africans were sold. The third side: the ships took sugar on board for sale back in Europe. So this was a three-dimensional trading agreement. It was over

these three trades that Europeans fought in the 17th and 18th centuries. The English and French nations wanted a monopoly of their colonies' trade. They had fought against Spanish monopoly; now they wanted to establish their own.

Mercantilism and Dutch commercial supremacy

Josiah Child, a late 17th century English economic writer, described the Dutch as the 'eternal prowlers' of the earth in search of a moderate profit by trade. Between 1620 and 1650 the Dutch were the main shipping carriers for the Caribbean. Dutch shipping facilities were available to every English and French colony, as was Dutch commercial expertise. The Dutch West India Company, which was formed in 1621, began a process of direct trading with most non-Dutch colonies in the region. By helping others, they were helping themselves. The settlers on Barbados and St Christopher could not have developed their sugar economies without Dutch commercial support. They supplied the planters with hardware goods, capital and credit, and took their sugar on good terms. The Dutch were welcomed in every British and French colony until the second half of the century.

The administrators of the French and English colonies operated a kind of 'free trade' system. It was only after the 1650s that they tried to establish a monopoly and control navigation. The assistance given to the French by the English in the Caribbean was not only financial. Both the French colonies of Martinique and Guadeloupe took in large numbers of Dutch settlers, most of whom had been thrown out of Brazil by the Portuguese in the 1640s and 1650s. It can be said that the Dutch started sugar production on the French islands by bringing in the necessary technology and capital.

The Dutch brought an efficient commercial system into the region from their trading posts at St Martin, St Croix and Curaçao. On top of this, they quickly forced their way into the trade in enslaved Africans by establishing fortified trading posts in West Africa. By the 1650s they were the leading suppliers of enslaved Africans to the Caribbean. In the 1650s they dominated both the sugar trade and the trade in enslaved Africans.

chapter 4 | *Other European settlement and rivalry*

By the mid-17th century, the wealth created by sugar and slavery in the Lesser Antilles was so great that imperial governments began to create systems that made sure that they controlled this wealth. The Spanish threat was now effectively over, and the Kalinago were on the retreat. The Anglo-French Dutch alliances had now outlived their usefulness, and the struggle for the largest share of the Caribbean economy was brought to a new level.

Each imperial government wanted exclusive trading rights with its colonies, and saw foreign merchants as smugglers. The French and the English created complicated commercial systems to ensure their monopoly over their colonies. This system became known as the mercantile system. The principles and provisions of this system were as follows:

a. Goods could only be imported into or exported from a colony in the ships belonging to the colonizing power of the colony.
b. The exports of the colony should only be sold on the home market.
c. Only the goods of the colonizing power should be sold on the colonial market.
d. Colonial goods should be given first priority on the home market.
e. Colonies were not to establish any manufacturing industry to compete with industries in the colonizing power.

The colonies and the colonizing power were seen as one unitary economy from which all foreigners were to be excluded or given a secondary and restricted role. This was called mercantilism.

The English mercantile system

Oliver Cromwell could be considered the father of English mercantilism because he first translated these principles into a legal structure. The system that he began to establish in the early 1650s became known as the 'old colonial system'. When he died in 1658 the Restoration government of Charles II continued to build this system with greater effectiveness. Remember that the Dutch were the main carriers of English colonial goods, so the Dutch merchants had to be replaced with English merchants. A consequence of these laws was economic conflict and eventually war between the two nations.

The English aimed to break Dutch commercial dominance; the Dutch aimed to maintain it. Cromwell started out with the Navigation Laws of 1650 and 1651. These laws said that non-English ships were banned from trading in English colonies, unless they had a licence. Only English ships, with a majority of English crew members,

could transport colonial produce. These ships had to sail first to English ports. The Dutch fought back and the first of the trade wars between the two nations began in 1652. This was the start of the Anglo-Dutch rivalry for commercial dominance in the Caribbean. The Navigation Laws, primarily against the Dutch, were strengthened by Charles II in 1660, 1661 and 1663.

Fig 4.4 Oliver Cromwell

The 1660 law said that all colonial goods, which were going to a wider European market, had to pass through an English port for assessment. The 1661 Tariff Act gave preferential treatment to English sugar on the home market. The 1663 Staples Act strengthened these provisions. In 1663 the English established their first large company for the African slave trade. This was the Company of Royal Adventures Trading into Africa. It was given a monopoly of the colonial market. These companies made a large dent in Dutch slave-trading operations, and by the 1680s the Dutch were no longer the dominant commercial force in the Caribbean.

French mercantile laws

In France, mercantile laws were passed in 1661 with the appointment of Colbert as a finance minister. These laws closely resembled the laws passed by the English. The French also wanted to break Dutch commercial dominance over its colonies. In the French islands this dominance was almost total, since 90 per cent of the shipping of Martinique and Guadeloupe in the 1640s and 1650s was Dutch. Colbert had a plan that involved not only expelling the Dutch from the colonies, but also using these colonies to renew France's naval and shipping facilities.

Colbert gave a monopoly of all trade to the French-colonised Caribbean territories to the French West India Company. A series of other companies held monopolies to supply enslaved Africans to the Caribbean, beginning with the 'Company of Royal Adventurers Trading into Africa'. Most of these monopolies fell into difficulties. A series of laws prevented the Dutch and English from trading with French colonies. However, this did not prevent the contraband trade continuing.

Colbert also saw the colonies as the exclusive property of the French state. Foreigners could not own property in them without imperial permission. This provision was specifically anti-Dutch, since the Dutch owned most of the sugar mills and warehouses. This system became known as the l'exclusif. Colbert's Caribbean policy helped French shipping to develop. In 1662 France had only four ships trading in the Caribbean; in 1683, she had some 205. In 1676 no foreigners sold sugar in France, but the Dutch were not excluded from trading with the French in the Caribbean. Unlike the English, the French did not have as much naval power to enforce their policy, and much Dutch trading continued, though it was in a quieter way.

2 European nations challenge Spanish monopoly

Losing Jamaica

In the second half of the 17th century, the Spanish monopoly in the Greater Antilles came under a much more systematic and organised attack from the English and French. Cromwell worked out a programme to drive the Spanish out of the Indies once and for all. This plan was called 'the Grand Western Design', and it was to bring the northern Caribbean under English rule and establish English supremacy in the region. The plan was organised by Admiral Penn and General Venables in 1654-55. They recruited some 4,000 men from Barbados and the Leeward Islands, who became the rank and file of the invading army. These men were mainly indentured servants and small farmers.

In April 1655 this army attacked Santo Domingo. But this unprepared and 'makeshift' army was driven back by the Spanish. To prevent total embarrassment, what was left of the army attacked Jamaica, which was the least defended of the Spanish islands. They took control after a short period of weak resistance from the Spanish settlers. This was the first naval and military operation against an important Spanish colony that succeeded. It was brought about by the English state, and was not therefore in the tradition of privateering raids.

The loss of Jamaica to England had a significant impact upon future Caribbean colonial relations. The Spanish had not taken the colony very seriously as a settlement, and its loss was more symbolic than real. Spain was beginning to lose its large islands. The English were now within a few miles of its prime islands – Cuba and Hispaniola. The loss of Jamaica also signalled the rise of the English as a Caribbean super power. By the 1760s Jamaica, after some 50 years of being a pirate camp had become the richest colony in the Caribbean. It formed the foundation of English economic power in the region.

Sharing Hispaniola

From their base at Tortuga, the French pirates *flibustiers* paved the way for the undermining of Spanish control of Hispaniola. The Spanish had beaten the English off the island in 1655, but the French pirates succeeded in making a settlement, sandwiched between the Spanish on the eastern portion of the island and Cuba on the west. The colony thrived and there was very little the Spanish could do about it.

The settlement became known as Saint-Domingue. In 1665 the French Company of the Indies established D'Ogeron as governor of Tortuga and he became the overseer of Saint-Domingue. His duty was to convert Saint-Domingue into a stable farming settlement, while keeping the *flibustiers* as military protection. The English and French had now lost all military respect for Spain in the Caribbean.

By the 1670s Saint-Domingue was producing maize, cotton, tobacco and cacao for export by the French Company of the Indies. Saint-Domingue expanded, but Spain refused to recognise it. Planters came from Martinique and Guadeloupe to establish a sugar industry. In the 1680s they exported sugar and the economic potential of the colony was recognised by the French.

In 1684 Governor De Cussy was given orders to ensure that pirating did not interfere with the agricultural expansion of the colony. He did not succeed in this but the

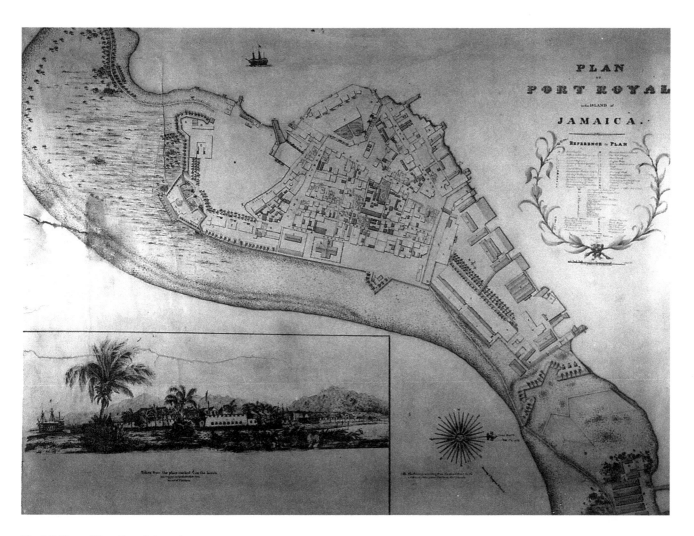

Fig 4.5 Plan of Port Royal, Jamaica

next governor, Jan Baptiste de Casse, was more successful. He organised the pirates into an army and sent them out on missions to attack the Spanish and English, so that the planters on the island could farm peaceably. In 1694 French pirates attacked and ransacked Jamaica, and in 1697 they captured the Spanish settlement at Cartagena in present Columbia.

In 1697 Spain was forced to recognise the settlement, and the colony of Saint-Domingue gained importance. This was a great blow to Spain – she was now forced to share her 'mother colony' – the centre of her Caribbean empire.

Spanish Caribbean

As late as the 1740s the economies of the Spanish Caribbean looked similar to the economies in the 16th century. Their main features were under-population; small, decaying towns; scattered cattle ranches and a few sugar mills. Their export bases were weak. Most of what they produced was for use in the colony and not for export. The main exports remained unchanged – tobacco, dyewood, hides and a little sugar. The Spanish did make an effort to revitalise the Spanish Caribbean economy. They formed a series of monopoly companies, but this seemed to worsen the problem. The 1728 Caracas Company was given a monopoly of trade to Venezuela, and in 1740 the Havana Company a monopoly of trading to Cuba. The 1755 Barcelona Company was given similar powers over Puerto Rico and Santo Domingo.

These monopoly companies exploited the settlers. So the settlers generally rejected them and preferred to trade with contraband traders. The Spanish islands were trapped in an outdated Spanish economic policy that stopped their development. The rigid monopoly system stopped the islands from getting the kind of commercial boost they needed to become more productive. It was only when the British occupied Cuba in 1763 (for 10 months) that the Spanish colonies were exposed to the full force of commercial capitalism.

The *Asiento* system

The plantation system would not have been as profitable as it was if it did not rely on an active trade in Africans. During the 18th century, the Europeans fought each other for the right and privilege of shipping enslaved Africans to the Caribbean. They fought on the West African Coast and in the Caribbean over their prize commodity – enslaved Africans. The table shows the number of enslaved Africans imported into the leading Caribbean colonies by the Europeans.

Enslaved Africans imported to the Americas, 1701-60			
	1701-20	1721–40	1741-60
Spanish America	90,002	90,000	90,000
Jamaica	53,500	90,000	120,000
Barbados	67,000	55,300	57,300
Saint-Domingue	70,600	79,400	158,700
Martinique	33,800	42,900	70,100

Source: P. Curtin, *The Atlantic Slave Trade: A Census*, pp. 216-234.

English, French and Dutch companies aimed to supply Africans exclusively to their own colonies, and sell extras to the Spanish colonists. Spain of course had no slave-trading contact in West Africa. But to supply the Spanish colonies with enslaved workers, companies had to get a contract, or the *asiento*, which was first given to the Portuguese in the mid-16th century. It was over this *asiento* that the English, French and Dutch fought wars.

In 1702 the French won the Spanish *asiento* through a tender placed by the French Guinea Company. The English did not like this and proceeded to make sure that the French did not enjoy this privilege. War resulted between France and England. These wars were fought mainly in Europe, but the Caribbean also experienced some fighting. The French were defeated, and in 1713 they gave up the *asiento* under the Treaty of Utrecht.

The English took the *asiento*, under the initiative of the South Sea Company. What France had won by bargain, England took by war. But the English also had great difficulty with the *asiento*. Dutch interlopers undermined the South Sea Company's market, and the Anglo-Spanish

Fig 4.6 Havana in the 1840s

chapter 4 | *Other European settlement and rivalry*

war in 1718 and 1727 disrupted the company's management. The English lost a quantity of property in the colonies. In May 1739 the Spanish government abandoned the *asiento*, and in October war broke out between Spain and England.

In 1750 the Spanish government was forced to pay the South Sea Company £100,000 cash for damages it had sustained during these wars. However, by this time England was the leading supplier of enslaved Africans to the Caribbean and in the race for the 'Black cargoes' had beaten the French, Dutch and Portuguese. In 1763 the British occupied Havana for ten months. In this time the Cuban settlers experienced for the first time the impact that a powerful merchant class could have on a colony's development. The interaction between the English merchants and the Cuban planters had an almost revolutionary impact upon the Cuban economy. The Spanish imperial government observed this development, and over the second half of the 18th century, used Cuba as a testing ground for the restructuring of its own colonial economic policy.

England occupies Cuba

In the ten months that England occupied Cuba, they sold over 10,000 enslaved Africans in Cuba, and the amount of shipping increased by over 400 per cent. Between 1520 and 1760, only about 60,000 Africans had been sold in Cuba. But between 1760 and 1820 the British imported some 40,000 Africans, and Havana became one of the most active ports in the Caribbean.

Spain did not have the money needed to finance Cuba's development. England had that money, and began to invest in Cuba. Sugar output rose from a mere 2,000 tons per year in the 1740s, to over 10,000 tons per year in the 1770s. In 1789 England declared Havana and Santiago free ports, which were open to all European merchant capital and shipping. In 1793 this 'free port' arrangement was extended for another six years. The British made similar arrangements in Puerto Rico and Santo Domingo, with similar economic results. British and Dutch commercial capital started the economic changes in these islands. In the 16th and 17th centuries colonists had emigrated from the islands to the mainland colonies. Now this pattern was reversed as hundreds of colonists emigrated from the mainland colonies to Cuba and Puerto Rico.

Havana became the thriving commercial centre of the Caribbean. The agricultural revolution in Cuba and Puerto Rico had begun. By the 1840s Cuba was the largest supplier of sugar in the world. This signalled the total success of commercial capitalism in the Caribbean.

3 Spanish counter-attack

In the first half of the 17th century, Spain was aware of its own military weakness and could not respond to these new enemy settlements and alliances. Spain could not launch any systematic attacks upon the settlements, but confined herself to occasional and random raids. She still clung, however, to her theory of 'exclusive rights' to the Caribbean and refused to recognise these settlements. Only when settlements were made close to the Main, or to the larger islands of the Greater Antilles, did Spain pull herself up to launch organised and powerful counter-attacks.

In 1629 a Spanish squadron attacked and temporarily chased the English and French out of St Christopher and Nevis. In 1635 Spain recaptured Tortuga, and Providence in 1641. The Spanish succeeded in keeping both the English and French out of the Windward Islands of Trinidad, Tobago, Grenada and St Lucia. However, their success was due more to Kalinago resistance than Spanish defence.

By the 1640s the Spanish had lost the energy and resources needed to drive the 'enemy' out of the Caribbean. The Spanish never attacked Barbados, which was the most developed of the eastern Caribbean colonies. They seemed to have a healthy respect for the colonists on that island. The Barbadians were confident and made great economic strides. In fact, Spanish merchants occasionally stopped at Barbados and traded. In this way Barbados was recognised as a separate colony. Yet Spain refused to officially accept these colonies. After the 1640s Spain could not in any significant way change the pattern of French, English and Dutch colonial development in the region. She merely watched her empire being slowly worn away as the 'enemy' strengthened its power.

4 Resistance of the Kalinago in the Eastern Caribbean

The invasion of the Lesser Antilles by Europeans led to the launching of a long drawn-out war with the Kalinago and the united Kalinago-African Garifuna. Over time they adopted different strategies and methods to pacify them, but still kept the position that the Kalinago should be enslaved, driven out, or exterminated. The English and French wanted to pacify the Kalinago for two separate but related reasons. The first reason why the English and French wanted to pacify the Kalinago was that they needed the lands occupied by the Kalinago for large-scale sugar production. So by resisting the land takeover

Kalinago were confronting the full force of European colonialism.

Secondly, European economic activities in the Caribbean were based upon the enslavement of indigenes and imported Africans. The main role these and other non-Europeans had within the colonies was to serve. However, in the Lesser Antilles Europeans were not successful in reducing a large number of Kalinago to chattel slavery or other forms of servitude. Unlike the Taino, Kalinago labour could not be controlled because their communities were difficult to discipline. It was not that the Kalinago were more militant than the Taino. Rather, the nomadic life of their small communities allowed them to make more effective use of the environment in a 'strike and sail' resistance strategy. The Kalinago were not prepared to surrender either land or labour to Europeans and so were in a better position than the Taino to strike back.

Mainly because of the Kalinago's effective war of resistance, which disturbed all Europeans in the region, the Europeans began to target the Kalinago with a propaganda campaign. The Taino were called 'noble savages', but the Kalinago were described as 'vicious cannibals'. In this way Europeans tried to justify their genocidal war against the Kalinago. The Spanish and later the English and French prepared detailed volumes calling for 'holy wars' against 'les sauvages'.

This literature, which dates back to Columbus in 1494, denies the Kalinago's humanity. Jean-Baptiste du Tertre, Sieur de la Borde, and Père Labat were all late 17th century French reporters of Kalinago lifestyles. In their writings the Kalinago are presented as a people who would 'prefer to die of hunger than live as a slave'. Labat, who commented most on their cultural attitudes, found them to be 'careless and lazy creatures', not at all suited mentally to difficult labour over a long period of time. In addition, he considered them a 'proud and indomitable' and 'exceedingly vindictive' people whom 'one has to be very careful not to offend'. From this comes the popular French Caribbean proverb, 'fight a Kalinago and you must kill him or be killed'.

Labat noted that the French discovered, like the Spanish before them, that it was always best, if possible, 'to have nothing to do with the Kalinago'. But this was not possible. The French had to establish relations with them. Labat noted that the Kalinago knew 'how to look after their own interests very well'. 'There are no people in the world', he stated, 'so jealous of their liberty, or who resent more the smallest check to their freedom'. Altogether, the freedom of the Kalinago disturbed the Europeans. There was a general view that no European nation could live on the same island with them without being compelled to destroy them, and drive them out. Labat also stated this view.

In 1624, the English and French started to establish agricultural settlements in St Kitts at the same time. In 1627 the English moved on to Barbados, and between 1632 and 1635 to Antigua, Montserrat and Nevis. The French concentrated their efforts at Martinique and Guadeloupe. The first three years at St Kitts were difficult for both English and French settlers. They were harassed and attacked by Kalinago soldiers. By 1635 the French at Guadeloupe were involved in a long battle with the Kalinago.

War

The French were the victors in their war with the Kalinago at Guadeloupe. This encouraged them to expand their colonial missions during the remainder of the decade. However, in the war they did not gain effective control of the Kalinago-inhabited islands of Grenada, Marie Galante, and La Desirada. Meanwhile, in 1639, the Kalinago easily fought off a small English expedition from St Kitts to St Lucia in the Windwards, in the heart of Kalinago territory. The following year the Kalinago launched a full-scale attack upon English settlements at Antigua. They killed 50 settlers, captured the governor's wife and children, and destroyed crops and houses.

The English settlements in the Leewards struggled to make progress against Kalinago resistance. At this time Barbados alone went ahead uninterrupted. Unlike their Leewards counterparts, early Barbadian planters easily expanded their plantations, made a living from the exports of tobacco, indigo and cotton, and feared only their indentured servants and a few enslaved Africans. By 1650, after their huge success in cultivating sugar cane with enslaved Africans, the island was considered the richest agricultural colony in the hemisphere.

The English and French colonists in St Kitts were determined to keep up with their Barbadian competitors. So they were first to use a joint military front to fight Kalinago resistance. Despite the fact that they both claimed exclusive ownership of the island, in the 1630s they entered into agreements to combine forces against Kalinago communities. On the first occasion, they 'pooled their talents', and in a 'sneak night attack' killed over 80 Kalinago and drove many off the island. After celebrating the success of their military alliance, the French and English continued their rivalry over the island until 1713. At this time ownership of the island was settled in favour of the English by the Treaty of Utrecht.

The Kalinago had been successful in holding on to an important portion of the Windwards, and they had successfully weakened the planting settlements in the

Leewards. These things fuelled the determination of the English and French to destroy them. By the mid-17th century, European merchants, planters and colonial officials were in agreement that the Kalinago 'were a barbarous and cruel set of savages beyond reason or persuasion and must therefore be eliminated'.

At this time it also became clear that there needed to be an 'absolute monopoly' of the slave-based plantation system in the Caribbean. No 'alternative system' could be tolerated. So, what Richard Dunn referred to as 'Kalinago independence and self-reliance' was a major problem for the Europeans.

By the mid-17th century, the need for a full-scale war against the Kalinago assumed greater urgency with the English and French. The English were first to successfully establish sugar cultivation and slavery, and so it is not surprising that they took the lead in trying to remove the Kalinago. Also, the English had the largest number of enslaved Africans in the region and they would not be able to keep efficient control on their plantations if Kalinago resistance persisted.

It did not take long for the Africans to become aware of the Kalinago struggle against Europeans, and to realise that they could possibly secure their freedom by fleeing to Kalinago territory. Labat, who studied inter-island African marronage in the Lesser Antilles during this period, stated that enslaved Africans knew that St Vincent was easily reached from Barbados, and many escaped there 'from their planters in canoes and rafts'. Between 1645 and 1660, the Kalinago generally took 'the runaway enslaved back to their masters, or sold them to the French and Spanish'. However, as the Kalinago came under more intensive attack during the mid-century, Labat noted, their policy towards African Maroons changed. They refused to return the Africans, he stated, and began regarding them 'as an addition to their nation'.

Labat estimated that by 1670 over 500 Barbadian runaways were living in St Vincent. This community was strengthened in 1675 when a ship carrying hundreds of enslaved Africans to Jamaica via Barbados ran aground off the coast of Bequia. Survivors came ashore at St Vincent and were welcomed in the Maroon communities. By 1700, Labat stated, Africans outnumbered Kalinago at St Vincent. In 1675, William Stapleton who was governor of the Leewards, noted the significant presence of Africans among the Kalinago. He suggested that of the 1,500 native bowmen in the Leewards 'six hundred of them are negroes, some runaway from Barbados and elsewhere'.

Kalinago-African relations
Throughout the second half of the 17th century, Europeans tried to exploit the relations between Kalinago and Africans, which were sometimes strained. The Europeans did this by encouraging the Kalinago to return runaway Africans to their owners. As African and Kalinago mixed, there were more and more families in which the male was an African Maroon and the female a Kalinago. This caused problems between the two ethnic groups. In other words, male Africans and male Kalinago competed for female Kalinago. Both the French and English said that occasionally Kalinago leaders asked for their help in ridding their communities of Africans.

By the 17th century, the group of mixed race persons were now known as the Garifuna or Garinagu. This group was increasing rapidly, and by 1720 there were more Garifuna than Kalinago and Africans in St Vincent. At this time joint African-Kalinago military expeditions against the French and English were common both on land and at sea. The full-scale attack on the French at Martinique during the mid-1650s, for example, involved both African and Kalinago warriors. They attacked French settlements at Grenada during the same period and kept them in a weak and defensive condition. Labat also noted that in the 1670s both Africans and Kalinago repelled English attacks from Barbados on St Vincent.

The presence of Kalinago communities on the outskirts of the slave plantations was a major problem for enslavers because the Kalinago nurtured and encouraged African resistance. This joining of the Kalinago anti-colonial struggle and the African anti-slavery struggle represented the twin forces that threatened the very survival of European settlement mission in the Windwards. So Europeans wasted no time in adopting a range of measures to suppress the Kalinago.

In 1664 a Barbados document called 'The state of the case concerning our title to St Lucia', described the island as being 'infected' with Kalinago who were 'abetted by the French' in their war against English settlers. In this document, Barbados enslavers were trying to reject French claims to the island. The Barbados enslavers stated that they had bought the island from Du Parquet, the French governor of Martinique, who had bought it from the Kalinago in 1650 for 41,500 livres. In the same vein, in 1668, Thomas Modyford the governor of Jamaica and former Barbados governor and sugar magnate, described St Vincent, which was another Kalinago stronghold in the Windwards, as a place which 'the Indians much infect'. These statements show us that England was preparing their society to accept a genocidal offensive against the Kalinago that London merchants were eager to finance.

But the English and French knew that a full-scale war would be costly, in human life and in money. In 1655, for example, Captain Gregory Butler informed Oliver Cromwell, the Protector, that the settlement at Antigua could not get off to a good start because of frequent 'molestations' by Kalinago, who at that time seemed to be in alliance with the French.

In 1667 Major John Scott, an imperial soldier, reported that he led an expedition against the Dutch settlement in Tobago with the help of a party of Kalinago. In the second Dutch War, from 1665 to 1667, France and Holland formed an alliance against the English in the Caribbean. In this war the Kalinago played an important role in shifting the balance of power between Europeans by fighting with the French and Dutch, while at the same time using this opportunity to expand their own war of resistance. In June 1667, Henry Willoughby was stationed in the Leewards. He informed his father, William Lord Willoughby, governor of Barbados, that when he arrived at St Kitts he received 'intelligence' of further atrocities committed by the Kalinago against the English. He said that these Kalinago atrocities were 'instigated' by the French but that the Kalinago nation effectively used them to serve their own ends.

The Willoughby Plan
The English and French sent agents to negotiate with the resisting Kalinago. Remember that the Windwards was the last island frontier. So the first diplomatic effort by the English to establish a foothold in Kalinago territory in the Windwards was the Willoughby Plan of 1667. William Lord Willoughby, governor of Barbados, had long recognised the great financial gain that he, Barbados, and England would have if the Windwards could be converted into slave-based sugar plantations. For more than ten years the sugar kings of Barbados had been demanding more land on which to expand their operations. Since the 1630s the Kalinago had repelled small-scale military expeditions. As Willoughby was not yet organised for a large-scale military assault, he chose to rather send diplomats to start negotiations with Kalinago leaders.

Peace treaty
In response the Kalinago showed some flexibility, as is often the case with peoples involved in long-term struggles. Willoughby wanted the Kalinago to sign a peace treaty that would remove any obstacles to expanding the plantations which used enslaved labour, and that would promote English interests. The Kalinago were suspicious and vigilant. In 1666 the Kalinago were tricked by the English to sign a treaty which actually signed away their 'rights' to inhabit Tortola. The English then drove them off the island. The Windward Islands were the Kalinago's last place of safety. Now they had nowhere to go.

On 23 March 1667, Kalinago leaders of St Vincent, Dominica and St Lucia met with Willoughby's delegation to negotiate the peace. At the signing of the treaty were Anniwatta, the Grand Babba (or chief of all Kalinago), Chiefs Wappya, Nay, Le Suroe, Rebura and Aloons. The conditions of the treaty were everything the Barbadian enslavers wanted. It said:

a. The Kalinago of St Vincent shall ever acknowledge themselves subjects of the King of England, and be friends to all in amity with the English, and enemies to their enemies.

b. The Kalinago shall have liberty to come to and depart from, at pleasure, any English island and receive their protection therein, and the English shall enjoy the same in St Vincent and St Lucia.

c. His Majesty's subjects taken by the French and Indians and remaining among the Indians, shall be immediately delivered up, as also any Indian captives among the English when demanded.

d. Negroes formerly runaways from Barbados shall be delivered to His Excellency, and such as shall hereafter be fugitives from any English island shall be secured and delivered as soon as required.

Within two months of the Kalinago-Willoughby treaty, a party of 54 English colonists from Barbados arrived at St Vincent to set up a settlement. The Kalinago, Garifuna, and Africans objected to their presence, drove them off the island and broke the treaty with Barbados.

The collapse of the Willoughby Plan
The collapse of the Barbados diplomatic initiative angered Governor Willoughby, who swiftly moved to the next stage of his plan – a full-scale military offensive. Once again the Kalinago proved too much for Willoughby, and the expedition returned to Barbados having suffered heavy losses.

Governor Stapleton of the Leewards stated his fear for the lives of Leeward Islanders, including those who worked in a silver mine in Dominica under an agreement with the Kalinago. Some of the Barbadian European community also offered their criticisms of Willoughby's war effort. In 1676, Governor Atkins described the war effort as a 'fruitless design'. He said the overall result of the war was that there remain 'no likelihood of any plantations upon Dominica, St Vincent, St Lucia and Tobago'. Meanwhile, the Antiguans were forced to keep soldiers on guard as a protective measure against Kalinago soldiers.

Governor Stapleton, talking about the collapse of the Willoughby Plan, and considering the prospects of English settlements in the Leewards and Windwards, argues that only the destruction of 'all the Caribbean Indians' could be the 'best piece of service for the settlement of these parts'. In December 1675 a petition to the English government sought to raise soldiers to go into Dominica to 'destroy' the Kalinago.

Stapleton was frustrated because he could not protect the lives and property of Leeward Islanders. He wrote to the English government saying, 'I beg your pardon if I am tedious, but I beg you to represent to the King the necessity for destroying these Kalinago Indians. We are now as much on our guard as if we had a Christian enemy.'

If their destruction cannot be 'total', insisted Stapleton, at least we must 'drive them to the main'. However he was aware that the Leeward Islanders could not finance a major war effort. They were also aware of the Kalinago's ability to obtain 'intelligence' with respect to their plans. (It was widely believed that some Europeans spied for the Kalinago.) Given these two circumstances, Stapleton instructed the English government to order the French Barbados government to help prepare the grand design against the Kalinago. Barbados, he added, was closer to the Kalinago 'infested' islands of St Vincent and Dominica. Also Barbados was wealthy and so war would be the 'best piece of service' they could offer England while there was friendship with the French.

On 11 April 1713 England and France settled their 'American' differences with the Treaty of Utrecht. At this time the Kalinago were still holding on to a large amount of territory. Although some Europeans lived in St Vincent and Dominica these two territories were still under Kalinago control. Also the Kalinago were fighting a war to keep their space at St Lucia, Tobago and Grenada. The French feared that successful English settlement of Dominica would lead to the cutting of communications between Martinique and Guadeloupe in times of war. So they continued to assist the Kalinago with information and occasionally with weapons in their anti-English resistance. The best the English could do was to continue to settle private treaties with the French, as they had done during the Peace of Ryswick in 1667, which allowed them to go unharmed to Dominica for the sole purpose of buying lumber from the Kalinago.

The Kalinago keep territory

The Kalinago were successful in keeping some of their territorial sovereignty. By doing this they managed to maintain their freedom from European enslavement. Other native Caribbean peoples suffered large-scale slavery at the hands of Europeans, but the Kalinago were never found in large numbers working the mines, latifundia, or plantations in the Eastern Caribbean. Although the Spanish raid for enslaved people in the 16th century did take many Kalinago into the Greater Antilles to supplement Taino labour gangs, European-controlled productive structures in the Eastern Caribbean were not built and maintained with Kalinago labour.

Between 1492 and 1730 the Kalinago population in the Eastern Caribbean fell by as much as 90 per cent, but they had done much to 'preserve and extend their independence'. By this time, adult Kalinago in St Vincent and Dominica, 'did not exceed 2,000' and soldiers were 'too weak in numbers to do any serious harm' to European colonies. Nonetheless, colonists in the 'outlying districts' still had reason to believe that Kalinago soldiers could take them by surprise any night and 'cut their throats and burn their houses'.

In 1762 the English government gave instructions for the launching of a military offensive against the Kalinago at St Vincent and a major naval force arrived at the island. The English governor of St. Vincent reported that the Kalinago fought against the English settlements as soon as they saw the fleet approaching. They killed 72 men and wounded 80; another 110 lost their lives to diseases within a month of the outbreak of war. However, the Kalinago could not hold out against increasing English military pressure. So in 1773 Chief Chatoyer and 27 other leaders found it necessary to settle a peace treaty with the English. The Kalinago were promised amnesty and sovereignty over a stretch of land in the north of the island (35 per cent of the island) in return for their allegiance to King George III.

Defeat

Peace could not be maintained. An uneasy political situation existed because of the expansionist desire of the sugar plantation sector and the persistent racist attitudes of the English. Another opportunity for Kalinago resistance came when the American revolution further divided France and England. French and British reactions to it in the Caribbean weakened European military capability. The Kalinago had rejected the treaty of 1773 and in 1776 declared war against the English. The English, however, were better prepared this time to handle the possibility of an alliance between the Kalinago and the French. The enormous build-up of English military power in the region after 1789 and during the French Revolution, easily swept away Kalinago resistance. The English, in the end, defeated both the Kalinago and the French in Caribbean battles.

The final defeat of the Kalinago in St Vincent and St Lucia in the 1790s drew whatever poison was left from the arrows of the Kalinago in the Dominica community. Joseph Chatoyer, paramount chief in St Vincent, was executed during a bloody clash with English soldiers in March 1795. Hundreds of Kalinago fled for safety to Dominica. About

5,000 were rounded up by English troops and herded together on the tiny island of Balliceaux in the Grenadines. Here they waited for imperial instructions about where their final destination would be. One third of them starved to death on the island while waiting. The others were transported to Roatán, an island off the coast of Honduras on which, it was said, not even iguanas easily survived. The Spanish eventually took them to what is now Belize.

The transportation of Kalinago from St Vincent and St Lucia left the Dominica community a split and militarily defeated nation. In 1804, the lands in St Lucia and St Vincent that had been given to the Kalinago in a treaty with the British government were given up to the crown. In Dominica, the surviving community tried to survive in the rainforest and took whatever advantage they could find in selling their craftware in towns and their labour on neighbouring plantations. By refusing to give in to European military pressure, the Kalinago had kept the Windward Islands, which were on the edge of the slave plantations, more or less the same for 200 years. In so doing they made a significant contribution to the Caribbean's anti-colonial and anti-slavery tradition.

To sum up

The plundered wealth of the Caribbean world was displayed by Spanish colonisers before the envious eyes of other European nations. Spain derived enormous wealth, power, glory and prestige globally from its Caribbean exploits. European maritime nations developed strategies and policies to capture a share of the spoils from Spain. By the middle of the 17th century, Spain was on the defensive as a colonial power, and the balance of military might had shifted. The enslaved Africans and the displaced indigenous community fought wars of resistance against all Europeans. They sought to secure freedom from slavery, to protect their lands and labour, and to establish independent communities. The demand for liberty and the forces of slavery created a culture of conflict in the Caribbean. Instability was the norm.

Revision questions

1 Why did other European nations form rival alliances against Spain?
2 How effective were rival alliances against Spain by 1700?
3 Describe the attitudes of the Kalinago to the Europeans.
4 How extensive and effective was Kalinago resistance?
5 What were the main shifts in political power among Europeans in the Caribbean between 1600 and 1800?

Chapter 5

Europe and the spread of chattel slavery in Africa

'Ambush in the night, they are trying to conquer me.'
(Bob Marley)

Much has been written about Africa's history before the transatlantic trade in enslaved Africans, showing the important contributions Africa made to world development through its contact with other major civilisations of the world. The transatlantic trade in Africans came about after centuries of mutually rewarding contact with the outer world during which many fundamental changes took place in African civilisations. Africa was in the forefront of the Neolithic agricultural revolution. Africa made many of the scientific discoveries of crop farming for large-scale food production and the rearing of animals. Africa was also at the forefront of the discovery and popularisation of early technological revolutions in metal science. These developments allowed populations to expand and complex political and social systems to develop. By the end of the Middle Ages, West Africa, Asia and Europe were dealing with the challenges of political governance, economic expansion, and community organisation in basically similar ways; and they were achieving similar results. These achievements were already familiar and recognisable by the time the Europeans arrived to trade and conquer in the mid-15th century.

In this chapter we will learn about:
1. Classical Africa in comparison with Europe
2. Early African development: African scientific and technological developments
3. The main West African states when West Europeans arrived in the mid-15th century
4. The decline of European slavery
5. The rise of slavery in Africa
6. The impact of the transatlantic trade in Africans on Africa

1 Classical Africa in comparison with Europe

An important feature of the ancient civilisation of West Africa was that its people, its goods and culture moved all over the world. So there was an exchange of scientific ideas, technologies and cultures between Asia, Europe, the Mediterranean, and West Africa, particularly in the areas of agriculture and industrial production. This exchange of knowledge shows the extent to which world cultures interacted with each other. Everyone was enriched by this experience; and it is against this background that the modern world saw the tragic crime against humanity – the transatlantic trade in Africans.

In recent years many different scholars have tried to look at the importance of Africa's cultural features and global connections before the transatlantic trade in enslaved Africans. They criticise the European scholars who deny the positive global influence and cultural impact of Africa on world development. Many European scholars used race and colour to explain why European culture was more advanced than African culture. But recent scholars show the powerful role that ancient Egyptian civilisations played both within Africa's and early Europe's cultural development.

The Senegalese scholar, Cheikh Anta Diop, challenges and weakens centuries of European thought on these issues. He argues that the ancient Egyptian culture is to African culture what ancient Graeco-Roman culture is to European culture. He shows that the Nile Valley civilisations were essentially the product of the black African world, mainly from West Africa; and that despite the racist writings of some European scholars, Western Europe drew intellectual and cultural nourishment from the Nile Valley and other African civilisations at the height of Greek and Roman civic advancement.

Many scholars, in antiquity and in recent times, had known and stated this. The famous classical Greek scholar Herodotus, for example, wrote about the black racial identity of the ancient Egyptian peoples. Following Diop's lead many western researchers are presenting more balanced, scientific perspectives. Martin Bernal, for instance, has skillfully demonstrated how European scholars from the 18th century onwards, deliberately made up descriptions of Ancient Greece in order to write black Africans out of the history of Egypt and, also out of Europe's cultural tradition.

Bernal's research partly focuses on the African identity of ancient Egypt. He explores how Greek culture borrowed from the Africans in Egypt and the Levant in the 2nd millennium BC – i.e. from 2100 to 1100 BC. However, Bernal says that the concept of race is not useful in these arguments because the Egyptians themselves – and most of the people of the ancient world – did not think in terms of race. He concludes:

> *Nevertheless, I am convinced that, at least for the last 7,000 years, the population of Egypt contained African, southwest Asian and Mediterranean types. It is also clear that the further south, or up the Nile, one goes, the blacker and more Negroid the population becomes. I believe that Egyptian civilisation was fundamentally African. Furthermore, I am convinced that many of the most powerful Egyptian dynasties which were based in upper Egypt – the 1st, 11th, 12th, and 18th – were made up of pharaohs whom one can usefully call black.*

Bernal argues that it is well established that classical Greece and Rome were intellectually fed and culturally led by the more advanced Africans in Egypt. However, some European scholars wish to show that primarily Europeans and people other than Africans created classical Greek and Roman culture. They want to deny that there was an African culture in Egypt, and also deny that Egypt had cultural connections with West Africa. Finally, Bernal says, they want to deny that people with dark skins stimulated the cultural advancement of Europe.

In the classical period, the Africans in Egypt led the way in the mathematical sciences. Early Europeans wondered about the mathematical achievement associated with the design and erection of the pyramids at Giza and elsewhere. Diop has argued that the famous Greek mathematicians, Archimedes and Pythagoras, came by Egyptian mathematics.

Fig 5.1 The pyramids at Giza, Egypt, North Africa

According to Diop, most of the scientists who gave Greece its scientific fame were persecuted scholars. They fled from Greece and took refuge in Egypt and other parts of north Africa, where they found a learning environment. The list includes Anaxogoras, Socrates, Aristotle, and Plato. Unlike Greece, the African Egyptians generally encouraged research in the sciences, philosophy and arts.

Bernal's writings support Diop's argument that West African societies were an important part of Egyptian culture. People from sub-Saharan Africa interacted with Egypt centuries before the 5th century western Europeans did. Bernal argues that the plants and animals that West Africans used in farming brought about the Neolithic agricultural revolution in Africa. This was an influential event in world history and Europe benefited from it too.

2 Early African development: African scientific and technological developments

The evidence we have of agricultural development in West Africa from around 5000 BC shows that this was one of the great moments in world history, and one of the outstanding achievements of Africans. From earliest times, African and Asian agriculture benefited from each other and developed along similar lines.

Agricultural development

West African connections with others in the world remained strong. Bernal says that between the 1st and 8th centuries AD, Asian yams, cocoyams, bananas, and plantains reached West Africa from the Near East. Through long distance trade millet, beans, wheat, rice, oil palm, and yams were spread all over West Africa three centuries before the Portuguese arrived. So the idea that the African economic world did not develop is a myth. West Africa was in social and economic contact with other continents during and after classical ancient times. West Africa was also part of the later rise of an early global trade network that centred on the Mediterranean.

It seems that cattle rearing was introduced into West Africa via Asia and Egypt in about 5000 BC. By the 10th century, the Fulani of northern Nigeria, for example, were well known for their mixed farming – of both cattle and plants.

Africa's history of metal mining and trade in metal goods also shows how much contact they had with the world – centuries before the modern era of European colonisation. We have evidence of iron working at Nok, northern Nigeria, which dates back to 500 BC. This shows that iron technology and trade in iron goods had spread all over West Africa by the 4th century AD. A great centre of trade in iron goods was Oume in the southern Ivory Coast, and Oyo in southwest Nigeria. The Awka and Nkwerri people were travelling ironsmiths who traded between the southern Ivory Coast, southwest Nigeria, and the entire Igbo country.

Fig 5.2 Terracotta head from Nok culture, Northern Nigeria

Gold industries

Gold was mined in West Africa as early as the 1st millennium. By the 8th century AD the West Africans traded extensively in gold throughout the Sahara and into the Arab world. The Arabs demanded more and more gold. This stimulated the gold mining industry and the production of gold goods in West Africa by the 10th century. These industries continued into the present time. By the 14th century, West Africa was Western Europe's main supplier of gold. Gold was a major currency in Africa, Asia, the Mediterranean, and Europe, and it gave West Africans open access to international markets. But the wealth from the gold industry remained in the hands of the West African kings and nobles. They were a political elite who worked in much the same way as European kings and nobles.

Fig 5.3 Gold jewellery worn as insignia by senior officials of the court of the Ashanti Kings, 18th-19th century AD.

By 296 AD the Romans in North Africa were issuing gold coins using gold from Sénégal. Arabic writers for the period 788-93 AD refer to the gold of Ghana as decorating royal palaces and the costumes of men and women. In 1067-68 the Spanish geographer, al-Bakri, used the stories of travellers to write about Africa. He described the colourful gold usage of the people of Ghana, but noted that enslaved people and gold were also part of the same trade. African rulers could influence the countries they came into contact with because of their wealth in gold. An example of this is in the well-documented pilgrimage by King Mansa Musa of the Mali Empire to Mecca in 1324. the Egyptian scholar, al-Omari, recorded that the Mali King bought so many goods in Cairo that he weakened the exchange rates by flooding the financial system with gold.

Other industries

Like gold, salt was a major West African export to the Mediterranean and Europe. In the 10th century Songhai

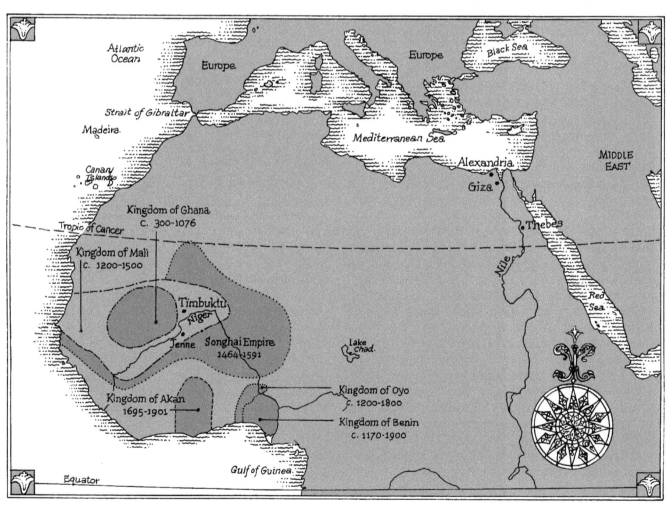

Fig 5.4 Ancient African kingdoms

chapter 5 | Europe and the spread of chattel slavery in Africa

became a well-known international centre for the salt trade. West Africa also had a thriving textile export industry as early as the 8th century. A.G. Hopkins notes that the West African production of cotton cloth, silks, woollens and raffia grew when Islam spread into the savannah. Contact with Islamic merchants in the 9th and 10th centuries enabled West Africa to export to European markets. By the 12th century, Hopkins concludes, cotton goods from the Western Sudan were well-known in Europe to the extent that the Mandingo words *bouracan* or *bougran*, were used to describe certain types of cloth. At the end of the 16th century the university town of Timbuktu within Mali was known for its textiles technology and for being an entrepot for grain, cattle, and vegetables.

Trade centres

Fig 5.5 The mosque in Old Jenne in Mali

Old Jenne is a well-known case of a large town that became a major trade centre. It is at a site in modern Mali that has been excavated by archaeologists. The settlement existed by the 3rd century BC, and was a substantial town by 400 AD. Archaeologists have found evidence of trade with the Mediterranean that shows that Old Jenne was part of a complex network of intercontinental trade. A thousand years later, in the 14th century, Mali was an Islamic State. In 1352-53, the great traveler, Ibn Battuta, admired Mali's social and economic development. By this time, Mali traders were in contact with traders in East Africa who gave them access to Indian, Chinese, and Persian markets. Battuta found cowrie shells from the Indian Ocean in Mali. These shells were used as currency in most of West Africa and had been in circulation as money for over 300 years. This indicates a long-established contact between West and East Africa.

So, centuries before the Portuguese began to kidnap West African people for the transatlantic trade in Africans, West Africa was an important participant in international trade. The evidence we have from about 1000 BC clearly shows that West Africans traded with Europe, Asia, and the Mediterranean long before the rise of Arab imperialism in the 7th century. When the Arabs invaded the empire of Ghana in 1077 West African international trade across the Sahara was well established. Certainly, West Africa was the leading supplier of gold to the European economy by the 12th century when gold replaced silver as the main currency. The European cities of Genoa, Florence and Venice all dealt with West African suppliers through intermediaries in Cairo who were described as 'Black,' Arab, and Jew.

Diplomatic missions

Economic relations and political diplomacy went hand in hand. There is evidence of diplomatic relations in West Africa in the early 10th century writings of al-Saghir. He refers to a 9th century Imam of Talbert in North Africa who was sent to a West African city state that has been identified as Gao. In the 11th century, al-Bakri described the mosque in the royal capital of Ghana, and indicated that the Ghanaians had diplomatic relations with the Almoravids of Morocco.

Ibn Khaldun describes a diplomat being sent from the ruler of Borno and Kanem to Tunis in 1257. This is the earliest known example of a diplomatic mission between countries. It is believed that the diplomat introduced the giraffe to Tunis. In the 14th century, Mansa Musa, King of Mali, exchanged embassies with the Marinid Sultans of Morocco. In fact, when King Abul of Morocco died in 1352 a memorial service was held for him in Mali.

Even the Portuguese in the 15th century tried to make contact with the political elite of coastal West African states through diplomatic missions. This was their earliest strategy, namely to win the political confidence of West Africa's leadership, which was important to merchants and monarchs alike. At the end of the 15th century, the King of Portugal sent two diplomats, Rui de Sousa and Simao de Silva, to the King of Congo. The Portuguese also sent a delegation to the Fula King in Upper Guinea in the 1490s, and had two ambassadors in Mali.

In the 9th century Arabic literacy spread in West Africa. More and more people learned to read and write in Arabic. At this time West African diplomacy focussed on trade and cultural matters. Remember that al-Bakri wrote about

Ghana in 1067-68. He noted that the king's interpreters, his treasurer, and most of his foreign ministers, were Muslims. Ahmad Baba, an Arab scholar, also described the diplomatic, trade and cultural exchanges between the Niger region and Andalusia in the 12th and 13th centuries. Other sources suggest that books in Arabic sold in Timbuktu for more money than other goods because people had an intense desire to learn more about the wider world.

The Portuguese and Spanish, then, arrived in the 15th century against the background of an old, well-established history in which West Africa had connections with the wider world and followed the main patterns of international development. So there is no truth in the idea that West African society was closed and out of contact with a wider world. West Africa had achieved an effective international commercial reputation, and at the time of the Portuguese arrival was prepared to build on this.

3 Main West African states in the mid-15th century: Ghana, Mali and Songhai

We know the names Ghana and Mali as two modern African states. But they were also names, as was Songhai, of powerful medieval states in Africa before the western Europeans made contact in the 15th century. They all had strong governments, prosperous economies, and trading contact with Europe via the Mediterranean. The modern boundaries of these states have been redrawn. The ancient empire of Ghana is about 1,000 miles north of present-day Ghana.

Ghana was known as the 'land of gold'. The gold, however, was mined in the sub-regions known as Wangara and Bambuk, outside of the political boundaries of Ghana. From about 950 to 1450 AD, Arab writers provide us with a lot of detail of the gold trade as well as West African relations to the European economy.

The Soninke rulers of Ghana bought gold from Wangara with salt, textiles and copper, and sold it to the Arabs as 'middlemen'. As imperial rulers, however, the Soninke rulers imposed taxes on gold trading, and politically protected the Wangara region from outsiders. The trade in enslaved persons was a minor activity in the empire, and was not an important source of wealth for the Soninke. It is important to note, however, that in the trans-Saharan caravan trade, the buying and selling of gold and enslaved people went hand-in-hand.

The attack upon Ghana by the Almoravid Muslims in 1042, the fall of the capital at Kumbi Saheh in 1076-77, and the final collapse of the empire in 1203, led to the expansion of both slavery and slave-trading. When the Islamic Mandingo empire of Mali rose out of the ruins of Ghana in the mid-13th century, under King Sundiata, this led to the political inclusion of Wangara and Bambuk, the two gold mining regions. Slave-trading was also not a major source of wealth for the Mali rulers, whose focus was on the sale of gold and on the expansion of their territory.

Under the monarchy of Mansa Musa, grandson of King Sundiata, who came to the throne in 1307, the Mali empire captured the imagination of the Mediterranean and European world. The extensive Arab literature on Mali was made widely available in Europe. This literature told of compelling images of gold wealth and education at the university of Timbuktu. Mansa Musa's pilgrimage to Mecca in 1324 became fabled for the impact his gold-laden caravan had as it passed through Walata and Tuat on the way to Cairo.

When he died in 1332, Musa's Mali was considered to be a wealthy, commercially dynamic, and a well-organised state. It had a reputation throughout Europe and the Mediterranean for culture and learning. His son, Maghan, lacked his father's political skills, and the state began to disintegrate. With it came political chaos, and many communities became vulnerable to slave-raiding. The Mandingos were still trying to hold the empire together when the Portuguese arrived in the mid-15th century. They even asked the Portuguese for their help.

The Songhai was a subordinate state of Mali for a short period between 1325 and 1335 when it broke away and asserted its sovereignty. When Sonny Ali, the famous Songhai king, came to the throne in 1464, he set about dismantling what was left of the Mali empire and conquered Timbuktu in 1468.

Shortly after the death of Sonny Ali, Askia Mohammed rose to power. This was associated with Songhai's emergence as a powerful state. Askia is credited with the modernisation of the commercial economy, the creation of an efficient administration and the rebuilding of Timbuktu, Benne, and Walata as centres of learning. According to Margaret Shinnie, 'gold continued to flow northward, together with enslaved people, ivory, ebony, and ostrich feathers, and in exchange came manufactured goods of copper and iron, brassware, sword blades from Spain and Germany, cloth and of coarse salt.'

By 1515 Askia had created one of the largest and wealthiest empires in Africa, stretching from the southern border of Algeria to the forest lands in the south, to the Atlantic in the west. The Moroccans, however, were

chapter 5 | *Europe and the spread of chattel slavery in Africa* principal enemies of the Songhai state. They did their best to stop its growth and influence. By 1590, as the Europeans penetrated deeper into inland economies, Songhai was collapsing under Moroccan military pressure. The failure of such political units to consolidate, as was the case with England and Spain, was the fuel that fired the trade in humans.

As an empire, Songhai was larger than many European states. When Sonny Ali ruled it between 1464 and 1492, it covered about 1 million square kilometres. This is greater than the size of France. The Arab literature that describes the expansion of the empire suggests that while slaves were taken in the process of waging war and annexing territory, the pursuit of slaves for sale was not an important goal. Nowhere is it stated that either Sonny Ali or Askia Mohammed were concerned with slaving as a significant activity.

Historians have suggested, however, that Songhai might have been the exception rather than the rule. They say that when the Portuguese arrived, most Africans lived in medium and small states, and these states were located in the most densely populated areas. Medium size states covered between 50,000 and 150,000 square kilometres. This is about the size of England and Portugal which stand at 150,000 square kilometres and 90,000 square kilometres respectively. It was then more typical to have small states, then populated with between 3,000 and 30,000 people. This was the political circumstance along the area that became known as the Gold and Slave Coasts, as well as along the Gambia River and Niger Delta, and the Kwanza River in Angola.

Recent research has also shown that West Africa's economic development on the eve of the transatlantic human trade was not very different from the conditions in Europe. The trade in humans did not bring into the region any vital goods that the Africans themselves could not produce. In effect, political elites in West Africa shifted their interest to the transatlantic human trade, not because it would sponsor or stimulate indigenous development, but because they could acquire exotic goods which they regarded as luxuries.

The early transatlantic trade in Africans saw the arrival of goods in Africa from Europe such as textiles and metal products, mostly iron and copper bars that were used to produce swords, knives and domestic utensils. Many parts of West Africa could and did produce iron and textile goods for sale. So that the exchange of persons for goods was not about meeting basic needs. Rather it was about the greed of elites. When the Portuguese arrived in Senegambia, the local iron and copper industry was well established, producing trade items of good quality. Africans were long recognised as skilled textile makers.

Early Portuguese traders bought both iron and textiles in one part of Africa to sell to another. Indeed, many of the producers of these goods were slaves within the local division of labour.

The political elites of small coastal and river states, especially, saw the trading presence of the Portuguese as a way to enrichment, and to build protection from inland empires. At first, Portuguese merchants found it easier to get enslaved Africans than to get the gold that they desired more. Muslim merchants were reliable suppliers of enslaved Africans and more and more often the local elites were prepared to negotiate the sale of captives that they got in their raiding missions.

The region of Central Africa also became a main source for supplies of enslaved Africans by the mid-15th century. This was mainly because of the existence of many states like Congo that engaged in on-going political and military conflict that produced large numbers of prisoners who were sold as enslaved persons. In this way, by the end of the 16th century, the Portuguese had established and expanded a major slave-trading network in the Angola area.

So, when the Europeans arrived, they fitted into the patterns of both localised and long-distance slave trading. African elites responded to the European demand for enslaved labour, and did so with respect to European demand for gold. As long as prices were attractive, the rise of human trading between some African and European elites was assured.

The expansion of slavery as a system to own and accumulate wealth in Africa during the 15th and 16th centuries, is associated with the disintegration of large nation states, such as Ghana, Mali and Songhai, and the expansion of small states. The ruling elites saw slave owning as a principal way to consolidate their power and prestige.

The arrival of the Portuguese during the 1440s did not begin the process of extensive slave trading. It merely served to create a wider context for the trade in humans. At first, though, the Portuguese engaged with it on a small scale. It was only at the beginning of the 16th century that Europeans began in important ways to determine and reshape the content and context of the slave-trading commercial culture.

4 The decline of European slavery

When the Roman Empire finally collapsed in the 9th century, European slavery still remained an important institution throughout Europe. By the 12th and 13th centuries, the enslaved were still considered valuable possessions in European, Asian, and African societies. However the meaning of the term slave changed and varied. One person's right to another person's labour was seen as different and separate from one person's right to own another person as property. In the 14th century European chattel slavery rapidly declined as a labour system, and was not practised widely after this in Europe.

More and more people thought that persons outside their family, religion, race, and nation could be enslaved. The Christian Europeans and the Muslim Arabs began to organise a more formal trading relationship with West Africa. The religious views of each group shaped the systems of slavery that were used. Spain and Portugal knew about the labour system of Islam that was used within North African culture. So these two countries especially led the way in the trade in enslaved humans and experimented with different forms of slavery in West Africa. Eventually they settled for the system of chattel slavery. This is the system where a person is legally and officially recognised as the property of someone else.

5 The rise of slavery in Africa

In Europe, the Mediterranean and in Africa there were different forms of human bondage. Wherever agriculture grew and long-distance trade was encouraged, enslaved labour was used. The spread of Islam in Africa also helped the trade in enslaved people to grow. Many of the great Islamic kings of Mali and Songhai, in particular, kept large armies of enslaved people to protect their empires. In the early 16th century, Africans traded enslaved people for horses as part of an enormous military build-up along the Middle Niger and the River Sénégal. In Benin, kings and nobles used large gangs of enslaved people in the mining of gold. In these economies enslaved people who were employed in large-scale agriculture and as the private property of their owners, came to symbolise wealth and prosperity.

Traditional slavery
In most of West Africa, slavery was used to bring an outsider into the kinship system of a society. Before an

Fig 5.6 *Slave felucca*

chapter 5 | *Europe and the spread of chattel slavery in Africa*

outsider could become a full member of a family or kin, he or she served as an enslaved person. So to enter a family then, one had to serve the family. Slavery, therefore, was a temporary condition. It was a position that one did not remain in, but passed through.

So slavery was as much part of a process of family and kinship building, as it was a system of labour. These enslaved were seen as future members of the dominant group. The social relationship between the enslaved and owners took this into consideration. It was understood by everyone that even a person who was captured in war, or reduced to slavery because of having committed a crime, could still achieve freedom in a family.

In most cases the enslaved had social rights and responsibilities. They had a right to family, cultural identity, and ultimately, freedom. People were not enslaved because of their race, colour, culture, or intellectual capability. Slavery was not about being inferior or having less worth than anyone else. However, this tradition changed in the early 15th century when slave markets were developed where Arabs and Europeans were the main buyers. Now chattel slavery became the system that was expanding.

Some scholars argue that, even in this traditional system of slavery, many enslaved persons were still doomed to lifelong slavery in families where they were isolated from the rest of society, sold many times and generally ill-treated. Also the growing influence of the transatlantic and trans-Sahara slave trades was changing the traditional system. The implication of this was that new economic forces were changing the nature of slavery in Africa.

Many African states engaged in slave raiding, wars, and other conflicts, in order to capture persons to sell to Europeans as slaves. But Africans in their communities were never enslaved in the ways they were in European colonies. The societies into which the Africans were imported by Europeans did not see them as human and tried to enforce their inferiority in relation to white skinned people.

Portuguese slave trade

In the early 15th century, the Portuguese began, on a small scale, the trading of enslaved people from West Africa to Europe. Prince Henry the Navigator was an influential figure in this development. He was concerned with both gold and slave trading. At this time there were rumours of huge economic opportunities at Timbuktu on the Niger. This drove Prince Henry's Portuguese merchants to introduce major military and trading expeditions. One enormous effect of these visits to Guinea was the organisation of slave trading as an international business. The Portuguese sold Africans in Europe, the

Mediterranean, and the Atlantic islands of Madeira, the Canaries, Cape Verde and the Azores. The Portuguese commercial network quickly developed in Guinea, and slave trading took on new and larger dimensions. By the 1440s, gold and slave trading were established along the River Sénégal.

It was no easy matter, however, to obtain Africans for enslavement. At first many Wolof kings along the River Sénégal opposed slave trading. So kidnapping Africans became the main way to get large numbers of persons to enslave. The Portuguese introduced the raiding of villages and the stealing of inhabitants as a way of conducting the slave trade business. This method spread wherever the Portuguese made contact with people along the coast of West Africa. To some extent they were building on the old tradition of village raiding and kidnapping which the Tuareg established to sell Africans to meet Arab and Mediterranean demand for enslaved persons.

Africans initially resisted as best they could, but the Portuguese superior military capability made this difficult. In 1448 the Wolofs made an organised attempt to ward off Portuguese kidnappers. This led to the killing of Vallarte, a Danish member of Prince Henry's inner circle, off the Coast of Goreé Island. The Portuguese, however, were persistent.

Europeans said that West Africans were different in physical appearance, dressed differently, possessed unfamiliar cultural characteristics, were black-skinned, and were therefore a backward and inferior race. They used cultural and ethnic differences as the basis of prejudicial treatment. Africans, the Europeans said, were inferior and could be legally enslaved. This argument was used to justify the transatlantic trade in enslaved Africans.

The Portuguese and Spanish Imperial Crowns approved of African enslavement in the Americas. They allowed settlers to legally use Africans as chattel. The prominent supporters of both the Crowns were granted royal licences to import Africans as slaves into the colonies. With the genocide of Caribbean natives almost complete by the 1580s, the trade in enslaved Africans to the Spanish Caribbean became a major way in which people could get rich. The development of the sugar industry in Cuba, Hispaniola, and Puerto Rico, and the many mining expeditions into the interior of these islands, encouraged the trade to expand.

Meanwhile, by the mid-16th century the Portuguese had established a large-scale sugar plantation economy in Brazil, using enslaved Africans. By 1600, Brazil was the largest producer of cane sugar in the world and dominated the European market. The sugar plantation business was based on the labour of over 100,000 enslaved

Fig 5.7 *Trading in enslaved persons*

Africans. Twice as many were also imported into Spanish colonies between Mexico and Chile to develop agriculture and mining industries.

The French, English, Dutch, Danes, Norwegians, Swedes, and Germans also wanted a share of the profitable trade in Africans. They all declared war on the Portuguese attempt to control and monopolise the trade, and on Spanish determination to own the Americas. Portuguese slavers were not safe on the Atlantic Ocean, and by the mid-16th century neither were their West African forts and trading stations. The French made significant early progress against the Portuguese on the Sénégal River and on the Gambia. In the 1530s, the Englishman, William Hawkins, was also busy establishing slave trading links on the Gold Coast as well as sales outlets in Brazil. Queen Elizabeth I of England issued a pronouncement saying that she was against the

kidnapping of Africans by her British subjects. However she approved of the practice of officially buying enslaved Africans.

Dutch trade in Africans

At the end of the 16th century the Dutch, led by Bernard Ericks, established a slaving network on the Gold Coast. By this time getting access to gold and ivory required complicated negotiations with African suppliers. So the Dutch decided to focus their attention on the trade in humans rather than in gold and ivory. Ericks' plan was to secure a slave trade link with the sugar producers in Portuguese Brazil because the demand for enslaved could not be met by Portuguese traders. Other Dutch merchants, like Pieter Brandt and Pieter van der Broecks built up slave trading networks along Loango Bay (on the southwest coast of Africa) between 1599 and 1602. In 1607 the Dutch

chapter 5 | *Europe and the spread of chattel slavery in Africa*

West India Company was established, and later the Guinea Company that established a trading fort at Mouri, about 12 miles east of Elmina (a major slave-trading station on the Ghana coast) on the Gold Coast.

The Danes and Swedes expressed a keen interest in the transatlantic labour trade. King Christian IV of Denmark and King Gustavus Adolphus of Sweden met with officials of the Dutch West India Company and discussed ways to enter the trade. Adolphus approved the formation of a South Company to trade in Africans. The Danes followed with a company of their own. Copenhagen equipped ships to sail to Guinea and offload human cargoes in Virginia, Brazil and the British Caribbean. The Swedes participated in a number of joint ventures with the Dutch. They supplied slave ships and crew, while the Dutch provided captains and finances.

Swedish soldiers protected the forts built in Africa to protect the captured Africans who were waiting to be traded. By the 1640s the Danes were sending slave ships to Guinea. And in 1651 they contracted the Gluckstadt Company to expand the trade. The *Neldebladet* was the first Danish ship to supply Africans to the Caribbean in 1643. Jens Lassen, the Secretary of the Exchequer in Copenhagen, owned it.

Like the French and Dutch, the Swedes and Danes fought for a greater share of the trade in Africans on the Gold Coast. They also built forts and between them supplied over 50,000 Africans to the Caribbean during the 17th century.

In 1635, after a series of failed slave trading businesses, the French government established the Company of the Isles of America. The aim of the company was to supply Africans directly to its Caribbean colonies. However, by the mid-1640s Dutch enslavers had control of the slave market on the West African Coast, as well as the Caribbean and Brazilian markets. Between 1645 and 1670, the demand for enslaved Africans, and White indentured servants, in the English and French West Indian colonies increased at an amazing rate. The enormous expansion of sugar production in the English colonies of Barbados, St Kitts, Antigua, and Jamaica, and the French colony of Martinique, demanded enslaved Africans at a level that the colonising nations could not deliver. The Dutch effectively filled this shortfall.

In the 1640s the Dutch took possession of Elmina, the Portuguese fort. (The Portuguese, in retaliation, drove the Dutch out of Brazil in 1647.) However, the Dutch never regained effective control of the trade in Africans on the Gold Coast. Instead, they moved into Angola and exported over 10,000 Africans per year from Luanda. First the Dutch established trade and kidnapping arrangements on the Gold Coast. Then they strengthened control over the West

Indian markets by supplying the French and English with Africans on favourable credit terms. These developments helped to promote Holland as the leading commercial and financial power in Europe.

In the 1640s and 1650s the Dutch West India Company had no significant rival. In 1670 there were over 100,000 Africans in the English West Indian colonies, most supplied by the Dutch. They also delivered over 50,000 Africans to Spanish America during this period. So within 100 years of Columbus' visit to the Caribbean, Africans were the main form of forced labour in the Americas. White labour, which had been imported from Europe under contracts of temporary servitude, proved to be insufficient. The Caribbean indigenous population was crippled and could not reproduce itself. By 1650 the Spanish colonies had over 375,000 enslaved Africans; some 30,000 were in the Central America region, and about half this number in the islands of the Caribbean.

6 The impact of the transatlantic trade in Africans on Africa

The transatlantic trade in Africans was a reign of terror unleashed upon the African continent. Initially the enslavers focused mostly upon West, Central and Southern Africa. But by the end of the 18th century enslavers had reached the eastern coast of Africa in search of persons to enslave. Their activities had a devastatingly negative effect upon local community and national life. It disrupted the economic and financial order; agricultural production; the way communities had managed food scarcity; political organisation; and the social and psychological well being of inhabitants. The transatlantic human trade was the outcome of Europeans undermining the material and cultural development of Africans. The fact that Africans themselves participated in the trade deepens, rather than lessens, the meaning of this crime against humanity.

The African trade affected the different parts of Africa differently. But all were distracted from their paths to development. Some small societies were completely destroyed. Those that simply refused to participate for long periods of time were assaulted militarily until they did. One example is the kingdom of Benin between the Igbo in the east and the Yoruba in the west. Societies that chose to benefit from the relationship with European slavers found it necessary to attack the communities of neighbouring states.

In these attacks the number of people who were killed or crippled, especially the elderly, the very young, and women, were far more than those who were finally

Fig 5.8 Slave coffle – captured Africans being taken to a trading post.

shipped across the Atlantic. Once some local kings could see that the trade in Africans was profitable, they increased slave raiding to meet the demand. Where possible, Europeans used kings to work with them as business partners.

After centuries of having an organised community life, millions of people had to go back to being nomads. In doing this, the people lost their ability to manage food production and distribution. They became more vulnerable to famine caused by drought and had little access to fertile land. Along the rivers, for example, where there had been large-scale farming, now became danger zones because of the high risk of being kidnapped. These circumstances restricted and undermined growth and development in sub-Saharan Africa.

The transatlantic trade in Africans caused a major depopulation of West and Central Africa – the skills and competencies of millions of people were lost. In some places population levels fell dramatically, in others they were reduced to a slower rate of growth. Seventy per cent of the people were sold across the Atlantic. This meant that there was very little chance for normal growth to take place in most African places, and community life was seriously affected everywhere.

So we can say that the transatlantic trade in Africans:

a. weakened the economic potential of many African communities and threw them off their development path.

b. destroyed and corrupted political institutions, and systems of governance

c. created immeasurable levels of fear, social contest, warfare and dishonour. And it undermined moral and civic practices in community life and culture

d. meant there was a massive drain of skills, abilities, and the general pool of human resources needed for sustainable development

e. created within some societies an impulse to rebel against the European presence that could have been beneficial in some areas

f. had a significant impact on gender roles in African societies because of the removal of more men than women.

Traders in Africans introduced a massive number of weapons into West Africa which created an arms build-up. For many states, their security and defence became linked to involvement in the trade. The export of humans as slaves was made possible because of the increase in heavily armed states that carried out raids upon neighbouring countries. The militarily powerful Guinea slave-trading states – Akwamu, Denkyira, Asante, Whydah, and Dahomey – developed their fighting character and power during the era of the trade in Africans.

Some rulers and their administrators were business partners of European slavers. Together they created an economic culture that destroyed the quality of life for

chapter 5 | *Europe and the spread of chattel slavery in Africa*

Fig 5.9 A depiction of the trading in human beings in Africa

most Africans. In the late 18th and 19th centuries European abolitionist groups accused European traders of corrupting the African political elites, and said that the slave traders should be condemned because of this. Europeans could see the material benefits of trading in Africans everywhere within their societies. However most ordinary Africans did not experience it in this way. Rather, they saw evidence around them of terror, flight, rebellion, and general mayhem. Many scholars have ignored the experiences of ordinary inhabitants, and have focused only upon the decision-making and spending patterns of rulers. This means they have disregarded the experience of ordinary inhabitants, which is essential for historical inquiry and judgment.

To sum up

The transatlantic trade in Africans, which forcefully removed between 10 and 20 million Africans, significantly increased levels of social conflict, political rivalry, warfare, and economic distortion in most of West and Central Africa. These conditions were extremely harmful to economic development. The arms build-up caused political instability and a military presence. It threw off balance traditional trade patterns and marketing systems in West and Central Africa, and it guaranteed the dominance of slave-raiding and trading within economic life. Africa was well-placed for economic development at the end of the 15th century, just like Europe and Asia. But it was interrupted by the reign of terror known as the transatlantic human trade from which it has yet to recover.

Revision questions

1 'Pre-modern Europe took much more than enslaved labour from Africa.' Discuss.
2 'West Africa before the transatlantic trade in Africans was developing economically in ways familiar to Europeans.' Discuss.
3 Which European Nations were the principal organisers of slaving in Africa in the 16th and 17th centuries?
4 What was the impact of the transatlantic trade in enslaved Africans on West African society and economy.
5 'West Africa lost much of its human skills to the Americas through the trade in enslaved inhabitants.' Discuss.

Chapter 6

The transatlantic trade in enslaved Africans

'Old pirates yes they rob I, sold I to the merchant ship.'
(Bob Marley)

By the beginning of the 18th century the transatlantic trade in enslaved Africans had become an organisationally complex and financially sophisticated business. To recruit, ship and sell over 12 million people the slavers needed effective planning and they needed to be able to use financial tools and institutions. For most of the time between 1500 and 1870 European royals, as well as political and commercial leaders, pooled their financial resources to invest in the trade.

In this chapter we will learn about:
1. The commercial and financial organisation of the trade in humans
2. Prices and profits in the trade
3. The debate over the size of the trade and the main participants
4. The Middle Passage and the mortality rate of Africans
5. Resistance by Africans to the transatlantic human trade
6. The impact of the trade on Africa, Europe, and the Americas.

1 Commercial and financial organisation of the trade in Africans

At the height of the trade in enslaved Africans, in the mid-18th century, Europeans were shipping some 90,000 Africans each year to the Americas. Up to the 1650s, ivory and gold were Africa's leading exports to Europe. By 1700, these items were less than 10 per cent of Africa's exports. Enslaved persons were now the leading export. African sellers exchanged these persons for a range of European, American and Asian goods. Textiles constituted about 65 per cent of the goods shipped from England to Africa to pay for enslaved persons. About 35 per cent of these textiles were East Indian fabrics. Among them, the Portuguese, English and French shipped about 80 per cent of the Africans to the Americas.

When they traded formally, African sellers sold about as many enslaved persons to the Europeans as the Europeans managed to kidnap. The relationship between African sellers and Europeans, however, was not a simple one. Some African leaders went to war with their neighbours to make sure they had enough captives for sale and to protect their own communities from war with the Europeans. Kidnapping, war, community raids, and market trading, went hand in hand. The process was driven by the increasing Atlantic demand for persons to enslave.

The prices paid for enslaved persons in West Africa varied over time, and from place to place. These prices showed the same patterns that we could expect in any commodity market. The relationship between kidnappers, African sellers, European buyers, and each of their agents, was an ever-changing one that produced different prices from voyage to voyage. Some African rulers and nobles benefited from the trade and took taxes, while others opposed or ignored the trade as best they could. So the size of the trade at any one place was determined by the efficiency of kidnappers, the attitudes of local political elites, and the organisational capacity of European slavers.

Kidnapping was the organisational part of the trade. European slavers did not always participate personally in the kidnapping operations. They paid African agents to kidnap people on their behalf. Sometimes entire communities were converted into paid armies working on behalf of European slavers. The Europeans often paid African agents in cowrie shells, which was a common form of money used in West Africa, India and parts of Europe.

The triangular pattern of the transatlantic human trade

The triangular pattern of the transatlantic trade was part of why it was such an efficient business. Ships would leave the Americas with colonial produce for Europe. Merchants in Europe would then equip the ships for enslaved Africans. When they left Europe for Africa, the shippers would buy goods to exchange for enslaved Africans, and a large quantity of devices to secure them during the Middle Passage. These devices included leg and neck irons, and mounted cannons.

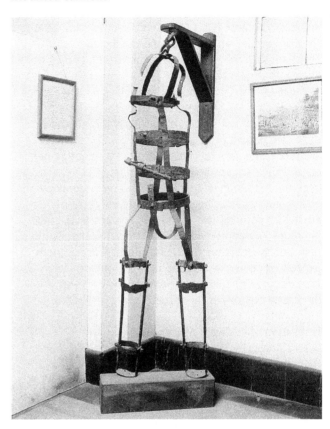

Fig 6.1 An iron gibbet, used for punishing enslaved persons

Ships were made of wood and designed to make full use of wind power. The typical ship would be about 200 tons, built to withstand the hardships of at least ten voyages to Africa and to carry 5,000 enslaved persons in its career. The ships were generally given names that ranged from Christian saints to other deities, such as Venus. The more fashionable shippers in the 18th century named their ships after lovers or Greek gods. Apart from the captain, 40 or more sailors, a doctor, cooks, and artisans manned a slave ship. The ships were in fact floating maximum-security prisons.

Negotiating the price
Traders made very accurate financial calculations of what it would cost each ship during a voyage. Participants in the business were expected to know these costs and calculate the income. The ship captain, almost always male, was

generally an employee of the shipping company. His employer(s) gave him precise instructions about the collection of enslaved persons. He would be told to go to a particular place in Africa and to negotiate for the purchase of a given number of enslaved persons. Often there was room for him to use his own initiative by reading local situations. He could decide, for example, whether to practise kidnapping or to negotiate with another European agent. The owner(s) of the ship set out the price ranges within which the captain should negotiate with the African agents or factors, as they were known on the coast.

Most Africans who found themselves on slave ships were people who had been kidnapped, left defenceless and kinless by raids upon their villages, or they were prisoners of war, or victims of political and judicial authority. Scholars have estimated that about 45 per cent of the Africans sold were political prisoners, 40 per cent were kidnapped, and the remainder were convicts of the law system. The trade in Africans certainly stirred up political instability and social chaos, and facilitated a cycle of warfare and social crime. As a result of the disruption to communities, many more people saw how the kidnapping was done. It was a vicious cycle, and over time these developments increased the size of the trade.

Inspection of enslaved Africans

Before slavers bought the enslaved persons, they insisted that they be washed and closely inspected. Captain Richard Willing of England wrote that he hired a mulatto African in the 1810s who could tell an unsound captive at a glance. He handled the naked bodies from head to foot, squeezing their joints and muscles, twisting their arms and legs, and examining teeth, eyes, and chest, pinching breasts and groin without mercy. The Africans stood in pairs, stark naked, and were made to jump, cry out, lie down, and roll, and hold their breath for a long time. After they were bought, factors, as agents on the coast were called, secured the enslaved for storage and shipment. Africans were often obtained along rivers deep in the interior. So they had to be taken downstream by canoes or by land, while they were heavily guarded. Factors delivered cargoes of Africans to ship captains or stored them in safe houses or forts until the ships arrived. At some time during this process Africans were branded with hot irons on their shoulders, arms, or chest. This was so that they could be labelled for transportation and storage.

Branding the enslaved

Africans who were bought for the Royal African Company of England were branded DY. This stood for Duke of York,

after the President of the Company. The Spanish firm, *Compaña Gaditana*, branded enslaved persons with the letter d, and the Middelburg Commerce Company of Holland used the letters CCN. The German company, the Brandenburg Company, branded the enslaved on the right shoulder with the letters CABC.

Fig 6.2 Branding of an African woman

2 Prices and profits in the trade

In the 17th century the Spanish said they preferred to buy Africans from Senegambia (the trading area along the Sénégal and Gambia Rivers), the Wolofs and Mandingos, because they were said to be intelligent, diligent, and multilingual. In the 18th century the French said similar things. This influenced what other Europeans preferred. They seemed more than satisfied with the Congolese who were described as robust, keen to please, peaceable and loyal. The Brazilians preferred Africans who were blackest in colour, without tribal marks on their faces or filed teeth. They were not keen on brown skinned Africans.

The slave trade, then, was carried on as a result of a massive organisational, financial, and political effort. The over 12 million Africans shipped to the Americas were only a part of a larger number of victimised people. Do not forget that in order to deliver over 12 million people to the Americas between 1780 and 1850, some 21 million people

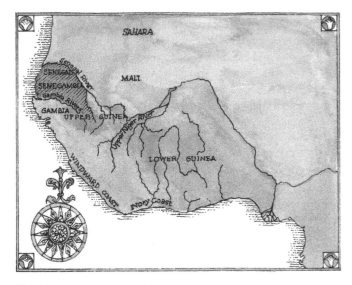

Fig 6.3 Map of Senegambia

commercial, and management effort, marks it as one of the most elaborate projects of the modern era.

Who were involved in the trade?

The trade in 'Black gold', as Africans were called, emerged as one of the most profitable transnational businesses of the early modern era. Slave trading was big business; it used advanced management and state-of-the-art investment instruments. It was not a poor man's business. People needed huge amounts of money to participate in the trade. There were many small traders, who could function because they pooled their resources through partnerships and other investment strategies. Large companies handled most of the trade. Many of them were granted royal contracts with monopoly rights. The most popular method of doing business was free trade and this opened the door to hundreds of participants. However the big firms were more effective in setting out organisational frameworks, determining prices, and establishing patterns of trading conduct.

The trade in humans attracted the rich and famous, men and women, from all the major European commercialising nations. It did so because it was profitable, and unlike

had been probably captured. The remaining people died or were kept enslaved in Africa, or they were scattered when they tried to run away or rebel. The scale of the operations required for this trade, together with the global financial,

Fig 6.4 Auction of enslaved people

Fig 6.5 *The Portuguese fort at Elmina, where the enslaved were kept*

many other trades, investors and managers could make a quick fortune. In all the imperial countries of Europe, monarchs, merchants, aristocrats, politicians, priests, farmers, soldiers and others who had money, contributed to finance the transatlantic human trade. Slave trade companies invested in ships and forts on the African Coast. They employed managers, brokers, agents, and captains to make fortunes for their owners.

In 1664, Jean Baptiste Colbert was concerned that contraband slavers had driven the state-owned company, the Company of the Isles of America, into bankruptcy. So he established a new corporation that could secure effective government control over the trade to the French colonies in the West Indies. He called it the Sénégal Company, and he raised three million livres from private individuals to finance it. In addition he secured a promise from the King for an equal amount of money and the French government agreed to put up two million livres. At this time La Rochelle was the leading French slave port, but Bordeaux and Nantes soon got involved as the trade expanded.

The English Royal Adventurers Company of 1663, headed by King Charles II, also had shareholders including all the leading investors of the time. Cape Coast became the Company's main station in Africa. In its first four years the company made an annual income of over 100,000 pounds on enslaved persons, and twice as much on gold. Then the company ran into problems with debt collection. So the Royal African Company replaced it in 1672. The new Company easily raised 111,600 pounds from 200 shareholders. One of the shareholders was John Locke, the famous philosopher of the theory of liberty. He invested

600 pounds in the first three years. Apart from Cape Coast, the Company opened slaving stations at Commenda, Accra, Aga and Ana Shan, along the coast of Ghana.

The Royal African Company spent large sums of money to kit out each voyage to Africa and to secure Africans who were sold in the West Indies for about £18 per female and £20 per male. Between 1672 and 1690, the company sold at least 100,000 enslaved Africans in the West Indies – about 25,000 taken from the Windward Coast (Liberia), 25,000 from the Gold Coast, 15,000 from Whydah, and the rest from Senegambia, Angola, Benin and Calabar. Persons would not have invested if they did not expect attractive profits.

The Scandinavians also wanted their share of the profits from the trade in 'Black gold'. Louis de Geer, a much-admired financial leader from Liege, and a known trader in iron works, set up a partnership with Samuel Blommaert, the established slaver from Amsterdam. Blommaert's ships operated from Gothenburg under the name of his trade company, which was formed in 1649. The business was headed by Henrick Carloff, who was an experienced slaver and who built Fort Carlosburg on the Gold Coast, within sight of Elmina. Carloff's venture attracted investments from as far as Lithuania (part of Poland) from the Duke of Courland. But Carloff soon ran into problems with his Swedish employers. He had to renegotiate a deal with the Danes before the war broke out between the two nations. Working for the Danes he built two forts on the West African coast, Christiansborg and Friedrichburg. He soon left them and became a broker for the French.

We do not know very much about the German involvement in the human trade. They made several attempts in the 17th and early 18th centuries to establish a stronghold in West Africa. The Germans used mainly the Dutch as their allies and sailed German ships under the Brandenburg Company flag. Germany had no colonies in the Americas, and so the German ships sold their enslaved persons mostly to the Danish settlements in the Virgin Islands. They did make an effort to establish a colony in Tobago, but the resistance of the Kalinago, informed by Dutch intelligence, made them abort this project.

No one would have invested if they did not expect attractive profits. Slavers swarmed around the coast of Africa like bees around a hive. We know a lot about the kind of profit Europe's largest companies were making, as well as the profit that the small family businesses and partnerships made. French and Dutch merchants made substantial profits, but not as much as the British. The records of 100 slaving voyages that were sent out by the Dutch *Middelburgsche Commercie Compagnie* between the 1730s and the 1790s show an average return of a modest 2-3 per cent. Some voyages made up to a very attractive 20 per cent and others experienced 10-15 per cent losses.

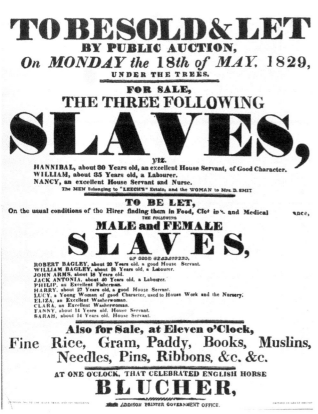

Fig 6.6 Advertisement for an auction of enslaved people

We can make a number of important observations:

a. The human trade was, in general, a profitable business for investors
b. Profits changed over time and place, and even between ships within a single fleet
c. Many voyages made losses, but investors remained optimistic because they thought they could make a big profit the next time.
d. If the investors made a loss in the sale of humans, then they could still make a profit from other commodity sales
e. The human trade offered profits, prestige and power to companies, governments, and individuals
f. Profits were sometimes made quickly, and were invested in plantation lands in the Americas, or converted to commercial and industrial capital in Europe
g. Few, if any, other investments in Europe offered the possibility for quickly making a large fortune
h. The average profit levels for most firms do not accurately show the true nature of wealth they were accumulating
i. Profits from the human trade were often interlocked with returns on other commodity trades, such as gold and ivory.

j. The present call for reparation for slavery is based partly on the huge profits made from the trade in enslaved Africans.

By the middle of the 18th century, the English had established themselves as the group that could get the most profits from the human trade. In British America slave prices were generally lower than in the French colonies. The Dutch had no major Caribbean agricultural colonies, except Suriname, so they tried to sell their enslaved Africans cheaper than the British and French slavers in their colonies. England had a more advanced industrial and commercial economy than the other Europeans. This was reflected in their lower unit costs. In other words, the English could outfit slave ships more economically than their rivals because most of the goods put on board for Africa were either locally made or acquired in their Asian and American colonies.

Average price of an enslaved person in Africa and the Caribbean, 1670s - 1780s		
	£	£
Years	African	Caribbean
1670s	3	15
1690s	10	20
1710s	15	20
1720s	16	22
1730s	12	25
1750s	15	30
1760s	13	30
1770s	18	35

The records of the large Dutch trading establishments show that average returns in the 18th century fell below 6 per cent, and for the French averaged between 6 and 8 per cent. However, we must bear in mind that the trade in humans was only part of a wider imperial network that included the New World, Asia, and Europe. The colonies would not be profitable without enslaved Africans. The Portuguese knew this all too well after they had lost Brazil and then regained it again from the Dutch in the 1640s. The Portuguese slavers set up a complex financial relationship with Brazilian sugar and coffee planters. This arrangement assured the Portuguese slavers that once the planters had collected their debts they would get a very attractive return on their investments. The true indicator that shows us how profitable the trade in humans was, is that it lasted for nearly 400 years. In addition, the main ports of Europe from where the trade was conducted bloomed as economic centres with thriving surroundings.

3 Size of the trade and main participants

It is very difficult to calculate the numbers of Africans removed from the continent and transported across the Atlantic. Explaining why and how millions of people were forcefully removed from their societies and enslaved against their will is an easier task than establishing precisely how many. Many scholars insist that it is very important to know the precise size of the trade in order to assess the magnitude of the business undertaking and its impact on Africa, Europe and the Americas.

Estimates of the numbers of Africans sold into the transatlantic trade in Africans have ranged from about five million to about 30 million. In the past two decades scholars have focussed on the work of Philip Curtin who in 1969 published the first attempt at a comprehensive census of the trade. Curtin estimated that about 10 million Africans reached the New World between 1500 and 1900. He suggests that maybe 12 million were shipped out, and about two million died on the way. Curtin's figures have generated enormous controversy. African scholars accuse him of downplaying the figures, but when they try to revise his analysis their figures are not very different.

The scholars who revised Curtin's work have tended to move the figure upwards. However, Joseph Inikori who is the only African scholar working on both sides of the Atlantic, and is a leading voice in this debate, has settled the figure at 15,4 million. Inikori's estimates add about 4,4 million to Curtin's calculations. Curtin's estimate for the British trade between 1701 and 1807 was 2,480,000; while Inikori suggests 3,699,522. This is a difference of 49,2 per cent.

The most recent estimate (1999) is presented in the form of a CD-Rom, *The Transatlantic slave trade: A database*, by David Eltis and a team of other historians. It refers to 27,233 voyages of enslaved persons between 1527 and 1866. In these voyages it is recorded that a total of 11,4 million Africans were shipped to the New World. Critics have already agreed that this is not an underestimation of the total volume of the trade.

Paul Lovejoy has estimated that six million Africans were shipped out in the 18th century alone. Of these six million, the shipping data show that about 40 per cent came from Angola and the Congo, 40 per cent from the Bights of Benin and Biafra, about 15 per cent from the Gold Coast, Sierra Leone and Senegambia, and the remainder from unknown places. The single largest purchaser of Africans was Brazil, which bought about 31 per cent of the total number of enslaved Africans. Brazil is followed by British West Indies which bought 23 per cent of the total; the French West Indies which bought 22 per cent of the total; Spanish America which bought 9 per cent; Dutch West Indies who bought 7 per cent; and British North America and the rest of the Danish West Indies which bought 6 per cent. About 60 per cent of all Africans sold came to the Caribbean. So the islands and continental communities of the Caribbean Sea were the largest single market for enslaved Africans.

Enslaved women

The gender profile of the trade in Africans tells us about the needs of Europeans. It is important to note that fewer African women entered the Atlantic trade than African men. The records that we have of European slave traders demonstrate this point forcefully.

Herbert Klein has done a comprehensive analysis of the records of Dutch slave traders, who in the 17th century also supplied French, Spanish, English and Portuguese colonies. This analysis shows that only 38 per cent of the enslaved Africans shipped were female. Klein analysed the records of the English and found a similar pattern. The general pattern, therefore, was clear. Between 65 per cent and 76 per cent of the persons shipped from West Africa as slaves to the Americas were male, with only slight variations across the region from Senegambia to Angola.

Carriers	Totals
English	2,532,300
Portuguese	1,796,300
French	1,180,300
Dutch	350,900
North Americans	194,200
Danish	73,900
Swedish/Brandenburger (other)	5,000
TOTAL	6,132,900

Source: Paul Lovejoy, 'The Volume of the Atlantic Slave Trade: A Synthesis', *Journal of African History* (1982), p. 483

Gender ratios of enslaved from different regions of Africa, 1764-88

African region	Percentage male	Percentage female
Gambia	72,1	27,9
Windward Coast	65,7	34,3
Gold Coast	66,8	33,2
Whydah	57,8	42,2
Benin	49,96	50,04
Bonny	56,5	43,5
Calabar	58,8	41,2
Gabon	68,8	31,2
Angola	68,2	31,8

Source: J. E. Inikori, *The Chaining of a Continent: Export Demand for Captives and the History of Africa South of the Sahara, 1450–1870* (Kingston, 1992).

The slave traders considered children high risk and low value and rarely targeted them. Less than 10 per cent of the enslaved sold were children. The records of the Dutch West Indian Company indicate that 9 to 14 per cent of its cargoes in the 17th century were children under the age of 14. However, over time as the economic frontier in the Americas diminished, children became slightly more attractive in some colonies. The result was a small increase in the number of children shipped in the late 18th and 19th centuries. Sometimes slavers could not avoid buying children in Africa, because they were grouped with adults, and they were offered at low prices. The numbers debate, however, continues to generate searches for new data and creative ways of making the calculations.

4 The Middle Passage and the mortality rate of Africans

Death and survival
The Middle Passage was much more than the transatlantic journey of millions of enslaved Africans; it was a symbol of the social division that separated the people of Africa and Europe. Also, it shows us how low humans can fall when they establish unjust relations with one another, and shows us their capacity for cruelty and insensitivity. So it is important to discuss both the psychological and physical aspects of the Middle Passage, as well as its economic and social significance and consequences.

Some 10 per cent of the Africans died before they arrived in the New World. This makes it necessary to speak about the mental torture and physical danger involved, as well as the power of survival demonstrated by those who lived. The survivors did not know where they were going or where they were when they arrived. Many of those who died held the religious belief that death on the Atlantic Ocean was not an end to life, but a means to return spiritually to their ancestors, to be reborn.

Scholars generally agree that the Middle Passage did not begin with the actual transatlantic voyage. It began with the capture and sale of Africans and ended with how they managed to adjust in the Americas. Scholars have identified six separate stages of the Middle Passage. These are:
a. Capture and enslavement in Africa
b. Journey to the coast and other departure points
c. Storage and packaging for shipment
d. Transatlantic crossing
e. Sale and distribution in the Americas
f. Adjustment in the Americas.

The separation of these stages allows us to analyse the Middle Passage in detail, particularly the experiences of individuals. Not all Africans survived each stage, and some experienced different stages more than once, and for different lengths of time. Also, from region to region individuals experienced these stages differently. Many Africans were captured and sold more than once before reaching the coast, and others were already enslaved at the time of sale to Europeans. Some were quickly taken to the coast and put on board ships that set sail, while others were stored in forts for long periods of time. In this time they could have been bought and sold to different European slavers, before setting out on the crossing. All of these circumstances influenced the conditions on the Middle Passage and determined the chances of survival.

Capture, enslavement and journey to departure point
In the period before the Atlantic crossing an enormous number of people died. Historians called the African coastal communities the 'White man's grave', but they were also a real cemetery for Africans. Many Africans gave in to brutality and terror, and the unfamiliar diseases that the Europeans and other Africans brought and against which they could not defend themselves. The conditions were a recipe for a high death rate and madness. Africans were afraid of Europeans as they thought they were cannibals; they were afraid of the ocean which many had never seen, there were strange diseases, physical brutality, psychological trauma, degradation by branding with hot irons for labelling, and general malnourishment.

Storage, packing and transatlantic crossing
The average length of the voyage to the Caribbean from West Africa was about 50 days. We need to add the 50 days to the 100 or more days it took to journey from inland points of sale and capture to the coast, and the 200 or more days that people remained in storage. The whole process of captivity and imprisonment took normally more than a year before the Africans were shipped out. A few ships made the voyage in less time; many took longer than 50 days because of the unpredictable winds, and the uncertain political and military circumstances in the Atlantic. The important issue here is that the voyage itself, the Middle Passage, was normally the shortest part of the entire journey to New World Slavery.

Many more Africans died in the crossing than on the coast. Indeed, slavers were used to losing up to 30 per cent of their cargo, and considered themselves fortunate when they lost less than this. Slavers spent a lot of time debating the best way to transport Africans across the

Fig 6.7 Captured Africans confined to a ship's hold

Middle Passage. Two methods were used, namely (i) loose packing and (ii) tight packing. Tight packing was based on the assumption that the slavers would lose at least 20 per cent of the numbers on board, and that it was more economical to pack the ship full to capacity and travel as fast as possible across the Atlantic. Loose packing was preferred by those slavers who believed that the more physically comfortable the enslaved were, the less chance they would have of dying. They chose to stock their ships up to about 75 per cent of capacity so that they could reduce the death rate to less than 10 per cent.

So slavers were divided by two schools of thought about how to deliver their human cargoes. However the evidence shows that neither method had any real impact on the death rate. The death rate varied among major African slave-providing areas. A study of 301 British slavers who supplied 101,676 enslaved to the British Caribbean in 1791-97 shows that the death rate ranged from 3 per cent for the Gold Coast to 11 per cent for the Bight of Biafra. The overall average death rate for this group was 6 per cent.

A Surgeon's (Joseph Buckhana) Journal of slave mortality gives an account of all the Africans that died on board the ship James, from Africa to the West Indies, 4 November 1788 to 8 February 1789.

Date of death	Description of enslaved	Cause of death
4 Nov 1788	man	inflammation of liver
29 Nov	man	dysentry
18 Dec	woman	suddenly
1 Jan 1789	man	dysentry
3 Jan	woman	dysentry
6 Jan	woman	lethargy
15 Jan	boy	dysentry
16 Jan	boy	dysentry
17 Jan	girl	dysentry
Jan 18	man	dysentry
19 Jan	boy	dysentry
28 Jan	boy	dysentry
31 Jan	woman	sulkiness
3 Feb	boy	lethargy
8 Feb	man	dysentry
Total slaves departed	154	70 men 46 women 23 boys 15 girls
Total death in Passage	15	
Arrivals	139	
% Loss	97	

Source: *English Parliamentary Papers*, 1789, Vol. 29; *Extracts of a Guinea Surgeon's Journal*, no. 632.

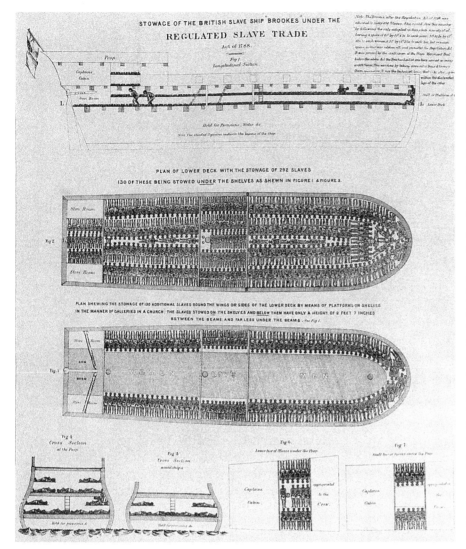

PLAN OF LOWER DECK WITH THE STOWAGE OF 292 SLAVES
130 OF THESE BEING STOWED UNDER THE SHELVES AS SHEWN IN FIGURE I & FIGURE 5.

Fig 6.8 *Stowage of British slave ship Brookes*

were thrown together on slave ships and exposed to new viruses. However, any first-time exposure to European diseases had greater effects. Outbreaks of yellow fever(s), scurvy, dysentery, measles, and small pox were known killers. Surgeons on board slave ships were expected to examine Africans for signs of sickness and disease. To protect the other Africans who seemed healthy, those diagnosed with disease were thrown over board. Maybe millions of African people were thrown to the oceans this way.

An important fact to note is that women survived the passage slightly better than men. We can see this difference quite clearly in the slave traders records. Scholars estimate that the overall death rate for men was about 20 per cent and for women about 15 per cent. They have given many different reasons for this difference. Some say that women can manage stress more effectively, and that they can withstand the effects of shock, pain, and malnutrition far better than men. Also, that their immune systems are more resistant to strange viruses. However, it seems more reasonable that women were already better adjusted to social oppression and physical domination, they had less restrictions in the passage, and they had greater access to the scarce nutrition on board.

Scholars have estimated that over 2,000,000 Africans lost their lives in the Atlantic crossing, and maybe another four million died as a direct result of capture and enslavement within Africa. It is important to note that millions of those who survived the Middle Passage died young, within a short time, in the New World. Many historians now accept the calculation that about 30 per cent of survivors of the passage died within the first two years of arrival in the Americas.

The result of the high death rates on the plantations was that Africans could not reproduce naturally. The most unique feature of African populations in the Caribbean and Brazil up to the 19th century was that they suffered a net annual decline. European colonial populations managed much better. In the United States of America the African population somehow succeeded in growing

Slavers did not fully understand the ways in which contagious diseases spread within confined environments. They also did not understand why exposure to diseases was fatal for some and not for others. So they dealt with the evidence as it appeared in individual cases. One important factor that did determine death rate was the length of the voyage. The number of deaths tended to increase rapidly after about eight weeks into the passage, whether the ship had departed from the Gold Coast or much further afield in Angola. The impact of epidemics was seen more clearly on long voyages, since with short voyages some infected persons died after arrival on the plantations rather than on the high seas. Also, when voyages went beyond the expected 50 days, food and water shortages increased the death rate.

The main cause of death was epidemics of contagious diseases. Africans from different disease environments

Fig 6.9 Africans thrown overboard the 'Zong'

naturally, as opposed to the African population in the Caribbean. In effect, the Caribbean holocaust, which began with the indigenous population, continued with the Africans for most of the slavery period.

Fig 6.10 View of Goree island, a major collection point for enslaved people

Rebellion in the Middle Passage

African resistance to enslavement was very different to the traditional way of protesting in West Africa. Chattel slavery was unfamiliar to most Africans. Africans resisted the European ideas about African inferiority, cultural disrespect, and reduction to chattel property.

From the beginning, the masses of African people turned against the trade in Africans. They did recognise that in some places, at particular times, their political leaders were forced to participate in the slave trade, or that they took the opportunity to accumulate wealth as clients to slavers. Given this, communities across the affected areas stood up against transatlantic slaving in the ways they best knew how.

As far back as 1475 a group of Africans captured a Spanish slave ship and killed its crew. This sent a strong message to Castile and its Dutch backers that the slave trading business would come across opposition from the majority of people.

Many African rulers and nobles who could not end the trade tried to reduce the violence and destruction of life. Some tried to outlaw kidnapping in their states and allowed only the sale of persons who were convicted for crimes and political prisoners. Dr C Wadstrom informed the English Privy Council in the 1780s of a case in which a King on the Gambia River forbade kidnapping. However, it

chapter 6 | *The transatlantic trade in enslaved Africans* was still practised by English slavers. They took the enslaved to an English vessel that left from Goreé. The ship was followed and captured by Africans who released the victims. They destroyed the vessel along with three other English vessels that were anchored in the harbour. Most of the crew aboard all the ships were also killed. In Upper Guinea, the Djolas and Balantas effectively resisted the trade in Africans up to the mid-17th century. This was because there was no strong, centralised leadership, and so the rulers and nobles could not ignore the will of the people and participate in the slave trade for personal gain.

Anti-slaving activities were an important political feature of West African politics. States passed formal anti-slaving policies and communities also got involved in mass resistance. So it is myth that only anti-slavery politicians played a role in the global anti-slaving campaign. The people who paid the highest price for standing up against the trade were the Africans themselves. They continue to pay a price because their struggle has been written out of history within eurocentric texts, and they remain invisible in the struggle to abolish slavery.

Rebellion showed how most Africans felt about their capture and enslavement. European slavers denied that Africans resisted the transatlantic trade by emphasising how the African rulers and nobles collaborated with them. But the evidence of rebellion – from general flight to armed resistance – is overwhelming. It indicates that the human trade existed in a context of deep mass opposition.

The fact is that the Europeans imposed the transatlantic trade in Africans upon African societies by using military terror. The evidence of a reign of violent military might is in the many European forts and 'castles' that form a chain link across the West African coast.

Despite resistance, Europeans managed to secure alliances with many African rulers and nobles. European slavers targeted those African leaders who resisted involvement for military attack. As a result of this military intimidation and the attractive material rewards offered by the Europeans, many African leaders participated in the trade against the wishes of their people. In some cases the decisions taken to participate related more to political survival than profiting, though over time this division became increasingly blurred.

African communities, however, learned how to defend themselves within this situation. They developed a culture of resistance against both the Europeans and the African leaders who were collaborating with them. So communities went against their leaders and their pro-slaving interests and established an opposition vanguard. People rebelled. They rebelled against the compliance of their political leaders and set in motion a culture of resistance that spread through communities. By so doing, they established an anti-slaving movement that was as important politically as the arrangements between rulers, nobles, and European slavers.

Fig 6.11 An African being restrained

5 Resistance by Africans to the transatlantic trade in Africans

We need to examine resistance to the transatlantic trade at four stages:

a. At the point of capture and sale
b. In transit to the coast, and in the barracoons
c. On board ships
d. On arrival in the Americas.

At the point of capture and sale

In 1730 Captain Adrien Vanoorn was a Dutch slaver and owner of the *Phénix* from Nantes in France. He and the captain of the ship, Laville Pichard, thought that they and their crew were safe at the mouth of the River Volta. The ship was docked at Queta. Pichard was busy negotiating the purchase of Africans from a client king of a river community. Without warning a group from the community appeared from nowhere. They burnt the ship and killed dozens of the crew. Many of the purchased Africans also lost their lives during the battle.

In 1758 Captain William Potter, a Liverpool slaver of the ship, *Perfect,* had a similar experience. He had almost completed the purchase of over 300 enslaved people and was preparing for sail to Charleston, South Carolina, an English American colony. The members of the community who had witnessed the sale attacked his ship on the River Gambia. The entire crew was killed in the assault. Ten years later, the ship, *Côte d'or*, a 200-ton vessel belonging to Rafael Mendez of Bordeaux, in France, was attacked on the River Bonny by warriors in rafts. The warriors were heavily armed with guns and knives. They boarded the ship and freed the Africans; the crew escaped with their lives when the attacking warriors fled as they saw an English vessel approaching.

In transit to the coast, and in the barracoons

The records of the English Royal African Company are full of stories of African rebellion on the rivers and coast. In 1703, for example, there is a record of Africans overpowering the guards in a fort at Sekondi, on the Gold Coast. They beheaded the supervisor. Also in 1703 reference was made to the capture of a European agent in Anamabo. The Africans forced him to buy his life for all the money he had available to buy Africans.

There are very clear descriptions of African resistance to the trade on the coast, especially in the forts. These descriptions show how Africans looked for every opportunity to free themselves. In 1727, for example, enslaved Africans succeeded in organising a rebellion in the Dutch fort, Christiansborg, on the Gold Coast. They fought Dutch soldiers and killed the manager of the fort. Many of the enslaved managed to secure their freedom. But those who were injured in battle and recaptured when the Dutch regained control of the fort, were put to death by being broken on the wheel. Their bodies were beheaded and thrown into the sea. This was a normal type of punishment for rebellious enslaved persons in the barracoons, the name given to the prisons where people were held while awaiting shipment.

On board ships

In 1765, Captain Hopkins of the *Sally*, arrived in Antigua, Caribbean. He told a story about the rebellion aboard his vessel four hours after leaving Calabar. He described how a number of the Africans were vomiting from seasickness and were allowed on deck. A few healthy persons were allowed to help them. These men then plotted to secure the freedom of the entire group. For several hours the Africans struggled to take the vessel, but Hopkins won by forcing 80 Africans overboard to their deaths.

In 1776, English Captain Peleg Clarke, described how Africans aboard his vessel that had just cleared the harbour in Accra rose up, struggled with the crew, and jumped overboard. Twenty-eight men and two women drowned, but six survived and were recaptured.

When Africans tried and failed to secure their freedom, slavers used the most gruesome punishments to serve as examples to the others. Fredericius Ovartus, the captain of a Danish vessel, suppressed an African uprising on board by cutting off the captives' arms and then legs, over a period of three days. This was in full sight of the rest of the enslaved people. On the fourth day, he cut their heads off. A French captain successfully put down a rebellion on board his ship by hanging the rebel leaders by their feet and whipping them to death. A Dutch captain survived a revolt by cutting off the Ashanti rebel leader's hands and then hanging him by his arms. The Ashanti leader was allowed to bleed to death in the sight of other Africans.

Hundreds of similar incidents were reported. But some of these events had greater impact on trade than others. One important case took place at Calabar in 1767. There were seven English ships waiting for their human cargoes on the Old Calabar River where captains and agents had established trading relations with the King of New Calabar. Five of the ships were from Liverpool, one from Bristol, and one from London. An armed group of over 30 Africans from Old Calabar attacked the English. However, the king's soldiers helped the English and the Africans were unsuccessful. The English beheaded the leader of the Old Calabar warriors, and then sold the survivors in the West Indies.

The Europeans in Africa, just like their counterparts in the New World, believed that beheading the bodies of

Africans before throwing them into the sea was the most effective way to stop the enslaved from committing suicide. Some Africans believed that at death the soul returned to the ancestors for rebirth. By beheading the Africans, Europeans tried to prevent the journey of the soul to the ancestors as the head and body were disposed of separately. But it was common for the enslaved to commit suicide as an act of resistance.

The journey across the Atlantic saw the continuation of these conditions of violent warfare. Slavers knew that the Africans would rise up at any opportunity. So they used maximum security on the journey. To ensure order the slavers used the terror of guns and cannons mounted on the deck, pointing at the slave holes. Africans were always on their guard and waiting. The records of the Dutch West India Company list 15 major revolts aboard ships in the years 1751-75. Most of these happened while the vessels were still close to the African coast. Hugh Thomas tells us that at least one uprising occurred every eight to ten journeys with the Dutch slavers, and one for every 25 voyages with the French slavers.

In 1770 the Africans aboard the Dutch slave ship, *Guinniese Vriendschap*, led by one Essjerrie Ettin, seized control of the vessel. But the Dutch warship **Castor** soon overpowered them. In 1751 Africans aboard the *Middelburgs Welvaren*, escaped the hole, and engaged the crew in a battle. There were 260 enslaved people on board. The captain recognised that the Africans had the advantage, so he ordered the cannon on board to be used against them. When the battle was over 230 Africans had been killed. On another occasion, Africans aboard the ship *Vigilantie* in 1780 overpowered the crew and took control of the ship. The crew fled in lifeboats leaving the ship, which was eventually captured by an English warship. In 1795 Africans seized control of the *Neptunius*. They tried to return to Africa. An English warship was alerted to the situation. They noted that it was not an English vessel, so they opened fire and blew it out of the water.

Slavers were not keen to report accounts of successful African rebellion. But a few such cases exist. One of the earliest incidents was reported in 1532. It concerned the Portuguese captain, Estevo Carreiro, of the vessel **Misericordia**. Carreiro was transporting 109 Africans between Sao Tomé and Elmina. Somehow, the Africans freed themselves, killed all the crew except the navigators aboard, and vanished. The navigators reached Elmina in a lifeboat. The Portuguese heard no more of the ship or its cargo. The 1752 story of the *Marlborough* of Bristol had a similar ending. There were 400 Africans on board from Bonny and Elmina on the Gold Coast. They rose up and killed 33 of the 35 crew. They kept two of the crew to assist with navigation and ordered them to return the ship to

Bonny. On the way to Bonny, the Elmina Gold Coast Africans objected to the journey. A clash between the two groups ensued in which 98 people were killed. At the end of the conflict, the Gold Coast group took control of the vessel, and headed for Elmina with one of the white navigators. They too vanished from history, as recorded by the Europeans.

On arrival in the Americas
These, and acts like these characterised the Middle Passage, and add to both its record of deaths and to the legacies of triumph and survival. The African's spirit of rebellion and struggle for liberty continued into the New World as a subsequent chapter will show. Throughout the world of slavery, African resistance inspired people to fight for justice and liberty. The anti-slavery movement of the Americas was a continuation of the struggles that took place in Africa and on the Atlantic Ocean. The Pan African movement in the mid-20th century that secured the decolonisation of Africa was part and parcel of this deeper, wider history.

Fig 6.12 Olaudah Equiano, an individual who was enslaved

6 Impact of the trade on Africa, Europe and the Americas

In the 16th century many parts of the western modern world economy were built around the transatlantic trade in Africans. The trade brought together the economies of western Europe, Africa, and the Americas into what became known as the Atlantic economy.

In the age of industrialism the trading system largely drove the development of this Atlantic economy. Many parts of this economic system were dominated by the trade in captives, by Africans, by the economic output of enslaved Africans (i.e. what they produced), by the money invested in slave production, and by the goods and services bought with the money created by enslavement. The investments in the transatlantic trade in Africans created new economic opportunities and a range of consumer goods. The Mediterranean was replaced by the islands of the East Atlantic as the main centre of wealth accumulation.

The moment large-scale African enslavement was introduced onto the East Atlantic islands of the Canaries, Azores, and Madeira, they became the area of huge economic activity. Remember that these islands had been colonised in the 15th century by the Portuguese and Spanish. By using chattel Africans on sugar plantations the Europeans produced a winning economic formula. This system was also used in the West Atlantic, the Caribbean and Brazil in the 16th and early 17th centuries. Chattel Africans enabled these appropriated lands to produce a surplus of sugar for world distribution.

The Brazilian economy, which was based on gold mining, coffee and sugar plantations, was made possible and profitable because of enslaved Africans. The Caribbean islands emerged as centres of wealth accumulation because of the enormous supply of enslaved labour. With so much enslaved labour, land and money Europeans could produce goods on a large scale. The trade in humans was their answer on how to best secure a long-term supply of labour. For this reason, chattel enslavement, which was no longer used by Europeans at home, was given a new life with respect to Africans in the Americas.

Without enslavement and the transatlantic trade that fed it, the potential economic value of the Americas could never have been realised. It was enslavement that made the rapid growth and development of economic activity in the Americas and Europe possible. Furthermore, it was through transatlantic trading in Africans that European entrepreneurs acquired and mastered the skills that they needed to manage a full-blown market economy.

In the 18th century, as a result of the trade and the Americas' dependence on enslavement for continued development, most of the business in the French Atlantic ports of Nantes, Marseilles, La Rochelle and Bordeaux was between those countries directly involved in the transatlantic trade in Africans. These ports, in turn, were connected to a global trade system that linked London, Amsterdam and Geneva to the Caribbean, Africa, parts of Asia, and the Mediterranean. The leading slavers were the main financial leaders in these port communities and held the highest political offices. They often influenced local and sometimes, national policies.

Important leading slavers

An important slaver in London in the 18th century was Humphrey Morice. He was a political and economic leader and this placed him apart as a major figure in London's economic life. He was:

a. A Member of Parliament
b. A governor of the Bank of England
c. A well-known owner of slave ships – all named after his wife and daughters.

Morice was also a business partner of Peter Beckford, Jamaica's leading sugar planter, and his son, William Beckford Jr. William was Member of Parliament for the city, and a powerful businessman in London. He was twice elected city Mayor and was a close friend of Prime Minister William Pitt (the elder). He was also an innovative leading London industrialist. These slavers took advantage of many of the important investment opportunities in British trade and manufacturing that were opened by the slave trade. At this time the view in the finance circles of London was that business prospects were limitless.

In Liverpool, the leading political and economic figures were also heavy investors in the slave trade. Sir Thomas Johnson, Member of Parliament and Mayor, was a 50 per cent owner in the *Blessing* – one of the largest slave ships in the city. There was also Foster Cunliffe, who made an enormous fortune from the slave trade during the 1730s, and was three times elected city Mayor. The Cunliffe family had extensive businesses in England and America. Foster had an office on the popular commercial street, Negro Row in Liverpool.

European economic development and the human trade

This Liverpool connection to the African trade helped its own economic development and the development of inland cities. Manchester grew as a major export town because of the transatlantic human trade. It became famous for its manufactured products that found ready markets in the African trade system. Its cotton goods, for example, dominated the Caribbean market, and were sold also to Spanish and Portuguese colonists in America. Its export values stood at £14,000 per year in 1739 and rose to over £300,000 in 1779 because of the phenomenal export trade to Africa, the Caribbean, and North America.

The leading Manchester cotton manufacturer and exporter was Samuel Touchett, a slave merchant. He was associated with the new machine technology that revolutionised the cotton spinning industry. He had industrial concerns in London, particularly in the shipbuilding industry.

In Liverpool, the largest shipbuilders were a firm called Baker and Dawson, who were slave traders in their own right. They had a licence from the Spanish government to sell enslaved Africans to Spanish colonies.

What was true of Bristol and Liverpool was also the case with Nantes. Slavers were important political and financial personalities with major investments in manufacturing and agriculture. A profitable activity for Nantes slavers was the sugar refinery business. Raw sugar was imported from the Caribbean to Nantes where it was refined for export. Every year the town exported as much as 25,000,000 livres of sugar to Holland, Germany, Spain, Sweden, Italy and Denmark.

Nantes also imported semi-processed cotton for refinement. A leading local slaver, René Montaudoin, led the way in finding export markets for Nantes cotton goods, in Africa and the Caribbean. Montaudoin was a major investor in *La Grande Manufacture*, a company that made dyed cotton, using indigo from the Caribbean. The Royal Glass Manufacture, one of his investments, specialised in making bottles for the trade in Africans. The Grous family also did well from the trade. They invested their profits from the African trade in rural properties that produced wines and brandies for the African and American markets.

By 1789 the Nantes economy relied on the African trade. Their investments in slavery were far more than their investments in other forms of commerce. The trade in Africans kept Nantes a major distributor of colonial commodities. Furthermore it was only the trade in humans that kept Nantes from declining to the level of a minor provincial port.

Robert Stein has argued that the trade in Africans also had an important role to play in the industrial development of Nantes. The slavers there invested heavily in a variety of related businesses. They financed local hardwares, textiles and shipbuilding industries with trade profits. Nantes in the 1770s was the largest shipbuilding port in France. Nicholas Arnous was both the leading slave trader and shipbuilder, and symbolised the link between the two businesses.

At least a dozen factories were built in Nantes during the 1760s and 1770s to manufacture the printed cloths the Europeans needed to exchange for enslaved Africans. By the time of the French Revolution this manufacturing of printed cloths was the leading industry in the town, and was owned by slavers. Nearly all the industries that developed in France in the 18th century had their origins in goods or commodities destined for the Coast of Guinea or for America.

In 1944 Eric Williams, the Caribbean historian, published *Capitalism and Slavery*, which is now a classic text on this subject. He argued that the profits and economic activities generated by the trade in Africans, the plantation trades and productions, produced the main spark that ignited the English Industrial Revolution. He also showed the relationship between French capitalism and slavery, but saw Britain as the country that benefited most economically from colonial exploitation. The Industrial Revolution, he said, was an explosion of manufacturing goods. This was made possible because of investment capital, supportive financial institutions, innovative entrepreneurship and new markets. The triangular trade, argued Williams, helped all these objectives, and gave the English economy the push it needed to completely change the way it produced goods. The evidence suggests that English exports provided a market for some 40 per cent of all British manufacturing production in the 18th century. The colonial market allowed English exporters to double their trade and this made up for the lack of growth on the European market. Indeed, the colonial markets in Africa, the Caribbean and America stimulated the new industries that led the way in the Industrial Revolution, and gave Britain a flying start with respect to industrialisation.

Exports of manufacturers from England (£)			
Annual Ave.	Continental Europe	Africa and Americas	Asia
1699-1701	3,287,000	473,000	111,000
1772-1774	3,617,000	3,681,000	690,000

Historians who have commented on the 18th century, state that the markets, profits, and financial skills that were generated by the Atlantic human trade triggered a growth in economic activity. The trade in Africans and all that it produced helped to establish Britain as the leading global military and naval power in Africa and the Americas. Britain's military and commercial confidence was based on its success in securing the lion's share of the 18th century trade in Africans and the Caribbean sugar market.

These achievements provided the business class and the state with a view about national and global development. When the financial centre of Europe moved from Amsterdam to London, this too symbolised Britain's success. Two banks, Barclays and Lloyds, developed rapidly from profits they acquired in the mid-18th century from the trade in Africans. Both of them later became important sources of credit for British industry and they both still function today as global financial institutions.

Not all scholars recognise how much the trade in Africans and colonial production based on slavery, contributed to European economic development. Some scholars have consistently argued that the financial inputs from the trade in Africans and from enslavement were minimal, and too inadequate to sponsor the level of industrialisation experienced in the 18th and 19th centuries. Others, however, have conceded that the Atlantic trade in Africans did make an important difference to the European economy, even if it did not completely transform the European economy.

The relationship between the plantation revolution based on enslavement and the English Industrial Revolution was positive and direct. The plantation revolution financed and advanced the Industrial Revolution. The flow of capital, enslaved labour, sugar and manufactured goods, turned the American colonies, Africa and Europe into a global web of transactions that stimulated economic growth in all the European centres. Also, the capital and trade that flowed because of plantation slavery became important for British economic development in the 18th century.

The Spanish and Portuguese did not show the same kind of economic results as the French and British. This was because they did not have the financial institutions to change their American loot into money that they could invest in their local industries. Also, the ruling class did not form investment linkages with the local business class to build an industrial economy at home. Perhaps a lot of this was because of the oppressive royal government in Portugal and Spain. In England and France capitalist leaders who wanted to enhance the economic potential of capitalist business, put kings and their aristocratic supporters to death.

Finally, when we argue that slavery was important for British economic growth, it does not mean that we are saying that slavery caused the Industrial Revolution. Rather, we are arguing that slavery increased economic activity in the Atlantic economy, and this contributed to sustainable development in Europe.

To sum up

The transatlantic trade in Africans was a major commercial and financial institution that required sophisticated managerial and political organisation. It was a modern commerce that used all the latest financial and commercial instruments and methods. It was a profitable trade, and this accounted for its attractiveness as an investment option, as well as its durability

But it was a crime against humanity. It brought immeasurable suffering to the enslaved Africans, and degraded all its participants, especially those who profited from it. It is possible to calculate and measure the size and profitability of the trade, as well as the sex and age composition of the enslaved Africans. Also, the impact of the trade upon West Africa, Europe, and the Americas can be measured, even though the measurements presented have generated academic controversy and intellectual contests. Such controversy has extended, it seems, to the call for reparation today from the descendants of the enslaved. Nowhere is this call more urgent than in Haiti.

Revision questions

1   Discuss the commercial and financial organisation of the transatlantic trade in enslaved Africans.
2   What factors determined the prices and profits in the trade in Africa and in the Caribbean?
3   How have historians sought to determine the mortality of Africans in the Middle Passage?
4   Give examples of successful attempts at resistance by enslaved Africans in the Middle Passage.
5   How and to what extent did Europe and the Americas benefit from the trade in enslaved Africans?

chapter 6 | *The transatlantic trade in enslaved Africans*

Chapter 7

The Caribbean economy and enslavement

'Didn't my people before me, slave for this country.'
(Bob Marley)

By the middle of the 17th century, the colonisers from Northern Europe realised that they needed to find a product that they could export. This was the only way to make a success of their colonies in the Caribbean. By this time also, the Eastern Caribbean islands were starting to cultivate sugar cane. While the cultivation of cotton, tobacco and food could be a success using a small labour force, profitable sugar cultivation needed large numbers of labourers.

The colonisers had already massacred and alienated the remaining indigenous Caribbeans. For various social and economic reasons, the numbers of European indentured servants could not keep pace with the demand for more and more labour on the sugar estates. Nevertheless, before enslaved Africans were imported to the Americas, it was the working-class Europeans that kept the economy going when elite Europeans could no longer find indigenous Caribbean labourers.

This chapter will look at how the growth of the sugar estates made use of working-class European indentured and enslaved African labour. It will also look at how Africans were found, and the implications of importing large numbers of enslaved persons direct from Africa.

This chapter will deal with:
1. The sugar revolution
2. How the sugar industry grew
3. Working-class European indentured servants
4. How the planters clamped down
5. Servant resistance
6. Enslaved Africans and production
7. Control of Africans

1 The sugar revolution

By the beginning of the 18th century, sugar had become the main staple in most of the Caribbean colonies. From the time Spain recognised St Domingue in 1697 to the beginning of the Seven Years War between England, Spain and France in 1756, sugar production in the Caribbean grew at a rate never seen before. As the following tables show, by 1770 the British and French, through their control of Jamaica and St Domingue, were benefiting from the export of sugar.

Sugar production in the Caribbean		
Territory	Output (annual average tons)	
	1741–45	1766–70
British	41,043	80,285
French	64,675	77,923
Dutch	9,210	10,126
Spanish	2,000	10,000
Danish	730	8,230

Source: Richard Sheridan, *The Development of the Plantations*, p. 23.

Sugar production in the nine leading territories, 1741–1770			
Territory	Size (Sq. miles)	Output (annual ave. tons)	
		1741–45	1766–70
St Domingue (Fr)	10,714	42,400	61,247
Jamaica (Br)	4,411	15,578	36,021
Cuba (Sp)	44,164	2,000	10,000
Antigua (Br)	108	6,229	10,690
St Christopher (Br)	68	7,299	9,701
Martinique (Fr)	425	14,163	8,778
St Croix (Dan)	84	730	8,230
Guadeloupe (Fr)	583	8,112	7,898
Barbados (Br)	166	6,640	7,819

Source: Richard Sheridan, *The Development of the Plantations*, p. 23.

2 The sugar industry grows

The Spanish had earlier tried to start a sugar industry in Hispaniola. But by the end of the 16th century it was very small. It was the English who began the serious sugar industry in the Caribbean and they started on Barbados in the early 1640s. Barbados was the most obvious place, given the political rivalry in the regions. By the mid-1630s Barbados was producing more sugar than its older sister colony, St Christopher, where Anglo-French rivalry and Kalinago aggression stopped the development of the sugar industry. The sugar industry needed economic stability and money invested in land, labour and technology – and this Barbados could offer.

Between 1643 and 1660 the economy of Barbados revolved almost completely around the sugar plantations. Sugar growing took up at least 80 per cent of the island's 100,000 acres. Only a few small planters carried on growing the staple crops of tobacco, cotton and indigo. Small pieces of productive land were brought together into large plantations. This meant that those small farmers who rented land were forced to give over their land to form these large plantations.

Land became more and more expensive as sugar production expanded. By the 1650s only the rich could afford good arable land. In addition, the demand for capital and credit was so great that the small planters could not compete with the planter elite. So successful small-scale farming became almost impossible in Barbados. As a result the planter elite began to control the island's politics and economy. All of this happened within 15 years of introducing sugar, which had become the most profitable product sold in Europe.

The sugar revolution created an economic transformation – the planter elite in Barbados became the wealthiest in the Caribbean, and the colony itself became the richest in the New World. Following the Barbados example, planters in St Christopher, Antigua, Montserrat and Nevis also started to cultivate sugar. However, it took about ten years for the sugar revolution to make a difference to the economies of the Leeward Islands. Even then farmers there never made as much money as the sugar planters in Barbados.

In the 1640s sugar prices in Europe reached their peak. This was because Brazil, the main supplier of sugar, was involved in a civil war. This meant that supplies to Europe were disrupted and so the price of sugar was pushed up. The Barbadians took advantage of this opportunity and became very wealthy. By the 1660s the market was beginning to normalise, and other West Indian planters that came into the industry received moderate prices for their sugar. By the time the French planters in Martinique and Guadeloupe joined the industry in the 1660s and 1670s prices had begun to fall – and the golden days of sugar were curtailed.

3 European indentured servants

In the first 20 years of colonisation the French and English employed mostly working-class European labour. Unlike the Spanish, they did not find any indigenous people whom they could enslave. So the tobacco and cotton plantations were worked by working-class European indentured labour and not by large numbers of indigenous people or Africans although the English in Barbados brought in some indigenous Guyanese. In 1652 it was reported that about 12,000 Europeans were working in the plantations in Barbados, and some 4,000 worked in the French islands. St Christopher also depended on a large European labour force for its economic progress. The majority of servants comprised males, with only about 25 per cent female.

Even though there were laws that protected free persons who worked on contract on the sugar plantations, these labourers were still treated as if they were enslaved working-class Europeans.

4 Planters clamp down

In the early years of English colonisation of the Caribbean, the Kalinago refused to become enslaved. This meant that the use of indentured servants as labour on the sugar plantations became more and more important. But these servants became restless and insubordinate as they realised that the indenture system was becoming more slave-like. They were unfamiliar with the conditions of Caribbean servitude and resented their living circumstances that were like those of enslaved Africans. Their contract owners complained about their unwillingness to work according to the terms of their contracts and about their hostile behaviour towards the overseers and managers.

To control and discipline indentured servants, and to establish their authority, colonial governments passed laws for the 'good governance of servants'. These laws called for very strict behaviour and severe punishments. If servants were insubordinate, a planter could call in the parish constables, the provost marshal, or, as a last resort, the parish militia. In the 17th century, officials used every aspect of the Servants Law to keep their servants under control. They felt that these servants, together with the enslaved Africans, were a threat to peace.

There is evidence in government records of the 1640s that indentured servants in Barbados were engaged in armed rebellion. This continued into the 1650s. For example, in 1656, Governor Searle learned that there were 'several Irish servants and Negroes out in rebellion in the Thicketts and thereabouts', arrogantly plundering the sugar plantations, and 'making a mockery of the law'. The Council sent a regiment to 'follow the said servants and runaway Negroes', and secure or 'destroy' them. The English viewed the Irish servants as a 'riotous and unruly lot'. Many Irish people were imprisoned or deported from the island for being opposed to the 'furtherance of the English nation'.

Governor Searle adopted a four-point programme to control rebellious, indentured servants. First, if any servant was found off his/her plantation of residence without a 'pass', 'ticket', or 'testimonial' signed by his/her planter, he/she was arrested and taken by any English person to the nearest constable. Here the servant was whipped and returned to his/her plantation. Second, if any unemployed servant was found on the island and could not give a good account of him/herself, he/she was arrested by constables. 'If they be of no fixed abode', they were put 'to labour for one whole year on some plantation'. Third, it was a legal offence for anyone to 'sell any kind of arms or ammunition' to Irish servants in particular. Fourth, any servants found in possession of arms or ammunition, 'either on their persons or in their houses, would be whipped and jailed at the Governor's pleasure'.

By the end of the 1650s the Barbados government accepted that it had failed to stop servant rebellion. The government then introduced tougher laws in the form of the Master and Servant Code of 1661. The code reflected what the English thought of the Irish servants in particular – as 'a profligate race', and 'turbulent and dangerous spirits', who thought nothing of 'joining themselves to runaway slaves'.

5 Servant resistance

Planters in Barbados became very concerned that their indentured servants were involved in revolts with enslaved Africans. But there is no definite evidence that indentured servants ever tried to participate in a large-scale violent protest by Africans. In reality, the poor European servants benefited in a small way from the enslavement of African people, and the Africans knew it. But the English were suspicious that they might support the Africans' rebellions and so wanted to bring in preventive measures.

In January 1692, Barbadian planters believed they had finally found sufficient evidence that indentured servants were involved in large-scale rebellious organisations of Africans. In the same month, enslaved Creoles (people born in the New World rather than Africa) plotted an island-wide conspiracy to defeat the planters and take control of the island. A small party of Irish servants was arrested and imprisoned for participating in the plot. The Assembly's Commission of Enquiry reported that the Africans had a strategy for obtaining arms and ammunition. This was to send 'five or six Irishmen' into Needham Fort and to give the guards strong drink and then unlock the stores. Of the Africans arrested for involvement in this plot, 92 were executed, four died of castration, 14 of miscellaneous wounds and four of unknown causes. No record, however, has been found concerning the trial or punishment of indentured servants.

English people in the Leewards feared that Catholic indentured servants would form an alliance with the French. They were particularly anxious about this with the political developments in the Leewards in the war years of the 1660s and the 1680s. Barbadians suspected that their Irish indentured servants were providing the French with military intelligence. So they tried to prevent them from running away to French settlements in the Windward Islands. Meanwhile, in the Leewards, Irish indentured servants had an important influence on the pattern of international events by contributing to important shifts in imperial power.

In January 1689 a new Irish-French military assault was launched in the Leewards. In the first week of February, Irish indentured servants in St Kitts plundered English estates in the name of King James II. The revolt weakened English forces, and the French took control of the colony. On receiving news of the protest, Leewards Governor Codrington immediately arrested a large number of Irish indentured servants. They were then deported to Jamaica, according to Codrington, 'lest they should serve us as they did' at St Kitts.

In Antigua the policy was to disarm the 300 Irish indentured servants and 'confine them to their plantations'. The Irish indentured servants at Montserrat, who were 'three to one of the English', openly declared their intention to desert their English employers and give over the island to the French. Sixteen were arrested, charged with treason, and sent for trial to the island of Nevis.

The English soon recaptured their island colonies, but settlers continued to live in fear of indentured servant-assisted French invasions. In June 1689 Joseph Crispe, a colonial official, reported from St Kitts that 'beside the French we still have a worse enemy in the Irish Catholics, who despite the law to the contrary, remain ... among us and openly exercise their religion'. In 1706 Lieutenant Governor Anthony Hodges of the Leewards noted that the French still 'flatter themselves' that regaining territory in the Leewards would be an easy matter – an impression 'derived from some confidence that the Irish here are in their interest'.

Against this background of fear, different governors continuously reported to officials in England that the English population was growing too slowly. Jamaica's Deficiency Law contributed to the demand for European indentured labour. The Deficiency Law provided that a certain number of European men must be kept on each estate in proportion to the number of African people. This law was strictly enforced. Planters took whatever indentured servants they could find to avoid paying the deficiency fee, and the Irish were most readily available. In 1703 the Assembly exempted from port charges all ships carrying 30 or more indentured servants – this was to help stimulate the import trade in European indentured labour.

6 Enslaved Africans and production

Enslaved population

The way the enslaved population was distributed across the Caribbean shows us the size of economic activity in the region and how quickly it expanded, particularly the sugar industry. The demand for enslaved labour showed how dynamic the economy was. The nature of economic activity varied from colony to colony. Some colonies experienced booms while others suffered slumps. The rise and fall of economic activity in any one colony over time meant a changing size in the enslaved population. In other words, the size of the enslaved community was sensitive to the market economy of the colony. The size of the enslaved population tells us about the trend in economic activity, its capacity to reproduce itself naturally and the volume of imports from Africa.

Enslaved population of the Caribbean, 1750 and 1830		
Colonies	1750	1830
British	316,891	684,996
French	281,658	202,940
Dutch	68,748	61,232
Danish	14,877	26,879
Spanish	42,697	359,458
Swedish	-	1,387
	724,871	1,336,892

In 1830, the British had the largest number of enslaved Africans. Over 450,000 African people had freed themselves in Haiti, otherwise the French would have had a similar number of enslaved people. The enslaved population was distributed as follows:

Enslaved Population 1830

British		Guiana	88,666	**Swedish**		St Eustatius	1,614
Barbados	82,026	Cayman	1,000	St Bartholomew	1,387	St Martin	4,000
St Kitts	19,094	Belize	1,898	**Sub total**	**1,387**	Aruba	393
Nevis	9,194	Bahamas	9,503			Bonaire	547
Antigua	29,600	Anguilla	2,600	**Danish**		**Sub total**	**61,232**
Montserrat	6,300	Barbuda	500	St Croix	19,876		
Virgin Islands	5,148	**Sub total**	**684,996**	St John	1,971	**Spanish**	
Jamaica	319,074			St Thomas	5,032	Puerto Rico	34,240
Dominica	14,706	**French**		**Sub total**	**26,879**	Cuba	310,218
St Lucia	13,395	Martinique	86,499			St Domingo	15,000
St Vincent	23,100	Guadeloupe	97,339	**Dutch**		**Sub total**	**359,458**
Grenada	12,551	French Guiana	19,102	Suriname	48,784		
Tobago	22,757	**Sub total**	**202,940**	Curacao	5,894	**TOTAL**	**1,336,892**

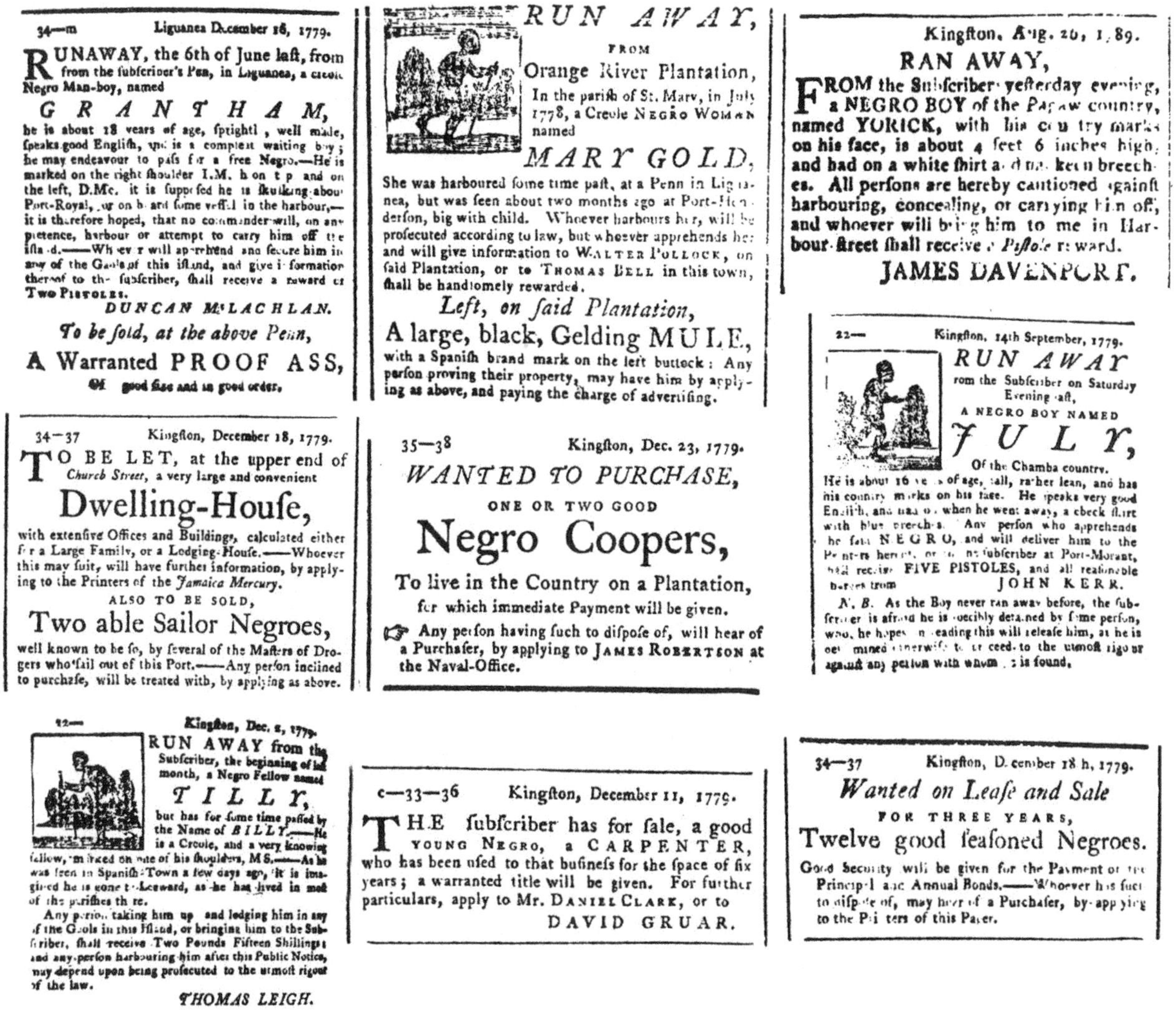
34—m Liguanea December 16, 1779.

RUNAWAY, the 6th of June laſt, from the ſubſcriber's Pen, in Liguanea, a creole Negro Man-boy, named

GRANTHAM,

he is about 18 years of age, ſprightl, well made, ſpeaks good Engliſh, and is a compleat waiting boy; he may endeavour to paſs for a free Negro.—He is marked on the right ſhoulder I.M. h on t p and on the left, D.Mc. it is ſuppoſed he is ſkulking about Port-Royal, or on board ſome veſſel in the harbour,—it is therefore hoped, that no commander will, on any pretence, harbour or attempt to carry him off the iſland.—Whoever will apprehend and ſecure him in any of the Gaols of this iſland, and give information thereof to the ſubſcriber, ſhall receive a reward of Two Pistoles.

DUNCAN McLACHLAN.

To be ſold, at the above Penn,

A Warranted PROOF ASS,

Of good ſize and in good order.

RUN AWAY,

FROM

Orange River Plantation,

In the pariſh of St. Mary, in July 1778, a Creole Negro Woman named

MARY GOLD,

She was harboured ſome time paſt, at a Penn in Liguanea, but was ſeen about two months ago at Port-Henderſon, big with child. Whoever harbours her, will be proſecuted according to law, but whoever apprehends her and will give information to Walter Pollock, on ſaid Plantation, or to Thomas Bell in this town, ſhall be handſomely rewarded.

Left, on ſaid Plantation,

A large, black, Gelding MULE,

with a Spaniſh brand mark on the left buttock: Any perſon proving their property, may have him by applying as above, and paying the charge of advertiſing.

Kingſton, Aug. 20, 1789.

RAN AWAY,

FROM the Subſcriber yeſterday evening, a NEGRO BOY of the Papaw country, named YORICK, with his country marks on his face, is about 4 feet 6 inches high, and had on a white ſhirt and ... breeches. All perſons are hereby cautioned againſt harbouring, concealing, or carrying him off, and whoever will bring him to me in Harbour-ſtreet ſhall receive a Piſtole reward.

JAMES DAVENPORT.

22— Kingſton, 14th September, 1779.

RUN AWAY

from the Subſcriber on Saturday Evening laſt,

A NEGRO BOY NAMED

JULY,

Of the Chamba country. He is about 16 years of age, tall, rather lean, and has his country marks on his face. He ſpeaks very good Engliſh, and had on when he went away, a check ſhirt with blue breeches. Any perſon who apprehends the ſaid NEGRO, and will deliver him to the ſubſcriber at Port-Morant, ſhall receive FIVE PISTOLES, and all reaſonable charges from

JOHN KERR.

N. B. As the Boy never ran away before, the ſubſcriber is afraid he is decibly detained by ſome perſon, who, he hopes ... reading this will releaſe him, as he is otherwiſe ... to the utmoſt rigour againſt any perſon with whom ... is found.

34—37 Kingſton, December 18, 1779.

TO BE LET, at the upper end of Church Street, a very large and convenient

Dwelling-Houſe,

with extenſive Offices and Buildings, calculated either for a Large Family, or a Lodging-Houſe.—Whoever this may ſuit, will have further information, by applying to the Printers of the *Jamaica Mercury.*

ALSO TO BE SOLD,

Two able Sailor Negroes,

well known to be ſo, by ſeveral of the Maſters of Droggers who ſail out of this Port.—Any perſon inclined to purchaſe, will be treated with, by applying as above.

35—38 Kingſton, Dec. 23, 1779.

WANTED TO PURCHASE,

ONE OR TWO GOOD

Negro Coopers,

To live in the Country on a Plantation,

for which immediate Payment will be given.

☞ Any perſon having ſuch to diſpoſe of, will hear of a Purchaſer, by applying to James Robertson at the Naval-Office.

12— Kingſton, Dec. 2, 1779.

RUN AWAY from the Subſcriber, the beginning of laſt month, a Negro Fellow named

TILLY,

but has for ſome time paſſed by the Name of *BILLY.*—He is a Creole, and a very knowing fellow, marked on one of his ſhoulders, MS.—As he was ſeen in Spaniſh-Town a few days ago, it is imagined he is gone to Leeward, as he has lived in moſt of the pariſhes there.

Any perſon taking him up and lodging him in any of the Gaols in this Iſland, or bringing him to the Subſcriber, ſhall receive Two Pounds Fifteen Shillings; and any perſon harbouring him after this Public Notice, may depend upon being proſecuted to the utmoſt rigour of the law.

THOMAS LEIGH.

c—33—36 Kingſton, December 11, 1779.

THE ſubſcriber has for ſale, a good young Negro, a CARPENTER, who has been uſed to that buſineſs for the ſpace of ſix years; a warranted title will be given. For further particulars, apply to Mr. Daniel Clark, or to

DAVID GRUAR.

34—37 Kingſton, December 18th, 1779.

Wanted on Leaſe and Sale

FOR THREE YEARS,

Twelve good ſeaſoned Negroes.

Good Security will be given for the Payment or the Principal and Annual Bonds.—Whoever has ſuch to diſpoſe of, may hear of a Purchaſer, by applying to the Printers of this Paper.

Advertisements from West Indian newspapers from the end of the 18th century

Fig 7.1 Advertisement for runaways and workers

Location and work life

The vast majority of the enslaved Africans were employed in agriculture – particularly sugar production. About 10 per cent lived in towns and the majority of them were females. Some colonies had developed large towns before their agricultural sectors were transformed by the sugar industry. In these cases, a large enslaved urban population was normal.

In Cuba, for example, before the rapid expansion of the sugar plantation sector, Havana's population of 40,737 was made up of about 30 per cent enslaved persons. By 1861, the population of the town had risen to 200,000 and only 15 per cent of these were enslaved. In 1788, in French St Domingue, only four per cent of the enslaved lived in towns. In Martinique and Guadeloupe the percentage was much higher: in 1835, 26 per cent and 16 per cent of the enslaved in these colonies respectively lived in towns.

In the British colonies less than 10 per cent of the enslaved lived in towns. The exceptions were Trinidad, Belize and Jamaica. In 1800 in Trinidad enslaved persons made up 4,000 of Port of Spain's population. In 1830, they were about 50 per cent of the urban population of Belize. At the end of the 18th century, Kingston was the largest city in the British Caribbean. In 1828 it had a population of 35,000 and about 3,500 of these were enslaved. About 6,000 of all the enslaved worked on sugar plantations – most of which were over 100 acres in size. Some 30 per cent worked on coffee, cotton, and cocoa plantations and livestock farms. The remainder worked in towns, or held occupations in the maritime sector.

In 1832 about 6,600 of the enslaved in Martinique worked on sugar plantations and about 30 per cent on coffee plantations. In Guadeloupe about 70 per cent worked on sugar plantations. In Cuba the pattern changed considerably in the 19th century. In 1827 an equal number of enslaved worked on sugar and coffee plantations, and a small minority of tobacco farms. By 1861, these ratios had been changed: 4,700 worked on sugar plantations, seven per cent on coffee plantations, and less than five per cent produced tobacco.

Jamaica in the 18th century was the largest British slave colony. Here, in about 1770 about 60 per cent of all the enslaved worked on sugar estates. In 1820 it fell to about 50 per cent when coffee production and cattle pens employed about 30 per cent. Barbuda and the Bahamas were not sugar producers. In 1820 more enslaved worked on coffee plantations than sugar plantations in Dominica. In 1833, 32 per cent of the enslaved in Dutch Suriname worked on sugar plantations and 28 per cent on coffee plantations. By 1860, 60 per cent of the enslaved were in sugar cultivation, and about 10 per cent in coffee production.

Fig 7.2 Planter and driver

Unemployment was not a feature of slave societies. All the enslaved were expected to work at least 18 hours a day, with one day a week to rest. In the cane-harvest time they seldom had a rest day and could work even longer hours. Children entered the production process once they had been weaned. From ages 4 to 5 years, enslaved children were given tasks such as collecting grass for livestock, chasing birds from crops, carrying water, and cleaning. The sick and infirm were carefully examined to make sure that their disabilities were genuine. The incapacitated, aged, invalided, diseased and insane generally did not have to do labour. At emancipation in the British Caribbean, 75 per cent of all the enslaved were classified as active workers.

Work was given to the enslaved based on their age, fitness, gender and colour. Most skilled and top supervisory jobs went to men. On the plantations there were the artisans, head drivers and mechanics in the mill. Men also worked in the 'Great House' as domestics, and were fishermen and watchmen. The skilled tasks that were given to women included sewing and nursing. There were slave drivers of gangs that were made up of young adults and children. Work was rarely given out based on place of birth although most African-born persons started as fieldhands. Mixed-race women were more likely to work

Fig 7.3 *Auction block: women and children being sold*

in the 'Great House', though most laboured in the field gangs that made up 70 per cent of the enslaved on an estate.

In the towns, most of the enslaved were females. They worked as washers, hucksters, seamstresses, shopkeepers, domestics, nurses, prostitutes, and in some clerical tasks. Many of these women were released from the plantations during the non-harvest time, and brought back for the harvest period. Some were forced to be the mistresses and concubines of urban men, as well as of plantation owners who kept town houses.

For most of the time the Dutch settlers focused on providing commercial services to other colonial powers, such as selling Africans and offering capital investments. However, most colonies emphasised the production of agricultural goods for global marketing. By the end of the 17th century, sugar accounted for about 90 per cent of the Caribbean export income. This also included rum and molasses as by-products of sugar manufacturing. In absolute terms, the total annual value in the Caribbean of sugar produced around 1700 was just under £1.8 million sterling.

Between 1700 and 1770 sugar production in the Caribbean jumped from about 1–2 million hundred weight to about 7.3 million cwt. This meant it grew each year at a rate of 2,600 cwt. Rum accounted for about 15 to 20 per cent of the value of plantation production. Sugar cultivation reached its financial peak about 1790. After this cotton and coffee began to feature more prominently in plantation output. These three crops dominated the Caribbean production for the remainder of the period of enslavement.

Enslavement and non-sugar economic activities

Although sugar was the dominant crop up to the 19th century and employed the major portion of the enslaved population in most Caribbean territories, it would be misleading to ignore the other economic activities in which the enslaved were engaged. Enslaved labourers planted other crops including cocoa, cotton, coffee, and indigo; they raised cattle, and also cut and transported logwood and mahogany. So, the raising of cattle and the cultivation of cotton, cocoa, indigo, food crops and coffee, were not confined to the pre-sugar era when large-scale slavery was not yet established (when they generated considerable profits for European settlers), but continued into the slavery period. Slavery was, in other words, not incompatible with small-scale agriculture, urban life or with an agricultural regime based on logwood, mahogany, the raising of cattle or the cultivation of agricultural crops other than sugar. In territories like Jamaica and Trinidad, almost 50 per cent of the enslaved population worked in activities outside of the sugar plantations. Franklin Knight tells that while in Cuba, nearly 50 per cent of the enslaved population worked directly on the sugar estates, with a significant percentage also involved in activities related to the sugar industry, a substantial proportion also worked in coffee, tobacco, food production and in urban occupations. We should note that historians including Barry Higman, Franklin Knight and Verene Shepherd have indicated that the character of slavery was different on non-sugar properties, and striking contrasts were evident between rural regimes of sugar and non-sugar properties.

For example, the work regime was less regimented on non-sugar properties, though the work was not exactly easy. The coffee and cocoa plantations had shade; and picking berries and pods, some of which were picked up off the ground, was much easier than cutting canes. The fieldwork done on coffee, cotton and cocoa plantations, says Higman, was equivalent to the work done by the second gang on sugar estates. Additionally, unlike the annual planting or ratooning on sugar estates, coffee trees needed to be replanted only every 12 to 30 years and cocoa trees after 100 years!

But sugar estates tended to use the gang labour system to a far greater degree than industries based on logwood, mahogany and cattle-farming where enslaved people often worked unsupervised and where task work was more usual. Sugar estates had far more resident Europeans than non-sugar properties. Vineyard Pen in Jamaica had just one European man, the overseer, and when he was away, the enslaved people were left unsupervised by any European. As non-sugar properties like pens and coffee farms were located at higher elevations than the lowland sugar estates, health conditions tended to be better and mortality rates lower. Enslaved people on pens were also better fed, with more access to protein and time to work on provision grounds.

Fig 7.4 Washerwomen

On Caribbean non-sugar properties, the enslaved tended to live in smaller units. Despite the differences, the factors used to assign tasks to the enslaved on non-sugar properties seemed remarkably similar to those used on sugar estates: health condition, gender, age, colour, skill level and whether the enslaved was African or Creole.

This section will provide an overview of slavery and non-sugar activities in the Caribbean.

COCOA AND TOBACCO

During the early period of settlement, as well as during slavery, there was some attention to crops like cocoa, tobacco, indigo and food provisions in the Caribbean. St. Domingue (Haiti) had over 50 cocoa (cacao) plantations in 1789, but this crop was secondary to sugar and coffee. In Cuba, tobacco became the principal crop in the region mainly west of Havana, in areas such as Pinar del Rio, San Cristóbal and Santiago de Cuba. Cuba's tobacco farms or *vegas* employed very few enslaved people, being cultivated mainly by European and free mixed-race people. In 1846, 40 per cent of the total number of tobacco workers in urban tobacco concerns were enslaved Africans. The numbers of workers on a *vega* (European and African) ranged from 4 to 20; and these workers planted, weeded, picked and cured the leaves, and prepared them for marketing.

In Trinidad, tobacco and cocoa were exported during the period of Spanish colonisation, but the majority of settlers in the 16th and 17th centuries engaged in subsistence agriculture. Tobacco cultivation began on a small scale in Trinidad during the 17th century, and it was sold to the Dutch and English ships which called to trade illegally with the settlers. The tobacco industry prospered for a while, with one observer noting than in 1611, foreign ships were seen in the Gulf of Paria awaiting shipments. But, says Bridget Brereton, this modest export industry was virtually destroyed by competition from the English colonies in North America and by the efforts of Spain to end contraband trade with foreigners.

In the later 17th century, cocoa, rather than tobacco, was the important export commodity. Indeed, cocoa was more important to Trinidad than to the other territories, especially after the 17th century. Jamaica had grown some cocoa when it was a Spanish colony, but cocoa production declined under the English. In 1668, a British officer reported that the cocoa grown in Trinidad was the best in the Indies. The early labourers were not enslaved African people, but the indigenous people who cultivated the crop on plantations owned by the Spanish. A fungus disease in 1725 all but destroyed the cocoa industry, which, until the

post-slavery period, never regained its pre-1725 importance. Still, sugar, which expanded after the 1790s, did not completely displace cocoa.

Spain ultimately became the leading importer of Trinidad cocoa, which along with cotton, accounted for 9.5 per cent of the total acreage, while coffee accounted for 6.4 per cent. Cocoa for a time fetched high prices because of its excellent flavour and during slavery was second only to the sugar cane as an export crop. Spain, the leading importer of Trinidad cocoa, dictated the market situation in Trinidad to the extent that price changes in Spain between 1820 and 1842 greatly affected Trinidad.

Still, as Brereton has shown, until the turn of the 19th century, sugar remained the principal export of Trinidad. It was also more heavily capitalised than any other industry. It was mainly in the post-slavery period that the economy became less heavily dominated by sugar, with cocoa, for example, emerging as an important export crop.

In Martinique, says Dale Tomich, while the cultivation of cocoa declined from 1,184 hectares in 1789, it remained relatively stable at about 500 hectares during the first half of the 19th century. Cocoa could be cultivated on most soils in almost all communes of the colony, but few plantations really specialised in producing it. The 1846 census, however, indicates only one. Cocoa cultivation suffered from natural disasters such as earthquakes; and from the 1830s, its cultivation was confined to small farmers.

During slavery, cocoa plantations used Africans as enslaved labourers. The enslaved did not have to replant cocoa trees annually. But when planting took place, the field workers cleared the land for planting. Field workers also weeded, pruned and then picked the pods at harvest time. The workers then broke the pods, extracted the beans, transported the beans to the drying platforms and, later, packed them in bags for the market. The enslaved also had to grow their own food on cocoa plantations.

COTTON

Cotton was produced in several colonies including Barbados, Haiti (St Domingue), the Leeward Islands, St Lucia, St Vincent, Grenada, Martinique, Trinidad, British Guiana and the Bahamas. Cotton remained a minor crop in most territories during slavery, however. For example, despite its potential to grow cotton, planters in Martinique preferred to focus on sugar; and only 2,726 hectares were in cotton in 1779. By the end of slavery, there was no cotton industry to speak about in Martinique. St Domingue fared better, with 800 cotton plantations in 1789.

French settlers developed cotton in Trinidad, while American Loyalists developed cotton in the Bahamas. While cotton was mainly for local consumption in

Trinidad up to the 1780s, it became an export, plantation crop, as in the Bahamas, by the end of the 18th century. Indeed, by 1788 cotton accounted for 70 per cent of the value of Trinidad's exports and was responsible for that island's initial prosperity as a plantation economy. However, the cotton production soon declined as crops were attacked by the boll weevil. Although, this disease was a setback for cotton production, it was temporary, as is evident in the 103 cotton estates that were present in Trinidad in 1796, producing some 224,000 lbs of cotton.

Like Trinidad, the Bahamas too experienced fluctuations in the cotton industry due to disasters. These fluctuations occurred between the period 1783 and early 1800s. In the initial stages the crop flourished. For example, in 1785, 2,476 acres of land produced 124 tons of cotton, and similarly in 1787, 3,050 and 4,500 acres produced 150 and 215 tons, respectively. Planters were filled with great expectations for the coming years.

However, the years following demonstrated that it would not be easy to produce cotton. There was a decline in cotton production due to attacks from the chenille and the red bug. In 1778 cotton fields succumbed to these bugs, thereby only producing 122 tons from 8,000 acres. Cotton production revived despite these adversities and, in 1790, 4,169 bales of cotton were exported weighing 442 tons. It seemed then that cotton was on the rise again, but it soon collapsed; thereafter, cotton went on the decline. By the early 1800s most cotton planters were in ruin.

The expansion of cotton in these islands could not be achieved successfully were it not for the enslaved men and women. Enslaved people cleared the land, prepared the field, sowed seeds, weeded soil, and picked the cotton. In the Bahamas, fields were cut and burnt using the slash and burn method, which many said destroyed the topsoil by removing the minerals. The fields were hoed and dug out in rows and filled with six or seven seeds. Many enslaved labourers found picking distasteful and hard because they had to carry baskets on their shoulders while they picked cotton.

LOGWOOD AND MAHOGANY

Logwood was a major export crop from Belize, but it did not sustain itself well and it later gave way to mahogany. British buccaneers used to attack Spanish ships near the coastline of Belize in the Bay of Honduras to get logwood from them. Logwood was very valuable as it produced a dye for the wool industry in Europe. These buccaneers, however, decided to shift from buccaneering to cutting logwood trees themselves. There was now more logwood on the market. In fact, there was a glut. This glut resulted in a decline in the market in the 1760s.

Mahogany then became the chief export crop from Belize. It was the Baymen, otherwise known as the British settlers in the Bay of Honduras, who decided to cut and export logwood and mahogany. In 1798 when Britain colonised Belize it renamed it British Honduras. (For the purposes of this discussion Belize will be used interchangeably with British Honduras.) The timber industry changed Belize in the 1770s when logwood trade shifted to mahogany. This shift created a new economy, society, and culture. The extraction of logwood was different from that of mahogany and engaged different methods and machinery. Logwood, a small tree that grew in clumps, required one Bayman with one or two of the enslaved to cut, while mahogany, a thick tree, required far more labour and machinery.

British Honduras kept the things that existed before the name change and so timber; logwood and mahogany remained major contributors to the economy, at least until the mid-20th century. The Baymen in Belize organised slavery for the extraction of timber. The enslaved were first recognised in Belize in 1724 shortly after Jamaica and Bermuda imported enslaved people. The enslaved population grew significantly and by the turn of the century constituted up to three quarters of the population, and the enslaved men's duty was to cut logwood and mahogany as their occupation. As the mahogany industry flourished there was need for more enslaved workers. After 1770s settlements based on enslaved labourers grew as hundreds of Africans were imported, either directly from Africa or indirectly from within the Americas. By 1776 the enslaved population was about 3,000, which was about 86 per cent of the entire population in Belize.

The timber occupation was different from the other plantation crops such as sugar and cotton. Timber created significant differences in slave patterns as they relate to work conditions and organisation of labour. There was a small involvement of Belizean enslaved labourers in agriculture and there was a distinct division of labour across genders, such that most men cut wood and most women did the domestic jobs.

The extraction of mahogany produced new jobs and titles such as huntsmen, axe-men, and cattlemen. All three jobs were critical to the extraction process. The huntsmen played a significant role that was invaluable to the master, for their task was to find the mahogany trees and report them to the master. The axe-men were the highly skilled enslaved men who trimmed trees, and the cattlemen were the enslaved men who drove and fed the animals used to truck the huge tree trunks.

Because the mahogany trees were far apart and remote, men were required to move from site to site for extraction. This meant that sites were temporary and that enslaved men were away from families for long periods of time; so logging had to be seasonal. After the logging season ended, however, families were reunited and celebrations took place at community festivals where the enslaved interacted with each other. The interaction among the enslaved created a new Belizean Creole culture.

Coffee

Coffee was grown in territories including Cuba, Jamaica, St Domingue (Haiti), Trinidad and the Windward Islands, in particular Dominica. In Cuba coffee was grown in the mountainous region of the eastern division in places such as Guanajay, San Antonio de los Baños, Cienfuegos and Matanzas. It was displaced from the plains of the central region by sugar.

Fig 7.5 Pulping coffee, Jamaica

Coffee was the second leading crop in the French colony of Martinique. At the height of its prosperity in 1789, it covered 6,123 hectares and 4,805 metric tonnes were exported to France. After 1815, as a result of natural disasters and French taxation policies, coffee plantations suffered neglect and deterioration and as the plantations declined, French planters replaced them with sugar estates. Coffee planters without capital had to sell off their enslaved workers and reduce cultivation or turn to food crops. Not until 1888 would coffee in Martinique experience a resurgence. In 1832, 10,918 enslaved people (compared to 32,719 on sugar plantations), were working on the island's 1,445 coffee plantations. In Trinidad, coffee was early cultivated by the French settlers; and there were 130 coffee estates producing 330,000 lbs of coffee in 1796. But, it was Haiti that was the leading producer up to 1793,

until the revolutionary wars there caused a drastic decline in Haiti's coffee industry. On the eve of the Haitian Revolution, St Domingue (as the colony was then called) had 2,500 coffee plantations.

The Haitian Revolution contributed to the expansion of coffee cultivation in many Caribbean territories like Cuba and Jamaica as some coffee planters fled Haiti with their capital and enslaved workers and settled elsewhere in the region. Coffee plantations were located at higher elevations and so never competed for space with the sugar estates. Like the owners of sugar plantations, the owners of coffee plantations included men and women, Europeans and free people of mixed-race. However, there were more free people of mixed-race, especially women, in coffee than in cane.

Most coffee plantations (called *cafetales* in Cuba) had fewer enslaved people than the sugar estates. The distribution of the labour force varied according to the size of the coffee holdings. The labour force for coffee holdings was organised in a similar fashion to sugar plantations. Enslaved people on coffee plantations were organised according to first, second and children's gangs led by drivers.

The enslaved men and women were assigned tasks such as weeding, clearing, and planting. During crop time they carried bags around their necks; they filled them with berries and they emptied them in huge baskets. They were expected to complete daily quotas such as three bushels or a barrel a day. Every Sunday, and some Saturdays, which were called 'Negro days' by the planters, the enslaved labourers could plant provisions or go to the market. Some were required, however, to look after coffee that was being dried on the 'barbecues'. They would get a day off in the week for their attendance on these days. It seemed then that enslaved men and women could bargain with their masters and mistresses for certain privileges.

Indigo

In the pre-sugar era, most Caribbean territories cultivated some indigo, a valuable blue dye-producing product. Indigo gave way to the large-scale production of sugar in most territories at the height of slavery. But it remained important in places like St Domingue way into the 19th century – though it did not receive as much recognition as coffee and sugar. In 1789, there were 3,000 indigo plantations in St Domingue, representing close to half of the territory's 7,000 agricultural plantations. The British and German textile industries purchased large quantities of indigo. Indigo initially faced competition from artificial substitutes. Afterwards, the textile industry realised that the dye was very important when it was combined with other dyes as indigo apparently enhanced the effectiveness of other dyes.

The Caribbean was not the first to export indigo. For a long time India was the only European supplier of indigo. During the 1780s St Domingue became a major exporter of indigo. Exports were up to 2,000,000 lbs per annum in St Domingue. Other countries like Guatemala (St Domingue's main rival) and Jamaica, also marketed indigo. Indigo was not marketed as premium product. It was marketed as a mass-market product.

Indigo employed much enslaved labour both male and female. Jamaica and St Domingue grew four varieties of indigo. In St Domingue the indigo shrubs were uprooted annually while in Guatemala they stayed in the ground for three years. As soon as they were uprooted new ones were planted at the beginning of the rainy season. Enslaved men would dig the holes and the enslaved women would place the seeds in the holes and cover them. The enslaved labourers paid great attention to the indigo plants, as they were not as sturdy as sugar cane. At harvest the plants were put in bundles and placed in basins where water was poured on them and left for fermentation between 12 and 30 hours. After fermentation, the liquid was drained into another basin where it was left to churn. After churning the coagulated mixture was put in bags to dry, then cut into cubes and further dried.

For some planters indigo was difficult to produce. While it did not require enslaved labour to work during the nights, it required them to work in the day. The work was so intense that many enslaved could not distinguish between holidays and work days. The plants were easily affected by insect-pests, weeds and heavy rains. It was even said that indigo dried out the soil more than other crops. It also required expert knowledge to judge the quality of the dye. To make matters worse, dyes which were of low quality were not saleable. It was not surprising when some planters shifted to planting other crops, such as cotton.

David Geggus maintains that the work regime on indigo plantations was less harsh then on sugar plantations. Planting, weeding and harvesting was all stoop labour, as with sugar, but there was no night work and much less heavy lifting. Planting did not require the digging of large holes, and the harvest doubtless lacked the fast pace dictated by the needs of the sugar estates.

SLAVERY AND PEN-KEEPING

Although most territories reared animals, livestock rearing was more important to Jamaica's and Antigua/Barbuda's economies than to any other Caribbean economy during slavery. In 1810, 14 per cent of the enslaved population in Jamaica were located on units called 'pens', a percentage that was greater than that of any other English colony, and 5 per cent of the enslaved in Antigua and Barbuda worked on livestock-producing units. Some of the owners of pens, the 'pen-keepers', were quite wealthy. They kept the sugar plantation supplied with work animals. The other territories relied to a far greater degree on imported cattle from North America. Jamaican sugar plantations used many 'cattle mills', compared to Barbados which kept mainly wind mills, and so needed a large supply of mill animals (cattle, but also horses and mules).

Pens utilised the labour of enslaved people. By 1832, the pens in Jamaica had an average of 99 enslaved people. The men worked with the large animals while the women looked after the smaller stock. Women did domestic work and planted provisions. Men were watchmen and couriers and they drove the cattle to the estate markets. The enslaved on pens were divided into three gangs, mainly along the same lines as on sugar estates. As on the sugar plantations, women dominated field labour while men dominated the skilled and supervisory occupations.

Other activities

Enslaved labourers in Cuba built boats. Others collected stones to build stone walls. In Berbice and Demerara-Essequibo some were fishermen and sailors. In the urban areas, where some of the enslavers were free Africans (like Berry-Burk Poore and London Bourne in Barbados), and free mixed-race (men and women), some of the enslaved were settlers retailing goods in town; some were transport workers as in Trinidad; and some were used in motels/lodging houses and taverns as servers, domestics and (in the case of enslaved women) as prostitutes. In 1803, in the Danish island of St Croix, 3,038 or 55 per cent of the total urban population comprised enslaved peoples. Brereton's records show that an unusually high percentage of Trinidad's enslaved peoples were urban dwellers, almost 25 per cent living in Port of Spain in 1813; and in the period 1817 to1820, 12 per cent of the enslaved population of Barbados lived in Bridgetown. From 19 per cent in 1832, the urban enslaved population in Martinique increased to 26 per cent in 1835, but had declined to 13 per cent in 1844. In Cuba in 1855, 19 per cent of the enslaved population (or 70,691), were in the urban areas compared to 81 per cent (304,115) in rural areas. It was the female enslavers, mostly those who were Europeans, who used urban enslaved women as cash-earning prostitutes. When these prostitutes had children, the owners could sell them and earn additional money. There were far more female than male enslavers in the urban centres, and the female enslavers tended to own more enslaved females than enslaved males. So it must be noted that enslaved labourers were not only used on plantations, but were also utilised in more sophisticated environments.

7 Control of Africans

The enslaved were constantly rebelling and resisting their enslavement, and so enslavers were preoccupied with the increasingly difficult task of keeping the enslaved in subjection. Some enslavers learned how to live in a state of severe social tension while all hoped that the enslaved would not rise up and destroy their lives, businesses and communities. Everywhere they invested considerable resources and much time in keeping the enslaved controlled, while at the same time making sure that their businesses were economically profitable. These objectives dominated the daily considerations of enslavers and their metropolitan sponsors.

Laws and regulations

Enslavers constructed an elaborate system of laws and regulations designed to secure obedience among those enslaved, preserve European supremacy, and define African insubordination as a severe offence. The enslaved people who broke the laws were punished. In addition to these laws, enslavers and imperial officials also designed and implemented a wide range of control methods and techniques. These measures were military, economic, social, psychological, judicial and ideological. Together they illustrated the complexity and magnitude of the task of social control.

The slave laws made sure that African people would be subordinate to European people. The legal principle was that Africans were really inferior to Europeans, and were therefore not entitled to freedom or social and material equality with Europeans. These laws were designed to degrade Africans as humans and to protect European privileges. Racism became the leading practice and belief system of Europeans. It was embedded within the laws and enforced by courts, armies and police. It had to be enforced, and it was done systematically with all the resources available to Europeans.

Mixed-race people

The 'European over African' principle sometimes needed a small adjustment to take into account any other social groups in the middle. Over time, mixed-race people grew in numbers and became a recognisable category in all enslaved societies. They represented the fact that humans would mate despite laws and politics which discouraged such intimacy. Enslavers made special legal arrangements for some of their mixed-race children to get freedom. Everywhere, slavery laws allowed these people to be freed or to have the opportunity to buy their freedom. These legal provisions also applied to Africans. But more mixed-race people could secure freedom than Africans. As a result all societies developed a middle category of so-called 'free Coloured people' who had special privileges set out by law, but who did not have equality with Europeans.

Europeans designed a social order that used the ideology of racism and European supremacy to separate people, and to establish lines and boundaries between them based on race and colour. They were very keen to establish the 'race' origins of everyone so that they could place them correctly within the society. Starting with the Spanish in the 16th century, they developed a system of colour-coding based on ethnic mixtures. This allowed them to define and socially locate everyone. The system of definition was as follows:

Black and White	=	Mulatto
Mulatto and Black	=	Sambo
White and Mulatto	=	Quadroon
Quadroon and White	=	Mustee
Mustee and White	=	Mustifino
Mustifino and White	=	Quintroon
Quintroon and White	=	Octoroon

A small number of mixed-race people became free and could move into the economic elite. In all societies, many of these people became leading enslavers and identified with European society and the principle of European supremacy. They tried to have legal equality with European people, but did not get this status until the very closing stages of slavery. As enslavers they had very contradictory relations with their African and European families. However, most mixed-race people remained in slavery as they could not get the support of their European family or raise the money to buy their freedom.

Fig 7.6 Enslaved female Quadroon

The free mixed-race elite

The free mixed-race elite developed their own identity based upon their property ownership of enslaved people and plantations as well as on their struggle for civil equality with Europeans. Although members of the elite were wealthy, they were still socially inferior to Europeans. They challenged their inferior position in colonial parliaments but they were seen everywhere by Europeans as potentially subversive and dangerous. This political circumstance was played out differently in every society. Europeans saw that control of the mixed race people was also a necessary part of maintaining the enslaved society.

Members of the free mixed-race elite were a political challenge for Europeans as well as for enslaved Africans, though for different reasons. Controlling the enslaved also meant managing the mixed-race people. Sometimes this meant it was necessary for Europeans to form tactical alliances with them against Africans. But these tactical alliances did not mean social acceptance.

Racism determined politics, and free mixed-race people knew that European society would never accept them as equals, despite their wealth and education. Also, they could not fully support the enslaved peoples' desire for freedom and this raised issues of distrust between them that often were of a domestic nature. In the end, European elites were reasonably successful in maintaining their

Fig 7.7 Free woman of colour and her slaves

social control of the enslaved, with and without support from the free mixed-race people. St Domingue and Grenada witnessed revolutionary upheavals by free mixed-race people for civil equality, but in general they were kept socially suppressed.

Different ways to control the enslaved

Basically there were two schools of thought as to where greater emphasis should be placed in implementing strategies for the control of the enslaved. A small minority group favoured a more relaxed and liberal set of policies based upon the principle of patronage. However, the majority believed in the aggressive use of power, coercion and terror. They were influenced largely by fear and prejudice. Social reality, however, dictated that a mixture of both views shaped policy and practice. In most places some enslavers recognised the need to offer incentives to encourage the enslaved to perform their duties peaceably and efficiently.

In all colonies, in the first instance, control of the enslaved was primarily the responsibility of enslavers. Laws were designed to arm European adults and some free mixed-race males, and to convert the entire free community into a massive police force. However it was understood that individual enslavers and their overseers, especially those with large numbers of enslaved people on isolated sugar plantations, could not suppress a large-scale armed revolt. As a result, it was not unusual for large-scale planters to maintain militia tenants on their properties. Their duty was to intimidate the enslaved, and in the case of revolt, to contain rebels until militia regiments could be called out and put into the field.

In the second instance, the task of controlling the enslaved was placed in the hands of militia regiments, garrison imperial troops, urban constables and specialist freelancing slave-hunters. When security on individual estates or in towns broke down because of rebellions, enslavers called upon these repressive forces to restore order and stability. The militia regiment generally consisted of able-bodied European males. In most places free mixed-race and free African people also served in the militia. Officer corps of prominent European enslavers nearly always led the regiments. Only Europeans were entrusted with such military leadership and high authority.

In addition, the militia regiments were required to police not only the enslaved, but all free inferior social groups. They were expected to conduct random searches, interrogate suspects, and in the final instance, crush protests of enslaved or free persons. In French St Domingue, Europeans, the *gens de couleur* (free mixed-races) and then enslaved performed militia service. They

***chapter 7** | The Caribbean economy and enslavement*

were also part of the *maréchausée*, a local police organisation established for general law enforcement.

In Spanish Santo Domingo and Cuba some poor Europeans found steady and rewarding employment as professional slave hunters. Together with their bloodhounds, they tracked down runaways and tried to uproot their Maroon villages. They usually worked on a commission basis and collected money rewards for each captured rebel.

In the Guianas, where the Dutch, French, and English established colonies, large numbers of enslaved people managed to disappear into the forested interior. Throughout the period of slavery, military corps of European and African soldiers, and native trackers, carried out long, drawn out operations to retrieve hiding runaways.

By the mid-1650s, as a result, of the sugar revolution English colonists were dependent upon enslaved labour. By this time Africans outnumbered Europeans four to one on Barbados and the Leeward Islands (Antigua, St Kitts, Nevis, and Montserrat). The role of militia regiments in maintaining social order assumed even greater proportions. In 1655, for example, Barbados planters in the St Philip parish informed Governor Daniel Searle that many of their enslaved had run away and were out in rebellion. On hearing this Governor Searle ordered the militia to 'endeavor to suppress or destroy them.'

Sometimes enslavers organised themselves into a militia regiment, but they generally did not think they were competent enough to quickly suppress any large-scale slave protest. So they were greatly comforted by the presence in their colonies of garrisoned imperial soldiers. For example, in 1790, on the eve of the St Domingue Revolution, militia forces in that colony comprised military companies (the *gens de couleur* forming 104 of them), but enslavers expressed confidence in the control of the rebellious, mainly because of the presence of 2,000 regulars of the King's army.

In the late 17th and 18th centuries troops were garrisoned at Antigua and occasionally at Barbados for extended periods of time. In both places, the enslaved recognised the significance of standing professional armies in their midst. In this period the enslaved did not revolt in these colonies. The conspiracies of 1692 in Barbados and 1736 in Antigua coincided with the departure of the garrisons.

The presence of troops strengthened the hand of enslavers and consequently weakened the hand of the enslaved. The timing of anti-slavery rebellions was often directly related to the weakening of military power. This was usually when the imperial troops left the colony. Taking Cuba as an example, Franklin Knight, the historian, suggested that during the entire 18th century the island had the strongest garrison in the Caribbean, and

experienced little overt anti-slavery protest. In 1795, however, there were a succession of revolts and conspiracies which culminated in the very extensive plot of Jose Antonio Aponte that reached fruition in March 1812. In this period, Knight argued, starting in 1793, the colonial garrison underwent a steady decline, as troops were sent to Santo Domingo, Florida and Louisiana.

The enslaved paid close attention to the troops who stood guard over them. The evidence we have from the English colonies shows that it was the deployment of hundreds of regular troops that reduced the anti-slavery rebellions. With these armies enslavers had a lot more power, which were used to defeat rebellions of Grenada in 1795 and Barbados in 1816.

Control of the enslaved in the towns

The towns posed certain special problems for enslavers in their attempts to work out appropriate mechanisms for the control of the enslaved. The economy of towns demanded that the enslaved be employed under less restricted and regimented social conditions. Urban enslaved persons worked in the domestic and service sectors, the retail and distributive trades, as artisans, and fishermen, and as sailors and imperial soldiers. They had greater freedom to pursue an independent life and they built complex social networks. In this social way, many were more 'free' than 'enslaved'. Europeans argued that this condition bred in them a desire to break the 'received codes of deference'.

Urban enslavers constantly complained of the insolence of their enslaved persons. They reported that the urban enslaved respected nothing and could not be governed, except by the lash of the whip or the dread of being sent into the fields of labour. The fear of being sent to the plantation was often enough of a deterrent for the domestic and the urban enslaved who saw labour in the fields as the worst possible experience.

Special policing and security arrangements had to be made, therefore, for enslaved persons in the town. In the Danish islands, for example, the 1755 slave laws provided that no enslaved person in the towns should be on the streets after 9:00 p.m. unless sent on an errand. In Dutch Curaçao, a 1745 law prohibited the enslaved from walking on the streets after 9:00 p.m. without a lantern and a night permit from their owners. They could also not play music or buy alcohol after 9:00 p.m. Everywhere the curfew was used to control the enslaved. Urban constables employed to patrol the streets enforced these curfews.

In Barbados there was a specially built prison, called the Cages, located in the centre of Bridgetown, the capital. This prison harboured and punished the enslaved who rebelled. In Jamaica, there were urban police known as town guards. They were stationed in Kingston under special town laws to deal with urban anti-slavery protest. Places of punishment, known as Workhouses, were also constructed under the 1780 Act. These places were for the detainment and punishment of the enslaved who rebelled. In addition, constables also functioned as freelance slave whippers. In Barbados they were called 'Jumpers', and could be called upon by individuals to flog the enslaved for a fee. This facility was widely used by slave owners who did not want to send their rebels to the cage (a detention prison) or workhouse.

Codes and laws

In all colonies, there were laws which laid the groundwork for these elaborate systems of repressing the enslaved. In English territories, these laws were passed by elected Legislative Assemblies which were dominated by elite enslavers. Imperial officials approved these laws.

In 1788, the English Privy Council allowed the principles of slave laws as follows:

> The leading idea in the Negro system of jurisprudence is that which was the first in the minds of those most interested in its formation; namely, that Negroes were property, and a species of property that needed a rigorous, vigilant regulation.
>
> The numerous laws passed in the different islands immediately upon their settlement, and for a considerable time after, with all their multifarious and repeated provisions, had uniformly this for their object. To secure the rights of owners and maintain the subordination of Negroes, seem to have most occupied the attention and excited the solicitude of the different legislatures; what regards the interests of the Negroes themselves appears not to have sufficiently attracted their notice.

Generally all the European Slave Codes contained similar ideas about Africans being an inferior race to Europeans. But there were also important differences. These differences can be traced back to differences in European societies, colonial circumstances, and enslavers' search for broadly similar solutions.

However, the main characteristic of this domination was brutality. The Spanish *Siete Partidas* did not express as fully the colonial desire for total power over Africans as did the French *Code Noir*. In the Spanish *Siete Partidas*, the need for strict guidance and control of the enslaved was not seen as being in opposition to the view that the enslaved were persons with a right to freedom.

The Spanish *Siete Partidas*

Indeed, according to Alfonso the Wise who framed these laws, freedom was the natural and desirable status of all humankind. The *Siete Partidas* has been called an 'extremely liberal Code' which accepted the 'personality of the slave' and held 'aloft the idea of liberty'.

In 1680 Spanish officials compiled a digest of colonial laws (a *recopilación*). This publication stressed the importance of police supervision to keep the enslaved under control. It stressed that the enslaved were to be policed because they were potential subversives. On the one hand it called upon colonists to baptise and free slaves, and it tried to enhance and protect their family lives. On the other hand, it also called for restrictions on African freedom. Africans people, whether free or enslaved, were seen as members of a dangerous and destructive caste, as well as a subject race.

The French *Code Noir*

King Louis XIV's officials created the French *Code Noir*. Just like the *Siete Partidas* this Code did not identify any conflict between the interests of colonists and the metropolitan government on the issue of controlling the enslaved. So it is worded in a way that protects the right of the enslaved to life and the owner's property rights in that life. However this Code was designed to give minimum protection to the enslaved, without encouraging insubordination. Under its provisions, the enslaved could legally make complaints to the Crown if they felt that their owners had maltreated them. As in the Spanish codes, the enslaved person in French colonies was to be baptised and raised in the Catholic faith, encouraged and allowed to keep family, and could pursue freedom. In addition the enslaved were not to work on Sundays or Catholic holidays.

Fig 7.8 Treadmill, Jamaica

chapter 7 | *The Caribbean economy and enslavement*

But the *Code Noir* demanded absolute obedience from the enslaved. The Code stated that the enslaved could not own property. It specified how much food and clothing the enslaved were allowed. It also specified the kinds of punishments enslavers could dole out to the enslaved, e.g. an attack on Europeans was a crime punishable by death. The Code said the enslaved were not to be tortured, but Article 42 allowed owners to chain and whip them. Under Article 161, the enslaved were not allowed to assemble unless owners agreed, not even for marriages. Under no circumstances could the enslaved own or sell sugar cane (Article 18). Over time these provisions did not reflect the reality of enslavement on plantations and in urban life. Enslavers used the enslaved as they wished and brutalised them with no respect for the laws, which offered them the minimum protection as humans.

English laws

While the *Siete Partidas* and *Code Noir* attempted to balance the need for repression and protection of the enslaved, English laws carried no such concern. Rather, underlying the English laws was a need to constantly be aware and on the lookout. These laws recognised 'a state of war between Blacks and Whites'.

Until the final years of slavery English enslavers denied that the enslaved had any civil rights. They believed that denying them civil rights was the best way of making them subservient. For most of the period of slavery, the enslaved in English colonies had no legal identity, no right to family life, leisure time, or religious instruction, and no access to legal institutions if they wanted to protest or take legal action against their owners.

The Barbados Slave Code of 1661 served as the blueprint for colonists in Jamaica and the Leeward Islands. This Code clearly illustrates English opinions on the control of the enslaved. Africans are described as 'heathenish', 'brutal', and 'a dangerous kind of people' whose 'naturally wicked instincts' should at all times be suppressed. The 1688 Code was the Code under which the enslaved in Barbados were governed for the entire 18th century. Settlers in the Windward Islands (St Lucia, St Vincent, Tobago and Dominica) also copied this Code. Under this Code, Africans are defined as 'of a barbarous, wild and savage nature', 'wholly unqualified to be governed by the laws, customs and practices of the English Nation'.

English slave laws showed the early settlers' deep insecurities in relation to Africans. They put to death any enslaved person found guilty of serious offenses or suspected of being so. They also used torture as a public spectacle to deter potential offenders. Under these laws, the enslaved could be gibbeted, castrated, branded with

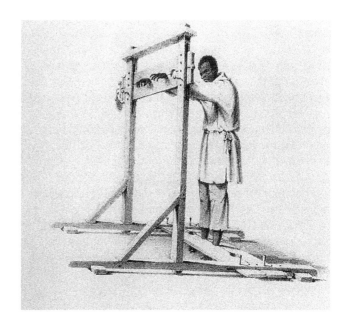

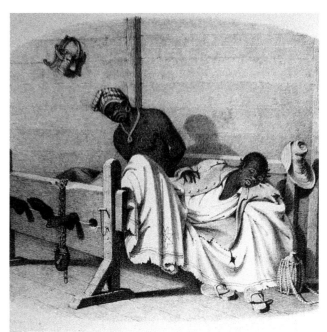

Fig 7.9 Punishment of enslaved people: the stocks

hot irons, dismembered and locked in dungeons for unlimited periods as punishment for insubordination.

Under the slave system, Europeans who killed their human chattel while administering punishments committed no criminal offense. The murder of an enslaved person by an owner was punishable by a fine of £15. It was only at the end of the 18th and early 19th centuries that the murder of an enslaved person became a crime punishable by death in the British colonies.

Danish laws

Danish settlers in the Virgin Islands of St Croix, St Thomas and St John debated at length what to do about the rebel behaviour of the enslaved. Their laws also reflected the urgent need to suppress the enslaved. Like those passed in other parts of the Caribbean, Danish Laws became more severe as the ratio of African to European people increased. The Code of 1733 for example, revised the Danish laws of 1672 and 1684. This new Code introduced punishments that included hanging, dismemberment, and branding with hot irons for offences such as theft and 'insolence'. Before, these offences were punishable by flogging and specified periods of imprisonment. Following the English lead, the Danish also introduced protection for enslavers who suffered any economic losses that resulted from 'just' punishment of the enslaved. In other words, enslavers who killed their human chattel while administering punishments committed no criminal offense.

Dutch laws

The Dutch legal provisions for the control and regulation of the enslaved and other subordinate social groups were similar to those of the French. The Dutch West Indian Company formulated these laws. They were determined to enforce the suppression of the enslaved and their use as alienable property. However, at the same time they insisted that enslavers were obliged to provide for the social, educational, and religious guidance and instruction of the enslaved.

In all the popular stereotypes about the severity of slave control methods, the Dutch emerged as the 'cruelest' enslavers of all Europeans. However, this reputation is more about the demographic, physical and social circumstances of Suriname than about the Dutch culture. The Dutch constantly dreaded the revolts of the enslaved and their constant marronage to the interior forest. Because of this enslavers adopted brutal and harsh methods of controlling the enslaved.

In 1762, the Dutch looked carefully at their slave laws and criticised them because they offered the enslaved some protection. They called for harsher measures and made the following protest to Governor Crommelin: 'although an owner should never presume the right of life and death over the slave, it is imperative that the slave continues to believe that his master has that right, as it would be impossible to control them if they were aware that their masters were liable to punishment or the death penalty for beating a slave to death'.

So the overall trend was for enslavers to adopt, over time, broadly similar methods and techniques for the control and regulation of the enslaved.

Fig 7.10 *Beating an enslaved person, Suriname*

chapter 7 | *The Caribbean economy and enslavement*

Cultural control of the enslaved

In addition to the written laws, in all colonies there were also unwritten laws that strengthened enslavers' control over their human chattel. This was especially evident in enslavers' attempts to make the enslaved firmly understand that as Africans they were racially inferior to Europeans.

In 1801, Barbados Creole historian John Poyer provided a very precise statement about the English idea of African inferiority and how it impacted on the social structure. He stated:

> In every well constituted society, a state of subordination necessarily arises from the nature of civil government. Without this no political union can long subsist. To maintain this fundamental principle, it becomes absolutely necessary to preserve the distinctions which naturally exist or are accidentally introduced into the community. With us, two grand distinctions exist resulting from the nature of our society. First, between the White inhabitants and free people of colour, and secondly, between masters and slaves. Nature has strongly defined the differences [not] only in complexion, but in the mental, intellectual and corporal faculties of the different species. Our colonial code has acknowledged and adopted the distinction...

Symbols denied

As a way of applying these racist ideas of inferiority, Africans were denied any symbols or signs that showed their achievements. For example, laws were passed that prohibited the enslaved from buying, selling, bartering and cultivating certain crops, or from wearing fine clothing without permission from European authorities.

These laws were passed to:
a. Prevent the enslaved from accumulating money and possessing property
b. Remove African competition from European businesses at the lower end of the economy
c. Control the movement of rural enslaved persons into towns to attend markets.

The enslaved in Barbados were not allowed to use stone to build their huts, and in Bermuda only the Governor's human chattel had permission to wear silk, lace, ribbons, rings, bracelets and buckles. Similar provisions existed in the Danish islands. All these laws were passed to impress on the enslaved a sense of respect for all White people.

Dehumanisation

Everywhere, Europeans used animal and demonic references when speaking about Africans. These anti-African sentiments increased over time as Europeans needed a clearer sense of their racial domination over Africans. Europeans tried to make enslaved persons feel worthless and to make them feel increasingly dependent on them. By attempting to dehumanise Africans, Europeans hoped to increase their social domination and economic exploitation over Africans.

Religion as a form of control

From Cuba in the north to the Guianas in the south, some enslavers used Christianity to promote African submission. They also used Christianity to justify slavery as an acceptable way of life. Catholic enslavers in the Spanish and French territories, like their Protestant counterparts in English and Dutch colonies, carefully selected, interpreted and censored scriptures from the Bible for the enslaved. Religious instruction was designed to encourage the enslaved to be docile and meek. At first English colonists were hostile to the policy of converting Africans to Christianity. Later they adopted this policy, but only once they were assured that missionaries would instruct the enslaved that God had willed their lowly position, and that unless they performed their allotted tasks well they would suffer eternally in a fiery hell.

Divide and rule

Apart from the laws and codes, enslavers also used personal survival strategies based upon their experiences with enslaved Africans. For individual enslavers on large estates, for example, legal codes, militia regiments, overseers and racist ideologies, were of little immediate use when hundreds of their human chattel took to arms. These enslavers used the principle that prevention was better than cure. They devised strategies to socially and politically divide the enslaved.

Over time, in most places, enslavers boasted that they were familiar with the ethnic origins of Africans and their cultural peculiarities. They believed they could use these things in their control strategies. In 1657, Richard Ligon, the Barbados sugar planter, outlined this general point:

> It has been accounted a strange thing that the Negroes being more than double the number of Christians that are here, and they are accounted a bloody people... would have power or advantage... and commit some horrid massacre upon the Christians, thereby to enfranchise themselves, and become masters of the island. But there are three reasons that take away this wonder: the one is, they are not suffered to touch or handle any weapons: the other, that they are held in such awe and slavery, as they are fearful to appear in any daring act; besides, there is a third reason which

*stops all designs of that kind, and that is, they were
fetched from several parts of Africa who can speak
several languages, and by that means, one of them
understands not another.*

Despite the fact that enslavers had discovered island-wide conspiracies in 1675 and 1692, in 1694 an official observed that 'the safety of the plantations depends upon having Negroes from all parts of Guinny who not understanding each others language and customs, do not and cannot agree to rebel, as they would ... when they are too many Negroes from one country'.

This view was supported by enslavers in Martinique, who also believed that 'the disproportion of Blacks to Whites being great, the Whites have no greater security than the diversity of the Negro languages', which would be destroyed if it was necessary to teach them all French.

However the evidence does not convincingly suggest that these 'divide-and-rule' techniques of control were effective. The enslaved consistently organised attempts across ethnic lines to undermine and resist planter authority. The composition of runaway bands and the leadership structure of revolts were trans-ethnic, though in some instances one particular group appeared dominant.

Over time the enslaved populations became increasingly Creole and their ethnic differences were less obvious. Enslavers too recognised that the enslaved seemed more determined than ever to free themselves by whatever means possible. But many enslavers responded to this longing for personal freedom and general emancipation with more elaborate systems of patronage and amelioration measures.

The enslaved became more difficult to control over time. In both the towns and in the country, enslavers carefully selected which 'rights' and benefits they could grant the enslaved within the confines of their slavery. They granted some rights and benefits with the expectation that the enslaved would be more committed to peace and hard work. But these concessions were actually designed to ensure greater control and regulation.

Enslavers made concessions and adjustments in three basic ways:

a. They interpreted the slave laws in such a way that they could grant the enslaved rights, such as the right to attend markets, purchase their freedom, give evidence in courts against the Europeans, own property, have marriages and familial relations recognised by law, and have greater cultural autonomy
b. They allowed the enslaved greater access to skilled jobs, formal schooling and religious instruction
c. They passed laws which gave the enslaved a greater sense of their human worth; for example, the provision that the murder of an enslaved person by a White person was a felony.

The *Siete Partidas* and the *Code Noir* contained some of these measures. However, the English and Dutch only adopted them in the late 18th and early 19th centuries as a stop towards legally recognising Africans as humans.

Enslavers thus began to appreciate the basic managerial point that to establish and maintain satisfactory levels of labour productivity and social peace, it was necessary to give in to some of the demands of the enslaved. Some enslavers now tried to use persuasive bargaining instead of armed domination and terror as a form of social control.

A privileged group of enslaved persons

Enslavers helped to create a privileged group of enslaved persons that included artisans, supervisors and domestics. These people were allowed greater social rights and material benefits. Europeans hoped that these privileged few would appreciate these benefits to the extent that they would identify more closely with their enslavers and abandon their commitment to anti-slavery.

However, these reform policies brought mixed results to enslavers. Some say that they were reasonably successful, while others said that the enslaved who were the main beneficiaries were 'generally the first and greatest conspirators'. Ameliorative or reform measures, therefore, show us that the slave systems were maturing and at the same time that the enslaved too were more anxious about obtaining their freedom.

This was certainly the case in Barbados, Jamaica, Demerara, Cuba, St Croix, Martinique and Guadeloupe. Towards the end of the period of slavery enslavers tried ameliorative reforms to combat the intellectual, moral, political, and economic arguments against slavery. At the same time the anti-slavery struggle of Africans intensified. This left more and more societies less stable.

By the 19th century many enslavers were threatened by the fact that the enslaved were primarily concerned with greater day-to-day social freedom and general legal emancipation. Manager Sampson Wood of Newton Estate, Barbados, informed his absentee employer in 1796:

*(Slaves) are the most extraordinary animals to deal
with in the world, and indulgences are tried by us in a
thousand ways, the one consistent with all the forms
and tenderness and humanity and the other kept from*

excess, but there is no such thing as finding a medium that will hold for any time.

Education

A family of elite enslaved at Newton Plantation pressed Manager Wood for the right to have their children schooled. He agreed in principle, but thought it a 'bad policy in their situation to bestow on them the power of reading and writing. It is of little good,' he stated, 'and very frequently producer of mischief with them'. On this issue, Wood got his way that enslaved children should not be schooled. This reflected popular opinion at the time, even among the most liberal enslavers. They thought that granting the enslaved too great a concession could have a destabilising influence on society.

The governor of Martinique spoke for most Caribbean enslavers when he stated in 1789 that in spite of ameliorative measures, 'the safety of the Whites demands that the Negroes be kept in the most profound ignorance'.

In addition, in 1831 Robert Scott, a Jamaican proprietor, informed a Parliamentary Committee that the enslaved had become impatient of the control measures used against them, 'If you exact more from them than you ought to do, they will not submit to it, but they know very well what duty they have to do on a plantation and if no more is exacted, they are very easily managed and require no harsh treatment whatsoever.'

Fig 7.11 Different images of the dress of African women

Free communities support slavery

In most colonies, social relations within the free community were largely influenced by the ratio of Africans to Europeans. In places where Europeans were greatly outnumbered by the enslaved, the Europeans relied upon political alliances with free non-European social groups who stood to benefit from the existence of a well-controlled enslaved community. These groups spanned the full spectrum of the colour and class hierarchy of free society. They included all classes within the free mixed-race caste, poor Europeans, free Africans, and occasionally, Maroon bands. In the mid-18th century, in Jamaica, where Africans outnumbered Europeans by nearly ten to one, Europeans made significant civil rights concessions to mixed-race people for their loyalty.

In Barbados Africans outnumbered Europeans by four to one. Europeans believed that liberal relations with mixed-race people were unnecessary for the control of enslaved Africans. Indeed, in 1803, enslavers in Barbados debated a bill to reduce the amount of property which free mixed-race people could own. This bill was passed and only defeated when the Attorney-General suggested to the House that the Haitian State owed its existence to a revolutionary African–mixed-race anti-European alliance. He outlined the interest of Europeans and the need to control the enslaved in the following terms:

> *I am inclined to think that it will be politic to allow them (the free Coloured) to possess property. It will keep them at a greater distance from the slaves, and will keep up that jealousy which seems naturally to exist between them and the slaves; it will tend to our security, for should the enslaved at any time attempt a revolt, the free Coloured persons for their own safety and the security of their property must join the whites and resist them. But if we reduce the free Coloured people to a level with the slaves, they must unite with them, and will take every occasion of promoting and encouraging a revolt.*

In 1816 the Attorney-General's political perceptions were proven correct when the enslaved launched an island-wide rebellion to emancipate themselves. The free mixed-race elite assembled for militia service under European captains. They distinguished themselves for their bravery in combat against the enslaved. The following year Europeans rewarded their efforts by giving them the right to give evidence in court on all occasions. The mixed-race elite thanked the European Legislature for this, and assured them that they 'will be ready at all times to give proof of our loyalty and sincere attachment to King and institution and risk our lives in the defense and protection of our country and its Laws.'

In addition free Africans who worked as slave hunters, constables and militia scouts strengthened the pro-slavery forces. Some of them could not get employment in other areas, and so they accepted these occupations under the threat of starvation. Maroon communities and roaming bands also played a similar strategic pro-slavery role, even though there was a popular perception that their very existence symbolised revolt and freedom.

In the 18th century, for example, Jamaican Maroons signed elaborate treaties with enslavers in which they promised to return runaways and to assist in putting down anti-slavery rebellion. In return, the Maroons gained some official recognition of their free status within the wider confines of the enslaved society.

To sum up

The overall success of the control of the enslaved rested in the enslaver's ability to bind together most Europeans and free African and mixed-race allies to defend the system of enslavement. As long as European and non-European enslaver's saw African freedom as being completely opposite to their own interests, they were willing to support and reinforce each other to protect their privileged positions.

Nevertheless, enslavers believed that the final disintegration of the slave system was not because of their own weak socio-political control of the enslaved. They could not prevent the enslaved from rebelling and destabilising society, but they only lost one entire colony to their human chattel – St Domingue; and elsewhere there were pockets of territory that gave birth to at best semi-free Maroon communities. To the very end most enslavers argued that they were efficient users of enslaved labour and competent social managers.

Despite the fact that there were persistent revolts of the enslaved, enslavers did have an impressive record of socio-political control by a minority over a majority, over an extended period of time. The evidence suggests that they were effective mainly because the European enslavers had the balance of power and terror.

Revision questions

Study the table and answer the questions that follow:

Territory	Sugar output (annual average tons)	
	1741-45	1766-70
British	41,043	81,285
French	64,675	77,923
Dutch	9,210	10,126
Spanish	2,000	10,000
Danish	730	8,230

1 a Explain the increase in the sugar output in all Caribbean territories shown in the table between 1741 and 1766.
   b State two reasons why the British and French territories outpaced the Dutch and Danish in sugar output by 1770.
   c Explain why the output was so low in the Spanish Caribbean in the period 1741 and 1745.
2 'The value of land in Barbados rose rapidly as sugar production expanded'.
   a State two changes other than the one mentioned in the extract that accompanied the expansion of sugar in Barbados.
   b Explain how the changes mentioned in 'a' affected the lives of Europeans in Barbados.
   c State three ways in which the changes accompanying the 'sugar revolution' in Barbados affected the lives of Africans.

Chapter 8

Making and marketing sugar

'They made their world so hard, everyday the people are dying.'
(Bob Marley)

In this chapter we look at how sugar was made and how it was marketed.

We see the technological advances that were brought into the industrial and transport sectors of the sugar plantation. But we will also see that the agricultural aspects of the plantation remained traditional. Only a few planters in the Lesser Antilles engaged the new technologies so that by the end of slavery the majority of sugar cultivators in the Caribbean still used the same techniques and technologies as their predecessors had used in the 17th century.

By the middle of the 17th century sugar was the primary export staple in most colonies. No other crop brought in as much profit as sugar. The planters who were successful became some of the wealthiest people in Europe. In fact, a common expression in 18th century England was that a person was, 'as rich as a West Indian sugar planter'. What was true of England was also true of France.

In this chapter we will learn about:
1. Making sugar
2. Marketing sugar

1 Making sugar

The work routine

Caribbean environments are well-suited to the growing of sugar-cane. The perennial grass, popularly known in the region as 'cane', grows well in the fertile soils of the tropical zones. The combination of fertile soil and tropical climate is an important factor in determining the rate of growth and ultimately the size of the cane.

Until the end of the 18th century Caribbean planters grew the only type of cane that was known to Europeans. It was a variety that was indigenous to the South Pacific, which they called the 'Creole'. Its scientific description was *saccharum officinarum*. However, by the early 19th century a recently introduced variety was increasingly being preferred. This variety was called the 'Bourbon', or more commonly known in the English colonies as the 'Otaheite'. Captain Bligh from Tahiti imported this cane into the English colonies.

In the mid-16th century cane was widely grown by the Spanish at Hispaniola for sugar-making. Between this time and the early 19th century, only minor changes were made to the process of planting cane and the technology

for making sugar. The 'sugar revolution' that we read about in Chapter 7, and which took place early in the English colonies (Barbados, 1645-1660; the Leewards, 1655-1680; Jamaica, 1680-1730) and in French St Domingue during the mid-18th century, had shared farming and manufacturing techniques.

An important feature of the cane-growing and sugar making process was the length of time it took to complete. Newly planted cane took over a year and sometimes as much as 18 months to reach the stage where it could be reaped for the purpose of sugar-making. Planting was generally done when the rainy season arrived, and harvesting was done in the dry months. Cane-cutting would normally begin in the early part of the new year and extend into June. The Easter season was when the cane-cutting cycle was at its height. These are the driest months in the Caribbean.

Planting was done from September through to December, in the rainy season. After the harvest, not all fields were replanted with new canes. A process called 'ratooning' was common to all the sugar cane-growing colonies. A ratoon cane was one which was allowed to 'spring' from the harvested root. By cutting the cane an

Fig 8.1 Sugar-cane planting

Fig 8.2 *Planting cane with windmill in background*

inch or two above the root, 'buds' would 'shoot' from it, and grow to full length. This way a field of cane could be 'ratooned' three or four times. Ratooned cane would mature at a slightly faster rate, and could be ready for cutting in 12 months.

Ratooning, however, had its disadvantage. Unless the field was heavily manured and the soil kept fertile, each 'generation' of ratooned cane grew smaller and produced a falling sugar yield. So the planter gave much attention to the yield per field which was measured in terms of pounds of sugar per acre. For example, in 1786 at Worthy Park Plantation in Jamaica, the fields of newly-planted cane produced 2,210 lbs of sugar per acre; the fields of first ratoon produced 463 lbs per acre; and the fields of second ratoon, produced 305 lbs per acre. You can see the falling sugar yield.

After two or three years of ratooning a field was taken out of cultivation to prepare it for the planting of cane. It was common practice for the field to be left fallow for a year, sometimes longer. Cattle would be allowed to graze on it, allowing 'dung' to begin the re-fertilising process.

The end of 'fallow' and the start of planting required weeding, further manuring and sometimes the ploughing of the field. Digging 'cane holes' and 'trenches' for the planting of cane sprouts was the final stage of preparation. The drainage of the field was an important aspect of this exercise and was normally done at the same time. A waterlogged condition could ' wet rot' the planted cane, and so proper drainage was critical.

Throughout the Caribbean recorded evidence of the daily work routine of enslaved fieldhands suggests that these manual tasks took a heavy toll on their physical health. Overworked and generally malnourished, fieldhands, both male and female, bore the brunt of this kind of tough plantation work.

The enslaved workers were given primitive, makeshift instruments with which to prepare fields for planting and with which to dig drains in a range of very different environments. In Jamaica, many sugar estates were located in vast Liguanea plains where the soils were heavy. They were physically demanding to hoe, dig and plough. In the Leewards, most estates were situated in light, drier soils. In the Windward many estates were located on less stable hillsides and required the building of terraces and embankments. In colonial Guiana and Trinidad, the enslaved had to drain swamp lands and waterlogged river valleys and secure them from the threat of flooding. In Suriname the process of land reclamation was called 'empoldering'.

The wide variety of environmental conditions across the Caribbean created different types of work systems. In all instances the enslaved workers performed labour which was a high risk to their health. Not surprisingly, the death rate among field hands was higher than for other categories of workers and they had the shortest life expectancy. In effect, sugar plantation field hands were treated more like beasts of burden than humans.

Enslaved women as producers

In the Caribbean enslaved women were valued for their productive roles in the plantation system. Planters, for most of the slavery period, believed it was cheaper to buy new Africans than invest time and money to look after pregnant women, and young babies. They were more involved in the plantation system than enslaved mixed-race and free women. Therefore, the mindset that African women produced, mixed-race women served and European women consumed, began to develop. This was not strictly true as there were some working-class Europeans and mixed-race people, but it gives a general picture. They laboured in every area of plantation life, but very few were artisans, and fewer still, drivers (called 'driveresses', in fact). The inventory below shows the rare case of Old Dido on Unity Plantation in Jamaica who was a 'driveress'.

Table of Inventories, 1799 – Unity Plantation, St Thomas-in-the-East, Jamaica			
Occupations of Enslaved Males		**Occupations of Enslaved Females**	
Watchmen	3	Old Dido	Driveress
Muleminder	1	Bess	Grasscutter
Invalid	3	Betty	Washerwoman
Drivers	2	Rose	Fowlwoman
(including head driver)		Delia	Runaway
Stock-keeper	1	Juba	Housewoman
Fieldworkers	19	Sucky	Houseman
Fishermen	1		
Gardener	1	Fieldwomen	
Waitingman	1	and Girls = 21	
Children	3	Children = 6	

Source: Jamaica Archives 1/B/11/3/93: Inventories, 1799

Attempts were made in the 17th century to prevent enslaved males from becoming artisans. In 1682 a law was passed in Nevis prohibiting enslaved men from learning the trade of coopering (barrel making). As European indentured servitude ended and the number of European artisans on the estates decreased drastically, more and more enslaved men, mostly mixed-race, were 'promoted' to the status of artisans. Only about seven per cent of skilled slaves in the British-colonised territories were women.

Most enslaved women worked as field labourers on sugar plantations. In all the British-colonised territories,

except Jamaica, over 80 per cent of the enslaved workers were on sugar estates by the 19th century. Field labour dominated slave occupations in the British colonised Caribbean, except in Belize where forest industries dominated. At emancipation in 1834 in the British-colonised territories, 68.5 per cent of the formerly enslaved were classified as field labourers. In the 19th century in the French-colonised territories, 70 per cent of the enslaved were field labourers, while 20 per cent were skilled. One-third of plantation labourers were in the first gang.

OCCUPATIONAL DISTRIBUTION: SOME EXAMPLES

In 1789 the Worthy Park Estate in Jamaica had an enslaved labour force of 339: 162 females and 177 males. A little more than 43 per cent of the women worked in a field gang while just over 16 per cent of the men did so. In 1793, 44 per cent of the women were field labourers on the same plantation. On the La Ninfa Estate in Cuba in 1829, the situation was similar. In Barbados in the late 1700s the Codrington Estates employed two-thirds of the women in fields compared to half of the men. At L'Anse-à-l'Ane Estate in Martinique in 1772, the first gang consisted of 20 males and 40 females. Women did most of the field labour on coffee estates and livestock farms.

Inventory – Halse Hall Estate, Clarendon, Jamaica, 1802			
Occupations Males	number	**Occupations Females**	number
Drivers	3	Fieldworkers	61
Fieldworkers	47	(26%) or 55.5 of	
(including 6 boys in the small gang) (20%) or 38% of the total no. of males		the total females	
		Invalids	20
Watchmen	10	Housemen	16
Invalids	14	(in the Great House/overseer's house	
Housemen	3		
(in the Great House/overseer's house		Garden	2
Cattlemen	5	Midwives	6
'Doctor'	1	Stockwomen	5
Small stockmen	5	Total = 110	
Sawyers	2		
Grasscart	1	**Additional**	
Carpenters	13	in town	3
Coopers	10	at the kraal	7
Masons	6	children	45
Blacksmiths	3	runaways	11
Total = 123		watercarriers	3

Source: Jamaica Archives, Inventories, 1802.

chapter 8 | *Making and marketing sugar*

Inventory of William Hewitt Israel, late coffee farmer of Clarendon, November 18,1812

Name of enslaved	Occupations	Value (£)	Name of enslaved	Occupations	Value (£)	Name of enslaved	Occupations	Value (£)
William	head driver	100	Damon	small stock	100	Florina	field	120
R Davies	head mason	140	Peter	small gang	100	Industry	yaws	100
Philip	head carpenter	200	Bernard	small gang	60	Hagar	barbecues	100
Thomas			Benjamin	small gang	90	Warner	field	50
Powell	carpenter	180	Jimmy	small stock	60	Emma	field	140
John Reid	carpenter	180	Yaw	yaws	20	Abigail	field	140
John Hewitt	carpenter	180	Robert	yaws	50	Agnes	field	130
Phelix	second driver	140	Sandy	a child	30	Dolly	field	130
Damon	muleman	125	Dallas	a child	30	M	field	130
Tom	head cooper	100	Quaw	small gang	80	Jane	field	130
Yaw	third driver	140	John Smith	a child	50	Princess	field	130
Charles	field wainman	160	William	a child	50	Bridget	field	130
Daniel	cooper	180	Manuel	a child with yaws	30	An	field	100
Trouble	field and sawyer	140	Alexander	a child	50	Catalina	field	130
Thomas Gale	house	100	Charles Hutchinson	a child	20	Charlotte	field	130
Jack	watching	150	William Barton	a child	20	Hannah	invalid	no value
Cerophy	watching	45	Belias	a child with yaws	20	Sally	field	70
Duke	watching	80	Cuffee	a child	20	Clara	yaws	50
Duncan	mason	160	Andrew	a child	20	Violet	small gang	120
Cato	mason	160	Park	a child	20	Eve	small gang	100
Washington	field	140	Frank	a child	10	Edie	small gang	50
Cuffee	watching	90	Frederick	a child	10	Nelly	small gang	40
Negro	field	105	Philip	a child	10	Ann Grace	small gang	40
Stephen	field (runaway)	130	Old Nanny	midwife	30	Kitty Davis	small gang	40
Kent	field	140	Cuba	doctress	50	Sandra	small gang	40
Hector	field	140	Mossey	cook	50	Phibba	small gang	40
York	field and sawyer	140	Jenny Thomas	house	50	Lucy	small gang	40
Tim	-do-	120	Lettice	house	150	Mary	small gang	30
Prince	-do-	120	Mary Brown	house	100	Joan Johnson	small gang	30
Robert Herring	-do-	140	Louisa	small stock	60	Bessy Smith	small gang	30
Edmund	-do-	140	Mimba	house	40	Patience	a child	30
Davy	-do-	140	Rose	driveress	120	Tillor or Fillor	a child	20
Smith	yaws	70	Maria	minding yaws	60	Juno	a child	20
John	field	120	Dido	field	90	Polly	a child	20
Calder	field	130	Peach	field	130	Rossannah		
Jarvis	field	140	Delia	field	130	David	a child	20
Boston	field	130	Nancy Thomas	field	40	Molly	a child	20
Nelson	field and yaws	100	Margaret	field	140	Tammy	a child	20
Old Harvey	runaway	no value	Leonora	barbecue	80	Luchia ?	a child	20
George	barbecues	50	Judy	field	130	Mary Williams	a child	10
Allick	house	140	Julia	field	140	Jesse	a child	10
Cubina	field	120	Davies	field	140	Daphne	a child	10
York	field	80	Elise Charlotto	field	140	Abba	a child	10
Guy	watching	150	Berina	field	130	Lucky	a child	10
Watson	cooper	180	Elisa	field	130	Sophia	a child	10
Albert	mason	180	Sally	yaws	40	Phillis	a child	10
Cato	field	100	Nancy	field	140	Venus	invalid	30
Abraham	small stock	100				Duchess	field	130

Total number of slaves 142
Total value = £12,335,00

Source: Jamaica Archives JB/1B/11/3/121/:ff.145-148

Fig 8.3 Sugar crop – cutting cane

Several explanations have been put forward for the greater percentage of women working in the fields:

- once the forests had been cleared women worked as well as men in cultivation, harvest and manufacture
- their longer life expectancy also meant that they worked much longer in the fields
- planters did not see any inconsistency in enslaved women doing field labour as they did not regard them as delicate
- African women were accustomed to agricultural labour in Africa
- the men were needed in a variety of non-field occupations.

Organisation of field work

Fieldwork was generally undertaken by three gangs. The first gang, which comprised males and females usually 16 to 50 years-old, did the heavy work. The traditional view that first gang workers were adult males who did the heavy work is, therefore, not supported by the historical data. Lighter work was done by the second gang, which was made up of younger slaves between 12 and 16 years-old. In the French-colonised territories, the second gang included those recently arrived from Africa and new mothers; while in the Danish-colonised territories, workers deemed 'weak' (young or old), were also in that

gang. The third or children's gang was responsible for weeding and clearing the fields of twigs and debris. In Barbados the younger children's gang or 'pot gangs' tended animals and the 'little gang' weeded and collected grass. In Trinidad four year-old children started work in the 'vine gang' gathering brush and vines from the fields. Old women were the 'driveresses' of the children's or 'pickney' gangs.

Typically, the women worked a 12-hour day in these gangs, with breaks for lunch and sometimes breakfast, six days a week weeding, cane holing, carrying and planting. As one historian notes:

> Weeding, or 'grass picking' was considered one of the most laborious tasks required of first and second gang women. With hoes, and sometimes just their bare hands, women stooped in rows under the scorching sun to pick out the weeds growing among the young canes...when the daily tasks were not completed, it was not uncommon to see first gang women driven to complete them 'by moonlight'.
>
> Cane-holing and carrying manure to the fields were also important parts of work of first gang women. Both required strength and stamina, with driver's whip being used to stimulate their productivity...after the first gang had dug the holes and, assisted by the second gang,

cleared the weeds, manure mixed with decomposed cane leaves…was applied before planting the young canes. Carrying dung from heaps near the cattle pens to the fields was considered as laborious for women as holing. They had to walk, sometimes distances of one mile over a surface 'now rendered very uneven by the holes, the driver bringing up the rear, and often smacking his whip to increase their speed'…manuring was again on 'equal task to be performed in a equal time by people of unequal strength'.

Sundays were generally free. In the year before emancipation when plantations began to fail in the British colonised Caribbean territories, additional time was given increasingly for work on the provision grounds. At the same time demands for increased productivity made the work regime more brutal; in the British Leeward Islands, the workday was ten hours; workdays in Jamaica increased from twelve to sixteen during crop season; and after the French Revolution in the French-colonised territories, holidays were reduced to four. The most demanding work regimes were developed in early the 19th century where Cuban enslaved worked twenty hours per day during sugar crop and fifteen to sixteen hours daily during coffee harvest. Harvesting lasted six or seven months of the year.

Domestic work on plantations

Enslaved women, usually mixed-race and born locally (creole), formed the majority of household labourers in the British-colonised territories. It is believed that enslaved women who worked in the planters' households as domestics enjoyed a higher status than field women and that a common form of punishment was the sending of domestics back to the field. In his work on domestic service in Jamaica, Barry Higman has pointed out that:

Historically, the low status attributed to the domestic worker in Jamaica must be dated to about 1930. Before that time the 'house-servant' was said to rank high in the social scale, with a relative advantage in material terms throughout the period of slavery and down to about 1850. Jamaican domestic servants then constituted a quasi-caste, being allocated to the occupation on the basis of their colour and closeness to the Whites in phenotype and kinship. It was also the period in which males had their largest proportion. Deterioration in the social status of the servant occurred when domestic service became the most common form of employment for women (replacing agriculture); when the women employed became predominantly Black rather than coloured; and when the material living standards associated with the occupation

declined sharply compared to other forms of employment. It can also be argued that the tasks of the domestics became increasingly heavy and generalised between 1920 and 1970.

Certainly, some domestics had high status, with slave housekeepers being part of an elite within the plantation household. Some enslaved women achieved their highest status and greatest socio-economic rewards through household occupations. There is the example of Old Doll, her three daughters and her niece, who dominated domestic service on the Newtons' estate in Barbados from the mid 18th century to the 1830s.

For the majority of the enslaved domestics, though, working 24 hours a day under the constant supervision of those in the Great House could not have been easy. Some visitors to the Caribbean commented on the arduous work of some domestics, particularly the water carriers who had to make several trips a day to distant streams and rivers. Washerwomen and maids worked as hard as field slaves and the scars that were on the bodies of some of these women indicated that they suffered physical punishment. They also suffered sexual abuse by European males.

Female domestics were normally entered in plantation records as 'women in office'; similarly male drivers, artisans and housemen were defined as 'men in office'. Here is an example from Barbados:

Principal slaves at Newton Plantation, 1796

Men in Office		Women in Office	
Name	Occupation	Name	Occupation
Saboy	Driver	Doll	housekeeper
Great Tobby	Smith	Dolly	in the house
Little Tobby	Smith	Betsy	in the house
Mulatto	Carpenter	Jenny	in the house
Daniel	–	Kitty	in the house
Jack	Carpenter	Mary	in the house
William	Jimer	Mary Ann	in the house
Sawyer	Joiner		
Hercules	Mason		
Thomas	–		
Sayers	Cooper		
Bob	Cooper		
Toby	Boiler		
Gloster	Basket maker		
Cuffy	Smith		
Hillos	Cooper		
Cupid	House		
Ned	–		

The number of domestics varied according to the size of the colony and the total enslaved population, the economic status of the enslavers and the presence of resident planters, who maintained large homes. In Barbados in 1780, there were probably 15,529 domestics making up 25 per cent of the enslaved population. Enslaved women comprised over 50 per cent of these domestics.

Barry Higman found that 70 per cent of all domestics in plantation households were female. The women were concentrated in childcare, sewing, cooking and laundry. Enslaved women dominated domestic service except in the French-colonised territories, where most cooks were male.

The sugar mill

The plantation was also an industrial business in which sugar was manufactured for sale. The manufacture of sugar used the labour of different categories of the enslaved workers – the factory attendant and skilled artisan. The plantation consisted of both cane fields and sugar factories and as such was one of the most advanced and complex production systems in the world in the 17th century

Once the cane was cut, the enslaved had to carry it to the mill for crushing almost immediately. If not, the fermentation process would set in and drastically reduce the sugar crystal content of the juice from the crushed cane. So the mill was the first stop for the cut cane. Here it was crushed between heavy iron rollers (or wood rollers covered in iron) to extract the juice.

Enslaved field hands would take turns to feed the cane into the rollers by hand. This was very dangerous work. The records of many plantations contain cases of enslaved workers who received serious injuries or died on account of clothing or hands being caught in the rollers.

There were three types of mills on Caribbean plantations before the end of the 18th century – the watermill, windmill, and animal mill. Where estates could benefit from swift flowing rivers, waterwheels were built to drive the mills. These were common in Jamaica, Cuba, Guiana and the Windward Islands.

Windmills were mainly used in Barbados and the Leewards. But they were also used in colonies where watermills were the norm because not all districts had access to swift rivers. By turning the blades of the mill to the wind, power was generated to turn the rollers that crushed the canes.

Animal mills, powered by mules and cattle and sometimes by the enslaved, were also common. Windmills

Fig 8.4 Carting cane to the mill

chapter 8 | *Making and marketing sugar*

Fig 8.5 *Aqueduct used to supply water to the mill-houses, Mona Estate, Kingston, Jamaica*

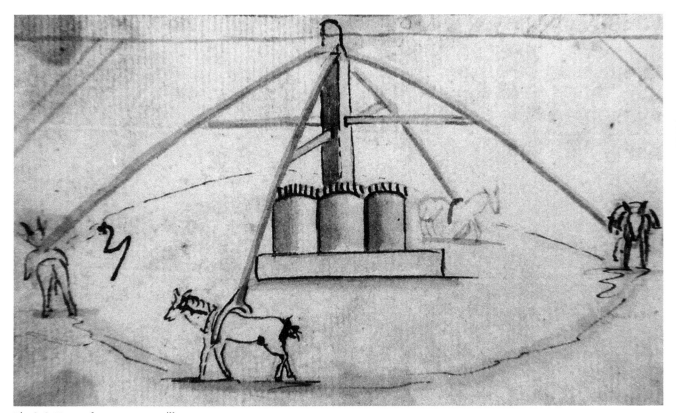

Fig 8.6 *Horse-drawn sugar mill*

were designed in a way that animal or human power could turn the rollers if the winds were insufficient. When the shaft of the mill was turned, the rollers would slowly rotate providing a slow but necessary motion. Richard Sheridan offers the following description of the working of the mills:

> Two slaves fed the mill, one stationed in front of the rollers to insert the newly-cut canes, the other behind to receive the crushed stalks and pass them back in order to extract the remainder of the juice.

With respect to the efficiency of the mill, he states:

> The mills were small and inefficient by modern standards. Only about 50 per cent to 60 per cent of the juice was expressed from the canes as compared with present day yields of 90 per cent to 98 per cent. A cattle or mule mill on the old model performed very well if it passed sufficient canes in an hour to yield from 300 to 350 gallons of juice.

From the mill the juice from the crushed cane travelled through pipes or gutters into the boiling house of the factory. Michael Craton and James Walvin describe the operations of the boiling house as follows:

In this steaming and smoking inferno it (cane juice) was crystallised by evaporation. After being held in one of several large reservoirs or 'receivers' the juice was first heated in shallow round pans called 'clarifiers', during which it was 'tempered' with lime. After tempering, the juice was boiled in a succession of progressively smaller hemispheric cast iron 'coppers', up to five in all, until it was ready to enter the 'tache' (tayche or teache), in which it was finally crystallised, or 'struck'.

So the estate boiler had to make very precise decisions in the sugar-making process. Almost certainly the boiler was an enslaved male, trusted by his owner, highly-skilled and valuable. He was the one worker who could decide at a stroke if the crop of canes would come to nothing. In other words, he could determined the potential for a profit or loss.

Craton and Walvin continue:

> The striking of the sugar was the most critical and delicate of the operations in a sugar factory. Only the most skilled and vigilant boiler men could tell the optimal moment for striking, testing the bubbling brown liquid between thumb and forefinger until it formed a filament of a certain length.

Fig 8.7 Boiling house

chapter 8 | *Making and marketing sugar*

The boiler decided when it was time to 'strike' – in other words he was deciding that the sugar was ready to granulate. The next stage in the process was to pour the granulated sugar into large copper 'coolers' which were surrounded by circulating water.

When cooled, the raw sugar was 'potted', that is, placed in large earthenware 'potts'. Then the draining process would begin. The remaining liquid molasses was allowed to be poured off, leaving the sugar in a dry state. At the end of the 18th century, most planters no longer used 'potts' but placed the sugar in large wooden barrels called 'hogsheads'. Most of these weighed over 1,800 lbs.

These 'hogsheads' were sent to the 'curing house'. A hole was made in them to allow the molasses to drain off over a period of several weeks. This process was still called 'potting'. It was after this stage that the dried sugar was ready to be weighed and exported.

Making rum

From the 'curing house', the drained molasses, which was a dark brown, thick fluid, flowed along pipes or gutters into the distillery where the rum-making process would begin. In most colonies the distillery was also called the 'still house'. Water and yeast were added to the distilled molasses to make the rum, which was an important product in the financial affairs of an estate. Some planters chose to export the raw molasses to be refined into rum in Europe, but this was rarely profitable and often not worth the trouble.

Muscovado and clay sugar

The sugar from many Caribbean plantations was not refined and was called muscovado. It was coarse in texture and dark brown in colour. The advantage of muscovado was that it stored and shipped very well. Some planters carried sugar through a semi-refined process and produced what was called 'clay sugar'. It fetched a better price than muscovado sugar in Europe, but still had to be fully refined before it became available to the household consumer.

The demand for labour and fuel on a sugar estate was at its maximum during the crop time. The combination of harvesting and grinding the cane brought enslaved field hands and enslaved industrial workers together during an intense period that lasted about three months. In this time the enslaved worked day and night, every day until the hogsheads were filled with sugar, and casks with molasses and rum. It was the time that the enslaved were most exploited. Crop-over festivals developed in most colonies. They tell us more about the enslaved's relief and survival than about their celebration that the planters were satisfied with the harvest.

Field hands had to be available to keep fires going under the boilers, day and night while the sugar was being made. Not every estate had a supply of wood on-site that could be burnt. Over time, most plantations used up the indigenous woodlands for building as well as for fuel. Richer estates imported timber and some coal from Europe. Less rich estates were innovative and used the dried 'trash' from the cane as fuel in the boiler-house. It was not as effective as wood or coal, but trash did the service for most estates in colonies where deforestation was advanced.

The introduction of steam power

In the 18th century the Industrial Revolution in Britain began. This involved the large-scale mechanisation of British industry. From the middle of the 18th century, the Industrial Revolution began to impact upon production in the colonies. Sugar producers became interested in the new technological innovations as one way to cut cost and increase profits.

Fig 8.8 Old wind-powered sugar mill that gave way to steam technology

The use of steam engines to generate power to drive mills became the single most important innovation that concerned sugar planters. Some Jamaican planters were already experimenting with steam power by the 1780s. But from the end of the 18th century into the 19th century, this new technology was adopted slowly by the estates.

The steam engine had many advantages over other mills that were driven by 'natural' power. It was more dependable during the high stress time of harvesting; it could go day and night for many weeks; it could be located in more than one place on an entire estate; and it was fuel-efficient.

The steam engine was not attractive to everyone throughout the region. This was because of the initial high costs of installation, technical problems with the machinery, the dependence on engineers to service the engines until the enslaved could be trained, and a general reluctance to be more innovative. So by the mid-19th century, most planters in the English and French colonies were still using waterwheels and windmills to grind their cane.

In the early 19th century, the mechanisation process was most advanced in the Spanish colonies particularly Cuba. But even here, progress was slow. In 1827 only 2,7 per cent of all the island's mills were driven by steam. By 1850 steam engines to grind canes were the norm on Cuban plantations. By 1860 between 70 per cent and 90 per cent of the island's mills were driven by steam. This development radically transformed the Cuban sugar industry, making the island the largest producer of cane sugar in the world by the end of the century.

The use of steam power to expand the volume of cane that passed through the grinding mill meant that other steps in the sugar-making process also needed to be mechanised. The major mechanical innovation that transformed the boiling house operation was the 'vacuum

Fig 8.9 *Caribbean sugar mill, Clarendon, Jamaica*

chapter 8 | *Making and marketing sugar*

pan' technology. The vacuum pan put the boiling process on a more scientific basis. This meant that the crystallising stage could be managed effectively on a large scale. The critical role of the boiler was now reduced. The mill could now take a much larger quantity of cane. This removed what had been a major restriction of the boiling house which could only handle a small quantity of cane.

Further mechanical innovations were made to the operations of the curing house. Traditionally molasses dripped from the hogsheads leaving the dried sugar crystals. This was a slow and lengthy filtration process, sometimes taking up to two or three months. But sugar cannot be crystallised in a wet, soggy state, so removing the molasses from the wet sugar was an important process. Technology was introduced to revolutionise the speed and efficiency of the curing house operation. This technology was the 'centrifuge'. This was a spinning device which pushed the excess molasses out of an inner drum leaving dried sugar crystals in the outer chamber.

Another important innovation was the railway which completely changed how the sugar plantations were organised in the larger colonies. The railway enabled the movement of sugar from the fields to the mill with greater speed and in larger quantities. This meant that the mill could now be located more strategically on the estate. Also, the sugar could reach the harbour for shipment more efficiently in terms of cost and time.

By the mid-19th century the railway was the main form of transport for cane and sugar on Cuban plantations. In Puerto Rico and Jamaica significant efforts were also made to invest in railways and to move away from carts drawn by animals. In the smaller islands like Barbados and the Leewards, railway technology had little impact upon the sugar sector. However, in Guiana and Trinidad it became increasingly popular at the end of the 19th century.

These new advanced technologies were not applied to the cultivation of sugar cane but only to the making of sugar. Consequently the agricultural part remained traditional. This created a contradiction within the industry.

Enslavers continued to rely upon the enslaved to manage these technologies, rather than on free workers. They increased the production of sugar by expanding to new lands rather than by increasing their sugar-cane yield through better soil management. Cane was still cut by the enslaved using hard swords known as machetes or cutlasses. Where slavery was abolished, most planters chose other forms of servile labour, such as indentured servants from Asia and, in some places, Africa.

2 Marketing sugar

The British way

The sugar crop generated an enormous amount of profit for planters. Of the English colonies, Barbados sugar planters were the first to experience this wealth. They did so in the mid-17th century by creating an economic boom which we now call the 'sugar revolution'. At the end of the century, planters in the Leeward Islands followed them. By the early 18th century the Jamaican planters had become wealthier than them all. Some of the wealthiest planters were absentees and lived in England. They sent out managers or hired them locally to run their business on their behalf. Less wealthy planters stayed in the West Indies and did the best they could.

This wealth was based on the fact that the European market for Caribbean sugar seemed limitless. In the course of the 17th and 18th centuries sugar became a common consumption item for millions of Europeans. Before this it was a rare and expensive commodity, that only the wealthy elite could afford.

The working classes in Britain, for example, used honey as their main sweetener. The elite bought sugar produced in the Mediterranean, the Middle East and Asia.

The Portuguese also began large-scale production in Brazil at the end of the 16th century but prices remained high in England because of taxes and duties imposed on 'foreign goods'.

In England and Wales the consumption of sugar increased about twenty-fold between 1663 and 1775. The vast majority of this was Caribbean sugar produced in English colonies. The massive expansion of sugar consumption had to do with population growth in Britain, rapidly falling prices of sugar, and increasing real wages for the average British worker.

The population of England and Wales rose from 4.5 million to 7.5 million over this period. At the beginning of the 17th century, sugar sold for about one shilling per pound. By the end of the century sugar prices fell to about six pence per pound. Retail prices in peace-time rose and fell at about this price until the end of the 18th century. Rising real wages for the average citizen in Britain allowed them access to many colonial goods and the consumption of tea and coffee became widespread, strengthening the demand for sugar. Sugar was also greatly consumed by the industrial sector, particularly the breweries and confectionery manufacturers. But first, the sugar had to find its way to the British retail market. It had to reach these markets at competitive prices, in good quality and with reliability.

There was big money in the marketing business. Apart from the sugar planter, the colonial and imperial governments both wanted their share in the form of tax. As the majority of planters lived in the Caribbean, they needed agents or brokers to handle the marketing aspects of their business in England. Some planters could do this within the family by training their own kin as agents and brokers. An absentee planter would be in England to handle this aspect of the business. But this was not typical, and most planters needed marketing arrangements in England to receive and distribute the sugar.

European colonial powers all developed similar views about the marketing of commodities produced in their colonies. None wanted the produce of rival imperial nations to undersell their own planters at home. All wanted to maximise the financial benefits accruing to the nation by excluding other nations when it came to marketing their goods. All European nations passed laws to keep the colonial goods of rival nations out of their domestic markets.

At the same time the European nations also tried to exclude goods and services produced by rival European nations from entering their colonial markets. The political principle was rival nationalism, and the economic principle was national monopoly. This arrangement was called the 'mercantile system', Each European imperial nation developed its own version of it that determined how sugar and other colonial produce from the Caribbean were marketed in Europe, North America, and elsewhere. The underlying theory of economic progress was that the size of trade determined the wealth of the nation; and that the size was limited in quantity. So a nation increased its share by reducing the share of rivals.

The marketing of Caribbean sugar was at the centre of these legal provisions. The West Indian planter enjoyed the preferential treatment his sugar received in England at the expense of sugar produced by the French in Martinique or the Portuguese in Brazil. But the imperial government wanted its share in the form of taxes and the Caribbean producers hated this imposition. They also disliked the restrictions imposed upon them with regard to whom they could do business with. Many preferred using Dutch merchants to English merchants; they found the Dutch more efficient and economical.

Most of all the English sugar planters hated the 4,5 per cent duty that they had to pay to the government on the average weight of a cast of exported sugar. They resented it when the colonial governments, started collecting this duty after 1663. They resented it even more after 1670 when this income was paid over to the imperial

government. Sugar planters tried all kinds of underhand methods to avoid paying this duty and to get around the mercantile restrictions.

The brokers or agents in England were less concerned about this matter because they received a commission on the sugar they sold on behalf of the planters. But the imperial government was determined to get its share of the sugar wealth and so it kept increasing duties and taxes on the imported commodity. The English parliament imposed additional duties on sugar exports in 1685, 1698 and 1705. When these duties were added to those of 1661, the total duty amounted to 3s. 4d per hundred weight for raw sugar and 11s. 1d per hundred weight for clayed, or semi-refined sugar.

As long as 'foreign' sugar paid a higher tariff, 'local' sugar looked more attractive on the British market. Sugar producers in Barbados, the Leeward Islands and Jamaica were happy with this. It meant that they had an effective monopoly of their domestic sugar market.

How did sugar planters enjoy this monopoly status that lasted throughout the period of slavery? The answer lies in the marketing mechanism called the commission agency system. Some commission agents were based in the colonies. They took the distribution pressure off planters by taking their sugar on consignment and marketing it for commission. But most commission agents were based in London. The system allowed planters to consign their sugar to an agent in London, whose duty it was to receive it and arrange for its warehousing and sale.

The agent took out his commission and kept the balance of the sale on the planter's account. In this regard he also functioned as a banker for the planter. But commission agents did more than receive and sell the planter's sugar. They provided a range of financial and commercial services to the planter. The planter would send them a list of supplies needed for the plantation, such as clothes for the enslaved workers and agricultural equipment and utensils. The agent would buy these items and send them off to the Caribbean, charging the purchase cost against the planter's account.

When the planter's account was overdrawn (too much had been spent), then the commission agent provided loans and credit facilities. When the planter was carrying a large credit balance (had a lot of money in the account), the planter could ask the agent to invest the money. In this role the agent functioned as an investment broker for the planter. So, the commission agent system was the main way that West Indian sugar reached the English market.

The commission agent also had to be protected from planters who could not pay their debts. Many planters would get credit from agents and then would not be able to pay it back. The 1732 Credit Act enabled England-based commission agents to bring legal action against Caribbean planters in both English and Caribbean courts in order to recover debts. In many cases this meant that the planter's estate or property was seized to cover the debt.

So commission agents were the life-line of the sugar planter. They provided a range of specialised services to the planter. These services ranged from financial arrangements to ensuring that grocers and refiners were well-supplied with the sugar they needed. This left sugar planters to concentrate on the challenges of production and the social and political management of the masses of enslaved workers.

The French way

In the 17th century, when the English parliament was developing the legal framework to introduce the principle of trade monopoly, the French were doing more or less the same thing. The French Minister in charge of colonial affairs was Jean Baptiste Colbert. In the 1660s he developed the 'colonial system' which the French called the *exclusif*. According to the *exclusif* the main purpose for the existence of the colonies was to increase the wealth of the mother country.

French sugar planters were allowed to sell their sugar only to French merchants, who had to use French ships only and could only operate from French ports. There was a sense of urgency in Colbert's approach. He was determined to exclude Dutch merchants from sharing in the wealth generated with French capital in French colonies.

The French sugar producers, like the English, did not like this system of control and restriction. Colbert, following the English, appeased the planters by offering them a guaranteed market for their sugar in France. From as early as 1655, raw sugar produced by rival imperial nations was heavily taxed if it was sold in France. Colbert taxed this sugar at such a high price, that few could afford it. The objective was to give sugar planters in Martinique, St Domingue and Guadeloupe a preferential arrangement for their sugar in France. With only a few changes, the 'exclusif' remained intact until 1861, when trade in colonial produce was liberalised.

The typical sugar planter was concerned with selling a million pounds or 250 barrels of sugar each year to a guaranteed market, for profit. The French planter, like the English planter, also had to decide if it was necessary to secure the services of an agent or broker who lived in the colony or in a French port town to market the sugar.

Many planters tried to market their own sugar by making arrangements to be in France when the sugar shipments arrived. There were other choices for planters who did not wish to take on this responsibility. They could sell the sugar directly to a ship's captain, or they could take the risk and sell it to a foreigner. In the early days most planters sold their sugar directly to ship captains and this system worked well for them. This was really an exchange system. The captain supplied tools, foods, garments, enslaved workers and other goods to the planter. The planter handed over the value in a fixed amount of sugar.

Selling sugar directly to foreigners was common but illegal. Smuggling was also common, particularly for planters in outlying districts. The English, Dutch and American merchants were keen to take French sugar in exchange for manufactured goods and enslaved Africans.

Most sugar, however, was sold legally within the French colonial system. Sugar was as popular in France as it was in England. The mass market was slower to develop in France. This placed pressure on sugar planters and merchants to look for markets outside the 'colonial system'. Much of the French Caribbean sugar was resold to Dutch and German agents and distributed by them all over Europe.

The largest planters, however, did their marketing in much the same way as the English planters. Some consigned sugar to a commission agent in France who sold it to retailers and wholesalers. Some planters preferred to have secure, long-standing arrangements with agents or merchant houses. Others preferred to look at the market each year before choosing an agent.

The agent working on a commission basis also served as a banker for the sugar planter. He kept the proceeds of sugar sales and made purchases for the plantation from the declining balance. Many agents extended credit to planters when there were negative balances on their account. French agents had a much harder time trying to get back their debts from planters, both in the colony and in France, because it was almost impossible for merchants to recover debt in the colonial courts which were controlled by planters or jurists sympathetic to the planters' needs.

Sugar planters protected themselves much more effectively in the French system than in the English system. In fact, towards the end of slavery, the French sugar planter was in a much stronger position to defend their preferential marketing arrangements than the English.

To sum up

The sugar producers of the Caribbean developed a global expertise in the large scale manufacture of sugar from the cane plant. During the 18th century they became the world's leading producers of cane sugar. Other products, such as rum and molasses were manufactured as additional outputs of the sugar plantations. Sugar producers tried to invest in the most up date technologies, but as sugar prices fell over the 19th century, this proved to be a challenging proposition. The marketing of sugar was made possible by a complex system of shipping and distribution. European and Caribbean merchants developed commercial expertise that enabled the sugar industry to survive over the centuries.

Revision questions

1   Discuss the nature of the field preparation involved in the planting of sugar cane.
2   How was the labour on a sugar plantation divided between enslaved men and women?
3   What impact did technological innovation have on the sugar making process?
4   How was Caribbean sugar marketed in Europe?
5   What was the nature of the relationship between merchants and planters in the Caribbean sugar industry during the 18th century?

Chapter 9

African culture and community life

'Two thousand years of history, Black history, could not be wiped away so easily.'
(Bob Marley)

The experience African people had with chattel slavery was the most extreme form of exploitation that any race of people had ever undergone. This was a unique form of domination in which one group of people defined and used another group as property; in which people were targeted for slavery because of their race; they were described as sub-human, and they were bonded to another for life.

But enslaved African people survived. They protected their humanity and identity; and over time they redefined themselves as a new, vibrant cultural force. As enslaved people they were never culturally dehumanised. Although this is what the enslaved owners wanted, they did not succeed.

African people adapted. They took on cultural customs and traditions that strengthened their ethnic identity. They developed attitudes and practices that shaped Caribbean civilisation. What is now called 'New World culture' is influenced by the ideas and customs of enslaved African ancestors. These are important achievements under extremely difficult circumstances and these achievements tell us about the energy and richness of African culture.

In this chapter we will examine the transatlantic trade in humans as a transfer of culture from one continent to another. In other words, as a movement of ideas, art, values, religion, science, and technology.

> In this chapter we will learn about:
> **1.** The transfer of culture
> **2.** Ethnicity
> **3.** Rites and rituals
> **4.** Dances, games and other celebrations
> **5.** Rebuilding family

1 The transfer of culture

Africans arrived from traditional societies with their own formed values and philosophies. They came to the Caribbean with developed views about politics, economy, society and culture. The Caribbean experience refashioned these ideas and values. This transformation was a major challenge for them as they were in new places that were often chaotic and unsettled, and these places were governed by violence and force.

Africans were undergoing three separate but related experiences:

a. Most of them were meeting other Africans from several different cultural and language groups for the first time. Many Africans got to know one another's cultures intimately for the first time because of transatlantic slavery. Of course, there had always been considerable movement of people throughout Africa because of trade, migration, wars and displacement. But in the Caribbean world, Africans from widely different backgrounds lived in the same households and communities for the first time.

b. Most Africans were for the first time exposed to different types of European cultures and languages. This exposure also happened within households and communities – in towns and rural areas. Many Africans passed from one European group to another and in the process they acquired different languages and cultural knowledge.

c. This cultural reshaping that Africans and Europeans experienced is called 'creolisation'. This process was also taking place in Africa. This meant that many of the enslaved who came to the Caribbean were already familiar with European culture. Some of them arrived already knowing European languages and European versions of Christianity.

Given these circumstances it was a challenge to keep African cultures relevant and alive. The enslaved wanted to create a life of their own, a life that was committed to survival and independence beyond the reach and understanding of enslavers. 'Creoles' came to be a dominant group and the different cultures had to adopt many different views and standpoints.

2 Ethnicity

When Africans arrived in the Caribbean they identified themselves ethnically, as Igbo, Ashanti, Wolof and so on. The Europeans would lump them together as 'Guiney Negroes' although over time they tried to recognise them as ethnic groups with different cultural identities. But the European categorisation of Africans was never accurate and this meant that Africans immediately were confronted with a challenge to their ethnic recognition. They managed to keep ethnic symbols and traditions deep into the slavery period. They did this by rooting them into community life and by adapting them to their changing circumstances. So Africans did not ignore their ethnic identity or lose it completely during the slavery period. Rather they used their ethnic identity in different ways to promote a greater, more relevant sense of self. The enslaved continued to describe themselves within ethnic identities – the records would refer to 'Ebo Jane' or 'Mandingo Jack', for example.

The idea of 'shipmates' or 'mates', for example, cut across all ethnic lines. The enslaved who journeyed across the Atlantic on the same boat became a new family, linked by the experience. In 1801 four Ashanti Africans ran away from their plantation in Jamaica. The newspaper, which carried information about them, made the following observation:

> 'They told some of their shipmates, whom they solicited to go with them, they would proceed to the sea by night, and remain in the bush through the night, and the first canoe they found by the seaside they would set sail for their country.'

The 'shipmates' took on the roles, duties and responsibilities of parents to their shipmates' children.

In 1819, a young Coromantee runaway in Jamaica was described as being hidden in Kingston, 'as he has both shipmates and countrymen in that city' who were his family. When a runaway woman in Kingston was caught the following year and was punished, the only way her owners could get her to eat and not starve herself to death, was to find her shipmate to talk to her.

Enslaved Africans searched for unity and solidarity within their community as a necessary part of their survival. In some cases Africans were from nations that had been at war with each other for some time. They brought with them hardened attitudes and feelings towards their enemies. The war between the Ashanti and the Fanti of Ghana between 1765 and 1766 resulted in many persons from both groups being captured and sold as slaves. They arrived in the Caribbean still wanting to carry on the war. However, these feelings had to give way, and gradually they did.

But up to the middle of the 18th century many anti-slavery rebellions were still organised along ethnic lines, particularly at the leadership level. Ethnicity offered the enslaved an important point of commonality, a basis for bonding. People from the same ethnic group trusted one another and this was important when planning revolts. People informed on one another and many revolts were betrayed. So the enslaved needed to find ways to build their confidence and loyalty to one another.

Ethnicity was an important binding force in the early years. In 1675 the enslaved in Barbados planned a revolt. The 'Coromantees' of the Gold Coast were said to be the leadership group in this revolt. Their plan was to establish a 'Coromantee' kingdom on the island under the leadership of King Cuffee. This form of government seemed logical to them, because most Africans came from societies that were ruled by monarchs. So it was not surprising that President Henri Christophe of Haiti crowned himself as King Henri I. It was also common in the Caribbean for the enslaved to show that they were of royal stock, and to seek the respect due to them by custom. So we can see that the concept of royalty became part and parcel of Caribbean culture. Monica Schuler shows that several revolts were Akan-led in 18th century Jamaica.

Fig 9.1 *Henri Christophe of Haiti*

3 Rites and rituals

The Africans had ideas about leadership that called upon the entire range of bonding practices within their cultures. Everyday practices included the use of blood oath rites, appealing to the powers of ancestral spirits, the use of magic, religion and science in the forms of voodoo and obeah, and 'swearing on the family's name'. These practices assumed important roles within most communities. 'Taking the swear', as it was called, was a powerful ritual used by Maroons to show their loyalty. The English enslaver, Thomas Thistlewood, stated that drinking 'grave water' – water mixed with dirt from the grave of family or shipmate – 'was the most solemn oath among Negroes'.

On a day-to-day basis the experience of slavery was more about death than about new life. On plantations and in towns more people died than babies were born. It was normal for 10 per cent of Africans on plantations to die each year. New imported Africans replaced them.

Fig 9.2 *Funeral – cemetery Paramaribo, Suriname*

Most West African cultures believed that when the body dies, the spirit returns to the ancestors before returning to the family as new life. The belief in reincarnation was common and had a great impact on social life in many ways. It helped, for example, to reduce the fear of physical death.

The records show that many rebels went to their death with no fear or remorse – some laughing in the face of their executioners, others singing and bidding farewell. For some suicide began the journey of 'returning home', a practice that was very common. Enslavers responded to suicide in two main ways:

a. They cut off the head of the rebellious and publicly displayed them on poles. They hoped that this would undermine the belief in the homeward journey of the soul.

b. They cut up bodies and scattered the parts to create the idea of a broken and fragmented spirit.

Africans saw death as the first part of the journey of the soul back to the ancestors. Here it would be prepared for its return to earth. So death was a moment of celebration, of joy and thanksgiving. In 1740, Charles Leslie tells us about an African Jamaican funeral. The family, he said, sacrificed a hog, which was quartered and a portion made into a 'kind of soup', put in a calabash, and waved three times. All then sat down. The musicians returned to their drums. Some women shook gourd rattles, others placed the soup at the head of the corpse and the rum at the feet and then filled the grave with earth. Then the celebrants ate and drank and sang all the way home.

In 1796 Dr George Pinckard described a similar event – the funeral of Jenny, an African woman in Barbados. He tells us that Jenny's fellow workers had 'full faith' that in her journey Jenny would 'meet her friends at their place of nativity'. He says that death for them was only a departure from their present to their former home, a mere change from a state of slavery to a state of freedom. At the graveside, an elderly woman chanted 'an African air' while a chorus sang 'not a solemn Requiem', but loud and lively. When the body was lowered, the Africans all shouted, 'God bless you Jenny, goodbye! Remember me to all friends to the other side of the sea! Tell 'em me come soon!'

It was common, also, for parents to name their children after departed relatives if they could see characteristics of the relative in the child. This was understood as evidence of the returned spirit. People would delay naming their children because they were looking for such characteristics in the child. Linked to these practices was the idea that the spirits of the dead were active in the affairs of the living. There was a huge amount of knowledge on this subject that was passed on through generations and understood as common sense. This knowledge of spirits being active in the affairs of the living was central to community social life, and was ritualised in several ways. So, the power of ancestors was central to African-Caribbean culture. To know ancestors was to know one's cultural identity. Even though over time the enslaved built up new forms of kinship and lineage, they still respected the idea of ancestral authority.

Fig 9.3 Enslaved people dancing

chapter 9 | African culture and community life

Fig 9.4 Enslaved persons dancing at festival time

4 Dances, games and other celebrations

Dance was the main ritual performance that Africans used to show ancestor recognition and celebration. The dancers were said to be 'spirit possessed' and had to inwardly understand and feel the intricate and demanding movements of the dance. Dancing was like a tribute or a memorial to the ancestors. In the Caribbean it was used to demonstrate that Africans had their own recognised ancestral culture that was still important to them.

Dances

In the 18th and 19th centuries, enslavers thought that bad weather, Sundays, and Christian holidays were just reasons to take the enslaved out of mainline production. However, not all the enslaved benefited from this. Senior domestics, supervisors and artisans on the estates, as well as many urban workers had a different pattern in their labour-leisure cycle.

Enslaved workers demanded from their enslavers the right to free time. Once they had achieved this, they shifted their attention to the more testing and vexing question of how it would be spent and organised. Some enslaved workers wanted to travel to other plantations or towns so that they could participate in planned events. In many colonies enslavers had strict dress codes for the enslaved that prevented them from appearing with lavish finery. Many laws were passed to prevent the enslaved from decorating themselves with silks, fine jewelry, and lace. Enslavers did not wish slaves to travel away from their homes dressed like free persons because fancy clothing was often used as a disguise by runaways.

Enslaved workers were allowed to travel around the colonies at nights and on weekends. They could attend dances and markets and to maintain kinship and friendship relations. Enslavers often issued them with passes or tickets to show that they had permission to travel.

Evening dances became a visible part of Afro-Caribbean culture. In 1789 William Dickson reported how busy the nights and early mornings were as the Africans travelled all over and took full advantage of their leisure time. 'Their contubernal connections are unlimited as to number and local situations', he stated. 'Both sexes are frequently travelling all night, going to or returning from a distant connection, in order, without sleep, to be in due time to go through a hard day's labour, after their nocturnal adventures'. He tells us that the enslaved workers travelled to family gatherings, to their lovers for sexual relations, for economic exchange, as well as to organise or enjoy dances and festivals.

In 1790 G. Franklyn supported Dickson's observations concerning the movements of the enslaved workers in their leisure time. He said: 'Nothing will at any time, restrain them from pursuing their amours or their amusements. Dancing they are passionately fond of; and they will travel several miles, after their daily labour is over, to a dance, and after dancing the greatest part of the night, they will return to their owner's plantations and be in the field at the usual hour of labour'. Pinckard's observations during 1795-96, were similar: 'They are passionately fond of dancing and the Sabbath offering them an interval from toil, is, generally, devoted to their favourite amusement; and, instead of remaining in tranquil rest, they undergo more fatigue, or at least more personal exertion, during their gala hours of Saturday night and Sunday, during any four days of the week'.

Crop-over festival and dances

In the 18th and 19th centuries, Afro-Caribbean entertainment culture included the annual crop-over festival and weekend dances. Frederick Bayley, who visited Barbados in the 1820s, tells us that anti-slavery Europeans who spoke of the 'groans of the Negroes' would not believe the spectacle of 'an assembly of these oppressed people on their grand day of jubilee', which they call 'crop-over'. The crop-over festival, he continued, begins on the 'day on which the last of the canes are cut on a sugar plantation', during which 'flags are displayed in the field and all is merriment'. To begin the ceremony, 'a quart of sugar and a quart of rum are allowed each Negro on the occasion', after which 'all authority, and all distinction of colour ceases; Black and White, overseer and bookkeeper mingle together in dance'. On the plantations he added: 'It was common on occasions of this kind to see the different African tribes forming a distinct party, singing and dancing to the gumbay'.

The crop-over festival was a Caribbean affair. Mrs A.C. Carmichael, who witnessed the closing years of slavery in St Vincent and Trinidad, wrote in 1833 that crop-over festivals were widespread. In addition, Robert Dirks notes that the Jamaican crop-over, rather than coming at the end of the harvest, was often put off until the end of sugar-making. Then the work gangs assembled around the boiling house, dancing and roaring for joy. The overseer would distribute salt fish and rum and the 'feast would be followed by a ball'. This culture is captured in a 1754 poem by Nathaniel Weekes, a Creole Barbadian:

> There's not a slave,
> In spite of slavery, but is pleased and gay
> For this is their delightful, darling time!
> On all sides, hear the Dialogue obscene,
> The last Night's Theft, the adulterous Intrigue.
> And all the scandal of unmanner'd Tongue.
> While some to cheer their Toil, and laugh the Hours
> In merriment away, forth from their Throats.
> The Barb'rous unintelligible song.
> Unmusically roared.

There are some very detailed descriptions of Barbados crop-over celebrations. In 1798 Sampson Wood, manager of Newton Plantation in the Christ Church parish, reported that after the crop he would gather the enslaved workers and give them a 'dinner and a sober dance'. He justified the expense of this by saying that it was 'a celebration of Harvest Home after the crop'. In 1819 on the Codrington plantation, which was owned by the Church of England, a policy was adopted to celebrate 'crop-over' with a holiday for the human chattel.

Generally, there were two types of crop-over dances: those organised by the enslavers and held within their households; and those organised by the enslaved themselves – with or without their owners' permission. Pinckard offers limited comments on the second type of crop-over dance. The workers, he stated, 'assembled in crowds upon the open green, or in any square or corner of the town, and forming a ring in the centre of the throng, dance to the sound of their beloved music'.

In Jamaica, Trewlawny Wentworth added more details:

> Music and dancing, the Negroes love to their heart's core, although of late years, they have been taught by the missionaries to believe that they are inconsistent with morality. At this time, dancing was frequent in the Negro houses in an evening, and once a week, a more general assemblage took place under the auspices of one Negro, who invited people from the neighbouring estates. On such occasions, it was customary to ask leave of their master to ensure a license for a greater duration of their obstreperous mirth, which, from the usual vicinity of his dwelling to the Negro houses, he must necessarily hear.

chapter 9 | *African culture and community life*

Fig 9.5 Crop-over festival

Wentworth also stressed that parties organised by Africans were not illegal when the masters and mistresses gave permission. The slave codes of most Caribbean colonies allowed legal gatherings. Wentworth points out that it was convenient for owners to 'admit them according to the character of the applicant.' He says that providing entertainment was also 'profitable to the Negroes', and enslavers tried to regulate activities so as to avoid monopoly by any one enslaved worker on the estates. Wentworth explains the financial arrangements of these dances:

> Each Negro coming into the assembly paid half a bit, in order, partly, to meet the expense of a fiddler, who commonly charged as much as four and five dollars; and who, if not to be found among themselves, was always to be engaged from among the enslaved upon some other estate. If it happened, that the Negro giving the entertainment has inferior accommodation, he would borrow a more eligible spot from another, the dancing taking place in the house, and in the adjoining plot of ground.

Crop-over fêtes

Bayley's description of crop-over fêtes, which he said were usually held in 'a negro hut', tells us about the independent culture of the Afro-Caribbean. According to him, 'tea and coffee are first handed round, after which the musicians, consisting of perhaps three fiddlers, a tambourine player, and a man who beats an instrument called a triangle, commence playing, and the dancing continues for a while in the most lively and spirited manner'. 'After the dancing', he added, 'the group sits down to the supper table, the contents of which have all been stolen from the masters or mistresses.'

At the end of the evening, Bayley continues:

> The parties separate and each returns to his home; the masters know nothing of the matter: but if by chance, any of them are charged the next day with having been on such an excursion, they do not hesitate in declaring that they never left the house, and assert, with the most imprudent assurance, their total ignorance that even such an occurrence was to take place.

Organising anti-slaving activities

However, the Africans never abandoned their hope for general liberation and emancipation. The 'dance party' gave the Africans an opportunity to organise anti-slavery politics. There were two types of these 'political' gatherings: those at which the enslaved gave vent to their frustration in a social sort of way; and those that were used to plan revolt.

The data on the 1816 Barbados rebellion and the 1824 Jamaica anti-slavery conspiracy illustrate the different natures and functions of such dances.

On Easter Sunday, 14 April 1816, over 10,000 of the enslaved Barbadians, led by Bussa, took to arms in an act of self-liberation.

Enslavers claimed that they were shocked by the suddenness of the event. They believed that the social and cultural liberties that they had given the workers should have protected them from such an onslaught. At the same time they explained that the cause of the revolt was the many freedoms granted the enslaved, such as permission to travel to attend dances.

Edward Thomas, Manager of Bayley Plantation which was the home of Bussa, stated that he had long provided many 'free' days for the enslaved to have 'dances' which, unfortunately, opened their appetite for greater rights.

Thomas Nurse, Chief Overseer at the River Estate, argued that the many social liberties and material comforts the enslaved enjoyed were the main causes of rebellion. It is a 'fact well-known', he said, 'that workers have had frequent dances and feasts, at which all were well (and some expensively) dressed'. Thomas Stoute, Manager at Mapps Estate, also explained the outbreak of violence by referring to the extensive social activities allowed to the enslaved. He said:

> I conceive, as far as I am able to judge, that the Insurrection was produced by the Negroes (in the first instance) abusing those indulgences which, for many years past, owners of the enslaved in this Island had been in the habit of granting them, such as having constant parties and dances on Saturday and Sunday evenings (at which they were most gaily attired).

James Maycock, a practising physician in the parishes, was physically affected by the revolt. He stated, 'the frequency of dances, and other meetings of that kind, no doubt, enabled the disaffected to mislead their associates'. Lewis Young, Maycock's medical colleague and an estate owner, gave a similar account of the rebellion. He said:

> As to the causes which produced the Insurrection, I am of the opinion that it was partly owing to the many indulgences – suffering them to keep cattle, and some own houses – to have large dwelling houses – great and frequent entertainments, with dancing, costly apparel, trinkets, etc. – had become more impatient of restraint...

Jamaican enslavers also spoke about the African peoples' use of 'free' time. On 28 January 1824, charges 'to enter into a rebellious conspiracy' were heard in a Montego Bay, Jamaica, court-house. The prosecution said that the dances the enslaved had organised in their homes in order to plan rebellion were illegal. They referred specifically to two dances held in the pre-Christmas period – one at Mary-Ann's house and one at John Cunningham's house. Mary Ann's home was described as a regular dance venue with the enslaved workers from distant estates attending to drink rum and dance into the early hours of the morning.

In this trial Jamaican slave owners debated just how much the enslaved had established a social life of their own. They painted for the jury images of them freely holding nightly parties and interrupting their dancing to drink to 'Wilberforce's health' during the Christmas season.

Judge Vaughan instructed the jury that dances were allowed by the slave laws, and that free men of good character often attended these dances. He reminded them that the legal question before them, however, was whether the enslaved used these night dances to plan 'sedition, conspiracy or rebellion'.

Judge Vaughan noted that several witnesses had given evidence that at these dances the enslaved did state that they 'would fight for their freedom', and that 'they and the White people are now on a footing'. 'All these expressions', he instructed the jury, 'must be termed criminal and rebellious'. It took one hour of deliberations for the 12-man jury to reach its verdict after the three-day trial. They found the enslaved guilty of 'attending meetings for the dangerous purpose of obtaining [their own] freedom, and the freedom of others by force'. Those enslaved persons who were found guilty of the most serious charges were executed; but many were whipped, imprisoned and deported as convicts from the island.

Dances were events planned for social amusement and recreation, as well as venues for political organisation. Freedom in its fullest legal sense was never removed from the top of the African peoples' agenda. Cultural activity amongst them were a leisure activity, but celebrations were also about freedom.

Holiday celebrations
Gombay festival

The highlight of the Christian holiday season was the colourful appearance and performance of the Gombay

chapter 9 | *African culture and community life*

which was a festive time of music and dancing that had its roots in Africa. Africans painted their faces, decorated their heads with flowers and brightly coloured ribbons, and went from house to house singing and dancing, and playing musical instruments. Sometimes they wore masks, and danced to the drumming of the Gombay. The drummers were highly skilled. This was an art that was learned and was part of the African heritages of different ethnic groups.

The Gombay was a Caribbean festival that was seen yearly in many colonies, particularly Bermuda, the Bahamas, the Virgin Islands, Jamaica, Belize, and parts of the Leeward Islands. Most Europeans were hostile to African festivals and were particularly critical of the Gombay. But Africans refused to give in to critical opinions of their culture. An editorial in the Bermuda *Royal Gazette*, 26 December 1837, for example, made the following hostile comment:

> *the savage and non-sensical exhibition of the Gombay, practiced here by the idle, should be done away with as a thing not suited to a civilised community, and highly dangerous to passengers on horses or in carriages.*

In the Virgin Islands, the government tried to control the Gombay Festival. In 1733 it passed a law that, 'all such fêtes, balls, dances, and divertissements with Negro instruments should end at sundown or at 8:00 p.m. on moonlight nights.' In St Thomas in the 1760s the governor extended the time limit to 10:00 p.m.; after this time Africans needed police permission to continue, but in no circumstances was the use of Gombay drums permitted.

At all fêtes the Gombay drum carried the beat. At these events the enslaved Africans were allowed to dress in fine clothes and fancy jewellery. In the Danish Virgin Islands, the government objected to the enslaved people dressing in silks and wearing gold, as only the European elite were expected to do so. In 1780 they passed a 'Sumptuary Law' that prohibited the enslaved from wearing gold, silver, precious stones, silk, lace, and other expensive fabrics. All such items were prohibited to field and house slaves alike. Any enslaved person caught wearing such items was arrested; the offending articles were said to be stolen goods and handed over to the slave owners.

Other societies passed 'Sumptuary Laws' that prescribed the kind of clothing the enslaved could wear, and prohibited them from dressing in silks, lace, and fine cottons. Often the police and magistrates confiscated their

Fig 9.6 Detail from a painting depicting Gombay festivities

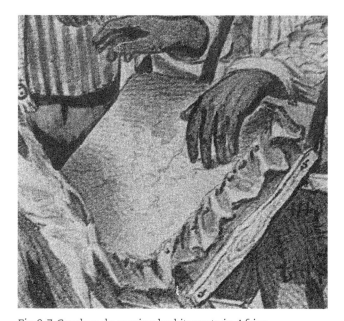

Fig 9.7 Gombay drumming had its roots in Africa

expensive jewellery, but these actions had little impact on the enslaved because they were so determined to 'look elegant and smart' on their festive occasions.

Joncanoe or John Canoe dance

In the Christmas season Africans in Jamaica, the Bahamas, Belize, Antigua and elsewhere performed the 'Joncanoe' or 'John Canoe' dance, one of the more well-established cultural rituals. The enslaved performed this ritual using elaborate headdress and masks, to show the relationship between the spirit world and social living. It is believed that this ritual had its origins at Axim, a major enslaved trading port on the Gold Coast. John Barbot, a traveller to the coast, named the mask worn by people for the spirits of the dead, the 'canoe'.

The Antigua Joncanoe or 'Junkanoo' as they called it, was mostly performed at Christmas. In 1774 Janet Schaw describes it as a rebellious affair that worried the Whites:

> It is necessary, however, to keep a look out during this season of unbounded freedom; and every White man on the island is in arms and patrols go all round the different plantations as well as keep guard in the town.

In St Vincent Africans also celebrated at Christmas with the Junkanoo festivals. Carmichael describes it during the early 19th century:

> They flour each other's Black faces and curly hair, and call out, 'look at he White face! and he White wig!' - with many other jokes of their own. ...about eleven in the morning, a party of Negroes from Paradise, the

adjoining estate, came to wish us a good Christmas. They had two fiddlers, whose hats and fiddles were decorated with many coloured ribbons. Negroes formerly used to be inclined, I was told, to rioting and fighting upon Christmas Day, but now they all go to church.

By the late 18th century in the Bahamas Junkanoo was part and parcel of African arts and culture and was associated with Christmas when 'Negroes have been seen beating their tambourines and dancing the whole day'. A Mr Farquharson noted in 1832 that his human chattel 'go abroad to see some of their friends and some stay at home amusing themselves in their own way through the day, but all of them are at home in the evening and had a grand dance and keep it up until near day light'.

Fig 9.8 Junkanoo festival – white faces and white wigs

The Kumina dance

Like the 'Junkanoo', the Kumina dance was a core element of culture in Jamaica and other places with large Akan (the area now known as Ghana) populations. It is a dance that allows the living to connect with spirit ancestors. The Kumina was a 'healer' dance, when rival doctors called forth the spirits with the help of Gombay drumming. The Jamaican Maroons integrated these rituals into their philosophy and science of life and preserved them from the local powers of the enslavers.

Spirit religion

Spirit-based religions were a core element in African culture. Examples of these were obeah and myal, religions based on the belief that it was possible for the living to use ancestral spirits to determine the future, and to shape the nature of social events.

European governments outlawed these religions in all Caribbean societies and punished people who practised them with death. However, the anti-obeah and anti-myal laws that the government passed made little difference to the power of the belief within African communities. Africans visited their myal leaders as well as obeah and voodoo priests for cures for illnesses, the removal of curses and bad luck, to bless children, in search of insights to personal futures, and for general counselling. They also went to their myal leaders for help in settling conflicts by imposing harm on others, using poisons, and for carrying out of punishments in the process of seeking social justice.

Spirit leaders were expected to promote resistance to slavery by providing visionary leadership and a psychic advantage over the enslavers. In the Haitian Revolution, the role of voodoo in achieving solidarity, loyalty, and extraordinary bravery in the face of death and destruction, is well known. In Jamaica during the 18th century, myal was part of the Maroon rebellion, and enslavers in the western areas were terrified of the influence of myal men, who were called doctors. When the enslavers caught them, they were often condemned and brutally executed.

In Jamaica myal practitioners incorporated some Christian beliefs and practices into their religion, as did voodoo in Haiti. The power that led to resurrection was worshipped and celebrated, and was infused with the Baptist faith. Voodoo and the Catholic belief in spirit possession were very similar.

Formal social affairs

Some gatherings of the enslaved were formal social affairs. They were designed not only to imitate European elite society, but also to be better than it in style and elegance. In some colonies these events were called 'Dignity Balls' and were extravagant affairs with an entry fee. Once people had paid the fee they could eat, drink and dance all night. Women were usually beautifully dressed in fine clothes and jewellry and all kinds of alcoholic drinks were available. Europeans would wonder where these items came from, and how enslaved women obtained their flowing ball gowns. An officer in the British army described a 'Dignity Ball' in Bermuda in 1830 as follows:

> When dancing was over the company was ushered into the supper-room where a table was set out covered with a profusion of cakes, preserves, wines, etc; that the Black women appeared in full costume, lace, satin and flowers; and that, in short everything was conducted with the same taste as in the higher circles of society. They had Spanish dances and quadrilles; country dancing not being considered genteel.

The music was provided by African musicians on violins, fiddles, flutes, and drums. In 1823 James Stewart noted that some slaves, particularly elite households, identified more with European cultural expressions so as to disassociate themselves with African forms of cultural expressions. He wrote:

Fig 9.9 Miss Dignity attending a Dignity Ball. Illustration by anonymous 19th century traveller

In a few years it is probable that the rude (African) music will be altogether exploded among the creole Negroes, who show a decided preference for European music. Its instruments, its tunes, its dances, are now pretty generally adopted by the young creoles, who indeed sedulously copy their masters and mistresses in everything. A sort of subscription balls is set afoot, and parties of both sexes assemble and dance country dances to the music of a violin, tambourine, etc... But this improvement of taste is confined to those who are, or have been, domestic about the houses of the Whites.

Stewart's observations about Jamaica refer to the Caribbean trend of African cultural survival. Pinckard, writing about Barbados in 1796, was hostile to African cultural expressions when he made the following statement:

They assemble, in crowds, upon the open green, or in any square or corner of the town, and, forming a ring in the centre of the throng, dance to the sound of their favourite African yell. Both music and dance are of a savage nature, their songs which are very simple, (are) harsh and wholly deficient in softness and melody.... While one Negro strikes the Banjar, another shakes the rattle with great force of arm, and a third sitting across the body of the drum, as it lies lengthwise upon the ground, beats and kicks the sheepskin at the end, in violent exertion with his hands and heels, and a fourth sitting upon the ground at the other end, behind the man upon the drum, beats upon the wooden sides of it with two sticks. Together with the man upon the noisy sounds, numbers of the party of both sexes bawl forth their dear delighting sound with all possible force of lungs,... a spectator would require only a slight aid from fancy to transport him to the savage wilds of Africa.

Bayley stated how the enslaved Africans, to the annoyance of Europeans would 'sit' up during the greater part of the moonlight nights, chattering together, and telling 'nancy stories'. He added furthermore, 'A nancy story is nothing more or less than a tale of ghosts and goblins, which pass with the negroes by the appellation of Jumbees.' He then commented on their 'grand day of jubilee, which they call crop-over'.

In the late 18th century, he added, 'it was common on "crop-over" to see the different African tribes each forming a separate party, singing and dancing to the Gumbay, after the manner of their native Africa'. He added that the festival was now less African.

Other pastime favourites

There were other pastimes that were favourites among the enslaved community. They enjoyed stick-fighting, particularly when contestants were competitive and prepared to dominate each other for a prize. Cock-fighting and card-gaming were also popular. Most societies passed laws that prohibited the enslaved from gambling, either with dice, cards, or betting on horses. Such laws had little effect in the face of determined communities. In effect, almost everything that the enslaved did by way of organised leisure became a crime for the White government. Storytelling and the playing of 'warri' - an ancient African game – the government did not mind, largely because they were quiet, homebound events.

Sports and games
Bat and ball: Origins of West Indies cricket

Early on in Caribbean enslaved society ball sports and team games were very much present in the form of organised cricket. As an English game cricket had its origins dating back to the early medieval period. It found its way into the Caribbean with the British army during the war against Napoleon's France. Cricket was introduced by garrisoned soldiers and played between officers and their men. The Africans watched the game, learned its rules and soon could perfect it. From the late 1790s onwards Africans had plenty of opportunity to practise cricket. Some enslavers encouraged them. Africans took keenly to the game, even though they were excluded from formal sporting contact with Europeans.

Africans developed their own game using homemade instruments. Coconut branches became bats, though harder woods were also used. For balls they used a variety of small fruits, and sometimes made them from cloth held together by string.

It is not surprising that the Barbadian planters were most determined to entrench cricket culture. They had already defined their island home as 'Little England', and held onto the view that they were Englishmen in a far-flung 'shire'.

In the early 19th century, the print media in the colonies helped to popularise the cricket culture. In the newspapers, games were announced alongside references to the sale of enslaved workers and price lists for sugar and other goods. In Barbados and the Leeward Islands, troops who were waiting for instructions to put down rebellious Africans or to keep out the army of Napoleon played cricket. The game helped them handle the stress of war and, more importantly, to imagine through play that they were back at home.

The earliest references to an organised cricket match within the Caribbean press appeared in the *Barbados Mercury* and *Bridgetown Gazette* on 10 May 1806 and 17 January 1807. This last entry was an announcement by the treasurer of the St Ann's Garrison Cricket Club inviting members to a special dinner after a game. Two years later the *Gazette* carried notice of a 'grand cricket match to be played between the Officers of the Royal West Indies Rangers and Officers of the Third West Indian Regiment for 55 guineas a side on the Grand Parade on Tuesday, 19 September'. The match was arranged to start 'immediately after 'gunfire' on the morning and continue until 8 o'clock a.m., then to resume at 4:30 p.m.' The Royal Rangers were required to wear 'flannel and blue facings' and the Third Regiment were to wear 'flannel and yellow facings'.

It seems that St Ann's Cricket Club was a pioneering British Caribbean cultural institution. Europeans in Barbados welcomed it. The owner and editor of the *Barbadian*, Abel Clinckett, wrote in May 1838:

> *We understand that to promote the gratification of the soldiers of St Ann's Garrison, as well as the sake of their health, the Commander of the Forces has sanctioned their engaging in the truly British, and manly sport of cricket. A great match, we are informed, will be played on Monday next at 6 o'clock (a.m.) - the 78th Regiment against the Garrison.*

This was a single-inning game. In the next week it was reported in the same paper that the 78th Regiment had won the game having scored 91 runs to the Garrison's 53. An important issue to be noticed here is that the Garrison team was made up of lower-ranking soldiers. This attracted the attention of Mr Clinckett when he stated that such social mixing of men of different classes showed 'the good feeling' that officers had for their soldiers.

The St Ann's Club can claim to be the nurturer of Barbadian and British Caribbean cricket. Again, the Barbadian newspaper informs us that in 1849 'gentlemen' in the parish of St Michael, in which the garrison was located, had formed themselves into two 'well organised cricket companies' – the 'City' and 'St. Michael' clubs. The editor described the first game between these clubs as an affair watched by 'highly respectable ladies and gentlemen' that 'evinced great spirit and extreme goodwill'. The game was played on a specially prepared field at Constant Plantation, owned by Mr Prettijohn, who also provided tents and refreshments for spectators.

The enslaved community was encouraged to use their 'free time' in any sort of cultural activity that did not suggest resistance. Any cultural expression that Europeans feared or considered rebellious was outlawed. So by the end of slavery there was an entertainment system within the African communities, and cricket was an important part of it.

5 Rebuilding family

Enslaved Africans arrived in the Caribbean with no family members to recognise or welcome them, and no kinship system to absorb and define them. They were torn from their family and kin. They could never reconnect or communicate with those they knew. Many adults had wives and husbands. Children had uncles, aunts, cousins, and grandparents. In African community elders took responsibility for the integration of children into the wider kinship and community.

Family life was at the centre of their culture and everything revolved around it, from identity and social status, to material well-being, health and a long life. Africans understood life through the eyes of family and community. But only their memories, values, attitudes, and ideas survived the Middle Passage. With these memories and attitudes they tried to rebuild a new life, the best they could, in this hostile environment.

Enlavers argued that the Africans were sub-human with no emotional links to kith and kin, and no commitment to family values. This was part of their attempt to justify the crime of the trade in humans. For most of the slavery period, Europeans saw the African family as an obstacle to their wealth accumulation. The practice of slave-trading and slave-owning tried to undermine the African family. The enslaver owner had the power to determine the life and death of an enslaved person. African parents had no authority over their lives or those of children.

Orlando Patterson, the Jamaican sociologist, has argued that the main feature of slavery was that it cut off the enslaved from family, lineage, community and heritage. The enslaved were people who were biologically disconnected from family links and so they were made honourless, degraded, and stripped of ancestral identity. Africans in the Caribbean began their new lives with a rebuilding challenge, a desperate effort to establish family and kinship.

For most of the slavery period the marriage of an enslaved person was not recognised by Europeans in the society. In many cases there were severe penalties for those who married when they were discovered by their enslavers. Africans took their domestic ceremonies underground, and this forced them to operate in a secretive way. The African family, then, was considered by Europeans an irrelevant, unimportant and sometimes a criminal institution. Sometimes the enslaved were given permission to live as couples in a household as a special concession for loyalty and good conduct. However, this was a privilege that could be suddenly withdrawn and forbidden. Even when enslavers informally recognised a marriage or a couple, they still did not allow couples to control the lives of children who could be readily sold without the knowledge or consent of the parents. At the best of times a few fortunate enslaved persons earned domestic rights and privileges, and worked very hard to maintain them.

Under the law the enslaved was classified as property and so could not own property. So, under the law it was not possible to recognise any contract that the enslaved entered into, whether domestic or financial. They had no legal identities as human beings. This was especially so for women who were commonly raped and sexually exploited by enslavers. The 'justification' for this was that it was not possible to rape property, and so unrestricted sexual access to their human chattel was part of the enslaver's right of property. The law, then, did not interfere with a property holder's right to enjoy the use of his or her property for sexual exploitation. This meant that the African family had no protection under the law. It became common for European settlers, like the enslaver, Thistlewood, to emotionally and sexually abuse the enslaved.

However, in some societies enslavers realised that their society could be more stable and they could heighten economic productivity on their estates by recognising and encouraging Africans to form family units or to live together. By the end of the 18th century, it was common in most colonies for the enslaved to live together in a household. However this was still seen as a privilege granted to them for docile behaviour. It could be withdrawn as a punishment for insubordination.

It is within these settings that historians have examined issues such as: how common it was for the enslaved to live in family groupings; what was the nature of these relationships; to what extent did they use African domestic systems or did they adopt and adapt European ways. It is true that slavery shattered family values and cultures, however there is a debate about the degree to which Africans recovered and established stable sustainable, domestic lives.

Evidence from the plantations of Jamaica shows that the nuclear family system was attractive for the enslaved, but very often the conditions of their lives did not allow them to achieve its minimum requirements. The sexual imbalance within the society, the frequent buying and selling of adults and children, the sexual exploitation of women by overseers, managers, owners and some supervisors, weakened interest in domestic union.

Michael Craton has shown that most of the 10,000 Bahamian enslaved workers in the cotton industry in the 1820s lived in 'simple nuclear families'. This was because both the enslaved and enslavers had a clear interest in this arrangement. This, however, was not the case in Trinidad, British Guiana and St. Vincent at this time. Most of the enslaved in these societies lived alone in huts and experienced high death rates on the newly-established sugar plantations. But at this time, the Bahamian enslaved achieved a natural growth rate of 16 per 1,000 per year – the highest in the region.

Elsa Goveia's work on the Leeward Islands in the 18th century demonstrates that when the African family existed, it consisted of a mother and her children, all belonging to the mother's owner. The nuclear family was not well formed in the Leewards. The Methodist and Moravian Churches did try to promote 'Christian monogamy' but with little success.

In Barbados after the 1770s there was a serious effort by enslavers to 'breed' a local labour force. One way of doing this was to encourage the enslaved to live in nuclear families – father, mother and children in a single household. Enslavers offered the enslaved incentives to create an interest in this arrangement. Parents were offered better housing, animals and the promise not to sell young children. Mothers were offered cash for delivering healthy babies, and so were midwives. Young married couples were offered their own huts, a crib and sometimes animals of their own.

Gabriel Debien's research on family life in Martinique is also very useful. He used the records of a single sugar plantation, *L'Anse-a-L'Ane*, from 1743 to 1778. For most of this period the estate had about 56 males and 52 females – this was a typical gender distribution for the colony at the time. Debien found that most enslaved persons lived in nuclear families. On this estate there were about 52 known nuclear families. They produced 215 babies, 4.1 per couple. They were fewer female-friendly headed families than those with married couples who produced more babies. The population, however, did not grow naturally because of very high infant death rate. Between 1762 and 1777, for example, 29 out of the 58 babies born on the estate died within three years.

Barry Higman's work on Jamaica shows just how many nuclear families produced more deaths than births. Examining three estates, Old Montepelier, New Martinique, and Shettlewood Pen, he found that about 52 per cent of the 864 enslaved persons lived in nuclear households (a man, a woman, and their children).

Fig 9.10 *An obvious caricature of the Bahamian enslaved family*

mother as the property of her owner. The husband or father could live on another estate. He was a visiting spouse, not necessarily by choice but by circumstances. So the mother's household was listed as a mother-child unit.

Many families were closely linked and adults parented children other than their own. Many extended families were headed by matriarchs or women, who exercised considerable authority over men and women.

One such family for which good records exist is that of 'Old Doll'. She was an established matriarchal figure who was the retired housekeeper at Newton Plantation in Barbados at the end of the 18th century. Several features of Old Doll's family are emphasised by the plantation records: first, the low profile of men as fathers – neither Doll's father nor husband(s) are mentioned; second, the predominant role of women in decision-making and other aspects of family life.

As a former housekeeper Old Doll occupied her remaining years protecting and directing the lives of her children and grandchildren – both males and females. As head of the extended family, her authority was respected by all, including her younger mulatto half-sister, Mary Ann, who 'lived' with a British man with whom she had seven children. Mary Ann used her influence to make sure that her younger brother, George Saers, who was the estate's head cooper, made arrangements for her young sons to be professionally trained. Uncle George took all four of his nephews under his wing as apprentice coopers. All of Doll and Mary Ann's sons were trained as craftsmen, and their adult daughters protected from field labour.

Old Doll's family was very successful in achieving elite status. There was such severe competition for the few highly prized occupations on the estates, that these elite families closed ranks and reinforced their advantage.

Old Doll's family held together closely and struggled as one even though colour was a critical factor in achieving status and creating different lifestyles between African and mixed-race communities.

Old Doll was frequently negotiating on behalf of her sister's 'White' children, while her sister's enslaved

Enslaved people, Higman showed, did the best they could to keep families together. The Christian nuclear family was common by 1800 when missionaries began their campaign in the colonies to have slave marriages and families recognised by the church.

In Cuba, according to Moreno Fraginals, nuclear families among the enslaved were rare because couples were so often broken up. The typical family unit was mothers and their children living in a household. Planters tried to encourage nuclear families so as to increase the population but did not succeed. The incentives they offered were inadequate. Women carried a very heavy load on sugar estates. Pregnant women received few rewards for giving birth and their children were not withdrawn from the slave market.

In general, then, all types of family systems developed in the Caribbean. Most common, however, was the mother and children household. The children stayed with the

workers assisted both parts of the family. It was certainly Old Doll's social authority that held the family together as a surviving unit rather than Mary Ann's status as grandmother of 'White' children. Also the weak image of men that comes out of the documents reinforces Old Doll's status as head of the family, and reinforces the fact that women were by no means always 'second class' individuals within the enslaved yards.

Despite this, by the end of slavery the Christian-style nuclear family was a rare institution within African communities. With family reunions taking place on weekends and at nights, Africans looked forward to a time when they would be permanently united. This can be supported by evidence from the post-slavery period which illustrates that much of the so-called African 'vagrancy' was actually individuals desperately searching for and reuniting their families.

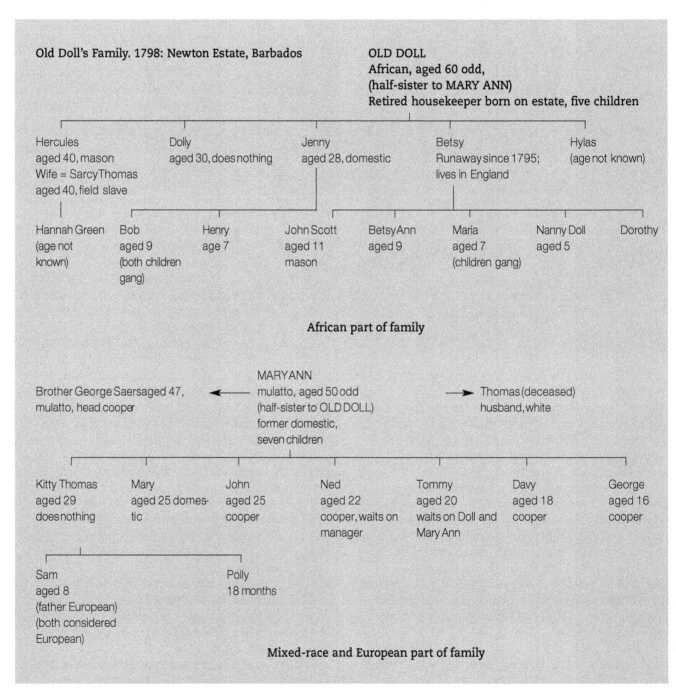

Old Doll's Family. 1798: Newton Estate, Barbados

OLD DOLL
African, aged 60 odd,
(half-sister to MARY ANN)
Retired housekeeper born on estate, five children

Hercules
aged 40, mason
Wife = Sarcy Thomas
aged 40, field slave

Dolly
aged 30, does nothing

Jenny
aged 28, domestic

Betsy
Runaway since 1795;
lives in England

Hylas
(age not known)

Hannah Green
(age not known)

Bob
aged 9
(both children gang)

Henry
age 7

John Scott
aged 11
mason

Betsy Ann
aged 9

Maria
aged 7
(children gang)

Nanny Doll
aged 5

Dorothy

African part of family

MARY ANN
mulatto, aged 50 odd
(half-sister to OLD DOLL)
former domestic,
seven children

Brother George Saers aged 47,
mulatto, head cooper ←

→ Thomas (deceased)
husband, white

Kitty Thomas
aged 29
does nothing

Mary
aged 25 domestic

John
aged 25
cooper

Ned
aged 22
cooper, waits on manager

Tommy
aged 20
waits on Doll and Mary Ann

Davy
aged 18
cooper

George
aged 16
cooper

Sam
aged 8
(father European)
(both considered European)

Polly
18 months

Mixed-race and European part of family

chapter 9 | *African culture and community life*

To sum up

In this chapter we have discussed the trade in enslaved Africans as a movement of culture, of ideas, art, values and religion from Africa to the Caribbean. We have seen how Africans used various means to ensure that their cultural identity thrived – ethnic groupings, rites and rituals, dances, games and celebrations, and the rebuilding of new family groupings. All these were part and parcel of the enslaved people's resistance to their conditions. In the next chapter we will continue with this theme by looking at their economic and physical survival on the various islands.

Revision questions

1   Explain why African people were able to maintain their culture under enslavement.
2   How did enslaved people spend their time when they were neither working for their enslavers or in their provision grounds?
3   What is meant by the term 'creole culture'?
4   How did African religions shape the community life of the enslaved population?

Chapter 10

Surviving enslavement: wealth and health factors

'We are the survivors, the black survivors.'
(Bob Marley)

Enslaved people used different strategies and tactics to survive their enslavement. Just like free people they tried to increase their wealth by participating in the economy as producers and distributors of commodities or goods. This was with and without their enslaver's permission. Although they were the primary victims of colonial economies, in which they were defined and used as property, nevertheless generations of Africans managed to identify and pursue their own material interests. They combined their work as field hands, artisans, domestics or whatever with their own productive and commercial activities. In this way those enslaved made economic decisions as 'free' persons.

Surviving enslavement was a significant achievement by those enslaved. A high death rate was the norm among both adults and infants. Other features of slave systems were low birth rates, low female fertility, and a serious imbalance in the sexes with there being more males. Many of those enslaved were malnourished, could not work because of disease and poverty, were subjected to unrelenting hard work and physical cruelty. All these things told the story of a race caught in a genocidal trap. In addition, their devastating exposure to unfamiliar diseases, and chronic inability to withstand familiar diseases because of malnutrition, persistent stress and physical abuse added detail to the journey of death.

In this chapter we will learn about:
1. The ways in which the enslaved pursued an economic life of their own
2. The ways in which the enslaved survived slavery

1 Enslaved people pursue an economic life of their own

Africans were accustomed to huckstering – the sale of food or other goods they produced on a small-scale. Huckstering was certainly as much part of their culture as other more well-known parts of African-American life, such as religion and the arts. They were attracted to huckstering because of their social isolation and because of the difficult conditions under which they lived because of slavery. Huckstering gave those enslaved the opportunity to improve the quantity and quality of their nutrition in environments where most people were malnourished. It allowed them to possess and later own property. It enabled them to make profitable use of their leisure time, and it afforded them the chance to travel and normalise their social lives as much as possible under highly restrictive circumstances.

In the Leewards, and Barbados especially, the planters had a policy to 'restrict the land at the disposal of those enslaved to small house plots', to import food for them, and include 'some food production in the general estate program'. In Martinique and Jamaica owners allotted their human chattel large tracts of land, which were not suitable for cane production and which were located in the foothills of the mountain ranges. These plots were called provision grounds or *polinks* in Jamaica. Enslavers encouraged the enslaved workers to produce their own food here. Apart from these provision grounds which were generally located miles from their homes, in Jamaica the enslaved also cultivated little 'house spots'.

Jamaican and Martiniquan enslaved workers became experienced peasant farmers on these provision grounds that they cultivated, and eventually dominated the food marketing system. Europeans came to depend heavily upon this produce and, as a result, there was no on-going legal attempt to arrest the enslaved or do away with their commercial activities. By the mid-18th century, the enslaved formally dominated the provisions market.

Jamaica

The enslaved of Jamaica managed to create an agriculture of their own. This enabled them to market as independent entrepreneurs a wide variety of foods such as tree crops, vegetables, herbs, roots, and craft materials. They sold their surpluses or extra food for cash in local markets or exchanged these for other goods and services. They kept the money from these commercial transactions. Market day for most of slavery was Sunday. Saturday was either a full working day on the plantation or a day when they could work their provision grounds for part of the day.

The provision grounds were normally some distance from the workers' villages on the plantations. An observer of a provision ground noted:

> When a tract of Negro-provisions regularly planted, is well cultivated, and kept clean, it makes a very husband like and beautiful appearance and it is astonishing of the common necessities of life it will produce. A quarter of an acre of this description will be fully sufficient for the supply of a moderate family, and may enable the cultivator to carry some to market besides.

Not all provision grounds were on reasonably good soil. Some enslaved workers struggled to plant and harvest crops on rocky, hilly, infertile land, with no protection from winds or heavy rains that washed away the soil.

Generally those enslaved were not supervised while working their provision grounds. This was an area of their life that offered them considerable freedom to make decisions. William Beckford, writing in 1790, noted of the work on provision grounds:

> All kinds of ground provisions and corn as well as the plantain, successfully cultivated in the mountains; but as this is done by the Negroes in their own grounds and on the clays which are given them for this particular process, it does not enter into the mass of plantation labour.

Beckford continued:

> They prepare their land, and put in their crops on the Saturdays that are given to them, and they bring home their provisions at night; and if their grounds be at a considerable distance from the plantation, as they often are to the amount of five or seven miles, or more, the journey backwards and forwards makes this rather a day of labour and fatigue, than of enjoyment and rest. On these occasions they move with all their family, into the place of cultivation; the children of different ages are loaded with baskets the infants are flung at the backs of the mothers..... the provision grounds in the mountains, or polinks as they are called in the Island produce all kinds of fruit and garden stuff of coffee, coco, ginger, and other minor productions of the country.

The unsupervised production of food crops by those enslaved provided the very basis of an open market system. The size of trading was increased because some enslaved persons preferred to produce minor handicrafts, some raised livestock, and some planted crops directly for sale. In

1662 a market place was legally created at Spanish Town. Initially those enslaved did not trade goods on it, but by the end of the century they were selling goods at a 'Saturday market at Passage Fort'. The first legal recognition of the enslaved as marketers came in 1711 when the law made provisions to punish those convicted by magistrates of 'hawking about and selling goods' other than foodstuffs. They were to receive no more than 31 lashes.

The enslaved were not allowed to trade in beef, veal, mutton and saltfish. They were allowed, however, to sell fruits, vegetables and poultry in markets. In 1735 a law provided that enslaved people who 'carry about and sell all manner of provisions, fruits, fresh fish, milk, poultry, and other small stock of all kinds' must have a 'ticket from their owner or employer'.

Fig 10.2 *Market woman, selling poultry and vegetables*

non-plantation owners. Finally legislators came to terms with the power of the culture, and allowed those enslaved to sell and buy goods, not only in the country markets, but also in the towns. Edward Levy described a Kingston market in 1774 as follows:

> At the bottom of the town, near the water side, is the market place, which is plentifully supplied with butchers meat, poultry, fish, fruits, and vegetables of all sorts. Here are found not only a great variety of American, but also of European, vegetables: such as peas, beans, cabbage, lettuce, cucumbers, French beans, artichokes, potatoes, carrots, turnips, radishes, celery, onions, etc. These are brought from the Liguanea Mountains, and are all excellent in their kind. Here are likewise strawberries, not inferior to the production of our English gardens; grapes and melons in the utmost perfection: mulberries, figs. and apples, exceedingly good, but in general gathered before they are thoroughly ripe.

He continues:

> In short, the most luxurious epicure cannot fail of meeting here with sufficient quantity, variety, and excellence, for the gratification of his appetite the whole year round. The prices are but little different from those of Spanish Town: but, where they disagree, they are more reasonable at Kingston, the supplies being more regular, and the market superintended by the magistracy. The beef is chiefly from the pastures of Pedro's, in St Ann; the mutton, from the salt-pan lands, in St Catherine's; what they draw from the penns in St Andrew's parish being very indifferent meat.

Fig 10.1 *Enslaved woman at the market place*

By the end of the 18th century, at the height of slavery in Jamaica, the selling and buying of goods by those enslaved was an established part of Jamaican economic life. Enslavers became dependent on these markets, as did the

chapter 10 | *Surviving enslavement: wealth and health factors*

By the end of slavery the produce that people enslaved produced independently and more importantly the buying power of the cash they accumulated were shaping social attitudes. Enslaved people had certainly won a considerable victory over those who argued that they were not industrious. As a result of their independent cultivation and marketing activities, people saw in their activities a readiness for freedom. Thomas Madden, writing in 1835, noted:

> To say that he is not industrious without reference to the object for which his exertions are employed would be an absurd remark; to say he is indolent, where his labour is exacted without reward, is to prove nothing. But where the Negro labours on his own ground, for his own advantage – where his wife and children have the price of his own commodities to fetch him from the market-town, no matter how many miles they have to trudge, or how heavy the load they have to bear – where the wages he received for his services are at his own disposal – where his own time is duly paid for, not in shads and herrings, but in money a little more than equivalent to the advantages he deprives his own ground of, by transferring his extra time to the estate he is employed on – the Negro is not the indolent slothful being he is everywhere considered, both at home and in the colonies.

Enslaved people, of course, understood very well that their independent economy was about their own 'freedom in action' but still within the limits of slavery. While enslavers benefited from these activities, the Africans were successfully demonstrating their cultural capabilities as a self-sufficient, self-directed community.

Martinique

Dutch refugees from Brazil introduced into the French colonies – especially into Martinique – the practice of giving those enslaved provision grounds, or 'Little Guineas'. So the provision ground allocation became known as the Brazilian system. The sugar plantations accepted peasant-like small farming by those enslaved on the provision grounds. From the mid-17th century this arrangement was established and enslavers gradually took the view that the enslaved workers were responsible for their own survival on their 'free' day.

Dale Tomich has shown that the system had its critics who argued that the custom of free Saturdays gave the enslaved too much freedom and independence producing in them too great a sense of liberty. The critics won the debate as far as the French government was concerned. The result was the proclamation of the Royal Edict of 1685, the *Code Noir*. By the Black Code enslavers were instructed to stop the practice of allocating gardens and to stop free Saturdays as a system of feeding people enslaved and to put in place a system of giving them weekly food allocations. This system was known as the *ordinaire*.

Enslavers objected to the instructions of the French government. They agreed that the *ordinaire* was an inferior system, as the gardens allowed both enslavers and those enslaved to maximise their interests. The French government ordered the governor to enforce the system but he lacked the resources and the public co-operation to do so. Enslavers spoke about the infringement of their property rights and that those enslaved pressured them to maintain the old system. As a result the *ordinaire* practice did not develop as the norm, while gardens and free Saturdays were normalised by the end of the century.

In 1784 and 1786 the *Code Noir* was reformed. The changes did not legalise free Saturdays, which remained outlawed but supported the policy of granting those enslaved provision grounds and called for effective regulation of these. It was now legislated that each enslaved adult was to receive a small plot of land on which to establish a subsistence farm. The thinking of the French government was that the produce of the provision grounds should supplement the *ordinaire* and not do away with it. The French government continued to oppose the custom of those enslaved having free Saturdays and as late as 1828 restated the policy by a Royal Ordinance.

By 1828 the link between provision grounds and free Saturdays for the marketing of surplus produce was so well-established that the law gave way to the accepted custom. Other, periodic attempts by the government to suppress the trading culture of those enslaved were ineffectual, and enslavers continued to encourage those enslaved to grow and sell their own produce as independent farmers and marketeers. Gradually the *ordinaire* was phased out and enslaved persons were encouraged to use as much land as their families could cultivate. All of this meant that there was more and more unsupervised activity which spilt over into even larger markets.

Now 'free' society could use enslaved persons in a commercial culture, which became its main way of securing fresh foodstuff. There was now a network of markets established around the produce of enslaved people. This showed the effect they had upon society and on the economy. The substantial market towns such as those developed at Lamentin, Francois, Trinite and Robert proved their independent economic culture. Enslaved persons visited these towns on Saturday, and gave them life and vibrancy.

Fig 10.3 Market girl, Barbados

According to A. Soleau, the Frenchman who described the slave society in French Caribbean colonies during the 1830s, on some Saturdays there were as many as 6,000 enslaved busy buying and selling and discussing 'matters unimaginable'. 'Have you seen them', he asked, 'very well-dressed and presenting the exterior signs of material well-being. The men have trousers, shirts, vests, and hats of oil skin or straw. The women have shirts of Indian cotton, white blouses, and scarves, some of which are luxurious, as well as earrings, pins, and even some chains of gold'.

Nevertheless, criticisms of the system continued. One argument was that it allowed those enslaved to get many material comforts, such as fine clothes and jewelry, money to purchase their freedom, and generally developed in them a taste for property that would lead to a demand for freedom. Supporters of enslaved people made the counter-argument that their independent economic activity gave them a stake in the colony, developed in them a strong sense of personal responsibility, and strengthened civil society through the building of inter-racial relationships.

The system allowed enslaved people also to travel long distances, maintain friendships and family ties beyond their limited plantation world; it provided the circumstances for social gathering and discussion; and it enabled them to come into contact with a wider cross-section of the free community.

Importantly, those enslaved knew that their economic culture and its social effects would be the basis of the new life that the anti-slavery movement were speaking about. They felt within the moments of each day the laying of the foundations for their future freedom.

In July 1845 the French government passed reforms to the *Code Noir* that allowed for the abolition of the *ordinaire* and the formal recognition of the provision grounds. This was a first step in the movement towards emancipation. The changes meant that those enslaved could legally own property and had rights to the produce of their labour. These rights could be defended in court. Tomich argued that the new civil code merely regularised what was already a customary practice and gave it the sanction of law.

But there was more. A Royal Ordinance of 5 June 1846 placed those enslaved in a position of having freedom to choose between, on the one hand, a provision ground and free Saturdays, and, on the other, the *ordinaire*. The French government gave the colonial government permission to ensure that enslaved people's choice would be respected and properly implemented. The result was that the *ordinaire* had to be recorded so that it could be scrutinised and the provision grounds had to be of good quality and no more than one km from the plantation.

In places such as Vauclin, Maria, Sainte Anne, Diamant, Anses d'Arlets, Trois Ilets, and parts of Carbet, poor soils and dry weather hampered the effective use of provision grounds. A public debate developed in the colony on this matter involving the colonial administration and the public sector. They urged enslavers to make available to those enslaved the 'ordinaire' in order to produce more food. They were also urged to find creative solutions such as securing better lands for those enslaved in distant parts, and to provide them with better agricultural implements.

Few enslaved persons chose the *ordinaire*. With abolitionists such as Victor Schoelcher being fully supportive of the provision grounds and free Saturday model, this system became linked to all discussions about how best to implement general emancipation of the enslaved.

The 'Little Guineas', then, had produced an economic and social culture that provided the basis of an independent African life. Slavery was abolished in the French colonies in 1848. The 'Little Guineas' were used as part of the rationale for abolition as Africans had

Fig 10.4 *Enslaved men in town*

Barbados

demonstrated their interest in freedom and had put in place part of the economic system for independence.

The experience of those enslaved in Barbados was somewhat different in scale and character. Barbadian workers had no provision grounds. They were fed plantation stocks, which were either imported or locally produced. The overseers allocated to the enslaved imported salted meat and grain grown on the plantation. They received this sometimes on Friday night, but mostly on Sunday morning. Those enslaved possessed only little house spots, generally no more than 25 square yards, on which to root their independent production and marketing activity.

Several visitors to Barbados paid attention to the relationship between the food allowances that the enslaved received and their huckstering. Pinckard notes that enslaved people's diet consists of 'mostly guinea corn, with a small bit of salt meat or salt fish', which served for 'breakfast, dinner and supper'. This diet, he added, was 'for the most part the same throughout the year', though occasionally they received rice, maize, yams, eddoes, and

sweet potatoes. Sometimes those enslaved sold these allocations and used the proceeds to 'buy salt meat or vegetables'. When those enslaved were asked why they preferred to sell or barter their food allocations, Pinckard declared, they would commonly express themselves, 'me no like for have guinea corn always! Massa gib me guinea corn too much – guinea corn today – guinea corn tomorrow – guinea corn every day – me no like him guinea corn – him guinea corn no good for guhyaam'.

In 1808 John Poyer agreed with Pinckard that people in slavery would generally 'barter the crude, unsavoury, substantial allowance of the plantations for more palatable and nutritious food'.

Pinckard, however, recognised that enslaved people did not rely fully on their food rations to create supplies to sell at market. Rather, he observed, 'those who are industrious have little additions of their own, either from vegetables grown on the spot of ground allotted to them, or purchased with money obtained for the selling of a pig, the goat, or other stock raised about their huts in the Negro yard'. He regarded it as 'common for the slave to plant fruit and vegetables, and to raise stocks'. At one hut on the Spendlove estate, Pinckard 'saw a pig, a goat, a young kid, some pigeons, and some chickens, all the property of an individual slave'. He observed the advantages of these activities for both enslaved and enslavers. He thought garden plots and livestock gave those enslaved 'occupation and amusement for their leisure moments', and created 'a degree of interest in the spot'.

Thirty years later Bayley's account of enslaved people's domestic economy was similar to Pinckard's account. He emphasised that they raised poultry and animals, as well as cultivated roots, vegetables and fruits. He described the 'small gardens' attached to huts of those enslaved as 'pretty well cultivated'. For him, 'the slaves have always time' to cultivate their 'yams, tannias, plantains, bananas, sweet potatoes, okras, pineapples, and Indian corn'. To shade their homes from the 'burning rays and scorching heat of the tropic sun', noted Bayley, those enslaved planted a 'luxuriant foliage' of trees that bear 'sweet and pleasant fruits, such as the mango, the Java plum, the breadfruit, the soursop, the sabadilia and the pomegranate'. In 'every garden' could be found 'a hen coop' for some 'half dozen of fowls' and, in many, 'a pigsty', and 'goats tied under the shade of some tree'. Bayley also observed that while the animals were 'grazing or taking a nap' a watchful 'old Negro woman was stationed near' to ensure that 'they were not kidnapped.'

Selling goods was enslaved people's main way of raising the cash they needed to buy other goods. Many produced goods specifically for sale. Sunday was their main market day (until 1826 when it became Saturday), although it was customary for 'respectable overseers and managers' to grant enslaved workers time off during the week when work was not pressing so that they could sell their valuable goods.

The established Anglican Church was never happy with Sunday marketing. In 1725 the catechist at Codrington Plantation informed the Bishop of London, under whose See Barbados fell, 'In this Island the Negroes work all week for their masters, and on the Lord's Day they work and merchandise for themselves; in the latter of which they are assisted, not only by the Jews, but many of those who call themselves Christians.' He said that efforts made by the estate's managers to prevent Sunday trading were unsuccessful, and many insubordinate persons among those enslaved went to their beds 'with very sore backsides unmercifully laid on'. The catechist suggested that the 'force of custom' among enslaved people would inevitably break through 'managerial resolve'. In other words, those enslaved would win in the end.

Fig 10.5 Street vendors

chapter 10 | Surviving enslavement: wealth and health factors

Descriptions of huckstering show the extent to which those enslaved affected the colony's internal economy. In the late 18th century, Dickson reported that people were seen all over the island on Sundays walking several miles to market with 'a few roots, or fruits, or canes, sometimes a fowl or a kid, or a pig from their little spots of ground which have been dignified with the illusive name of gardens.' J A Thome and J H Kimball who witnessed the ending of Barbados slavery in the 19th century, had much to say about the role of the enslaved and free in the internal marketing system of Barbados.

Thome and Kimball were impressed by the picture of these 'busy marketeers', both 'men and women, 'pouring into the highways' at the 'crosspaths leading through the estates'. These plantation hucksters were seen 'strung' all along the road 'moving peaceably forward'. Thome and Kimball described as 'amusing' the huge amount of products those enslaved were transporting, such as 'sweet potatoes, yams, eddoes, Guinea and Indian corn, various fruits and berries, vegetables, nuts, cakes, bundles of fire wood and bundles of sugar canes'.

Enslaved women were in the majority. Thome and Kimball mentioned one woman who had a small black pig doubled up under her arm and two girls, one with 'a brood of chickens, with a nest coop and all, on her head', and another with 'an immense turkey' also on her head. Thome and Kimball were impressed with the 'spectacle' of this march to the Bridgetown market. They were also impressed with the hucksters' commercial organisation, especially the way in which their information network spread the news concerning the start of the market.

The hucksters – enslaved and British

Many urban enslaved persons sold goods for their owners, mainly non-agricultural foodstuffs such as cakes, drinks, and a range of imported goods. According to Bayley, many Bridgetown inhabitants gained a livelihood by sending enslaved persons about the town and suburbs with articles of various kinds for sale. Most of these hucksters were women. They carried 'on their heads, in wooden trays, all sorts of eatables, wearables, jewelry and dry goods'. Bayley also spoke about the social status of free persons who directed enslaved hucksters. Most, he stated, were less fortunate British settlers, however it was also common for members of 'the higher classes of society' to 'endeavour to turn a penny by sending their slaves on such money-making excursions'. These enslaved hucksters sold exotic items such as 'pickles and preserves, oil, noyau (a skin cream), anisette, eau-de-cologne, toys, ribbons, handkerchiefs, and other little knick-knacks'.

Most of these items were imported from the neighbouring French island of Martinique.

Poor Europeans lived on the outskirts of plantation society. They developed the most important contacts with enslaved hucksters. From the 17th century onwards, many of the women labourers, most of whom previously were indentured servants and their descendants, made a living by selling home-grown vegetables and poultry in the urban market. They were largely Irish Catholics and the predominantly English Protestant community discriminated against them. The Catholic women formed their own communities in backcountry areas of the parishes of St Lucy, St John, St Andrew, St Joseph, and St Philip. Here they cultivated crops as subsistence peasants on a variety of rocky, wet and sandy, non-sugar lands. Descriptions of their huckstering activity were very similar to those of enslaved people.

Dickson studied the poor European settlers closely and offered a detailed account of their huckstering culture. He said that labouring Europeans, both men and women, 'till the ground without any assistance from Negroes'. The 'women often walk many miles loaded with the produce of their little spots, which they exchange in the towns for such European goods as they can afford to purchase'. Their gardens were generally larger than those used by enslaved persons and so was the amount of commodities they traded. But despite the African people's disadvantage, they still offered their British hucksters stiff competition, especially at the Sunday markets.

The relationship between those enslaved and British hucksters was complex. Both Dickson and Pinckard commented that there were similarities in their marketing patterns and customs. White women hucksters were typically seen carrying baskets on their heads and children strapped to the hip in a typical African manner. This suggests some degree of cultural transfer between the African and British hucksters. Dickson stated that some British hucksters owned small stores in the towns and most of them depended upon the exchange of goods with Africans. These hucksters, he said, 'make a practice of buying stolen goods from the Negroes, whom they encourage to plunder their owners of everything that is portable'.

Dickson made a strong moral plea for the protection of enslaved hucksters in their unequal relationship with British hucksters. Until 1826 enslaved persons had no legal right to own property, and they suffered frequent injustices in their dealings with the British. Many British hucksters, Dickson stated, 'depend for a subsistence on robbing the slaves' by taking their goods 'at their own price' or simply 'by seizing and illegally converting to their own use, articles of greater value', which the 'poor things may be carrying to market'.

Laws trying to undermine huckstering by those enslaved

At first legislators thought that it was possible to stop the enslaved from going 'house to house' to sell their 'goods and wares'. The 1688 Slave Code, for instance, said that Justices of the Peace must identify English hucksters and warn them against doing business with enslaved hucksters. The law also empowered Justices to take legal action against English hucksters who disobeyed their orders.

In 1694, an assemblyman who considered the 1688 Slave Code insufficient, introduced two bills designed to remove enslaved hucksters from the internal market economy. The first bill prohibited 'the sale of goods to Negroes' and the second prohibited 'the employment of Negroes in selling'.

The bills never became law but persistent complaints from small-scale English cash-crop producers, urban shopkeepers, and other competitors of enslaved people kept the subject at the forefront of discussion concerning the 'governing' of those enslaved. In 1708 the first of many 18th century laws was finally passed which tried to undermine African huckstering. This 1708 law tackled every aspect of African huckstering. The preamble to the Act linked huckstering to insubordination and criminality among the enslaved. It stated that 'sundry persons do daily send their Negroes and other slaves to the several towns in this island to sell and dispose of all sorts of quick stock, corn, fruit, and pulse, and other things' with the result that the slaves 'traffick among themselves, and buy, receive and dispose of all sorts of stolen goods'. So the 1708 law prevented any English person from sending or employing a slave to sell, barter, or dispose 'of any goods, wares, merchandise, stocks, poultry, corn, fruit, roots, or other effects, or things whatsoever'.

Any offending English person found guilty could be fined £5, while enslaved persons who were convicted for selling or bartering could receive 'one and twenty stripes on his or her bare back upon proof thereof made by any person'. Hucksters were allowed to sell stocks to their owners, overseers and managers, and 'milk, horse meat or firewood' to any person. But this concession was also granted on terms that dehumanised the huckster and symbolised criminality because the huckster had to wear 'a metalled collar' locked about his or her neck or legs. The collar had to display the master's and maker's name and place of residence.

In 1733 the island's Assembly passed a new law to strengthen and expand the 1708 Act. This time the law listed the foodstuffs and other items that hucksters were allowed to sell. It also enlarged the range of commodities

Fig 10.6 Enslaved woman wearing metal neck-collar

that the enslaved workers could not trade, either on their own or for their owners. This law was undoubtedly a response to the growing number of enslaved hucksters in the years after 1708. It suggests that the government saw hucksters as a threat to the efficient control of the enslaved and a threat to its own dominance in the economy. The list of commodities that constables and market clerks were empowered to confiscate from enslaved hucksters now included sugar cane, 'whole or in pieces, syrup, molasses, cotton, ginger, copper, pewter, brass, tin, corn and grain'. The law was particularly concerned for the welfare of poor European settlers and small planters as their profits were badly affected by intense competition from the enslaved. To protect these persons, the Act made it unlawful for the enslaved to plant crops for the use of anyone but their enslavers. Cotton and ginger were singled out and any enslaved person found selling these two crops could be charged for selling 'stolen goods'. In addition, Europeans who bought these items from enslaved hucksters could be prosecuted for receiving stolen goods. The 1733 Act was amended in 1749, making it illegal for enslaved people to assemble 'together at huckster shops' for any reason.

chapter 10 | *Surviving enslavement: wealth and health factors*

Still those enslaved refused to obey these provisions and so they were ineffective. For example, in 1741 the manager of Codrington Plantation reported on the attitudes of his human chattel towards these laws. He said that nothing short of 'locking them up' could keep the Africans away from the markets and such an action would probably result in a riot.

So in spite of these laws enslaved persons continued to take an active role in the internal marketing system. In 1773 the legislature came under pressure from Bridgetown merchants who claimed that enslaved and British hucksters posed unfair competition for their businesses and was a public nuisance on account of the noise and litter those enslaved created.

Established Bridgetown merchants remained dissatisfied with the measures against enslaved hucksters and lobbied for still tougher measures. In 1779 a new law aimed to end the 'traffick carried on by slaves' and limit the number of free hucksters – British, mixed-race, and African. For the first time British hucksters were subject to official regulation and were placed in the same category as free mixed-race and free Africans. All free hucksters now had to get a trade licence from the treasurer at an annual cost of £10, in addition to a processing fee of 25 shillings. This levy, which was also a way of earning income for the government, tried to get rid of minor hucksters.

By the beginning of the 19th century the huckster market was an established institution within the colony. Visitors described it as colourful, exciting and attractive. In 1826 the 'Sunday and Marriage Act', which was aimed at speeding up the conversion of the enslaved to Christianity, finally outlawed Sunday markets. Saturday became the major market day until the present time.

After slavery was abolished hucksters continued to dominate the food provision market, although plantations also sometimes sold food directly to the public. As in other Caribbean colonies, former enslaved persons took to other types of work, but huckstering remained an attractive occupation. It was an economic niche which they had identified and protected during slavery. In freedom it became the foundation upon which many households survived.

2 The enslaved survived slavery

The very act of surviving enslavement was a major triumph for Africans. Survival was a very difficult task especially in a system that was designed to get the maximum labour out of a short period of life from adults,

and that considered the aged and the youth as liabilities. For most of the slavery period in the Caribbean the economic policy of enslavers was clear. It was cheaper and more economical to buy Africans from the ships than to bear the cost of locally 'breeding and rearing' the enslaved. The price of imported enslaved persons ranged from £16 to £70 between 1650 and 1800, at the height of the slave economy. Enslavers thought this was reasonable in relation to the profits they got from their businesses.

As a result of this labour policy enslavers were not that interested in a female labour force. They did not want women to reproduce and so they discouraged women from child-rearing by refusing to provide them with pre-natal and post-natal care. Women worked in the field and gave birth when the time came. In a very short time they were back at work with infants on their backs. There are several reports of enslaved women being whipped for stopping work to nurse their babies. Infant death rates were therefore very high, and many women died in childbirth or shortly thereafter.

Fig 10.7 *Enslaved woman forced to stop breastfeeding and return to the fields*

The slave system, then, for most of the period was not designed to encourage child-rearing or survival into old age. Children, the aged, and the infirm, were seen as a cost to the plantations, which must be removed. However, after the 1780s the price of enslaved Africans began to rise significantly. In the 1790s the sugar boom collapsed. Both of these things increased the cost of production in the British Caribbean. At that point the enslavers turned their attention to the issue of 'breeding locally a slave force'.

As a result of these policies, the most striking feature of the enslaved African population in the Caribbean was that it did not grow by natural means. It declined naturally, and it was sustained by huge numbers of new imported Africans. The enslaved population in the southern American states grew naturally owing to the fact that their work routine was not as physically destructive and to the fact the enslavers promoted family life among the enslaved. More Africans died than were born, and they died at a faster rate than people were born. This meant that Africans were driven onto a genocidal path. Without new Africans they would have died out completely.

Historians have acknowledged that the genocidal conditions in which Africans lived in the Caribbean shows that their slavery experience was the most brutal and severe in the Americas.

So, surviving slavery was a significant achievement by those enslaved. There was a clear link between nutritional poverty and enslaved people being vulnerable to disease. Caribbean enslaved workers were malnourished and overworked. The diets they received were inadequate for good health and could not help them keep even reasonable health, given the hard labour they were expected to perform. Enslavers tried to cut their costs by working their human chattel to the maximum with the bare minimum food supply. Their management policy was based on the idea that 10 good years from an enslaved person who was fed, clothed and housed at the minimum subsistence cost was good business. The food supplied to those enslaved was just sufficient to keep them alive. The fact that they could work up to 18 hours per day, sometimes seven days a week, for ten years was a miracle which shows the extraordinary capacity of humans to rise above adversity.

Furthermore, the quality of the food supplied was nutritionally very poor which made them vulnerable to a number of diseases that plagued only those enslaved. They lacked sufficient calories, calcium, vitamin A and B and fats in their diets – all these were important to perform and survive the work regime expected of them. These nutritional deficiencies were associated with the prevalence of what became known as 'Negro diseases' that debilitated and killed Africans, adults and children, with an alarming frequency on the plantations and in towns.

The records of enslavers and medical practitioners are filled with descriptions of these 'Negro diseases' such as 'yaws', 'lock-jaw', or neonatal tetanus, 'sore eyes', dropsy, and beri beri, or dirt eating. Lock-jaw was a major killer of infants. Beri-beri did not spare adults who ate dirt in search of a mineral intake. Beri-beri and dropsy were seen as the primary killers of Africans in Puerto Rico, Cuba and Jamaica. These diseases were confined exclusively to Africans and were the result of chronic malnutrition. In Jamaica these diseases were described as common upon almost every plantation and accounted for about 50 per cent of all deaths.

To prevent enslaved people from eating dirt, enslavers would place a metal gag over their faces covering their mouths. Slave owners did not understand that the enslaved had a nutritional deficiency disease. They thought that dirt eating was part of an attempt to commit suicide or to get sick so as to avoid work. Some African people thought that the disease was part of an obeah or voodoo spell cast on them. But it was just a disease that created addiction to dirt as a mineral supplement. The symptoms were quite common; the enslaved appeared 'languid and listless', 'short of breath', 'bloated with appetite', 'palpitations of the head', weak and giddy. Children appeared 'weak and rickety', and severely infested with hookworm. Often the hookworm was confused with what was described as 'dry belly-ache' which caused enormous intestinal pain, convulsions and epileptic seizures.

European doctors wrote that enslaved Africans were dying at a shocking rate from diseases. In Jamaica, on the Worthy Park Estate, between 1811 and 1834, dropsy and dirt eating accounted for 16 per cent of the 222 deaths. Between 1817 and 1830, dropsy claimed about 15 per cent of most Africans on plantations in Jamaica. Between 1796 and 1825 in Barbados on the Newton Plantation 'dropsy', 'consumption', 'fits', and 'dirt eating' accounted for about 14 per cent of the more than 300 deaths.

At Newton Plantation the record of infant deaths in the short period, between 1744 and 1748, shows the sugar plantation as a 'killing field' for the enslaved Africans:

In 1744 Betty Occo miscarried, but Little Murriah and another Betty successfully gave birth to two sons; Little Murriah's Drummer lived past 1748, but Betty's child died of 'fits' on his tenth day of life. In 1745 Joan's daughter was born on 7 Feb. and died on 12 May; Occo's daughter began life on 13 Feb. and died on 13 July; Molly's boy was born on 7 July and died on 14 July; Bennebah's daughter lived only from 3 October to 10 October; Arnote's son, Cudgoe, lived only to 1748 and Moll's baby daughter, Moroat, lived only to 1748. Mercy's daughter, Mary, was the only one of the seven youngsters born in 1745 who survived at least three years. One of the three children born in 1746 died in the same year. The two children born in 1747 outlived their second years, and six of the seven babies born in 1748 lived past 31 December of that year. Thus ten of the twenty-two children born in the years from 1744 to 1748 died before the close of the period.

Most of these children would have died of neonatal tetanus, beri-beri and a range of nutritionally related diseases that were an endemic feature of enslavement in the Caribbean.

The general record of disease and death tells us about an enslaved people who were ravished by nature and terrorised by management. We know the (crude) rate of decline among them. In Barbados, the annual rate of decline among those enslaved was 4.1 per cent between 1676 and 1700; 4.9 per cent between 1701 and 1725, and 3.6 per cent between 1726 and 1750. In Jamaica for the same periods it was 3.1 per cent, 3.7 per cent, and 3.5 per cent respectively. The data from Worthy Park estate in Jamaica show that during the sugar boom of the 1790s the death rate rose from 3.0 per cent to 5.7 per cent, and that in the last two decades of slavery it settled at about 2.6 per cent. At the same time the birth rate was a mere 2.3 per cent – a natural decrease of 0.27 per cent in other words, or approximately six enslaved persons were born every five years out of a population of about 500.

Overwork, cruelty, and the loss of life because of frequent rebellions, all contributed to the natural decline. Only in Barbados did Africans achieve a natural growth rate by 1800. This is mainly because there was a good balance of males and females for most of the 18th century. This was unique. The shortage of females in most societies meant there could be little female fertility in an environment where women were not encouraged to reproduce most of the time. All other Africans suffered a natural decline. Epidemics of small pox and measles from time to time devastated the African population. Low birth rate and high infant death rate constituted a formula for natural decline.

To sum up

Populations, unless subject to catastrophic external forces, such as famine and disease, tend to grow naturally. Birth rates tend to exceed death rates, and growth becomes a natural occurrence. In the Caribbean the enslaved population did not grow naturally. Indeed, for most of the period, in most colonies, decline was the norm. Societies came to depend upon importation to maintain population levels. Without the transatlantic trade in Africans the enslaved population would have declined making the economy non-viable.

But the Africans had an interest in suppressing their fertility, birth rates and reproductive capacity. Enslavers did not always understand this; some explained the weak growth performance in terms of disease, resistance, overwork and inadequate nutrition. Others spoke of the Africans' refusal to reproduce as part of their opposition to enslavement.

Revision questions

1 Why was the huckstering activity of enslaved Africans considered an act of resistance?
2 Compare and contrast the ways in which those enslaved in the English and the French Caribbean experienced involvement as petty traders.
3 Which diseases took the greatest toll on African life?
4 What was the relationship between malnutrition among enslaved Africans and their mortality?
5 Did enslavers take measures to reduce the death rates and increase the birth rates among enslaved people?
6 a Why were provision grounds allocated to enslaved peoples?
  b How did the provision grounds benefit those enslaved economically and socially?

Chapter 11

Revolt and marronage

'He who fights and runs away, lives to fight another day.'
(Bob Marley)

Every slave system was politically unstable. Everywhere those enslaved revolted and anti-slavery conflict was extremely common. From Canada in the north to Argentina in the south, the story of anti-slavery rebellion is a story of people demanding their democratic civil rights and freedom. This is the contribution Africans made to the struggle for human rights and democratic freedom in the Americas.

By demanding freedom in all the colonies, enslaved Africans supported the view of Enlightenment thinkers in Europe. Everywhere the words 'freedom' and 'liberty' were associated with the protest of Africans. They gave these political ideas real social meaning.

In this chapter we will study the resistance of enslaved people in Caribbean history. We will concentrate on marronage. In the next chapter we will look at armed revolt.

In this chapter we will learn about:
1. African anti-slavery politics
2. Marronage as resistance

1 African anti-slavery politics

African anti-slavery politics has received much attention in recent years. Historians have studied and compared hundreds of rebellions. Their research has focused on the following:

a. The African/Creole origins of the leaders
b. The social and political ideas used in the rebellions
c. Organisation and planning of the rebellions
d. Successes and failures of the rebellions
e. General and specific impact of the rebellions
f. The Haitian revolution and Maroon communities
g. Gender and resistance.

Historians have identified three stages of resistance among the enslaved in Caribbean history. The first stage (1500-1750) relates to the experience of early plantations. The second stage (1750-1800) concerns the developed plantation society. The third stage (1804-1838) relates to the age of abolition and emancipation debates in European parliaments and is linked to the impact of the Haitian revolution.

Within these three general stages, historians have described three types of resistance. First, there were acts of day-to-day resistance. These were generally not designed to overthrow the slave system but to make it less efficient so as to quicken its eventual demise. Second, there were a large number of plots that were discovered by enslavers. Monica Schuler has shown that in these revolts certain ethnic groups, for example the Akan, dominated the leadership. The Fon and neighbouring groups from Dahomey were dominant in the Haitian Revolution. In some 19th century revolts, the Hausa from Northern Nigeria, who followed Islam, were prominent. In fact, we have underestimated the role of Muslim Africans in Caribbean history, a gap that historian Sultana Afroz is working hard to correct. Third, there were successful wars – from long-term marronage as in Jamaica and Suriname to the Haitian revolution.

Historians have researched extensively the highly planned rebellions as these are considered to be the most advanced anti-slavery acts. According to Robert Dirks, there are references to about 70 planned rebellions of those enslaved in the English colonies between 1649 and 1833. Of this total, Dirks states that about 32 rebellions were not fully implemented because they were discovered by the enslavers, and some existed only in the enslaver's imagination. Michael Craton lists about 75 acts of recorded rebellion between 1638-1837, some of which were actual rebellions and some did not take place.

Chronology of Resistance, 1638 – 1837

Numbers of enslaved people involved:
A = dozens; B = hundreds; C = thousands; D = many thousands

PROVIDENCE

1638	B	Christmas. General slave rebellion.

BARBADOS

1649	A	Servile revolt reported by Ligon, possibly involving slaves as well as white servants.
1675	B	June. Coromantee plot led by Tony and Cuffee.
1683	A	November. Plot involving mainly African slaves.
1686	B	February. Plot involving mainly African slaves.
1692	C	October. Afro-creole plot, led by Ben, Sambo, and others.
1701	B	November. Afro-creole plot.
1816	D	Easter. Bussa's rebellion, centered on St. Phillip's parish.

BERMUDA

1656	A	November. Plot led by Black Tom and Cabilecto.
1673	B	Christmas. Plot led by Robin and others.
1720 – 1731	A	"Poisoning Plots," including the one allegedly directed by Sarah Bassett.
1761	B	October. Island-wide plot led by Mingo and others.

JAMAICA

1655 –1670	B	Resistance by "Spanish negroes" Lubolo, de Serras, and others.
1673	B	Revolt of Coromantee slaves, Lobby's estate, St. Ann's parish.
1676	B	Large-scale running away, St. Mary's parish.
1678	B	Revolt on Duck's estate, St. Catherine's parish.
1685	B	July. Revolt on Grey's estate, Guannaboa Vale.
1690	B	July. Revolt centered on Sutton's estate, Clarendon parish, led by Cudjoe the elder.
1730 – 1740	C	First Maroon War, involving Cudjoe the younger, Nanny, and many other leaders.

1742	A	Christmas. Coromantee plot, St. James's parish.
1745	B	New Year. Plot, mainly by African slaves, St. David's parish.
1760	D	Tacky's revolt, dominated by Coromantee slaves, originating in St. Mary's parish at Easter but spreading widely through island around Whitsun.
1765	A	November. Coromantee uprising, St. Mary's parish, led by Blackwall.
1766	C	Coromantee uprising, Westmorland parish.
1776	C	July. Afro-creole plot, Hanover parish, led by Sam, Charles, Caesar, and others.
1791 – 1792	B	Island-wide slave unrest after news from Haiti.
1795 – 1796	B	July – March. Second Maroon War in Trelawny and St. James's parishes.
1806	A	Plot in St. George's parish.
1808	B	Mutiny of the Second West India Regiment and plot in Kingston.
1815	B	Christmas. Ibo-led plot, St. Elizabeth's parish.
1819	B	Epidemic of running away throughout the island.
1823 – 1824	C	Widespread plots and unrest, especially in Hanover parish, where it was popularly called the "Argyle War."
1828	A	Expedition against a troublesome band of runaways behind Dromilly estate, Trelawny parish.
1831 – 1832	D	Christmas. "Baptist War" in western Jamaica, led by Samuel Sharpe and others.

ANTIGUA

1685 – 1700	B	Widespread running away and maroon activity.
1701	A	Christmas. Revolt by Coromantees, Greencastle estate.
1729	A	Christmas. Plot centred on Crump's slaves.
1735 – 1736	C	October. Island-wide Afro-creole plot, led by Tackey and Tomboy.
1831	C	Widespread unrest and arson after banning of the Sunday markets.

ST. KITTS

| 1690 | B | Slave uprising in conjunction with French invasion. |
| 1778 | B | Easter. Abortive Afro-creole plot. |

| 1835 | C | Widespread unrest over apprenticeship. |

GUYANA

1763	C	Cuffee's rebellion in Dutch Berbice (preceded by slave revolts in 1733, 1749, 1752, 1762).
1795	C	Slave revolt in Dutch Demerara, in conjunction with maroons.
1823	D	August. Rebellion on East Coast, Demerara, led by Quamina, Jack Gladstone, and many others.

BAHAMAS

1734	B	September. General slave plot revealed by Governor Fitzwilliam.
1787	A	Armed runaways lurking in Blue Hills, New Providence.
1830	A	June. Pompey's revolt, Exuma Island.
1832 – 1834	B	Widespread unrest in Exuma, Eleuthera, Cat Island.

BELIZE

1765	A	September. Revolt of Cooke's slaves from Jamaica.
1768	A	July. Revolt on New River.
1773	B	Easter. Revolt on Belize River.
1813	B	Disturbance on New River.
1820	B	Easter. Revolt on New River, led by Will and Sharper.

GRENADA

| 1765 | B | Slave revolt followed by widespread maroon activity. |
| 1795-1797 | D | Fèdons rebellion, involving majority of islands slaves. |

ST. VINCENT

| 1769-1773 | C | First Carib War, with Black Caribs led by Chatoyer. |
| 1795-1796 | C | Second Carib War, under leadership of Chatoyer and Duvallè. |

TOBAGO

1770	A	November. Revolt at Courland Bay, led by Sandy.
1771	A	June. Revolt at Bloody Bay.
1774	A	March. Reevolt at Queen's Bay.
1801	B	Christmas. Afro-creole plot, centered on western half of island.
1807	B	December. Proto-peasant unrest, with march on Government House.

DOMINICA

1785-1790	C	First Maroon War, under leadership of Balla, Pharcell, and others.
1791	B	New Year. Revolt of windward slaves.
1795	B	May. Colihaut uprising, involving some slaves.
1802	B	April. "Black Man" mutiny of the Eight West India Regiment.
1809-1814	C	Second Maroon War, led by Quashie, Apollo, Jacko, and others.

TORTOLA

1790	B	May. Revolt on Pickering's estate.
1823	B	Second Pickering slaves' revolt.
1830	B	April. Revolt of Lettsome slaves.
1831	B	September. Islandwide slave plot led by Jacob Kierney and others.

ST. LUCIA

1796-1797	C	Brigands' War, involving many slaves.

TRINIDAD

1805	B	Christmas. Plot among francophone slaves around Careenage and Maraval.
1837	B	Daaga's mutiny in the First West India Regiment.

SOURCE: Michael Craton, *Testing the chains: Resistance to slavery in the British West Indies*

This record of resistance tells us that there was hardly a generation of enslaved persons in the region that did not confront their enslavers with arms in pursuit of their freedom. So we can see the relations between the enslaved and enslavers as an ongoing psychological war with occasional bloody battles.

Some enslaved persons knew about the anti-slavery ideas and strategies that were being lobbied for in metropolitan Europe, whether they were in St Domingue (1790s), Barbados (1816) or Jamaica (1831). There is evidence to suggest that enslaved persons saw their anti-slavery actions as connected to these European anti-slavery ideas and movements.

Some 400,000 Africans gained freedom in St Domingue through revolution. This shows that more enslaved persons freed themselves than were freed in any single colony by a European parliament. To this list we must also add the many Maroons who lived in Caribbean mountains and forests as self-liberated persons.

Eric Williams suggested that when metropolitan anti-slavery lobbyists intensified their campaign in the late 18th century, so did those enslaved of the Caribbean. By 1833, he said, 'the alternatives were clear', emancipation from above or emancipation from below, but emancipation.

By 1832 the anti-slavery activists demonstrated that the enslavers could rule only through extreme repression. But European parliaments were not prepared to pay the economic or political costs of this repression. So they tried to resolve the explosive situation by passing emancipation laws.

The writings of Richard Hart on anti-slavery rebellion in Jamaica illustrate that there was an unrelenting determination for freedom among Africans. Gordon Lewis says that Caribbean enslaved persons made a huge intellectual contribution to the philosophy of freedom. He found a grand Caribbean anti-slavery tradition whose actors were not only Africans and mixed-race, but also native Caribbean and a few Creole Europeans. He does not take away from the anti-slavery achievements of Europeans, such as Wilberforce, Clarkson, Buxton and Schoelcher, but he does suggest that Toussaint and Dessalines, Nanny of the Maroons, Nanny Grigg, Sam Sharpe, Tackey, Bussa, and other leaders among those enslaved, seemed more 'hell-bent' than the Europeans on destroying Caribbean slavery.

Haiti emerged regionally and internationally as the main symbol of freedom. According to David Geggus, the major European abolitionist did not openly approve of violent self-liberation by enslaved Africans. Wilberforce thought that the enslaved Africans in Haiti were still not ready for freedom and condemned what he termed the 'cruel' and 'dreadful' revolt.

Thomas Clarkson, however, spoke of Haiti as representing the 'unalterable Rights of Men' to freedom. For him the Haitians revolted against tyranny, and – 'acting like men', – fulfilled the most honourable destiny of humankind.

In 1802 the English poet William Wordsworth celebrated the value of Toussaint to humankind's search for liberty with his sonnet, 'To Toussaint L'Ouverture'

> *Though fallen thyself, never to rise again,*
> *Live and take comfort. Thou has left behind*
> *Powers that will work for thee; air, earth, and skies;*
> *There's not a breathing of the common wind*
> *That will forget thee; thou hast great allies;*
> *Thy friends are exultations, agonies*
> *And love, and man's unconquerable mind.*

But Wordsworth, like Toussaint, did not win popular support in Europe for his anti-slavery stance. English abolitionists rejected the revolutionary approach to freedom by the enslaved. That is, they did not support

Fig 11.1 The English poet Wordsworth

protests by the enslaved who tried to overthrow the elite class. They wished that the enslaved could be legally free and to some extent recognised as social equals to Europeans. But they argued that it was to the advantage of Africans that they were economically dependent and politically subordinate to Europeans.

So, from a Caribbean perspective, we should not see the struggle for freedom of enslaved people as being secondary to the laws around emancipation that were being debated in the European parliaments. The European actions were part of the final episode in what was an already very long struggle for freedom. But that struggle was pushed forward by its greatest sufferers – those enslaved. It was only in Haiti that the enslaved people overthrew the slave regime but, those enslaved throughout the region consistently rebelled in order to gain freedom.

2 Marronage as resistance

Wherever slavery existed so did marronage. The environmental conditions influenced whether enslaved persons fleeing bondage formed ongoing and sustainable 'Maroon societies'.

In some islands of the Eastern Caribbean the terrain was flat with no forest or mountain. In these places, such as the Virgin Islands, Barbados, and on Antigua, more rebels fled to freedom by sea seeking safety in other islands. These rebels have been described as 'maritime Maroons'.

In colonies with mountainous and forested environments, runaways could:

a.   defend themselves against the forces sent to get them back; or

b.   form large communities that were self-sustainable. There were many Maroon communities in the larger colonies such as Cuba, Jamaica, St Domingue, Puerto Rico, as well as in the mainland colonies of the Guianas and Honduras. Of all the Maroon societies of the Caribbean, and indeed the Americas, those of Jamaica and Suriname have been written about the most. The process of marronage in Jamaica began with the Taino who fled into the mountains as part of a strategy to resist Spanish colonialism. In the mountains the Taino were accompanied by Africans, who were also seeking freedom. The Blue Mountains, rising to 7,400 feet with impenetrable 'cockpits' became home to some of these Maroons. ('Cockpits' was the term used to describe parts of mountain ranges that were difficult to access and identify.)

Maroons

The process of flight from the scene of slavery was not always understood by those enslaved as part of a struggle against slavery. Sometimes the objective was to escape from slavery for a short while with the intention to return. This often happened when enslaved people wanted to avoid punishment, wished to visit persons some distance away and was refused permission, or were generally disturbed by developments in their personal lives.

There were many reasons, therefore, why those enslaved would wish some temporary respite from the plantation. When this option was chosen runaways became fugitives. They lived on other plantations or in spaces that offered hiding facilities. In most cases they were protected by friends and family. Sometimes they fled to the towns and lived in the underworld that offered cover and assistance. This type of activity has been described by historians as *petit-marronage*.

When, however, enslaved people fled to the wilderness, mountains and forests with no intention of returning, but to develop an anti-slavery posture and lifestyle, they were clearly engaged in something far more subversive. At this level they had a number of choices. They 'could go it' alone, form small bands that survived as mobile units, or participate in the creation of large, settled Maroon communities. This kind of activity has been described as *grand marronage*.

Dominica

Sometimes the environment determined what was possible and how effective options were. The Maroons of Dominica constitute a case in point. The mountainous terrain of the island allowed the Maroons much scope to

Fig 11.2 *Maroons in ambush*

move around in small fighting units, with no intention of returning to the terms of enslavement.

During the 18th century the Maroons took up an oppositional military stance against the enslavers but tried to create a political environment that allowed them to access the goods and services available on the plantations and in the towns. In this regard they were aware of how the Kalinago sought to establish an intermediary position that secured their freedom but enabled them to move about relatively unmolested.

But the fact of the matter was that the island was not large enough to enable them adequate social distance and independence from slave-based reality. Also, the enslaved African population was not substantial enough to supply frequent recruits in order to sustain a large-scale Maroon community. The Dominica Maroons nonetheless fought bravely to protect their freedom. They were not defeated until 1815 after a major military expedition against them by the English in what was described as 'the second Maroon war'.

Belize

The nature of regional politics was as important as the environment in determining the outcomes of these anti-slavery activities. The case of Belize is also instructive as it is a mainland country that offered enslaved people the best possible circumstances to form successful Maroon communities. Initially the colony was a part of the Spanish empire located as it is on the Yucatán peninsula. But it was a backwater both in terms of Spanish settlement and imperial economic interests. It was therefore a largely neglected place within the empire. In the 1620s the British, aware of the substantial forest resources and finding a market for mahogany in Europe, as

Fig 11.3 *African Caribs sign Treaty with British Military*

well as for logwood in other colonies, began settlement of the area. The Spanish harassed these settlers and their enslaved lumberjacks, but did not displace them. Eventually, in 1783 the Spanish ceded the colony to the British.

The entire project of 'logging and slavery' was not one that could be easily policed. The English settlers were scattered throughout the forest with enslaved lumberjacks that outnumbered them. It was a relatively easy matter to escape deeper into the forest, establish Maroon bands, and attack the slavers strategically.

The Maroon bands were fed with new members from both the Spanish and English settlements. This gave them more comprehensive information about European activities in the areas. Eventually, the Spanish, in an attempt to undermine the English settlement offered freedom to all Africans that fled across the border at the Rio Hondo to join Spanish settlements. It was an expensive and time-consuming exercise to track down and retrieve these runaways. Native people were sometimes paid as trackers to locate Maroon camps, but this method was unreliable. The English loggers themselves did not have the wealth to fund these retrieval operations.

The further evolution of nationalist politics in the Spanish colonies, driven by Simon Bolívar's independence movement, offered these Maroons alternative ways of looking at their future. When the new republics that emerged from Spanish colonies chose to abolish slavery in 1821, the enslaved community in British Belize saw an excellent opportunity to take flights to a different kind of freedom. They had this choice: they could continue to hide in the forests and endure the very precarious freedom or take flight to the Spanish republics where slavery was abolished.

For many runaways, the new republic offered the better chance to have the kind of life they found attractive. Not all Maroons wished to live as life-long soldiers or in a nomadic state. Many persons wanted to participate in the processes associated with building a new nation, and to see their children benefit from citizenship and nationhood. As a result, thousands who were engaged in Maroon activities in the forest, chose to cross the border into Guatemala to become free of the threat of capture and re-enslavement. This process effectively undermined the development of Maroon societies in British Belize.

Cuba

From the 1520s, when the Spanish settlement in Cuba began to import enslaved Africans, the process of rebellion and flight was recorded. Thousands of Maroons occupied the Cuban hills and offered enslaved Africans an alternative form of life. This kind of social existence had been long established by the Taino who at times harboured and assisted the runaway Africans in their anti-slavery struggle. Many Maroon communities were large enough to be recognised as complete societies. These were known as *palenques*. A recent study by Gabino De la Rosa Corzo has mapped the spaces occupied by 62 *palenques* in Cuba. These were located on the low mountain ranges west of Havana, in the highlands of Matanzas, and in the hills of the Sierra Maestra.

To be sustained, the *palenques* had to be well hidden and able to mount an adequate defense. Many of them were largely male communities engaged in strikes against Spanish settlements, not prepared for settled organised community life. A few, however, evolved as settled communities with their own internal government, farming systems and social organisation.

The Spanish settlers did all they could to eradicate the *palenques*. They did not succeed and through the 18th century, *palenques* became an even more prominent feature of the Cuban colonial landscape. They flourished during the sugar boom of the early 19th century because the plantations had now been flooded with enslaved Africans who saw in them opportunities for freedom.

The Guianas/Suriname

The Guianas, like Belize, offered excellent opportunities for enslaved people to take flight and engage in the formation of Maroon communities. The existence of a massive hinterland dominated by large rivers, an unknown rainforest and intimidating mountain ranges seemed ideal circumstances for Africans to keep their distance and maintain effective independence.

When the Dutch took over the colony from the English in 1667, they found that Maroon bands were already in existence. Some had settled near Para Creek, a tributary of the massive Suriname River, and were called the 'Condi' people. There were several hundreds of them and Chief Jermes, who was determined to drive the English enslavers out of the area, led them.

The first Dutch Governor, Van Sommelsdijk, tried to succeed where the English had failed and opened peace talks with the Condi. Negotiations were settled in 1684 and the Condi and the Dutch settled into respecting their own spaces for over 50 years.

As the colony grew in size and importance as a sugar zone, both the Dutch and the enslaved African population rapidly increased. This development placed considerable stress on the political situation. More enslaved Africans fled into the interior to secure their freedom and formed new Maroon communities. The Dutch enslavers believed that the Maroon threat was now unbearable.

In the 1770s the English, French and Dutch began investing more heavily in sugar plantations on the coastal

Fig 11.4 'Bush Negroes' (Maroons), Suriname

plains of the Guianas. They all imported thousands of enslaved Africans to make this possible. Their documents show that the Maroon communities in the interior also began to grow almost in proportion to the size of the coastal settlement. The English, many of them planters from Barbados, where they were negotiating with the Kalinago and Maroon Africans in the neighbouring Windward Islands, developed a counter strategy to wipe them out.

The plan involved paying indigenes to track them and bring them back to the plantations, dead or alive. The Dutch West India Company that owned most of the coastal plantations paid both indigenes and free Africans to hunt Maroons. The company paid 300 guilders for every right hand of a dead Maroon.

The French were faced with a stronger challenge from the Maroons. These Maroons had taken over the region known as Lead Mountain, located to the west of the plantation settlement at Cayenne. So the French called in the imperial troops.

The history of the Maroons in Suriname, or Dutch Guiana, located between the French and English colonies, presents a fascinating case in the study of Maroon anti-slavery politics. Between the 1670s and 1740, the Dutch had transformed the area into a large exporter of sugar using the labour of some 60,000 enslaved Africans.

In this period, Maroon societies became so firmly established that the colony had acquired a reputation for having the highest death rate among those enslaved as well as the largest Maroon communities in the Americas. By 1740 the two largest groups of Maroons in Suriname were

now the Saramaka, who settled along the interior of the Saramacca River, and the Djuka, who occupied a place called Djuka Creek in the Marowwne River area. Another smaller but rapidly growing group was the Matuaris. Their villages were located deep in the forest that housed these rivers, but could not be seen by persons who navigated them.

They were larger than any Maroon societies in the Caribbean. Sylvia de Groot, a leading scholar of these Maroon societies, has estimated that in 1738 there were at least 6,000 Maroons in Suriname. Each of these large Maroon communities were made up of smaller groups known as 'lo'. The 'lo' was given a name to reflect the plantations from which the majority of Africans had escaped. They formed distinct settlements within the wider community. According to de Groot:

> Groups of people with the same background and interests clustered together and gradually formed matrilineal clans and extended families which claimed the same ancestors. Religion was a uniting force and an important source of strength. Priests therefore played their role in power struggles and decision-making.

They were expert farmers and fishermen, in very much the same traditions of ancestral Africa, though they benefited also from the agricultural science of the local indigenes. Their main food crops were manioc, potatoes, rice, corn, bananas, beans, sugar cane, and a wide variety of fruit and vegetables. They developed a system of farming that made them independent of the plantations.

Fig 11.5 Abeng player – the instrument was used by the Maroons to send messages

Maroon communities were so effective in defending their alternative forms of living for Africans, that Europeans were forced to formally recognise them and engage in diplomatic relations that led to the signing of peace treaties in the 1760s.

These treaties called for the Maroons to become allies of the Dutch in returning all new runaways. In turn, the Dutch offered formal recognition of their freedom and independence. The government recognised the freedom of Maroons by sending gifts every four years to Maroon leaders. This was considered a good deal by Maroon leadership.

The treaties signed with the Dutch in 1760 (the Djuka), 1762 (the Saramaka) and 1767 (the Matuaris), were therefore designed to end the war that had been ongoing between them for a century. The Dutch wanted safety for their settlers and property, and could not secure this by military means. They could not defeat the Maroons. The Maroons also wanted safety for their communities and freedom from the threat of re-enslavement.

But the peace that these treaties were expected to offer, proved difficult as long as slavery was ongoing. A new, but smaller group of Maroons, no more than 1,000 called themselves the Boni. They did not wish to be a part of the peace with the Dutch. They attacked Dutch settlements forcing the Dutch to use the terms of the treaties signed with the Saramaka and Djuka to seek their support in putting down the Boni.

The Dutch were denied assistance. But as the Boni grew in number and strength, they began to encroach on Djuka lands. This led to a war between them. In 1793 the Boni were crushed as a major political force. Differences between these two Maroon groups were soon resolved. But the Boni remained defiant in respect of the Dutch presence. As a result of their persistent anti-slavery position, the Dutch did not recognise the freedom of the Boni until 1860. New runaways were rarely returned and Maroon communities grew larger. Today many of these communities still exist and stand as monuments to the anti-slavery struggles and achievements of Africans in the Americas.

Jamaica

In 1655 when the English defeated Spanish forces in Jamaica and took control of the island, many enslaved Africans from Spanish settlements fled to the mountains and joined or formed Maroon communities. They defended their freedom with arms and raided English settlements for food, and new recruits. Two well-known Spanish-speaking Maroons were Juan Lubolo, alias Juan de Bolos, and Juan de Serras. They were leaders of Blue Mountain communities. In the cockpits the Africans learned much about survival skills from the Taino who they called the 'likkle brown men'.

These early Maroons participated in the politics of European and colonial rivalry. The Spanish offered them full freedom if they fought against the English settlers. The English Governor gave a counteroffer – their freedom and land if they joined the English cause. There was another choice: the early Maroons could declare their own freedom and independence and resist both Spanish and English colonialism.

In 1659, Juan Lubolo offered his loyalty to the English after Governor Doyley's troops tracked down and fought against his community on the southern slopes of Lluidas Vale. Lubolo's Maroons helped the English find the Spanish military camps near Ocho Rios under the command of Christobal de Ysassi. They also participated in the battle that resulted in the Spanish's final defeat, and the flight to Cuba of Ysassi from 'Runaway Bay'.

In 1662 Governor Lyttleton of Jamaica compensated the Maroons for their part in the battle, with 'grants of land' and the 'liberties and privileges of English men'. However, these freedoms and properties came with conditions:

a. The Maroons had to continue to submit to the English nation and be the enemies of their enemies
b. The Maroons had to raise their children in the English tongue
c. The Maroons had to assist the English in hunting and returning all runaway Africans and serve as a militia force in putting down rebellions among enslaved persons.

In November 1662 Lubolo was ambushed and assassinated by Juan de Serras who had offered his services to the defeated Ysassi. Without Lubolo's leadership this Maroon group was weakened and was no further force in Jamaican politics.

The Windward and Leeward Maroons

As the African population in Jamaica grew with the development of the sugar plantation system, the number of Maroons also steadily increased. The old groups, like the so-called 'Varmahalv Negroes', absorbed new recruits and established the 'Windward Maroon' communities in the eastern part of the island. Groups of runaways also fled to the mountains on the western side of the island and formed the so-called 'Leeward Maroons'. These Maroon bands maintained their freedom by resisting the slave system.

Fig 11.6 Nanny, the leader of the Windward Maroons

The enslavers could not stop the flow of plantation Africans seeking freedom in the Maroon communities. In 1673, the enslaved on the Lobby Plantation in the St Ann's parish, rose in revolt and killed many Europeans. They took guns and ammunition, and formed a Maroon community in the mountains of St Elizabeth and Clarendon. All efforts by enslavers to recapture them failed. Events like this were typical of Jamaican society throughout the 17th century.

By the 1730s there were thousands in the Leeward Maroons. They were under the leadership of Cudjoe and were a major political and military force in Jamaica. They had established an Ashanti-style warrior government with Cudjoe as leader who, together with his two lieutenants Accompong and Johnny, formed a War Council that kept the community in a state of military preparedness.

The leader of the Windward Maroons was Nanny, an African woman who was a spiritual icon and freedom activist. Today, Nanny Town, an important Maroon community, is named after her. Nanny was a great inspiration to the Windward Maroons.

Nanny's policy was that her community should accept all runaway Africans into their ranks. Their initiation ceremony was a declaration of loyalty to the community. As a result of this policy the Windward Maroons appeared more defiant of the slave system than the Leeward Maroons. The Leeward Maroons under Cudjoe were less inclined to accept runaways and did not initiate conflict with Europeans.

The policy of the Jamaican government was to destroy all Maroons. Their strategy was to divide the Leeward and Windward groups and turn them against each other. But the local forces of the enslavers were inadequate for this task.

In 1731 the Jamaican government imported 800 soldiers from the island of Gibraltar to launch an attack against the Maroons. The smallest targets were the Leeward Maroon settlements of Accompong Town in the northern parish of St Elizabeth, and Trelawny Town in St James – all deep within the western Cockpit Country. The larger targets were the more numerous Windward Maroons, whose settlements included Quao's Town, Guy's Town and Nanny Town.

The regular British troops had no easy access to any of these towns. The military expeditions were considered very dangerous and risky. The British said that Cudjoe's home in Petty River Bottom was so skillfully chosen that 'even without using their guns they could destroy such a force with rocks alone'.

The Gibraltar troops made no headway against the Maroons. They blamed defeat upon the mosquito that spread the yellow fever disease which took a heavy toll on

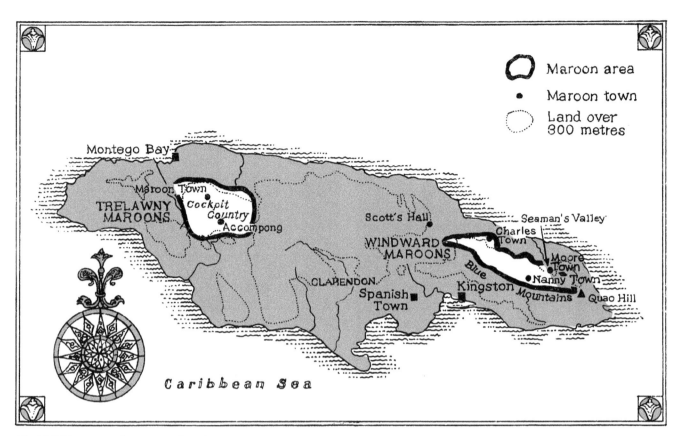

Fig 11.7 Maroon settlements on Jamaica.

them. The next strategy by the Jamaican government was to import another type of specialist; this time a group of the famous indigenous dog-carrying hunters from Central America called the 'Moskito Indians'. This plan was partly successful in that it assisted British soldiers to penetrate the mountain and reach the Maroon settlements.

The Moskito Indians, then, led the way. In 1732 after a bloody battle, the British troops took Nanny Town, the heart of the Windward Maroon. The Maroons counter-attacked and recaptured their town the following year under the leadership of Kissey. The Maroons went on to capture and occupy three plantations, cutting off communications with the main port town, Port Antonio. In 1734, the British struck back and after several encounters in which they lost several soldiers, the British captured Nanny Town in 1735. This time, partly in reaction to the Maroon capture of plantations, the British burnt the town and surrounding villages.

The inhabitants of Nanny Town and Guy's Town fled across the Blue Mountains. They built New Nanny Town to the east above the Rio Grande and renamed it Maroon Town in 1768. Most of the Maroons who journeyed westward joined up with Cudjoe's Leeward Maroons and settled in Accompong Town. Others gradually moved back into the St Mary's parish and established Crawford Town.

For some time after the loss of Nanny Town the Windward Maroons seemed pacified. The British now directed their efforts to the less numerous Leeward Maroons. Cudjoe had heard and witnessed the atrocities committed by the British soldiers at Nanny Town. He was also aware of how the Maroons in the mountains had low morale because of the defeat. Many of his men deserted, surrendered to the British, worked as spies and trackers, and gained freedom under colonial law. The British administration was always more inclined to negotiate with Cudjoe's Maroons rather than with Nanny's warriors who were less accommodating with slave owners.

In 1738 Governor Edward Trelawny sent Colonel John Guthrie to negotiate peace with Cudjoe's Maroons. He offered land and liberty under British law in return for their surrender. The British had no intention of bargaining from a position of weakness. So they launched an assault upon Cudjoe's settlement, which they captured and renamed Trelawny Town. Cudjoe was given a choice by the British: come in and surrender under terms, or face an outright military assault. Cudjoe signed the capitulation treaty on 1 March 1739. His troops were weakened by desertions to the British and by the threat of famine – the soldiers having burnt crops and destroyed provision grounds.

Fig 11.8 *Trelawney Town, largest settlement of the Maroons*

The document contained 15 clauses, most of which were intended to destroy Maroon military resistance, cripple their spirit of rebellion, and bring them under British colonial command. The British offered Cudjoe and his Maroons a 'perfect state of freedom and liberty'. However, those runaways who had joined Cudjoe's community in that same year were excluded from this treaty and handed back to their slave owners. According to the document, the Maroons were to submit to British government, return all future runaways, assist in putting down rebellions of the enslaved and foreign invasions, and to accept military instructions from colonial commanders.

In return for these services Cudjoe's Maroons would receive monetary payments from the British. By the treaty Governor Trelawny agreed to make available 1,500 acres of freehold land between 'Trelawny Town and the Cockpits'. The Maroons were expected to live off this land by selling their produce on markets once they had secured a huckster licence from the local authorities. They were not allowed to plant sugar cane, and while they could administer law among themselves, they could not impose the death penalty for any crimes.

Cudjoe was recognised as the chief commander of the Leeward Maroons, and his two brothers Accompong and Johnny, followed by Captain Cuffee and Captain Quao, were considered his successors. After this group, the Governor would have the power to choose Maroon leaders.

Fig 11.9 *Cudjoe making peace with Colonel John Guthrie*

This clause was the final undoing of the Leeward Maroon as an anti-slavery force. In addition, the treaty signalled their defeat and conversion into a military police force for the colonial administration.

In the same year (1739) the Windward Maroons were under the leadership of Quao and were still in rebellion. However they agreed to sign a peace treaty similar to the one that the Leeward Maroons signed. The entire Maroon leadership was converted into a police force, tracking down and returning runaways, suppressing enslaved rebellions, and constituting a military presence that served to terrorise enslaved persons in town and country. They roamed the highways as free Africans, armed but working for the colonial regime. Cudjoe was given the rank of Captain by the British and later promoted to Colonel for his role in putting down the 1760 rebellion of enslaved people in Westmoreland.

For the next 50 years Jamaican enslavers enjoyed the pacification of the Maroons. They expanded the sugar and cattle economy at an enormous rate. In the meantime the Maroons complained bitterly that the lands granted to them were inferior mountain soils on which they could not subsist. In 1776 they petitioned the government but this had no effect. Small British farmers also expanded their possession of the foothills, pushing the Maroons further up the mountain. The younger Maroon generations spoke out more and more about the inequity of the arrangement and were scornful of the deal made by Cudjoe.

When the Colonel died in the 1770s the political situation became more controversial. The enslavers and British farmers were contemptuous of the Maroons. This simply made the young Maroon leaders more and more determined to renegotiate the terms and conditions of 1739. They were humiliated by living with the terms and conditions of the 1739 Treaty that stripped them of honour. In 1793 Jamaica heard of the St Domingue Revolution. This revolution increased the confidence of the young Maroon leaders and by 1795 the Maroons took up arms in what became known as the Second Maroon War.

The Maroons believed that the political situation in Jamaica was ripe for a successful military attack upon the colonial regime. Africans throughout the colony were fascinated by the rise of Toussaint in the Haitian Revolution and the effectiveness of his leadership. There, the enslavers were on the run and African freedom seemed assured. The Jamaican enslavers were terrified of the power of this example and began to prepare for similar action amongst their enslaved persons.

Those enslavers who could afford it sent their wives and children to safety in Britain. They boarded up their houses at night and kept what military forces they had on the streets. It was a society living in fear, and the Africans

Fig 11.10 *Maroon monument for Cudjoe, Accompong, Jamaica*

knew this all too well. When two young Maroons in Montego Bay were publicly flogged for theft, this set off the rebellion. The Maroons ambushed the soldiers of the Eighteenth Light Dragoons and killed 34 of them including five men of officer rank. The war deepened. Only a few enslaved persons ran from their estates to join the rebellion, but those who did, fought with resolve. A local government official wrote:

At first the Maroons forced the enslaved persons to join them, but finding that many deserted from them, they now force no one, but receive runaways with great Triumph. It appears that their Ideas are that we shall be forced to Treat with them; for they say they never will have any other towns but the Cockpits. They add, that the French Fight the Buckras on the water and that now they were fighting on land, Buckras will have enough to do.

The British troops used the strategy of burning Maroon farms and destroying their food supplies. In this they were more successful than the Maroons were at recruiting enslaved persons. The British by then knew enough about Maroon settlements. The enslaved people also knew enough about Maroon politics: they distrusted and feared the Maroons. The Maroons received some support, but it was not enough to persuade those enslaved to abandon their enslavers.

On 10 October Leonard Parkinson, the feared military leader of the Maroons, retaliated against the British by attacking and destroying Amity Hall Estate with a small party. They killed the bookkeeper, the only British person they found. Here again those enslaved did not rally to the struggle. Parkinson made a plea to them but found they were not responsive. Wherever the Maroon rebels went they found congregations of unwilling enslaved persons. The Maroons could not mobilise them because the enslaved people distrusted them and were hostile to them because of the oppressive role they had played during the long peace.

By the end of the year the British had effectively crushed the Maroon rebellion. It stood little chance without the support of the enslaved population. In January 1796 the British imported hundreds of dogs from Cuba to track down rebels who refused to surrender. By March, the British had finished their mopping up operations. There were trials of Maroons that led to floggings, imprisonment, deportation and executions. The British community took the law into its hands and killed more Africans.

In July and August the British decided to deport Maroons who were still in captivity. Most of the British people on the island called for their exile. The British chose the cold lands of Nova Scotia in Canada to which to send them. The Black Caribs (Karifuna) of the Windward Islands, who also deserted the British in 1796, were deported to Roatán Island off the coast of Honduras. No one expected either group to survive and flourish. Finally the British transported both groups to Sierra Leone in West Africa as political convicts. In 1819, 123 rebels from Barbados who were defeated in the 1816 Bussa Rebellion joined these groups. The groups did survive. When slavery was abolished in 1838, they petitioned Queen Victoria through the Governor of Sierra Leone for permission to return to the Caribbean and some were allowed to return 'home'.

To sum up

Whenever there was slavery, there was resistance that often took the form of marooage. The enslavers tried to contain the flight of their human property. They used complex policing systems and severe punishments for

Fig 11.12 *Maroon warrior, Leonard Parkinson*

captives. But those enslaved were always seeking opportunities to take flight, and ultimately form Maroon communities that were able to take a stand and defend their liberty against the retrieving forces of enslavers. There was flight from the rural estate to towns; from valleys to mountains; from valleys, plains and towns to forest and other remote environments. Some of the enslaved took to sea, and sought refuge on other islands and mainland spaces. These were called maritime Maroons. As communities they fought wars to protect their liberty, and occasionally signed treaties of accommodation with enslavers and their governments.

Revision questions

1   What is meant by the term 'marronage'?
2   'Maroons were found everywhere that slavery existed.' Discuss.
3   How did Maroons protect their communities?
4   How did Maroons seek compromise with the slavery system?
5   What is mean by the term 'maritime marronage'?

Chapter 12

Armed revolt

'Get up, stand up, stand up for your rights.'
(Bob Marley)

We have seen that Africans in the Caribbean were persistent in their commitment to freedom, even though many died in the effort and despite the terrible suffering they went through. It is now commonly accepted that anti-slavery rebellion was frequently of a revolutionary nature. We can view the many revolts and plots as a '200 Years' War' – an ongoing struggle between those enslaved and their enslavers. This view can enrich our general understanding of the many forces that finally succeeded in toppling the slave-based regimes. In the previous chapter we focused on marronage, the establishment of Maroon societies, as one method of resistance by those enslaved. This chapter will focus on armed revolutions.

In this chapter we will learn about:
1. Tacky's War, 1760
2. The Berbice Revolution, 1763
3. The Haitian Revolution, 1791
4. The 1816 Emancipation War in Barbados
5. Emancipation War in Jamaica, 1831/32
6. Women and resistance

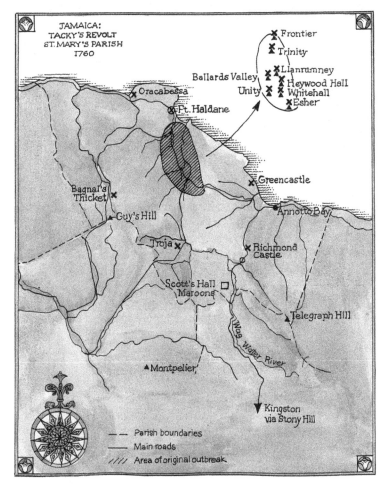

Fig 12.1 Tacky's revolt

1 Tacky's War, 1760

The first major 18th century war was that led by Chief Tacky in St Mary, Jamaica in April 1760. It began on the 7th April, starting on Frontier Sugar Plantation belonging to Ballard Beckford and spreading to Trinity, Esher and other plantations where there were large populations of 'Gold Cost' Africans. The Africans raided Fort Haldane in Port Maria for weapons and sought out and murdered several British enslavers in plantations such as Esher and Ballards Valley. They sought the collaboration of the Maroons to stave off the British military forces that were sent by the lieutenant governor to defeat them. It is believed that some Maroons looked the other way, but others acted as mercenaries for the establishment and engaged the rebels in a fierce battle. Martial Law had to be declared in order to help to suppress the war. But despite the suppression in St Mary, protests spread to St Thomas in the east and as far as Westmoreland. When it was all over about 40 to 60 British

were killed and some 1,000 Africans (including Damon, Kingston and Fortune) either deported to Honduras, executed, flogged and/or imprisoned. There is controversy over what happened to Chief Tacky. Oral history claims he escaped while colonial sources claim that he was captured and hanged. Jamaica was to be the scene of continuing African protest in the later 18th and 19th centuries.

2 The Berbice Revolution, 1763

How did the Berbice Revolution begin?

In the mid-18th century Suriname was the largest Dutch colony. In 1760 it had about 50,000 enslaved Africans, most of whom worked on large sugar estates. There were also smaller, neighbouring colonies to the west of Suriname – Berbice, Essequibo, and Demerara. Berbice was a company colony that was still in the early stages of development. The Directors of the Berbice Company were also its owners. There were only about 350 Dutch people in the colony who were responsible for the ownership, possession, and management of about 4,000 enslaved Africans. This means there were about eleven Africans to one European. The sugar plantations were privately-owned, and the colony had about 84 estate owners. The Directors of the Company owned about a dozen estates.

Like many other colonies on the South American mainland Berbice also had about 300 enslaved indigenes. These were persons who were supposedly captured in the Dutch wars. There were some free indigenous persons who had either made peace agreements with the Dutch or were licensed traders and food suppliers. Some supported the Dutch in their rivalry with other Europeans on the coast. Generally they helped the Dutch to police the interior frontier, tracked and returned runaway Africans, and worked as soldiers in crushing African revolt. In other words, they played a similar role to the one the Maroons of Jamaica performed for the British after the 1739 Peace Treaty.

In February 1763 the enslaved Africans in Berbice, led by Kofi, revolted and fought for their freedom. It was not the first time they had done so. Between 1733 and 1762 the colony had an ongoing history of rebellion and protests.

Like most of the African rebellions the war began as an action on one estate and spread to the estates of the other leaders. The first estate was Plantation Magdelenen on the Canje River. The Africans here killed the plantation manager and some other officers, before moving on to the neighbouring La Providence Plantation. There the manager escaped with his life but his house was destroyed and the rebels recruited more soldiers to join the war.

Within two weeks enslaved persons were rebelling on most estates on both the Canje and Berbice Rivers. Many Dutch people were killed and taken prisoners as the rebels moved from plantation to plantation. Those Dutch people who escaped did so by fleeing down the river to coastal forts and towns, or by taking the difficult overland route to Demerara. From the end of February until early December 1763 Africans took charge of the colony and were in command of its government.

Heavily armed Dutch troops arrived in November and after many bloody battles they defeated the rebels by 10 December. By the end of January 1764 the Dutch had rooted out other small pockets of African resistance. The rebels were tried under a military court and the punishments and executions were completed at the end of June.

When the enslaved people were in command of the government they immediately began the task of nation building. The first thing they did was to build a new system of government. The revolutionary leader was Kofi (Cuffy), who was identified as the mastermind behind the strategy to drive the Dutch out of Berbice. Kofi became the Governor of the colony. His second-in-command during the war was Captain Accra. Both of them were Akan men from Ghana. Accra was appointed the deputy Governor. They took up residence in the prestigious Council House at Fort Nassau, with all the official staff and ceremony.

Governor Kofi

Kofi had been enslaved on the Barkey plantation on the Berbice River. He had arrived in Berbice as a young boy, and was recognised on the estate for his intelligence and good manner. As a result of this he was trained in domestic service and taught the respected cooper's trade. The Barkey plantation was at the centre of the rebellion.

Governor Kofi, like Toussaint L'Ouverture later, was concerned with national development. He believed that the economy should be restructured and production restarted as trade was required to produce wealth and taxes for the government. He began to negotiate with the Dutch so as to meet these objectives. Kofi wanted to revive the plantations and produce sugar and rum for export. He wanted to become a statesman and nation-builder. Kofi was, however, like Toussaint, very clear and firm on the question of slavery. He stated that:

a. Slavery in Berbice was abolished forever
b. Berbice should be sub-divided into a free African state, and, if necessary, a Dutch colony
c. The campaign for freedom could not be turned back
d. Africans would fight as long as the Dutch sought to restore slavery.

Kofi knew that he was not in a position to stop the trade from Africa or abolish slavery in neighbouring colonies. So he modified his policy so that his ideas only applied to the region under his command. It was as compensation to the Dutch, he offered to sub-divide the colony.

Kofi wrote a series of letters to the defeated Governor Hoogenheim. The letters set out the anti-slavery policies of his government and at the same time indicated a willingness to recognise the interests of the Dutch outside of Berbice. Just like Toussaint, Kofi's compromises and attempts at reconciliation with the defeated enslavers and their government representatives were his undoing. In May he wrote to the former Governor and sent him a gift of gold buckles as a token for the inconvenience he had suffered. He indicated that there was no personal animosity towards him. He proposed a deal to settle the matter of their mutual interests in Berbice.

In one letter Kofi stated:

> *Cuffy, Governor of the Negroes of Berbice and Captain Accra send their greetings to Your late Honourable. We don't want war: we see clearly that you do not want war. Barkey, and his servants, de Graaf, Schook, Dell van Lentzing and Frederick Botgen, but more especially Mr Barkey and his servant, de Graaf are the principal instigators of the riot which occurred in Berbice. The Governor, I Cuffy, was present when it commenced, and was very angry at it. The Governor of Berbice asks Your Honour that Your Honour will come and speak with him; don't be afraid; but if you won't come, we will fight as long as one Christian remains in Berbice. The Governor will give your Honour half of Berbice and all the negroes will go high up the river, but don't think they will remain slaves. Those negroes that your Honour has on the ships, they can remain slaves. The Governor greets your Honour.*

Governor Kofi knew that his supporters might oppose his policy of seeking a friendly settlement with the Imperial Dutch. He admitted as much when he informed Hoogenheim that some of his close allies were bitter and would not rest until all and every European was destroyed or driven out of Berbice.

However, Kofi's political understanding of the situation did not save him from these very persons he recognised and described to Hoogenheim. While a letter written in May was on its way to Hoogenheim, groups within Kofi's camp were already planning further military assaults upon Daargradt, the only remaining significant Dutch settlement in Berbice. This group was led by Atta, also from Ghana. They were not prepared to negotiate with the Dutch, whom they believed were enslavers and opposed to African freedom. Atta and his group were determined to drive all the Dutch out of Berbice and completely free all enslaved Africans in the colony.

So the leadership of the freedom struggle was divided – broken into two separate camps that were now at war with each other. One group declared Atta its Governor, saying that Kofi was a compromiser and betrayer of the cause, the other group supported Kofi. June 1763 became a period of warfare between Africans. Most of Kofi's supporters were killed because Atta had the support of the majority since he had a policy of total war against all enslavers.

Kofi was defeated militarily, but rather than fall into the hands of Atta's warriors, he shot himself in a dramatic act of suicide. It was said that his loyal followers sacrificed two Europeans on his grave as a mark of respect for his leadership. Atta captured Kofi's deputy, Accra. He spared his life on condition that he worked for one of Atta's commanders. Accra subsequently escaped and surrendered himself to the Dutch. In return for his life and freedom he agreed to work for the Dutch as a spy and a soldier hunting rebels.

Governor Atta

Atta became Governor and selected a military council made up of other well-known soldiers – Kweku, Baube, Accabre, Kees, Goussari, Fortuin, Kwabena, and a few others. He did not seek to negotiate with the Dutch but declared war on their settlements and military installations. The Dutch reported that he was a powerful soldier. When his troops approached them in battle they would shout, 'Atta! Atta! Atta!' The Dutch described the soldier, Accabre, as a 'fellow with the bearing of a prince who also commanded considerable loyalty by leading by example'.

However, it was not easy for Atta to maintain unity among Africans. As the Dutch increased their military strength and began to invade territory under African control, they regained power. Meanwhile, Africans were running out of weapons and ammunition, and food was also in short supply. Low morale began to have its effect on the African fighters, and many surrendered to the Dutch in the hope of saving their freedom and lives.

Against this background of despair, unity between Africans increasingly took the form of ethnic bonding. Accabre became the leader of a 600 strong Bantu group, while Baube took command of the Guango people. At the same time, ethnic divisions increased the general tensions between Africans born in Africa and the Creoles. In fact, the suspicion and the tension between Africans and Creoles were the main reasons for armed conflict between African communities on the Berbice and Canje Rivers.

Under the pressure of these divisions and conflicts Atta's leadership fell apart. The warrior Goussari fled to the Dutch camp. He surrendered and agreed, just like Accra, to be a spy and soldier for the Dutch. These spies were sent into African territory as mercenaries to capture rebels and to encourage others to surrender. It was in this way that Atta was captured and delivered to the Dutch authorities.

By February 1764, one full year after Kofi's war was started, the Dutch were back in full possession of the colony of Berbice. The Dutch put the remaining rebel leaders to death after the Court of Criminal Justice had issued its judgments. The revolution was defeated, but many Africans had enjoyed at least a period of freedom. For a year they were effective rulers of their own country.

3 The Haitian Revolution, 1791

In 1804, after 13 years of civil war and revolution in St Domingue, the enslaved people emerged victorious and free. They became nation-builders when they declared the State of Haiti independent. For those enslaved in the Caribbean and beyond, this was the grand moment of redemption. Haiti was the new symbol of African liberation in the West.

On the eve of the Revolution St Domingue was by far the richest in the Caribbean, if measured in terms of production and trade. It was the world's largest producer of cane sugar. It supplied half of the cane sugar that was used in the Americas and Europe. Its coffee was sold all over Europe, as was its cotton and indigo. St Domingue, like Barbados in the mid-17th century and Jamaica in the mid-18th century, was the 'gem' of the colonial world.

St Domingue's wealth was made possible because of the brutal enslavement of over 400,000 enslaved persons – by far the largest enslaved population in the Caribbean. In the 1780s, a further 35,000 enslaved Africans were imported each year, making St Domingue the largest single slave market in the Americas. Plantations meant mass slavery. There were about 8,500 working plantations producing a range of goods for the export markets.

St Domingue's wealth was important to the economic and social development of France: it made up about 35 per cent of France's foreign trade; it provided the French upper classes with tropical goods and offered everyone cheaper sugar and coffee. Slave traders and investors in most French port towns grew rich from the trade in enslaved Africans. In addition, the colony offered important military strategic support to the French navy.

A small community of free peoples owned and managed this large enslaved population. They were made up of 42,000 European people and 35,000 free mixed-race people. Both the European and free mixed-race communities had deep class divisions, creating a caste-like society based on race and colour and European supremacy. Those who could afford it lived in France from the income they had made from their investments. Those who stayed behind dealt with the conflicts that arose from slavery, race and class prejudice.

The free mixed-race were called the *gens de couleur*. Most were poor but a few were very rich. The privileged few benefited from education and were professionals. But as persons of mixed race ancestry, the law declared them second-class inhabitants. As a racially oppressed group they were denied access to the high status professions such as high public office. They also could not own nor wear silks and expensive finery. However, the elite were still enslavers. For the most part, like the French people, their privileges and wealth were the result of the exploitation of enslaved workers.

The free mixed-race people were the first to launch a rebellion. Just like the entire region at this time, they demanded full civil rights. This meant legal equality with French people. They published their own 'Rights of Man' document in Paris, and engaged the government in a discussion about their civil rights. But remember that this was entirely a debate between the mixed-race elite and the French community.

In 1790 local French people rejected the request of free mixed-race people, and it seemed that there was no imperial support from the French government. Two of the free mixed-race leading members, Vincent Ogé and Jean-Baptiste Chevannes, assembled an army of some 350 mixed-race people and demanded legal equality from the Governor. The local militia crushed them and both leaders were killed by being broken on the wheel. The French government responded to this development by passing a law which recognised the equality of the free mixed-race people with French people, an action that drove colonial French people into opposition.

A civil war developed between the free mixed-race and French communities – both using the enslaved in their different armies. But African enslaved persons entered the war with their own agenda. They launched a major revolt against both French and mixed-race enslavers and demanded their freedom. They burnt, looted and killed many people as they went from plantation to plantation. By the end of 1791, at least 1,000 plantations were destroyed and hundreds of French and free mixed-race people were killed.

The free mixed-race people in the north were seeking revenge for the murder of Ogé and Chevannes. So they joined the enslaved African people against the French enslavers. In the southern and western areas the free mixed-race peoples took up arms against the French community, both groups again using armies of enslaved persons to advance their cause.

The enslaved rise

It was against this background of civil war between the free mixed-race and French communities and their mutual opposition to French domination, that those enslaved on 22 August 1791 launched the greatest revolt for freedom from slavery ever known.

For several weeks those enslaved, particularly those in the Northern Province of the colony, had been planning to fight for freedom. They had been organising long before the night of 14 August 1791, when they decided that the rebellion should begin.

Rebel leaders came from plantations throughout the central parts of the northern province – Port-Margot, Limbe, Acul, Petite-Anse, Limonade, Plaine du Nord, Quartier-Morin, Morne-Rouge and many others. On the night of 14 August they fixed the date as 22 August 1791 to start the freedom struggle. The meeting took place on the Lenormand de Mezy Plantation in Morne-Rouge.

The main leaders of the rebellion were described as enslaved persons with elite jobs, people in whom their 'owners' had trust and confidence. Most of them were drivers and overseers. The main leaders were Boukman Dutty, Jeanot Bullet, Jean-François, and Georges Biassou. Boukman and Jeanot were to lead the early assault, and Jean-François and Georges were to bring together and consolidate the rebellion.

Toussaint L'Ouverture, who later became the main leader, was at first given a low-key role as advisor. He worked as a coachman for the manager, Bayon De Libertas, on the Breda Plantation, and from his home there he kept in touch with Boukman, Jean-François and Biassou. Touissant was freed by the owner of the plantation at about the age of 30.

Boukman Dutty

In these early years, Boukman, originally from Jamaica, was the leading thinker and strategist. He was the one in command who gave the instruction to start the rebellion. Like Toussaint, he was a coachman by occupation, but unlike Toussaint he was not free. He belonged to the Clement Plantation, which was one of the first properties to be destroyed by fire during the revolution. He was also a commander in the French militia that had trained him in the use of European arms.

Boukman was an experienced organiser who understood the importance of unity and secrecy. He needed to guard against betrayal; spies had to be dug out and exposed. He believed that he needed to use spiritual powers to build courage. Boukman practised the African religion of voodoo, with its rituals and ceremonies. He was known as 'Zamba' – a spiritual leader within the voodoo faith. For his followers, he was larger than life and immortal.

A voodoo ceremony was organised to strengthen his leadership. It was held not far from the Lenormand Plantation, in a wooded area known as Bois-Caïmon. We now know this ceremony as the Bois-Caïmon ceremony – it was a political event that set the tone for the rebellion.

Boukman and a voodoo high priestess called Cécile Fatiman led the Bois Caïmon ceremony. She was described as an 'old Negress woman with strange eyes and bristly hair'. She was a Mambo or a voodoo high priestess. It was Cecile Fatiman who had the power to call up the spirits of the ancestors and the spirits of the African gods and to call upon them to speak through Zamba Boukman.

When this was done, Boukman rose and spoke. His 'voice of liberty' speech is one of the greatest orations of history and signalled the beginning of the Haitian Revolution. Boukman stated:

The good Lord who created the sun which gives us light from above, who rouses the sea and makes the thunder roar – listen well, all of you – this God, Hidden in the clouds, watches us. He sees all that the White man does. The god of the White man calls him to commit crimes; our god asks only good works of us. But this god who is so good orders revenge! He will direct our hands; he will aid us. Throw away the image of the god of the Whites who thirst our tears and listen to the voice of liberty which speaks in the hearts of all of us.

It was after this speech that the 'blood pact' was ritualised in solemn ceremony. This was when Cécile Fatiman killed the sacrificial pig and passed the blood for the rebel leaders to drink as evidence and proof of their secrecy, loyalty, resolve and commitment to fight until the death. The plans that the leadership approved on 14 August show a well-considered course of action. In fact, historians have described the planning as 'ingenious'.

The Acul district was first to go up in flames. The rebels burnt the Clement Plantation, then Tremes, Noe, Molines and Flaville, to the ground and killed dozens of their French personnel.

The Acul district served as a centre for rebel communications. From there the freedom fighters moved westward to the Limbe district via the Saint-Michel Plantation. Gathering strength in numbers, by 25 August they had pushed further west into Port-Margot. As they moved from plantation to plantation, they destroyed all the symbols of their enslavement – sugar mills, equipment, the homes of managers and owners, water wheels, barns and cane fields. With this policy of destruction they intended to completely ruin the slave economy.

By the end of August all the prime properties that represented St Domingue's colonial wealth and glory were destroyed by the hands that had built them. Over a hundred properties were destroyed by 25 August 1791 and by the 30th this number had risen to over 200. In addition, the freedom fighters completely ruined 1,200 coffee plantations. The damage was estimated to be at 40 million livres. Over 10,000 of the 170,000 enslaved persons in the northern province were sweeping though the countryside destroying all that the enslavers were proud of.

The enslavers, however, managed to prevent the capital Le Cap from falling into rebel hands. They repelled an assault led by Boukman and gave urban dwellers the kind of boost not experienced by rural dwellers. Boukman was killed by French people in battle. His death strengthened the determination of the enslavers in Le Cap. They cut his head off and displayed it on a stake in the public square in the town with the inscription, 'The head of Boukman, leader of the rebels'.

At first Boukman's death lowered the morale of his African followers. He was their esteemed leader. But in a short time they were ready to retaliate – head for head. There was now an even higher level of motivation to drive the French enslavers out of the colony. In November, civil commissioners arrived from France. This changed the nature of the political condition. They began negotiations between Africans and the French government. The majority of Africans did not want to negotiate. They wanted to fight to the end. Some leaders shared this view, but others preferred amnesty and a settlement.

In April 1792 the French government granted the free mixed-race people full civil rights as citizens. Now an alliance between free mixed-race and French people gradually began to emerge against the enslaved. For the first time since the civil war had begun the lines of rebellion were clear. The enslaved were now on the defensive. Thousands chose to surrender and both Biassou and Jean-François fled to the mountains. But by now the free mixed-race community wanted more than equality with French people. They wanted to be the colony's new elite.

In early 1793 the mixed-race people were backed by the French Republican government. They easily brushed aside the French people and assumed considerable power in the colony. In July they had massacred the French people in Les Cayes and under the leadership of André Rigaud took full power in the south. They restored control over the enslaved and rebuilt their economic base as merchants, planters, and professionals.

A major surprise was on the way for the mixed-race people. In August 1793 the French government abolished slavery in the Empire. The enslaved were once again encouraged in their struggle. However, the empowered mixed-race people and the remaining French people loudly objected. Leaders of the enslaved were still hiding out in the hills, moving among the Maroons, and seemed helpless to act. In addition the British and Spanish arrived to occupy the colony and restored slavery in most of the south and west despite the fact that the French government had proclaimed emancipation.

Toussaint L'Ouverture

Fig 12.2 Haitian leader, Touissant L'Ouverture

It was within this context that the African community threw up the great leader Toussaint Breda, who later changed his surname to L'Ouverture. He had served under the earlier leadership of Biassou and Jean-François and was an experienced organiser. He was a native of St Domingue, and had been enslaved, but enjoyed some privileges on the Breda estate. He worked as a coachman and head cattleman and developed an extensive knowledge of the colony. He also managed to acquire literacy and was a practising Christian.

Toussaint was described as a small, thin man, dark skinned with piercing little eyes, and with a sharp intellect. No one around him seemed to laugh. He was intense and serious in his mood. In groups or crowds he was reserved but dignified, mysterious but pleasant. He always seemed to be in full control of himself and of things around him. He was always fearful of being poisoned, and so ate very little. No one seemed to know

his thoughts and his actions were never predictable. He was a family man, married with children. His hobby was horseback riding. This craft served him well in his war days.

When Toussaint moved to the centre of leadership he brought attention to the anti-slavery feature of the civil war. His main concern was the liberty of Africans and he built an army with this objective in mind. His task seemed an almost impossible one. The Spanish and English occupation encouraged slavery, and the slave rebels in the mountains were experiencing famine and shortages of military equipment. The rebel soldiers that Toussaint held together were not highly motivated and most he described as being as 'naked as earth works'. But from his early years he was known as a tactical master, and this is why he commanded respect and loyalty amongst his followers. By the end of November 1794, his army included over 10,000 fighting men and women. Jean Jacques Dessalines, who had fought with him under Biassou, was his chief commander and his young nephew Moise a commander.

Over the next two years Toussaint collaborated with the mixed-race leader Rigaud to drive both the English and Spanish from the colony. By the end of 1798, they had defeated the English who were preparing to withdraw. The Spanish had withdrawn earlier. Both blamed their defeat on the outbreak of yellow fever. The result was the achievement of self-emancipation for some 100,000 persons in the west and north. But things were not so clear in the south where Rigaud was in full control.

With the 'foreigners' out of the way, the final stage of the civil war took shape. Toussaint was never satisfied with mixed-race people's dominance of Africans, and distrusted their attitudes to slavery. The feeling was mutual; Rigaud considered Toussaint an extremist. War broke out between the African and mixed-race forces. This conflict was known as 'The War of Knives'. Toussaint gave Dessalines instructions to defeat Rigaud and his troops. He showed no mercy and this earned him a reputation for ruthlessness. The mixed-race people were defeated, and Rigaud fled to France to save his life.

The fact that Toussaint's successful strategy was celebrated and honoured by friends and foes alike was an indication of his brilliant leadership. By 1800 Toussaint was in full control and abolished slavery throughout the colony. He was proclaimed the Governor of St Domingue and he made it clear that slavery would never be restored. However, as Governor his main task was to begin the rebuilding programme. Ten years of civil war, and five years of repelling foreign invaders had left the country in ruin. His top priority was to restore the productive sector and rebuild the plantation sector.

Fig 12.3 Haiti Republic letterhead

However, his plan had many problems. Africans saw the plantations as the home of their enslavement and refused to commit themselves to rebuilding them. The plantations needed labour and Toussaint used government pressure to get workers. When he invited former enslavers back into the country to assist the rebuilding process his followers resisted. His nephew General Moise led the movement against him. The rebellion was put down and Toussaint had Moise shot. Also, he promoted a multi-racial approach to progress and this weakened his followers' loyalty to his government. Africans were in no mood to see mulattos and Europeans regain property. Neither did they support the decision to execute General Moise. But Toussaint thought that these measures were necessary.

He led his troops over the border into Spanish Santo Domingo and annexed the colony. He was now Governor of the entire island of Hispaniola. He abolished slavery in the Spanish section and assumed even greater global status as a liberator.

If the Spanish appeared helpless, then the English and French did not. In October 1801 the British government approved plans for the invasion of St Domingue as they feared for the safety of neighbouring Jamaica. In February 1802 Napoleon sent 10,000 French soldiers under his brother-in-law, General LeClerc, into the colony to recapture the government and to restore slavery. He ordered that all properties were to be returned to their former owners and French rule restored.

The combined pressure of the English and French proved too much for Toussaint's leadership. He destroyed most of what he could and retreated into the mountains, leaving the towns to the invaders. He tried to organise a counter-attack but by April the resistance was broken. Thousands of soldiers surrendered, including leaders such as Dessalines and Henry Cristophe, who subsequently worked for the French. Toussaint also surrendered to French diplomats. He was later kidnapped by a French

Fig 12.4 Napoleon

military unit and deported to France to spend his last days in prison. He never met Napoleon, despite several pleas. He died in a French dungeon in April 1803.

When the French tried to restore slavery, the Africans and mixed-race people worked together to resist the invaders. With Toussaint removed from the scene, the leadership fell to Dessalines. The mixed-race leader, Alexander Pétion, agreed to work under Dessalines' command. This was a reminder of earlier days when Toussaint and Rigaud had collaborated to drive out the French.

Napoleon had sent 40,000 troops into the colony but they failed to regain effective control of it. By May 1803 they were retreating, beaten and disgraced by the African and mixed-race soldiers. Geggus tells us that since 1791 the English, French and Spanish had sent in some 70,000 soldiers to retain control of the colony and had failed. The leadership of General Dessalines was as successful as Toussaint's. The Europeans were driven out of the country, slavery was not restored, and the 'natives' were back in full command.

In 1804 Dessalines did what Toussaint had failed to do. He declared national independence and became the country's first president. The country was renamed 'Haiti' – the indigenous name for the island of Hispaniola. The state was officially proclaimed on 1 January 1804. It became the second independent nation in the Americas and the first in the Caribbean.

Building a free nation

Toussaint strongly believed that to rebuild a workable economy one needed diplomatic relations with the world powers. He understood that without trade there could be no wealth, and that trade depended upon producing commodities on a large-scale on the plantations. But he needed to build up good relations with the merchant class and investors in Europe so that they would put money and capital into the plantations and so that they would buy the produce.

Toussaint believed that it was possible and necessary to revive the plantations (with French people in charge if necessary). He hoped that the plantations would produce for Africans the wealth and general well-being that French people had enjoyed. On the other hand, for Dessalines, plantations were the root of the evil that had allowed French people and their mixed-race allies to hold Africans in captivity. These differences in belief were expressed at the level of government policy with respect to land ownership and distribution. Toussaint called for the restoration of properties to the French, Dessalines called for the complete economic dispossession of the French, so from the beginning in the government, there was a division over economic policy in Haiti.

Toussaint's constitution of 1801 clearly said that all individuals were equal, regardless of race or colour, and that any discrimination based upon these characteristics was illegal. General Moise had broken with Toussaint on the issue of equality between races when Toussaint had tried to equalise African economic empowerment by giving wide-ranging concessions to French people. Moise argued that Toussaint was prepared to accept that French people would own and manage property to the detriment of African people who had fought such a bloody war for their liberty.

The Haiti Independence Constitution of 1804 was clear on the question of race, identity and nationhood. It declared that all citizens, regardless of colour or race, must be classified as Black (but Europeans were not included). This was an attempt to remove the issue of colour from domestic politics because of its divisive power. No one should claim higher or lower status because of colour. This was a bold initiative. Dessalines, unlike Toussaint, was trying to build into the law a way of dealing with the race

Fig 12.5 Dessalines, Haiti's first president

and colour issues that had survived the war of liberation and were still present in Haitian society.

Article 12 of the 1804 Constitution denied foreign people, the French in particular, the right to own property. Europeans tried to find a way around this provision – they transferred their property into the name of supportive and related mixed-race people. Dessalines responded by cancelling these property transfers. This was his way of making sure that the newly-acquired political power of Africans was not compromised. According to his supporters, this was a reason for Dessalines' assassination on 17 October 1806.

Haitian leaders who came after Dessalines also tried to manage the relationship between race and economic power. They believed that key to the relationship was land ownership and the lack of it by Africans. On the one hand, land ownership and landlessness had long been linked to slavery. On the other hand, those Europeans and mixed-race people who were allowed to own land and other forms of property had political and economic power. So those people who historically were not allowed to own land, now had very little political or economic power.

The mixed-race people argued that Dessalines' constitution was an attempt to impose a African nationalist image upon a country that was in fact racially mixed. They wanted the racial mix and their own positions to be acknowledged. However, Africans viewed these arguments with suspicion. They believed that mixed-race people could easily be used by the French to restore slavery, especially if there was not one African nationalist image. The French had used Rigaud in this way, and large numbers of mixed-race people had supported LeClerc's attempt to restore slavery.

However, within the so-called mixed-race people's camp there were large numbers of 'Black *ancient libres*' – free Africans who were also opposed to the freedom of the mass of Africans.

After Dessalines' assassination Haiti split into two separate nations. It was the general political view in both the northern state – called the Kingdom of Haiti – and the Republic of Haiti in the south that Haiti was 'a symbol of Black dignity'.

Leaders spoke of themselves as the restorers or 'regenerators of Africa'. Henri Christophe addressed the issue of African liberation with passion. He argued that Haiti's task was to lead Africans into a new dispensation. Intellectuals in Christophe's government like De Vastey provided the historical arguments to strengthen Christophe's. In his typical poetic prose, De Vastey said:

Blacks as we are and yellow in complexion, bowed as we have been for centuries under the yoke of slavery and ignorance, assimilated to the condition of the brute; how resolutely ought we to exert ourselves; how much of perseverance, wisdom and virtue is necessary for reanimating our race to this moment enchained and in darkness.

De Vastey also played an important role in the development of Christophe's policy to promote anti-slavery activities within the region. From Toussaint to Boyer (who became president of the Republic of Haiti in 1810), Haitain leaders expressed a fierce anti-slavery stance. Remember that in 1800 Toussaint had invaded the neighbouring colony of Spanish Santo Domingo with an army of 20,000 and had liberated the Africans there, thereby removing slavery from the entire island.

France's reaction to the Haitian Revolution

There was little the French could do to restore the situation in Haiti. However, the Haitian leaders did recognise that they needed France to officially recognise their independence so that they could progress economically and socially. The French and Americans had banned commercial trade with Haiti. The French wanted to be fully paid out for what they had lost. They said that their colonial officials would fix the exact amount and they wanted this compensation before they would even start discussing their official recognition of Haitian independence. Other imperial powers were in agreement.

France would recognise Haiti but at the financially devastating cost of 150 million francs which was to be paid as compensation to French enslavers for the loss of their property during the revolution. In 1825 Haiti had completed negotiations with France.

It has been noted that 150 years later Haiti was still paying for its political recognition. In the 1870s an estimated 20 per cent of government income was still tied to paying off this debt. In some years as much as 60 per cent of total customs revenues were taken up to pay the debt. According to President Aristide, who has asked France to pay back this sum of money to Haiti, Haiti eventually paid a renegotiated sum of 90 million gold francs plus interest, equivalent to 21.7 billion US dollars.

The impact of the Haitian Revolution on the Caribbean

As the Jamaicans were so near Haiti, they probably felt the impact of the revolution more directly than others. The enslaved persons in Jamaica became more and more anxious about achieving their freedom, and at times wanted to follow the Haitian lead. At the same time the tensions in Jamaican society caused by increased levels of anti-slavery rebellions reached uncomfortable levels. Everywhere in Jamaica life had changed. The Jamaican Assembly debated the need to put measures into action to prevent restlessness amongst the enslaved who eagerly awaited arms and instructions from Haiti. But no arms or instructions were forthcoming from Haiti.

In July 1798 Governor Lord Balcarres and the Jamaican Assembly stated in a letter to the Duke of Portland, that the Haitian revolutionaries 'hold forth such an example to our Negroes here, as to place Jamaica in a new point of view, and to render her safety much more precarious and problematic than at any former period.' The governor added that the managers and landowners had no choice but to restructure and upgrade their armed forces 'to watch over the conduct of the Negroes on the several estates and plantations.'

Jamaican enslaved Africans such as the six who absconded from the boat *Deep Nine* in 1819, used every chance to seek freedom in Haiti by means of maritime marronage.

Further afield in the Caribbean, however, the impact of revolutionary Haiti was more chaotic. A general feature of the Antilles was that there was a definite increase in militancy by the enslaved whose support of the 'Black Jacobins' (named after the most radical group in the French Revolution) of Haiti was evident. Throughout 1791 newspapers carried reports about the state of affairs in the region: reports from Martinique on 15 February and from Dominica on 4 March indicated that many enslaved persons had 'taken up arms', 'were refusing to work', 'deserting the estates', and that Europeans were living in 'dread of the consequences'. In May the *London Times* carried a report of a revolt at St Vincent. In November they had a similar report about Guadeloupe and St Lucia.

In 1794 the enslaved people in Grenada revolted, led by Julien Fedon. This was a clear signal that African people were determined to fight for their liberty. The Barbados Assembly's report on the 1816 Bussa-led Revolution in which 1,000 African people had been reported killed, stated that the influence of the Haitian revolution was the main reason why the enslaved had adopted the revolutionary option. The report described the Barbados rebels as being under the influence of the rhetoric or public speeches of Haitian leaders. It said that they were waiting on support from Haiti for their rebellious design and that they had grown impatient when the long awaited messenger from Christophe (who had had himself declared King in 1816) did not arrive. Everywhere the example of Haiti occupied the thoughts of enslaved people but no other colony managed to duplicate the Haitian revolutionary experience. In Trinidad, sugar planters reported that the name 'Haiti' featured in many anti-slavery songs.

4 The 1816 emancipation war in Barbados

The enslaved in Barbados had rebelled before, for example between 1685 and 1688, and many had been executed. On Easter Sunday, 14 April 1816, Barbados experienced a major rebellion. This was the first of the three major revolts by enslaved people that took place in the British Caribbean between the abolition of the slave trade in 1807 and general emancipation in 1838. The other two rebellions happened in Demerara in 1823 and in Jamaica in 1831-32.

Most reports about the rebellion suggest that it began at about 8:30 p.m. in the south-eastern parish of St Philip. It then quickly spread throughout most of the southern and central parishes of Christ Church, St John, St Thomas, St George and parts of St Michael. There were a few smaller outbreaks of arson in the northernmost parish of St Lucy, but there were no skirmishes with the militia. There were also no reports of fighting between rebels and the militia in the eastern and western parishes of St Andrew, St James and St Peter. So more than half of the island was engulfed by the rebellion.

The rebellion was short-lived. Within three days it was completely suppressed by a joint offensive of the local militia and imperial troops stationed on the island. Some Black soldiers of the 1st West India Regiment were part of the imperial troops. Martial law was imposed at about 2:00 a.m. on Monday 15 April and was lifted 89 days later on 12 July. Mopping-up operations continued in May and June.

The death toll
The death toll was very unevenly balanced between African and British people. Governor Leith's report of 30 April stated that, 'It was impossible with any certainty to state the numbers who have fallen: but about 50 however are at present conjectured to be the amount'. He also estimated that about 70 of the enslaved Africans were executed under martial law, and that many prisoners remained in jail awaiting trial. By 21 September he had revised his estimates to 144 of enslaved people executed under martial law, 70 sentenced to death, and 123 sentenced to transportation.

An anonymous author who wrote about the rebellion (he probably wrote his account in September that year) suggests that the Governor's figures were a gross underestimate of the total fatalities. He estimated that just under 1,000 of those enslaved were killed in battle or executed by the Law. Colonel Best, commander of the Christ Church parish militia, stated that his men alone killed 40 rebels in battles during Monday and Tuesday, 15 and 16 April. According to Colonel Best the reason why many more Africans had to be executed in the field was because 'the numbers not only implicated but actively employed' were great. In addition, he stated, many of the Africans had to be executed because 'they were all ringleaders'.

Only one British militiaman, Private Brewster of the St Philip parish militia, was killed in battle. Several British people were seriously injured and many of the elderly died of exhaustion that was caused by the rebellion. During the clashes between enslaved people and the imperial troops at Bayleys and Golden Grove Plantations on the Tuesday morning, two of the 150 men of the West India Regiment were killed. The Assembly's investigative committee estimated that damage to property was about 75,000 pounds. Twenty-five per cent of the year's sugar-cane crop was burnt as the rebels extensively used arson to undermine the economic base of the planters and to give directions to their scattered units.

An island-wide conspiracy
The governor, the colonels of the militia and the commandant of the imperial troops were convinced that enslaved had organised an island-wide conspiracy to overthrow enslavers and to obtain their freedom. They

denied that the rebellion was limited in nature, or directed specifically against a section of the island's planter class. They also did not believe that the revolt was simply a type of protest action by those enslaved which was designed to better their social and work conditions. According to Colonel Best the Monday night was to be the beginning of an arsonist attack upon the slave-owning community. He argued that those enslaved were going to burn canes and buildings to the ground. Then, while everyone was panicking because of the burning, the enslaved persons were planning the 'murder of white men' across the island on the Tuesday and/or Wednesday. One captured rebel, who was tried by court martial, confessed that they had intended enslavers to cry 'Water!' on the Monday night and 'Blood!' on the subsequent nights. Those enslaved wanted freedom. The only way to get it, according to Nanny Grigg, an enslaved woman and a leading agitator at Simmons Plantation, 'was to fight for it'.

'General Bussa'

The armed struggle was led by an African-born enslaved man named General Bussa, the ranger at Bayleys Plantation in the parish of St Philip. *The Times* newspaper of Barbados in April 1876 described the rebellion as 'The war of General Bussa'. This view also exists in the folk culture. The parliamentary papers for 1876, which included the government's report on the labour revolt that year also referred to General Bussa.

We do not have much information about General Bussa. However, we know that for an African-born man to be the main leader of a predominantly Creole rebellion is important. In 1816 at least 92 per cent of the enslaved population was Creole, and all the other leaders of rebel groups were Creole and not African-born. In addition, the fact that an African achieved the status of head ranger on his plantation suggests that in 1816 he most probably was not a young man, as the slave trade was abolished in 1807. To become the head officer among the enslaved workers on estates, it generally took at least ten years for Africans to acquire the language skills they needed, as well as their owner's confidence.

Fig 12.6 *General Bussa*

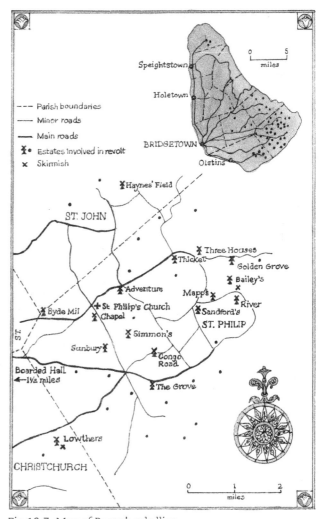

Fig 12.7 *Map of Bussa's rebellion*

We can also partly confirm General Bussa's military leadership in the rebellion by looking at the general movement of the armed battles. Rebel groups assembled at Bayleys Plantation on the Tuesday for the final showdown with imperial troops. This points to General Bussa's central role as the principal revolutionary leader. Rebels from all over the island came together at General Bussa at Bayleys, and it was there that the rebellion was finally put down by imperial troops. It has been said that General Bussa died while he was leading his rebel group in St Philip.

However, the Assembly reported that a free mixed-race, landless man named Washington Franklin had encouraged the enslaved to revolt. They referred to a confession by an enslaved man which stated that the rebels had intended to make Franklin the Governor in the revolutionary regime. But there is no reliable evidence that gives Franklin this leadership role. It is more likely that the St Philip militia used the opportunity of the rebellion to execute Franklin. British people within the parish had long considered him an insubordinate individual. He was arrested, tried for inciting rebellion, and hanged.

Information gathered from the confessions of the rebels suggests that there was a decentralised form of leadership. Each plantation was actively involved in the rebellion and was represented by a rebel group, which had one dominant leader. All the leaders met frequently to discuss strategy. Jackey, the enslaved head driver at Simmons Plantation in St Philip, and who reported to General Bussa, was mainly responsible for the overall coordination of these rebel groups. He convened planning meetings, most of which took place on his plantation.

The Assembly's report stated that Jackey frequently invited the leaders of rebel groups from plantations in St Philip, such as Gittens, Bushy Park, Byde Mill, Nightengale, Congo Road, and Sunbury, to his home to coordinate the details of the rebellion. John, the enslaved ranger at Simmons Plantation, was Jackey's chief messenger. John took messages to rebel groups throughout the southern and central parts of the island, and also kept General Bussa at Bayleys Plantation informed. James Bowland, a literate enslaved man belonging to the River Plantation in St Philip, confessed that John had been in frequent touch with General Bussa since March, and that he often took instructions to rebel groups in all the different parishes.

In addition to these leaders, three free mixed-race men mobilised the mass of enslaved people and spread rebellion propaganda. They were Cain Davis, Roach, and Richard Sarjeant. Davis held meetings with the enslaved on several plantations, such as River and Bayleys in St Philip, and Sturges in St Thomas. He spread the view among enslaved persons that their owners were opposing English efforts to have them freed, and that if they wanted freedom they had to fight for it, as Nanny Grigg suggested.

PRINICIPAL SLAVE ORGANISERS OF THE 1816 BARBADOS REBELLION

Name	Origins	Sex	Plantation	Occupation
Bussa	African	M	Bayleys	Ranger
King Wiltshire	Creole	M	Bayleys	Carpenter
Dick Bailey	Creole	M	Bayleys	Mason
Johnny	Creole	M	Bayleys	Standard bearer
Johnny Cooper	Creole	M	Bayleys	Cooper
John Ranger	Creole	M	Bayleys	Ranger
Charles	Creole	M	Sandford	Driver
Dainty	Creole	M	Mapp	?
Davy	Creole	M	Palmer	?
William	Creole	M	Sturges	Driver
Sandy Waterman	Creole	M	Fisherpond	Driver
Nanny Grigg	Creole	F	Simmons	Domestic
Jackey	Creole	M	Simmons	Driver
John	Creole	M	Simmons	Ranger
Mingo	Creole	M	Byde Mill	Ranger
Will	Creole	M	Nightingale	Ranger
John Barnes	Creole	M	Gittens	Driver
King William	Creole	M	Sunberry	Driver
Will Green	Creole	M	Congor Road	Driver
Prince William	Creole	M	Grove	Driver
Toby	Creole	M	Chapel	Driver
Little Sambo	Creole	M	Adventure	?

Source: Barbados House of Assembly Report.

The Assembly's report on the rebellion was published on 7 January 1818. The report reflected the general opinion of the planters that the rebellion started with the campaign for slave emancipation led by Mr Wilberforce. They accused him of having agents and spies in Barbados, who had informed those enslaved that the planters were trying to stop the process leading to their freedom, and so it was up to them to exert pressure by using violence.

Trials and executions

African people who were found guilty of either rebellion or looting could be executed. The military courts were set up at various points on the island. President of the House of Assembly, Spooner, had expressed concern that innocent people should not be implicated in the rebellion. At the same time he wanted to make sure that the military succeeded in effectively removing all the main rebels from society. In addition he asked the courts to consider that many Africans might have been forced to join the rebels for fear of being punished by them. Such Africans were to be separated from those primarily responsible for the organisation of the rebellion. If they were found guilty, then they must receive corporal rather than capital punishment.

The courts ordered that most of the guilty persons must be executed in areas where, during the rebellion, the 'public peace was maintained'. The logic behind this was that Africans who did not witness any violent conflict in the rebellion still needed to understand the consequences of rebellion. The courts decided that the most effective way to achieve this objective was to execute rebels in the parishes were people had not taken part in the rebellion. Most Africans in the parishes of St Peter, St Andrew, St James, St Joseph and northern zones of St Thomas did not physically take part in the rebellion.

Johnny, the cooper from Bayleys Plantation, was one of the primary leaders and a colleague of General Bussa. After he was captured, tried and condemned for rebellion, he was transported to the parish of St Peter and executed on Trent's Hill 'for the sake of an example to the Africans in that part of the island.' The Rector of the St James Parish Church, John Frere Pilgrim, attended this execution. He noted that shortly before Johnny died he confessed that he had joined the rebellion to fight for his freedom since the British on the island were not prepared to grant it.

A tradesman from Haynesfield Plantation in St John was found guilty of rebellion by a military tribunal in that parish. He was transported to a part of St Thomas and executed, along with William, the driver at Sturges plantation. Jack Groom, the driver at Haynesfield Plantation in St John, a main organiser of the rebellion, was found guilty and executed in the parish of St Joseph 'as an example to the Negroes in that part of the island'.

In this way the planters hoped to impress upon the Africans throughout the island the full reality of the consequences of revolutionary struggle. This policy was in line with how the Barbadian planters dealt with rebels. For example, during the 1675 rebellion which those enslaved aborted, the enslavers dragged the bodies of some captives through the streets of Speightstown in full view of slave crowds. They placed their heads on tall poles and left them there for public viewing.

Conrad Howell was in charge of several Courts Martial for seven weeks between 20 April and early June. He tried 150 captives, including the four free mixed-race men. The sentences he gave these captives were as follows: three of the four free mixed-race people were executed for rebellion, and one (Franklin) was executed for inciting Africans to revolt. Of the enslaved, 111 were executed, 11 received corporal punishments, 18 were acquitted, and ten sentenced to transportation. The trials continued into June and early July. Even after martial law was lifted on 12 July the planters were still not fully convinced that the rebels were fully rooted out. In mid-August large numbers of rebels were still held in prison as there was not sufficient evidence against them to bring them to trial.

After General Bussa

The rebels had lost the battle, but they did not accept that the war was over. The struggle against slavery continued although it was at a less organised level. In June 1816 a British Barbadian described the post-rebellion feeling among Africans, and outlined the dangers that these emotions posed for colonial society as follows:

> The disposition of the enslaved persons in general is very bad. They are sullen and sulky and seem to cherish feelings of deep revenge. We hold the West Indies by a very precarious tenure - that of military strength only. I would not give a year's purchase for any island we now have.

In September 1816 a small party of enslaved Africans was arrested for attempting to organise a second rebellion. Colonel Best who sat on the court martial which tried them, wrote:

> Murder was to have been the order of the day. As on the former occasion, the drivers, rangers, carpenters, and watchmen were chiefly concerned and few field labourers ... I am under no apprehension as to the consequences ... It is no longer delusion amongst the slaves ... I once thought before, I am now convinced that they were not entirely, if at all, led away in the last business by delusion. They conceived themselves to be sufficiently numerous to become the owners ... of the island.

According to Best, the captives confessed that in General Bussa's rebellion their tactics were wrong. They should not have engaged the militia in combat. Rather they should have aimed at and killed only the mounted officers. An enslaved person betrayed the September affair. He told the militia that the rebels offered him any position in their organisation that he desired. The ordinary soldiers would have been forced to flee.

Thomas Moody stated that the September affair, which originated in the parish of Christ Church, 'excited much alarm and uneasiness in the minds of the inhabitants'. However, when the secretary for the colonies requested that Governor Leith send all information he had about the rebellion attempt, he was told that the planned event should not cause alarm, 'and may more properly be regarded as the result of one or two turbulent men, disappointed at their failure, endeavouring ineffectually to reproduce insubordination.'

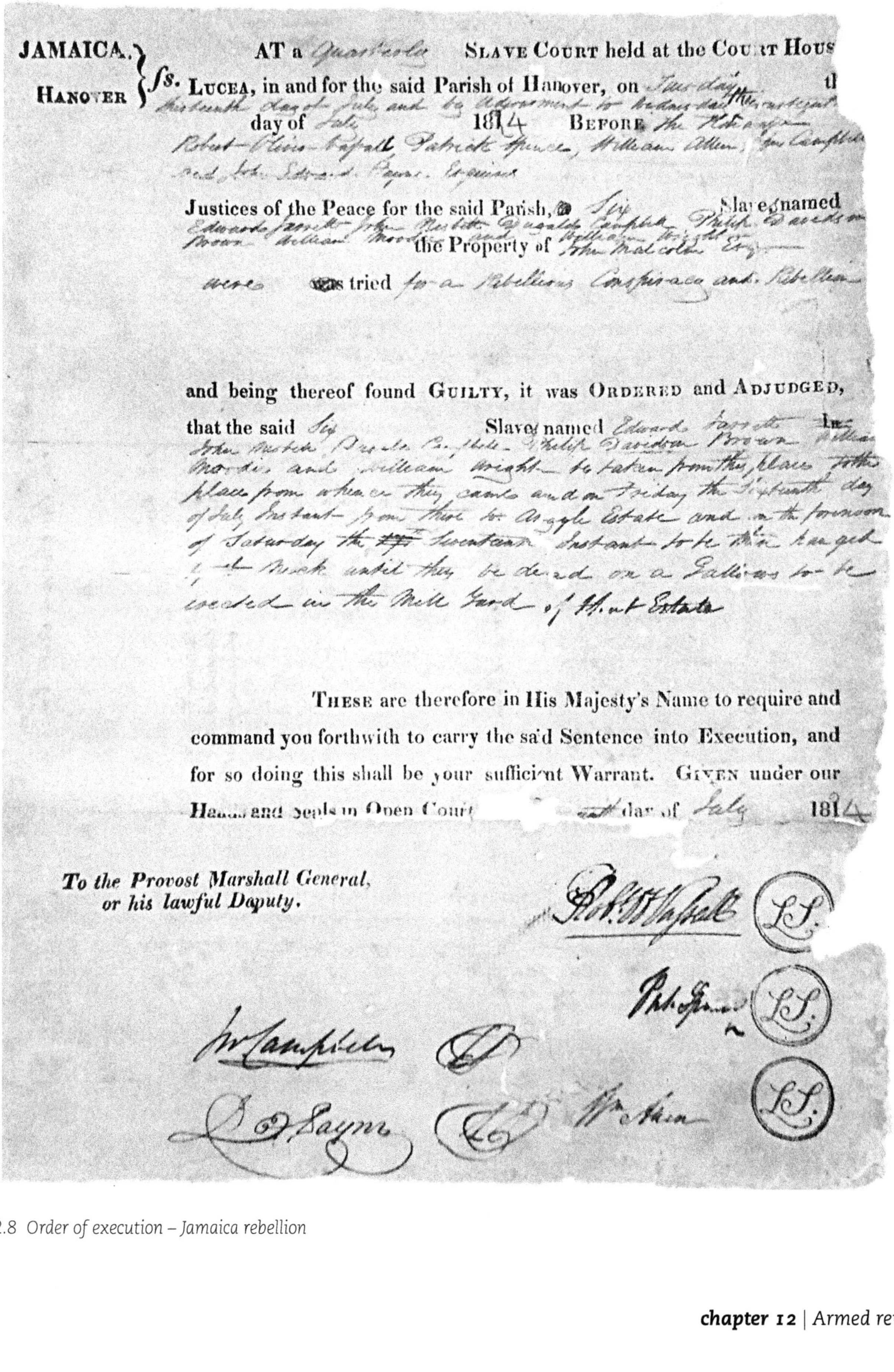

JAMAICA. } *ss.* **AT a** *Quarterly* **SLAVE COURT held at the COURT HOUS[E]**

HANOVER } **LUCEA, in and for the said Parish of Hanover, on** *Tuesday* **th[e]** *thirteenth day of July and by adjournment to Wednesday the fourteenth*
day of *July* **1814 BEFORE** *the Honble Robert Oliver Vassall Patrick Spence, William Allen, John Campbell and John Edward Payne Esquires*

Justices of the Peace for the said Parish, *Six* **Slaves named** *Edward Jarrett John Nesbitt Dugald Campbell Philip Davidson Brown William Moodie and William Wright* **the Property of** *John Malcolm Esq*

were **tried** *for a Rebellious Conspiracy and Rebellion*

and being thereof found GUILTY, it was ORDERED and ADJUDGED, that the said *Six* **Slaves named** *Edward Jarrett John Nesbitt Dugald Campbell Philip Davidson Brown William Moodie and William Wright be taken from this place to the place from whence they came and on Friday the Sixteenth day of July Instant from thence to Argyle Estate and in the forenoon of Saturday the Seventeenth Instant to be there hanged by the Neck until they be dead on a Gallows to be erected in the Mill Yard of that Estate*

THESE are therefore in His Majesty's Name to require and command you forthwith to carry the said Sentence into Execution, and for so doing this shall be your sufficient Warrant. GIVEN under our Hands and Seals in Open Court day of *July* 1814

To the Provost Marshall General, or his lawful Deputy.

Robt. O. Vassall (L.S.)

Patk Spence (L.S.)

Jn Campbell (L.S.)

J. E. Payne (L.S.)

Wm Allen (L.S.)

Fig 12.8 *Order of execution – Jamaica rebellion*

However, the abandoned September affair suggests that Africans persisted in their attempts to overthrow the planters' regime and in this way gain their freedom. It became clear to the planters that much greater repression was necessary to keep the Africans in subjection. John Beckles, Speaker of the House, summed up the debate by stating that the rebellious 'spirit' of the Africans was not subdued, nor would it ever be subdued.

5 Emancipation war in Jamaica, 1831/32

The Bussa-led Rebellion in Barbados in 1816 shook the enslavers into the deep realisation that African people wanted freedom without delay. Other rebellions confirmed that there were anti-slavery feelings in colonies other than those that relied on sugar plantations. For example, there was rebellion in Demerara in 1823, and in 1830 the Pompey revolt at Exuma Island, Bahamas. In Antigua, a rebellion in 1831 demonstrated that the enslaved had developed ideas about civil rights and were not prepared to give them up. When the government tried to outlaw the Sunday markets where enslaved persons bought and sold goods, those enslaved met this attempt with rebellion. Grenada, Belize, St Vincent, Tortola, St Lucia, Trinidad and Dominica, all experienced rebellions of one kind or another.

But the largest rebellion of all in terms of the number of African people involved, the size of the area affected, and the impact upon world opinion, was the 1832 Sam Sharpe-led war in Jamaica. The British had crushed a rebellion in the Second Maroon War in 1795-96. Thereafter, in 1806 there was a plot in the St George's parish, a mutiny of the Second West India Regiment, a plot in Kingston in 1808, the Igbo-led plot in St Elizabeth's parish in 1815, and the revolt in Hanover parish that became known as the 'Argyle War' in 1823. The Sam Sharpe-led war in 1832 clearly demonstrated that slavery could not be sustained in Jamaica.

Jamaica had the largest population of all the English colonies in the Caribbean. It contained some 320,000 enslaved persons out of a population of 380,000. Over 60,000 of those enslaved were involved in the war, which took place over the Christmas season in 1831. When it was all over, perhaps 900 of the enslaved and 14 British people and 3 free mixed-race were dead. Also, among the wounded, were 12 British and 2 free mixed-race. It was an extensively planned strike for freedom. It had a well-coordinated and recognisable leadership that expressed the politics of emancipation.

Damage during the war

The Jamaican Assembly published a report in 1832 setting out the damage done to property during the revolution. The list showed that 207 properties in the five western parishes, and 19 in other parishes suffered considerable damage. These properties were distributed as follows: 106 in St James, 41 in Hanover, 29 in Westmoreland, 21 in St Elizabeth's and 10 in Trelawny. Damage to property was also reported in Portland, St. Thomas-East, and St. Thomas-in-the-Vale. The properties that suffered greatest were Montpelier, Belvedere, Seven Rivers, Hazelymph, and Greenwich. Military operations were said to cost £175,000, and the total financial loss was £1,154,589.

Enslavers reported that the war began on the evening of Tuesday, 27 December 1831 with the burning of Kensington Pen outside Montego Bay. Other reports, however, state it began on Salt Spring Plantation, also outside Montego Bay, two weeks earlier. Enslavers suggested that the war did not come about because of any of the specific conditions of slavery but because of the political campaign for the emancipation of enslaved people in England. They blamed the Christian missionaries in Jamaica, as they had given Africans reasons to believe that emancipation was their right and that it was about to happen. Both the church missionaries and the British abolitionists denied responsibility for causing a war but enslavers remained adamant that Africans took their cue from the abolitionists.

In 1831 the free mixed-race people received full legal equality with British people in Jamaica. The enslaved Africans had good reason to believe that it was their turn next. On 22 December the Governor, Lord Belmore, published a proclamation that slavery was not yet abolished. He said that the belief of those enslaved that they were to be freed by the end of the year was incorrect. He urged them not to spread the rumour and to stop worrying about any pending freedom.

Non-conformist missionary preachers

The enslavers believed that these rumours about pending freedom came from non-conformist missionary preachers. They said that these preachers were encouraging enslaved persons to fight for freedom with high-pitched evangelical sermons. The Presbyterian, Wesleyan and Moravian missionaries managed to ward off these accusations by showing just how pro-slavery their sermons were. However the Baptists could not get rid of the charges. Their liberation theology set them apart as promoters of African people's rights to justice, equality, and equity. The

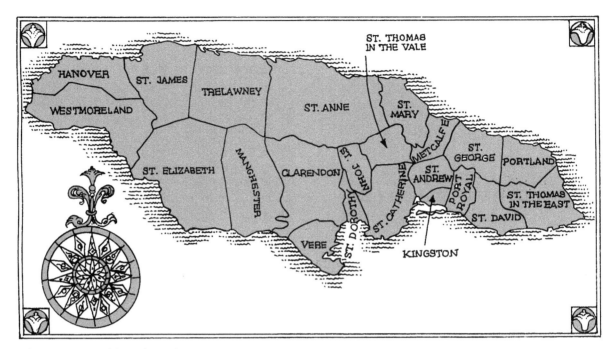

Fig 12.9 *The parishes of Jamaica.*

way they created their congregations was to empower African preachers who took the title of 'Deacon'. African deacons were sent out into the field to preach the principles of Christianity to other Africans.

African and British preachers within the Baptist movement did not demand immediate freedom and they certainly did not encourage the force of arms. But African congregations read between the lines and understood the preachers to be saying that the time had come for freedom.

They had taken this view long before the war began. By the middle of the year plans were well on the way and meetings were held regularly at the house of an enslaved man named Johnson, on Retrieve Plantation. During the height of the war, British Baptist preachers like William Knibb, and Burchell were jailed – some for up to six weeks. The Reverend Henry Bleby was not jailed, but he was captured by a British mob and was tarred and feathered. The Baptist chapels at Salter's Hill, and that of Knibb at Falmouth, which were always filled by African congregations, were destroyed by leading members of the British community while serving in the militia.

After the rebellion was crushed angry British people burnt over a dozen other chapels to the ground. They claimed that Baptists, Wesleyan, Methodists and Moravians encouraged the war. The Reverends Knibb and Burchell who were arrested at the Assizes (itinerant magistrate courts) had to defend themselves against the charge of incitement to war or sedition. When released Knibb sailed to England and Burchell to the United States.

The revolutionary planners

The revolutionary planners consisted of Samuel 'Daddy' Sharpe, the charismatic Baptist Deacon; 'Colonel' Johnson from Retrieve Plantation; 'Colonel' Campbell, a joiner at York Plantation; 'Captain' Robert Gardner, the head wagon man at Greenwich Plantation; 'Captain' Thomas Dove from Belvedere Plantation, who like Gardner, was literate, and George Taylor. Women activists and planners included Susan of Stracy Plantation, Bina, Charlotte of Moor Park Plantation, Eliza Lawrence, Ann Guy, and Kitty Scarlet.

Sam Sharpe

Sam Sharpe was the main leader both in terms of stating the objectives of the struggle and in the field as a commander. As a Baptist deacon he was given freedom of movement in western Jamaica and had built a solid reputation as an intelligent, articulate and compassionate man with considerable charm. At Retrieve Estate he spoke to the organisers about the plans for freedom. His comments were said to be spiritual in tone. It is said that British overseers in the Baptist Church, such as Rev. Henry and Rev. Knibb greatly admired Sharpe's character and personality, and had fallen to his charm.

But Knibb denied that he was an admirer of Sharpe or that he had ever made any such public statements about Sharpe. Bleby, however, who knew Sharpe well, and visited

Fig 12.10 *Attack of rebels on Montpelier Old Works Estate in the Parish of St. James, Jamaica 1832.*

him in jail while he was awaiting trial, wrote, 'I found him certainly the most intelligent and remarkable slave I have ever met with.' His description goes on:

> He was of the middle size, his fine sinewy frame was handsomely moulded, and his skin as perfect a jet as can be imagined. His forehead was high and broad, while his nose and lips exhibited the usual characteristics of the Negro race. I heard him two or three times deliver a brief extemporaneous address to his fellow-prisoners on religious topics, many of them being confined together in the same cell, and I was amazed both at the power and freedom with which he spoke, and at the effect which was produced upon his auditory. He appeared to have the feelings and passions of his hearers completely at his command; but when I listened to him once, I ceased to be surprised at what Gardner had told me. 'that when Sharpe spoke to him and others on the subject of slavery' he, Gardner, was 'wrought up almost to a state of madness.

Fig 12.11 *Reverend William Knibb*

Fig 12.12 Sam Sharpe

The trial of Sharpe took place on 19 April 1832. He was found guilty of rebellion or insurrection and was hanged on 23 May 1832. His final words are said to have been: 'I would rather die upon yonder gallows than live in slavery.'

Much of what we know of Sharpe comes from statements made by condemned enslaved persons and from his British Baptist colleagues and friends. Hylton, a condemned slave captive, spoke of his last meeting with Sharpe at Johnson's house. He said that he and others were 'spellbound' by Sharpe's speeches in which he referred to the 'manifold evils and injustices of slavery' and 'asserted the natural equality of man with regard to freedom'. He said that Sharpe told them, 'if the black man did not stand up for themselves, and take freedom, the whites would put them at the muzzles of their guns and shoot them like pigeons'. He also added that Sharpe had made it clear to them that they must have freedom, but if the 'bukra would pay' work would continue as normal. Without pay for their work, Sharp told them, they would have no choice but to fight for their full freedom.

Two other enslaved men, Robert Rose and Edward Barrett, said that Sam Sharpe took out his Bible at one secret meeting and placed it on the table. He then told them that 'we must be free; must not work again unless we get half pay'. The enslaved throughout Trelawny and St. James were in agreement and swore loyalty to Sharpe's leadership.

But African activists had clear ideas about why they fought as this extract from the testimony of William Binham demonstrates:

The Baptists all believe that they are to be freed; they say the Lord and the King have given them free, but the white gentlemen in Jamaica keep it back; they said if they did not fight for freedom they would never get it. I heard them all say this.

John Henry Morris echoed Binham's views when questioned after the suppression:

Q: *Can you state any matter or thing relating to, touching, or concerning the cause of the late rebellion among the slaves in this island*
Ans: *My opinion of the cause of the rebellion is, that it proceeded from the mistaken idea of the slaves that they were free, and from the proceedings of the British Government*

George Taylor seemed to have been particularly important and was described by the condemned prisoner Robert Morris as, 'a greater man than Gardner, Dove and McCail' and one who 'recommended "the thing", fighting for freedom.' Taylor, said Morris, was 'the head of the whole of this bad business began from Montego Bay ... the head amongst them'. James Gardner also hinted that while at first Sam Sharpe was the only ruler, others became important rulers subsequently. Other prisoners expressed the view that Tylor, not Sharpe, was the principal ruler. Indeed, George Taylor's name crops up time and again in confessions.

Robert Morrice, who confessed before Rev. Thomas Stewart on February 1, 1832 stated:

As I am now certain that I am going to die I am determined that those who led me to this shall be known, If I die, George Taylor must die also. ... The white people must send to the governor, and immediately lay hold of George Taylor. He is a greater man than Gardner, Dove and McCail. He recommended 'the thing', fighting for freedom, and he saw about the arms at Montego Bay. The head of the whole of this bad business began from Montego Bay, and Taylor is the head amongst them. ... I declare, as I am going to give up my life this day, that what I have just said is true.

chapter 12 | Armed revolt

The spread of the war

Plantations throughout western Jamaica were burnt and the Christmas sky became a sheet of flame. Within a week of war Sharpe's aides had established effective control of western Jamaica, and were preparing to move into the central and eastern zones.

Parish militias were called out on 28 December and Governor Belmore summoned a meeting of the War Council. They sent military units throughout the western parts. These military units set up camps at Black River, Savanna-la-mar, Lucea and Rio Bueno. They had instructions to support the retreating militias of St Elizabeth, Hanover, St Ann, and Wetmoreland. General Sir Willoughby Cotton, the Commander of the troops set up camp at Montego Bay on 1 January 1832. The following day, the Governor offered a $300 reward for the capture of 'General Ruler, Samuel Sharpe, or Tharp, alias Daddie Ruler Sharpe, or Tharp, director of the whole, and styled also Preacher to the Rebels, belonging to Croydon estate, St James'. He offered the same reward for Gardner, Dove and Johnson.

The battle of the bushes continued throughout western Jamaica for another month. As soon as the troops re-opened roads, the rebels ambushed soldiers and militias on them. They would 'strike and vanish in the air'. The revolutionaries ambushed the St James militia and attacked at Anchovy Bottom. General Cotton's men were also assaulted at Richmond Hill.

Maroon trackers

The general feared increasing fatalities and called upon the Maroons to honour their agreement with the government in which they had promised to assist in tracking and hunting rebel armies. Maroons from Moore Town and Charles Town were shipped into Falmouth to support those from Accompong. The Cuban tracking dogs were also used as they had been during the Second Maroon War.

The Maroon trackers were bounty hunters. Some of them collected prize money from the military command for amputated ears. The militia and troops burnt the houses of the enslaved, destroyed their provision grounds, and randomly executed captives in an effort to intimidate slave communities into surrendering rebel leaders or giving information as to their whereabouts. Some Maroons supported the revolutionaries, though.

The war is crushed

The militia fired rockets into the villages of the enslaved people and this proved effective. By the end of January the militia had overcome most of the rebel groups. On 29 January the Maroons captured 'Captain' Dehany, the untiring rebel leader who took the lead at this late stage. By this time Sam Sharpe was already in custody but we do not know if he was captured or if he surrendered. The Revolution was crushed. The Governor arrived at Montego Bay on 1 February and lifted Martial Law on 5 February.

Fig 12.13 View of the destruction of Roehampton Estate in the Parish of St James in January 1832

The execution of rebel leaders and some followers took place randomly. Those found guilty by court-martials were executed in public ceremonies. The Rev. Henry Bleby described the Montego Bay execution exercises like this:

At first shooting was the favourite mode of execution and many were thus disposed of. But when the novelty of this had ceased the gallows was put in requisition....The gibbet erected in the public square in the centre of town was seldom without occupants, during the day, for many weeks. Generally four, seldom less than three, were hung at once.. ..Other victims would be brought out and suspended in their place, and cut down in turn to make room for more, the whole heap of bodies remaining just as they fell until the Workhouse Negroes came and took them away, to cast them into a pit dug for the purpose, a little distance out of the town.

After sentencing, over 300 revolutionaries were executed and many more lost their lives on the battlefields of eastern and western Jamaica. The Governor found over 500 captives awaiting trial when he arrived at Montego Bay and more were arriving. He believed that none of them could avoid conviction. Most activists were hanged and maybe a third were shot. Some were deported as convicts to Canada and some were decapitated and their heads displayed on poles. Many were flogged, receiving between 10 and 500 lashes. Four women were hanged, including Kitty and Jenny from St James.

According to Michael Craton, the trial records also tell us a great deal about some of the occupations and identities of about 440 of the 627 persons who were charged. In general terms these persons could be categorised into occupation groups as follows:

Table 12.1 Occupations of charged activists

Occupations	Number
Fieldhands	271
Drivers	39
Headmen	35
Carpenters	48
Coopers	10
Masons	10
Blacksmiths	9
Hothouse doctor	1
Domestics	7

The data indicated the following groups in very general categories:

Table 12.2 Identities of activists

Africans		Free Black men	12
Average	37 years	Free Black women	2
Youngest	20 years	Free Coloured men	1
Oldest	70 years	White men	1

The war, then, was crushed within two months. Savage punishments followed as these examples from St James and Portland illustrate:

Parish of St. James, Jamaica SLAVE COURTS 1832

Names	To whom belonging	Sentence
Peterkin	Roehampton	Death
Barrett	Roehampton	100 lashes
Alias Geo. McClennan		Death
Wilson	Mgray?	Death
Samuel Sharpe	Samuel Sharpe, Esq.	Death
Alexander McIntosh	Leogan	Death
Thomas Hislop	Leogan	100 lashes
Prince	Vaughansfield	Death
Alexander Gow	Castle Wemyss	Death
Cyrus	Vaughansfield	Death
William Wilson	Anchovy Bottom	Transportation
Allick alias Alexander Milne	Chesterfield	Transportation
Billy alias Billy Mighty	John Baillie	Transportation
George Hellington	John Baillie	Death
George Miller	John Baillie	Death
Richard Bowen	John Baillie	Death

Courts Martial Parish of Portland (after the 1831/32 emancipation war)

Names	To whom belonging	Sentence
Geo H Cosens	Fairy Hill	Death
? Orr	Castle ?	100 lashes, 6 months imprisonment
John Taylor	Fairy Hill	50 lashes

Thomas Smith	Cold Harbour	200 lashes, 12 months imprisonment
Patrick Ellis	Mount Pleasant	100 lashes
Nicholas Simpson	Fairy Hill	Death
Solomon Atkinson	Fairy Hill	Death
Joseph Curry	Fairy Hill	300 lashes
Lambert Taylor	Fairy Hill	300 lashes
Frederick Fisher	Fairy Hill	150 lashes
George Murray	?	Acquitted
Richard Buckley	Fairfield	Death
Alexander Simpson	Fairy Hill	Death
Robert Markland	Zion Hill	Death
William Franklyn	Zion Hill	200 lashes
Thomas Williams	Zion Hill	?
Thomas Bells	Zion Hill	39 lashes

A Proclamation.

By His Excellency the Right Honourable Somerset Lowry Earl of Belmore, Captain General and Governor in Chief of this His Majesty's Island of Jamaica, and the Territories thereon depending, in America, Chancellor, and Vice Admiral of the same.

WHEREAS, Notwithstanding His Majesty's Royal Proclamation denouncing his high displeasure against all Slaves who should offend against the Laws by which they are governed, or resist the authority of their Masters or Managers, many slaves in certain parts of this Island, under the pretence that orders have been sent out by His Majesty for their emancipation, have proceeded to the most flagrant outrages and destruction of property: And, Whereas, the death of many of them, actually in arms, and the exemplary punishment already inflicted after trial upon several ringleaders in this Rebellion, must have convinced all Slaves engaged therein, that it is in vain to oppose the overwhelming force which is assembled to reduce them to obedience: And, Whereas, there is reason to believe that numbers are deterred from returning to their duty by a fear of that punishment which their rebellious practices merit, I have therefore thought fit, to issue this my PROCLAMATION, promising and assuring to all Slaves who have been misled by the misrepresentations of cunning and designing persons, His Majesty's most gracious pardon, Provided they do, within the space of ten days from the date hereof, surrender themselves at the nearest Military Post, or return peaceably to the plantations to which they belong, and resume their ordinary occupations, quietly submitting themselves and obeying all the lawful commands of their Masters or Managers: And I do hereby declare and make known, that all those principals and chiefs who shall be ....cted of having instigated or directed the destruction of the lives and properties of .... the peaceable inhabitants of this Island, are specially excluded from the benefit of this proclamation.

Given under my hand and seal at arms, at Montego-Bay, this third day of February, in the second year of His Majesty's reign, Annoque Domini, One Thousand Eight Hundred and Thirty-two.

Fig 12.14 Governor Belmore's proclamation

But the imperial government and the local enslavers understood that the system of slavery was near its end because of the extent of people's commitment to freedom, and the depth of their resolve. Enslaved Africans had made their position clear to the British Parliament who had been debating how to reform slavery rather than how to abolish it.

The 1831 revolution made many Parliamentarians understand that emancipation sooner rather than later was the only logical option if colonialism in Jamaica was to continue. In this way, Sam Sharpe's war brought about an earlier emancipation and built the Africans' confidence that they were agents of their own liberation.

6 Women and resistance

Enslaved women went to great lengths to secure their freedom. They contributed to the liberation of their families and the wider enslaved community. We have an example of this in a letter written by an enslaved woman in Barbados calling for her freedom. The letter was addressed to Thomas Lane, her owner who lived in London. It began as follows, 'My honoured master, I hope you will pardon the liberty your slave has taken in addressing you on a subject which I hope may not give you the least displeasure or offence'. The letter contained a request for freedom. It is dated 1804 and signed by Jenny Lane, a Creole Black woman.

The presence of women in the military vanguard of the Jamaica 1832 war did not escape the attention of the courts-martial or the magistrates in the civil trials. Some of the women who were sentenced to hang were pardoned but not all were that lucky. Most were given corporal punishment. Some received up to 300 lashes in addition to imprisonment.

The records of the civil trials and the courts-martial show that 627 persons were found guilty and charged. In a short time 344 of those convicted were shot by firing squad or hanged. Seventy-five females were among the convicted and as men found before, four were hanged.

Then there were women like Nanny of the Jamaican Maroons, and Nanny Grigg of the 1816 Bussa-led rebellion in Barbados, who took up arms in search of freedom. They did their best to improve their condition. All these women contributed to the tradition of struggle that enabled the enslaved community to survive and acquire freedom.

Natural rebels

Slavery was a system that was passed on at birth to the next generation of those enslaved. Children of enslaved women inherited their slavery. The European female could not be allowed to produce an enslaved child, whether African or European. This could only be the lot or fate of a child produced by an enslaved woman.

Children fathered by free African men or European men were born into slavery if their mothers were enslaved. European women and their children, because of their race, were not enslaved. Some European women had free-born children with enslaved men, as well as free African and free mixed-race men. Their children with African men enslaved or free were born into freedom.

So the system of slavery was organised upon the basis of race and sex. The enslaved woman had a life that was different from that of the enslaved man – and with important implication. Their experiences of slavery were very different from the experiences of enslaved men. Enslaved men had an advantage as they could father free-born children.

The millions of African women tried to oppose slavery with both their minds and their bodies. They used many strategies to negotiate and resist the harshness of slavery. There was nothing peculiar about Jenny's letter. There was nothing unusual about the enslaved woman in the British Virgin Islands who, in 1793, took a cutlass and severed her hand in protest against her enslavement. This case became famous in Britain and tells us volumes about the nature of women's anti-slavery attitudes.

The severed hand that was expected to work and feed the young indicates the relationship between resistance to work and the protection of sexuality. Enslaved women had the capacity to bear children and so they had to extend their resistance to slavery into sexual zones. Maternity and mothering were typical ways in which slave owners exploited enslaved women.

The 'breeding' policy

From the mid-18th century, when prices of enslaved Africans in the British Caribbean started to increase, the 'treatment' of enslaved persons became something of greater importance to enslavers. Their policy slowly shifted from 'buying' Africans to 'breeding' them on plantations. This social reform is described as the 'age of amelioration'.

In economic terms, amelioration meant that money that would have been spent on buying new Africans was now spent on maintaining the existing enslaved group. An aim of amelioration was to encourage enslaved women to have babies. It meant less work and better nutrition for pregnant and breastfeeding women, as well as the provision of some child care support from the enslavers. Enslavers offered enslaved women money for having healthy children. Enslaved midwives were also offered money to deliver healthy babies.

Offering money to women to have children meant that enslavers considered it possible to influence their social and sexual behaviour. Throughout slavery, plantation managers reported that they could not explain the low birth rates and high infant death rates. Most were suspicious that enslaved women were practising birth control. They did not know how women could stop being fertile. They generally believed that women had decided to resist having enslaved children. So because enslaved women declared reproductive opposition to slavery, the enslavers said that they were engaging in resistance through abortion and pregnancy prevention measures.

Some women appeared to be psychologically broken by the power of enslavers. These women expressed patterns of behaviour that others described as subservient.

Enslavers made reference to the kindness they showed some females. They also stated that the women's behaviour was often unpredictable. We see evidence of this in the cases when the enslaved appear before the courts. An example of this is in the records of the 1736 Antigua anti-slavery plot. Philida, the sister of Tomboy, the alleged leader of the Antigua conspiracy, was arrested and charged as a participant. She was accused of publicly making some 'virulent expressions upon her brother's account'. This was an action that surprised her owner who said that she was a loyal and faithful slave. She was also identified as the person who betrayed her brother.

Queen Mother

Philida's testimony shows that she was present at the meeting when her brother designed and discussed plans for the rebellion. Other women, most notably Obbah and 'Old Queen', were also present. It was said that Obbah performed traditional Akan rituals to strengthen secrecy and solidarity among the rebels.

There is a lot of information about the role of Queen Mothers in the resistance. Barbara Bush has said that 'women were in the vanguard'. Nanny of the Maroons was considered a Queen Mother who possessed considerable spirit power. It was said that she could use her body to repel the bullets of British soldiers and that she was unbeatable.

In the case of the 1736 Antigua plot, evidence indicates that 'Old Queen' may have assumed the role of a traditional Akan Queen Mother who had political influence with the enslaved. This was also the case with the Jamaica conspiracy of 1760 in which rebels declared that they intended to appoint Abena, the Akan slave, as 'Queen of Kingston'.

The relation between the Queen Mothers and the magico-religious leaders, the voodoo priestess in particular, is not always clear. But it was said the Queen Mothers were often given the task of ensuring loyalty, discipline and secrecy. It was believed that they had direct access to ancestral spirits and were respected for this power.

Hucksters and economic resistance

The economic culture of the Africans in the Caribbean became part of resistance strategies. Women provided consistent leadership in this. In West African societies women were dominant in the small-scale internal marketing of foodstuffs. Despite their enslavement in the Caribbean, this culture persisted. Huckstering of foodstuffs on street corners, in markets, and from house to house, was largely part of women's culture. They defended and expanded it in spite of hostile legislation to control, suppress and eradicate it.

Enslaved women grew crops, bought and sold foodstuffs, sold goods to plantation and urban stores, and bartered their food allowances for other goods and services. They did all these things despite the opposition of their owners and the laws in some colonies. When the enslavers tried to abolish the hucksters' market used by the enslaved in Antigua in 1831 this sparked off riotous behaviour by enslavers women. In the 18th century, Barbadian enslaved recognised the foolishness of the police and the laws against huckster women. They started issuing licences to the women to secure their control and regulation of the huckster market.

Newton's Plantation in Barbados was the home of Old Doll, the retired housekeeper. In 1796 she was described by Manager Wood as a 'perfect out-shop for dry goods, rum, sugar, and other commodities'.

Rebel women

Lucille Mair has written extensively about women's contribution to the anti-slavery movement. She has described those who organised and led rebellions as 'rebel women'. Nanny, leader of the early 18th century Jamaican Maroon band, takes pride of place. She is celebrated today as a Jamaican national heroine.

In Barbados, Nanny Grigg was one of the main organisers of the 1816 anti-slavery rebellion. She is described as the person who informed her fellow victims about the Haitian Revolution and its significance for them. It was said that she mobilised a cadre of enslaved males around her ideas.

An enslaved man named Robert stated that Nanny Grigg told the people on his estate that 'they were all damned fools to work, for that she would not, as freedom they were sure to get', and that the way to get it was 'to set fire, as that was the way they did it in St Domingo'.

Robert Dirks has argued that when enslaved people were discontented on the plantation, it was usually the

Fig 12.15 *Women and resistance, illustration from cover of Lucille Mair's book*

female gang members (field hands) who complained the loudest. Women earned the reputation for being the main cause of protests and the 'more unmanageable element of the workforce'.

Jacob Belgrave, for example, the mixed-race owner of a large Barbados sugar plantation, told the authorities that shortly before the April 1816 Bussa revolt he was verbally abused by a gang of enslaved women. The women accused him of being opposed to the British parliament trying to abolish slavery. During the revolt, those enslaved singled out his estate for special treatment. He claimed property destruction of £6,720, the third highest in the island. There were altogether 184 damaged estates.

Gender and anti-slavery

Females expressed a wider range of responses to their enslavement than males. This was because their experiences as enslaved women were more complex, both in their private and public lives. They had to protect themselves and their daughters from empowered European men sexually exploiting them. Rape was not a crime at that time. Under slave laws, enslaved women were property and the owner of property had a right to use 'such property' as he saw fit so long as it was not destroyed. Enslaved women were subject to this kind of reasoning by those who developed the slave laws. Some women ran away, murdered their attackers, committed suicide, and other such defiant acts. Many, however, were victims. But even then they did their best possible to find positive ways to interpret their misfortune.

We can learn a lot from the autobiography of Mary Prince, the well-known enslaved Caribbean woman who became an important anti-slavery political figure in London. She 'cared' for the children of a mistress, but did not lose her own identity in the process. She had a very strong sense of her own freedom and married without the permission of her mistress. For this she was horsewhipped.

Mary Prince tried to be a loyal worker. But at the same time she confronted her mistress with the idea that 'to be free is very sweet'. British people, she wrote, all had their 'liberty', and 'that's just what we want'. 'Freedom' and 'liberty' are words that appear like monuments on the pages of her book.

To sum up

The enslaved, both male and especially female, persisted in their struggle for emancipation. Their resistance took many forms, including marronage and armed revolts. They planned and plotted and waged wars until they had freed themselves.

Revision questions

1 'No slave society was politically stable'. Comment, using suitable examples of instability.
2 For any one of the following armed rebellions/wars,
    1763 Berbice rebellion
    1791 Haitian revolution
    1816 Barbados war
    1831/32 Jamaica war,
    a State two reasons for the outbreak.
    b Give the name of the leaders identified.
    c Examine the methods of organisation.
    d Examine the methods of suppression.
    e State the outcome of the rebellion for the enslaved peoples.

Chapter 13

Caribbean emancipations

'Emancipate yourself from mental slavery, none but ourselves can free our minds.'
(Bob Marley)

European-run Caribbean colonies were successful because of slavery. Slavery became the basis of a new civilisation. It took just about 100 years to complete the spread of slavery all over the Caribbean. It took an equal time to remove it from the entire region. Between the 1794 French Emancipation Decree (which followed the revolution in St Domingue) and the emancipation legislation of the imperial Spanish government in 1886, all European governments with Caribbean colonies passed emancipation laws. These laws made it a crime to enslave people.

In this chapter we will learn about:
1. The background to emancipation
2. The abolition of the trade in Africans
3. The system of ameliorating slavery
4. Emancipation in Haiti and its impact on the slave systems of the wider Caribbean
5. Emancipation in English colonies
6. Emancipation in French colonies
7. Emancipation in Danish and Dutch colonies
8. Emancipation in the Spanish colonies
9. Comparisons: emancipation in the USA

1 Background to emancipation

Passing Emancipation Acts was a slow, drawn-out process. The British passed an Emancipation Act in 1833; the French in 1794 and again in 1848 because they had re-established slavery in 1802; the Danish in 1848; the Dutch in 1863; and finally the Spanish in 1886 or the Portuguese in 1888. Each European government took its own decision around slavery and emancipation for its own reasons and when it wished. Colony by colony, the system of slavery crumbled. It finally disintegrated in the Caribbean when the Spanish Law was passed in 1886. The Iberians, the first to establish and legalise slavery in the Caribbean, were the last to abolish it.

Each European government arrived at emancipation as a result of many different pressures on it over time. No government willingly abolished slavery. Each was pushed to do so by a combination of political, economic, moral and cultural forces. In all these societies the debates around emancipation divided parliaments, and public opinion, and exercised the minds of public intellectuals.

For most leading Enlightenment philosophers slavery was a moral problem. They targeted slavery in the Caribbean and elsewhere as something that had to go so that moral authority could be restored in European civilisation. The leading intellectuals who wrote about the crime of slavery were people like Jean Jacques Rousseau (1712-78), François Voltaire (1694-1778), Denis Diderot (1713-84) and Charles Montesquieu (1698-1755) of France; Jeremy Bentham (1748-1832); Adam Smith (1723-90) and David Hume (1711-76) of Britain; and Thomas Paine (1737-1809) of the United States of America. As radical thinkers, and in some cases activists, these philosophers called for their societies to rid themselves of slavery.

The anti-slavery movement in Europe developed as a broad-based alliance of religious sects, politicians, radical philosophers and intellectuals, industrialists, workers' organisations and women's groups. Many organisations had a significant number of members who were African activists. Among the religious pressure groups were the Quakers, Methodists, Baptists and Moravians. In England, intellectuals, like Thomas Clarkson (1760-1846) and Adam Smith, and politicians like William Wilberforce (1759-1833) and William Pitt, made significant contributions to the abolition of the trade in Africans in 1807 and ultimately to the emancipation process.

In France, intellectuals like the Abbé Gregoire (1750-1831), the Abbé Raynal (1713-96) and the Marquis de Lafayette (1757-1834) were activists in both the anti-human trade and anti-slavery movements. These prominent personalities gave credibility to the emancipation campaign. By the end of the 18th century, then, slavery was under attack from several angles – the religious, the economic and the moral and spiritual. The French Revolution of 1789 and the St Domingue Revolution of 1793 took these ideas and movements to their logical conclusions. This resulted in the first phase of Caribbean emancipation legislation. In 1793 Leger Felicite Sonthonax, who was the representative of the French Revolution, announced in the French colonies the abolition of slavery. The law was formally adopted by the National Convention in 1794 and led to emancipation in St Domingue, Cayenne, Martinique and Guadeloupe.

Fig 12.1 British politician William Wilberforce

2 Abolition of the transatlantic trade in Africans

The debate on emancipation spoke about abolishing the buying and selling of people, and freeing all enslaved persons as two separate acts. Because of this there was a significant time difference between the abolition of the trade in Africans and general emancipation. In some cases between 25 and 57 years separated the two acts of abolition. This was certainly the case with the British and Spanish governments. The British abolished the African trade in 1807 and slavery in 1834. The Spanish technically abolished the trade in 1826, and slavery finally ended in 1886.

The thinking of religious groups, humanist philosophers and a smaller category of radical political leaders dominated European abolitionist movements. Many of these groups were not completely resolved about their condemnation of the trade. Most did not call for an outright, immediate abolition of the trade.

Some clerics and philosophers were critical of the trade in their published texts and speeches. However, few were committed to public demonstration to achieve abolition. In the 17th century Quakers in the English Caribbean colonies were not opposed to the trade in Africans or slavery in general, but called for moderation in the usage of enslaved persons. They asked enslavers to cater for the mortal souls of those enslaved, and make provisions for the freedom of those persons who were good and loyal. English enslavers saw the Quakers position as an attempt to undermine their full property rights in people enslaved. They persecuted the Quakers and drove them out of the Caribbean. They settled in the mainland colonies where members of their Church were much more tolerant of the human trade and of slavery.

Even though some European philosophers spoke and wrote on the question of human liberty, social freedom, justice and notions of the public good, they still supported and participated in both slavery and the trade in Africans. John Locke of England had a well-established reputation as a leading philosopher on the theory of liberty. Yet he was a business administrator and one of the main investors in the Royal African Company which was the leading English human trafficking corporation in the last quarter of the 17th century. In addition, he was an investor in a plantation in the Bahamas.

Thomas Hobbes, too, wrote extensively on liberty and democracy. But in his writings he justified slavery. He saw Africans as captives of war. So, he said that their enslavement was lawful and moral. The racism in the work of both John Locke and Thomas Hobbes shows how limited much of early English liberal philosophy was.

Voltaire, in particular, was scornful of the anti-intellectualism of racism. He ridiculed the idea that a so-called 'white race' was entitled to enslave a so-called 'black race'. He saw it as a sign of ignorance that people should consider human features such as skin colour, hair texture and facial structures important indicators of civilisation. He condemned enslavers for using such arguments to justify their trade in death. Rousseau, like Voltaire, saw European involvement in the transatlantic human trade as the worst modern corruption of the use of economic power and political authority. No one, they said, had a right to enslave another. Rousseau's voice and Voltaire's vision helped to generate an abolitionist feeling in France.

The philosophers' opposition to slavery was strengthened by the publication in 1776, in England of Adam Smith's book, *The Wealth of Nations*. Smith described enslaved workers as less productive and more expensive than free workers. This argument gave the anti-slavery politicians a powerful reason to support freedom.

Fig 13.2 *The French thinker Voltaire*

Fig 13.3 *Rousseau, whose voice helped the abolitionist cause*

England legislates the abolition of human trafficking from Africa

In 1783 the English House of Commons debated a bill to abolish the trade in Africans on moral grounds. The majority was against the bill because they argued that slavery was very important for the economy. Five years later a 'Committee for Effecting the Abolition of Slave Trade' was founded in England, led by Thomas Clarkson. The society agreed on a two-phased approach to abolition; first, they would abolish the trade in Africans, and second slavery.

Parliamentary support for the Anti-Slavery Society came from evangelical leader and Member of Parliament for Hull, William Wilberforce, liberal intellectual Charles Fox, and Prime Minister William Pitt. Clarkson presented evidence showing how unprofitable the human trade was, how it led to an enormous loss of life, and how it had damaged African and colonial societies. Fox stated: 'slavery itself, odious as it is, is not nearly so bad a thing as the slave trade.' Prime Minister Pitt agreed that the evil of the African trade should be removed as long as the financial interests of England would not be harmed, and could be developed in at least the medium term. The following year the British Privy Council launched an investigation into the transatlantic trade in enslaved Africans.

Fig 13.4 *Wedgewood mug with anti-slavery medallion which was the seal of the Society for the Gradual Abolition of Slavery*

The British finally abolished the transatlantic trade in African captives in 1808 when Parliament was persuaded that the national economic and political interest would best be served by the abolition.

The French abolish the trade in Africans

The French followed with the establishment of the *Société des Amis des Noirs*. This French abolitionist movement was led by Marie Jean Condorcet, Antoine Lavoisier, Jacques-Pierre Brissot, Honors Mirabeau, Etienne Claviere, Louis-Alexandre La Rochefoucauld and Jerome Petion. But the movement never had the same impact on the people of France as the British abolitionist movement did.

In 1791 the French National Assembly had debated and condemned both the transatlantic slave trading and the colonial slave owning. The assembly followed the British courts, although it took 20 years. They declared that any person who arrived on French soil would be free of slavery, but they continued to distinguish between slave trading and slave ownership. In 1794, the Convention in Paris abolished slavery but slave trading continued under law.

The Americans abolish the trade in Africans

The politically independent Americans took the lead in the abolition of the trade in illegally captured Africans. In the 1780s many states such as those in the Carolinas, Maryland and Virginia outlawed the importation of enslaved persons from Africa. In 1778 the legislature of Massachusetts debated an anti-human trade bill and in the same year the Virginians voted to free all illegally imported Africans.

The Danish abolish the trade in Africans

In 1792 the Danish government declared that from 1803 no trade in enslaved Africans would be allowed in its colonies. This enabled their Caribbean settlements to stock up with African captives and they did. More Africans were imported into St Croix and St Thomas in this time than during the previous 100 years. The government was clear on the issues. They said that the economic benefits of the human trade had fallen to such a low level that it was not worth the moral and political criticism and outrage. They said that the forts on the African coast, particularly Christiansborg Castle at Accra, were not profitable. Also, like the British, the Danes had shifted their slave labour policy from buying Africans to breeding Creoles. Colonists were encouraged to promote the natural growth of the enslaved population rather than purchase enslaved Africans.

The trade in Africans continues

The northern Europeans outlawed slave trading to their own colonies. However they were aware that slavers had found new, larger markets for their human cargo in the older colonial empires of Spain and Portugal. Indeed, in the 19th century, Spanish Cuba and Portuguese Brazil became the largest markets for captured Africans after

England, France, Denmark and Holland had abolished the transatlantic trade in Africans to their own colonies.

In 1800, the United States Federal government voted to make it illegal after 1808 for any resident or citizen to ship enslaved captives, or invest in any trading project that supplied enslaved Africans to a foreign country. As a result, between 1800 and 1808 there was a flood of Africans into the major slave-owning states such as Georgia. In addition, in 1802, Napoleon reopened transatlantic slaving into the French Empire. This policy reversal was celebrated by the consumers in Nantes, Bordeaux and Marseilles.

British and United States abolition of the transatlantic trade in Africans in 1808 brought in a new era – the era of Europeans illegally engaging in slave trading mostly to Cuba and Brazil. It brought into being an inter-colonial slave trade. Britain and America put political pressure on the Spanish and Portuguese governments to abolish slave trading in their Empires. In 1815 a British-Portuguese abolition deal was made and in 1818 the British made a similar deal with the Netherlands and Spain. However, slave traders ignored these deals and the governments of Spain and Portugal were not keen to enforce them. Enslaved Africans poured into Cuba and Puerto Rico in English, French, Dutch, Danish, Portuguese, and American ships. In 1818 the French, once again, abolished the trade in African people.

The Haitian government policed the high seas to suppress the illegal trade. In 1819, for example, a Haitian naval vessel, named *Wilberforce*, seized the Spanish slave ship *Dos Unidos*, off its coast. The ship was laden with enslaved Africans headed for Cuba. The Africans were freed and declared citizens of Haiti. The Cuban government demanded that President Boyer of Haiti return these properties. The request was ignored just like Pétion had refused to return the Jamaicans from the *Deep Nine* in 1819. In the 1820s thousands of enslaved people were shipped into Brazil each year. The transatlantic human trade was finally abolished by Portugal in 1831, but it was not until the 1850s that Brazil effectively refused Africans.

Cuban slavery

In this period of abolitionism, slavery took off as an economic system in Cuba. In 1830 there were twice as many sugar plantations in Cuba as in 1800 and the enslaved population was growing rapidly because they were imported from Africa. The Spanish government had legislated in 1826 that any African who could prove that he or she was illegally imported into a colony would be set free. However this provision was not enforced, just like the Portuguese law of 1831. In the 1840s Cuba became the leading cane sugar producer in the world, and again Africans were imported each year in their thousands. As in Brazil, it was not until the 1850s that Cuba finally ended the human trade.

European humanitarians were not the only ones who struggled against the trade in African captives. The literature of the time shows that Africans themselves were strongly committed to abolishing slavery. They knew that the transatlantic trade in Africans would not end until slavery itself was abolished. They did not separate the two activities: slavery relied on the trade in Africans for most of the period.

The abolition of slavery in Haiti

The greatest rebellion against the transatlantic trade in Africans and the inter-colonial trade in Africans came with the 1805 Haitian constitution. The leaders of Haiti were themselves mostly former slaves. They declared that any African or native Caribbean person who arrived in Haiti would be declared a citizen. This legal provision effectively abolished slavery and replaced it with the granting of citizenship and nationhood. This was the most significant development for Africans in the wider Atlantic world.

Enslaved Africans from all the societies of the Americas fled to Haiti as boat people in search of liberty, freedom and citizenship. Haiti became the Atlantic symbol of African diasporic redemption and liberation. Boatloads of people arrived on its shores, fleeing from slavery.

3 Ameliorating slavery

We have seen that the abolition of the transatlantic trade in Africans did not immediately lead to the end of slavery.

Slavery was still profitable. The enslavers put their economic interests above moral and philosophical criticism. However, they also tried to respond to this criticism in some way. Throughout the Caribbean enslavers reluctantly accepted a system known as 'amelioration' introduced by the British Government. This was a series of policies that were designed to improve the material and social conditions of those enslaved so as to encourage them to reproduce and breed. Through these policies the enslavers made an effort to be more responsive to the many demands of those enslaved and to have less power and authority in their lives.

The amelioration proposals said that pregnant women and infants should receive a better diet and nutrition and that enslaved females should no longer be whipped. The proposals stated that overseers and drivers should stop carrying whips in the fields and that they should keep a record of all lashes administered to enslaved males. All punishments should only be administered 24 hours after the offence when tempers had cooled. Furthermore, the proposals stated that enslaved people should get religious instruction and that church marriages between enslaved males and females should be encouraged. The enslaved people should get Saturday off as a market day so that they could attend church on Sundays. It cannot be said that the amelioration experiment worked well. The enslavers were angry and colonial legislatures did not want to implement the proposals because they objected to the imperial government dictating their labour relations, and because they believed that the reforms would make enslaved Africans insubordinate and rebellious.

The first step in the amelioration of slavery was the abolition of the trade in Africans. The next step needed to be the abolition of slavery. We will now return to look more closely at what happened in Haiti and its consequences.

4 Emancipation in Haiti and its impact on the slave systems of the wider Caribbean

In 1802 Emperor Napoleon Bonaparte restored slavery and withdrew the Emancipation Law of 1794. The enslaved Africans of St Domingue and other French colonised territories fought a bloody war of resistance, with the result that Emperor Napoleon did not succeed in restoring slavery in St Domingue. His troops and those of the English and Spanish were defeated by the emancipated people who had become free citizens when General Jean Jacques Dessalines proclaimed the Independent state of Haiti on 1 January 1804.

Haiti passed its emancipation laws and consolidated this freedom in its constitution at a time when the less profitable areas of the Caribbean slave system were undergoing important changes. When Haiti was pulled out of the Caribbean slave system it sent huge shock waves through the trade in Africans that threatened its future viability. It was a mortal blow. Despite great investment and management efforts to save the trade in Africans over the next two decades, the recovery process did not really work.

Three important developments took place within the slave system in the Caribbean and in Europe at the time of the Great Emancipation Initiative of the Haitian people.

a. Political attention in Europe was focused on the fact that Caribbean slave societies were the greatest destroyers of African life anywhere in the colonial world. After three centuries of importing over five million Africans, societies still relied upon the trade in Africans to increase the slave population. But after 300 years the Caribbean enslaved population was not growing naturally. It was naturally declining. This decline was compared with the earlier genocide of the indigenous Caribbean populations. If Africa was a 'white man's grave' then the Caribbean was a 'black peoples' grave'.

b. The Haitian Revolution took place at a time when in Western Europe, especially in England, industrial capitalism was developing. The factory was replacing agricultural production as the main source of wealth.

The industrial capitalist class saw the sugar plantation system as holding back industrial development in Britain because they still used the labour of enslaved Africans and their descendants rather than the new machine technologies. Sugar producers borrowed money in Europe to finance their production. They also needed European markets to export the bulk of their sugar. Also the new industrial capitalists saw the sugar planters in the Caribbean as a backward, old-fashioned, immoral business class. Industrial capitalism used the wage labour of people who were free. More and more the use of enslaved labourers was seen as primitive, economically inefficient, and socially undesirable.

The Haitian Revolution shook the Caribbean slave economy to its very roots. The market forces and political support of the new industrial period were also shaking the economy based on slavery. Economists agreed that slavery bred inefficiency, higher costs and a waste of resources. Respected political leaders preferred to identify with the new industrial system that viewed slavery as part of an old backward world. The slave economy also had no real intellectual support. In public places, influential moral and religious thinkers spoke about slavery's immorality and social destruction. They all came together to form the anti-slavery movement that gained mass support among workers and women. Workers saw slavery as being close to their own oppressive experiences.

c. The amelioration of slavery through the abolition of the transatlantic trade in Africans also affected the slave system. Enslavers in Brazil, the USA and the Spanish Caribbean could still get enslaved people from Africa. But the British Caribbean, which had large slave economies, could not survive without the ongoing African slave trade. Of the major sugar economies, only Barbados and to a lesser extent St Kitts, could maintain production and profitability without new supplies of enslaved Africans. Jamaica, the largest sugar producer, was in difficulty.

The English had recently acquired new colonies – Trinidad from the Spanish and Guiana from the Dutch. Both these colonies had tremendous potential as sugar colonies. However, they could not get off to a good start because of huge labour shortages. They imported thousands of enslaved people from Barbados, but this was still not enough. So, there was a huge problem in the overall productivity in the British plantation system.

The British had believed that if they stopped the supply of enslaved Africans to their colonies, the sugar producers would be forced to care better for those enslaved they had, encourage them to reproduce, adopt new management schemes, and would use machine technology to replace human labour. However this did not happen. There were more positive results in the Spanish colonies of Cuba, Puerto Rico and Santo Domingo and in Portuguese-colonised Brazil. The 1820s and 1830s was the age of the railroad and steam-driven sugar mills. Cuba became the Caribbean model of how to use this modern technology in a plantation system. In contrast, the British-colonised territories were models of the old technologies.

By the 1830s enslaved Cubans were producing more sugar than those in all the British colonies. The British colonies remained economically backward despite efforts in Jamaica to establish a railway system and steam-powered mills. In addition, it became clear in Britain that cheaper sugar could be obtained from Cuba and Brazil on the world market. It also came from the East Indies, especially Mauritius, where the sugar industry using Indian indentured labour and enslaved Africans, had taken off.

The railway system brought the sugar cane from distant fields to a centrally located steam-driven mill. The effect of this was transformative. The old wind, water and cattle-powered mills were inefficient. The steam mill was powerful and allowed large-scale sugar producers to grind more cane at lower costs. The saving they made in the production process led to lower sugar prices on the world market. This competitive advantage placed British producers in difficulty.

5 Emancipation in British colonies

The British built the strongest anti-slavery political movement in 18th century Europe. In the beginning its main leader was Granville Sharp (1735-1815). He was responsible for bringing to the court the circumstances of an enslaved man, James Somerset whose trial led to slavery being declared illegal in Britain.

Somerset was an enslaved man from Jamaica who was taken to Britain by his owner. Once there, he tried to secure his freedom. But his owner was opposed to this and tried to send him back to Jamaica. Sharp took the case to court. Lord Chief Justice William Mansfield heard the case on 22 June 1772. Mansfield ruled that 'the state of slavery' was revolting to British Law and so Somerset had to be set free. The Mansfield Judgement was a determining moment although British colonies in the Caribbean administered their own laws and so the Mansfield Judgement did not apply there. However, it did influence the thinking of judges in other European countries. In 1836 French judges made decisions in courts that outlawed slavery in France, and judges in Spain did the same in 1864.

Adam Smith made a name for himself as a leading Scottish political economist when he attacked the Caribbean slave system and the enslavers. Smith argued that the slave plantation economy was an inefficient one – it was wasteful, low in worker productivity and high in economic costs. He showed that free workers were more efficient and productive, and could produce cheaper commodities. The plantation as 'a business', Smith argued, did not make sense in how it operated economically. It was forced to keep workers who had no long-term reason or incentive to be efficient, and who had to still be maintained even when they were unproductive.

Smith presented a solid and compelling economic argument for the abolition of slavery. Economists had now joined philosophers and religious leaders in condemning slavery. They were a powerful alliance that was sure to win political battles in Parliaments where enslavers still had support for the world of slavery. However, by the middle of the 1820s the concept of a gradual movement to emancipation had taken root in British politics. The 1831 Jamaican anti-slavery rebellion helped to increase support for this path.

CLR James and Eric Williams have argued that by the mid-1800s the Caribbean slave system had already played its critical role in the rise of British industrial development and was no longer important. The sugar plantations in the British Caribbean colonies were no longer producing new wealth at the rate that was needed for growth and development in Britain. Rather, these plantations were high-cost and low-profit places. They were now a social and political embarrassment and an economic burden to the modernising Britain.

So the slave system had to go. It was now irrational to keep it by using social, political or economic arguments. Everyone always knew that slavery was immoral, but this had been overlooked because of high profits. Now it could not be tolerated politically when its profits were low and there were new, larger sources of wealth available.

Fig 13.5 Proclamation of emancipation, Spanish Town, Jamaica

Emancipation was the solution to this policy crisis. The lessening financial benefits of slavery were now considered not worth the moral cost. In the interests of the nation there needed to be a policy decision and action to remove the crisis that had developed. Consumer benefits and citizens' consciousness came together to win the political battle in the British parliament.

Legislation to begin to abolish slavery was passed by the British parliament in 1833. From 1 August 1834, the status of slavery would be abolished. This meant that people could no longer be classified as slaves. The former enslaved would now be classified as 'Apprentices' for a period of six years. After this they would be fully liberated. Only Antigua and Bermuda chose to go for immediate, full emancipation without the six-year transition period of 'Apprenticeship'. There, the enslavers who were in government, believed that they had sufficient control of the land and resources to keep their dominance over African wage workers. Also, the Antiguan slaves, despite a history of resistance, had never massacred Europeans in a large-scale rebellion. Europeans there were more confident that they would continue to rule in the future.

The enslaved were not given any money as compensation for their history of bondage. The British government did not think this was necessary. The Africans were expected to be grateful for their emancipation. As a people without the rights of citizens, compensation was not part of the emancipation process. An important part of British thinking around emancipation was the necessity to retain European supremacy in the colonies. Britain's main objective was to make sure that European rule would continue in all the colonies under a wage labour system.

However, enslavers received compensation. The British government believed that enslavers had lost their 'African' property and this was a serious political matter because the politics of 19th century British democracy focused on the protection of individual property rights. They drew on the principle that people should be compensated for the loss of property when the government ended such property rights. The enslaved were people who were defined and used as property. The British did not consider them worthy of compensation for their suffering and abuse.

So British emancipation was loaded with racist attitudes and policy positions. The government made available 20 million pounds sterling as compensation to slave owners for the loss of their property rights in the enslaved. This helped to settle enslavers' anxieties and fear for the future. At the same time freed people received no compensation and relied on the labour market to start a new life. As it turned out the Apprenticeship System was not workable because of the problems that came about from this 'oppressive emancipation' (see Volume Two).

chapter 13 | *Caribbean emancipations*

(EXTRACT FROM) CLAIMS FOR COMPENSATION, 28TH Sheet

Filed with the Assistant Commissioners for Jamaica (SAMPLE)
(Note that male and female, rural and urban enslavers claimed compensation)

Name and description of claimant or person in possession of slaves	Character in which the claim is made	Plantation or other domicile of slaves	Number of slaves	Parish in which slaves were valued	Number of claims and of valuer's return (i.e. page to look for details)
Allea, John, Clarendon	Owner		1	Clarendon	428
Burke, Patrick, St Johns	Owner		1	St John	162
Blair, John, St John &	{Trustees {and Lesee of	Hanson's Pen	95	St Catherine	597
Samuel, B. Hylton, St Catherine	{Elizabeth {Williams {Hanson	Hanson's Pen		St Catherine	597
Barker, Edward, Westmoreland	Owner in fee	Savanna-la-mar	1	Westmoreland	48
Bullock, Thomas, St John	Owner in fee	Brailsford Pen	1	St John	73
Boswell, Mary, St James	Owner in fee	Montego Bay	5	St James	810
Barlow, Oliver, St James	Owner in right of wife	Montego Bay	7	St James	209
Brooks, George, sen. Manchester	Agent of Antenette Reed	Enver Garden	2	Manchester	58
Brodie, Eliza, London	Owner in fee	Spring	2	Trelawney	186
Buckeridge, Catherine, Great Britain	Owner in fee	Salt Pond Hut Pen	23	St Catherine	527
Biggs, Jane, Manchester	Owner	Java	1	Manchester	478
Burke, Charlotte, Trelawny	Owner in fee	Falmouth	4	Trelawny	524
Cohen, Hymen, Great Britain	Owner in fee	Albion	322	Manchester	106
Cohen, Hymen, Great Britain	Owner in fee	Berlin	385	St Elizabeth	109
Cargill, Ann Moore, Kingston	Trustee on behalf of infants		5	Kingston	1401
Douglas, Eliza, St John	Admix. of M. Douglas		12	St John	229

6 Emancipation in French colonies

There were political and economic developments in France that helped to undermine the institution of slavery and the position of enslaved Africans within the French empire. France provides us with the clearest example of emancipation that shows how anti-slavery politics and free trade economics came together to destroy the slave system.

The French Revolution in 1789

The French Revolution in 1789 had produced a political situation in which slavery was now a contradiction to what the leaders were fighting for. How could revolutionary leaders maintain slavery in the colonies, but fight for the values of fraternity, equality and liberty for French workers at home? The national revolutionary government decided to abolish slavery in 1794 so as to remain true to the politics in France at that time.

Napoleon re-establishes slavery

As we have seen, in 1802 Emperor Napoleon Bonaparte re-established slavery. This was a signal that the revolutionary principles and values had been defeated. His government was once again associating its national economic development with the exploitation of the enslaved and the expansion of colonies. But in 1807 the decisions by Britain, Denmark and the USA to abolish the trade in Africans had considerable effect upon French politics. This gave new life to the anti-slavery movement and it embarrassed sections of French society who saw themselves as supporting the most immoral and backward institution within European civilisation.

The monarchy

When the Bourbon monarchy was restored to the French leadership this once more set the path to abolition and emancipation. Louis XVIII promised the British that he would abolish the slave trade. He did this in 1815. He also demanded that reforms be implemented in the slave societies so that there could be a gradual movement towards emancipation as the British had done.

In 1824 Charles X came to the throne. He campaigned to stop the illegal French trade in Africans and linked this campaign to the emancipation of the enslaved. The revolution of 1830 overthrew the Bourbon monarchy. Many abolitionists were brought to power within the new liberal government. In March 1831 the new government declared its intention to prevent all illegal slave trading and to open discussions about emancipation.

Steps towards emancipation

When the British emancipated their human chattel by law

Fig 13.6 The French revolution

Fig 13.7 King Louis XVIII

in 1833, the French abolitionist movement placed the French government under even greater political pressure to do likewise. These pressures mounted in the rest of the 1830s and into the 1840s. The government of Louis-Philippe favoured emancipation of all the enslaved persons in the colonies but could not decide on how best to implement this. The British system of apprenticeship, which was a phased approach to emancipation in which children, skilled and domestic enslaved were given freedom earlier than field hands, had already proved a failure. In the late 1830s and early 1840s the French debated how best to implement emancipation. However, from 1832 steps were being taken to show that the government intended to push towards emancipation. In that year the government abolished the high tax on the legal transactions by which enslaved persons were freed. They declared that the branding of those enslaved was illegal; and they demanded that there be a census of the enslaved population. In 1833 free mixed-race men were given full civil equality with Europeans and freedom was guaranteed to all Africans who arrived in France.

In 1834 the *Société pour L'abolition de L'esclavage* was founded in Paris. The leading economist, Hyppolite Passy, was a vice-president. Prominent intellectuals, like Alexis de Tocqueville, were members. In 1836 a resolution for emancipation was defeated on the grounds that more research was needed to set out the social and economic implications of emancipation for both Africans and Europeans in the Caribbean Colonies. In 1838 Passy proposed that all children born to enslaved mothers be considered free, and that all enslaved persons should have the right to buy their freedom at a price set by the metropolitan government. Passy's proposal did not succeed, but the public's support for emancipation was growing. They were getting impatient with the drawn-out process of abolition.

Two paths to emancipation

Despite resistance from those who favoured slavery, in 1840 the government took a step closer to abolition by attempting to improve conditions of an enslaved person's life. They passed laws which promoted education and Christian marriage among those enslaved, and laws to supervise and record the punishments that were allowed. Magistrates were asked to inspect plantations and report cruelties and violations of the laws. Also, in the same year, government established a commission of enquiry into slavery, headed by Duc de Broglie. This commission was to report on the measures that were required to implement an effective emancipation. After three years the commission reported two paths to emancipation:

a. The first path called for general emancipation after ten years with compensation for enslavers

b. The other path called for partial, phase by phase, emancipation starting with children, skilled slaves, domestics, and finally, the field hands.

The report reflected the division within French politics on the objectives of emancipation and freedom for African people. Public leaders debated which was a better strategy. They focused on themselves rather than on the enslaved. In the meantime economic developments were gradually wearing down the financial conditions and viability of colonial sugar planters. The rise of the beet sugar industry at home in France was providing a worthy replacement to colonial sugar. The beet sugar lobby was fighting for and winning equal, and later more favourable, financial and tax conditions that gave them a competitive edge over colonial sugar planters.

Economic conflict

By 1835 beet sugar producers could meet the demands of the nation for sugar, they could generate a surplus of sugar for export, and this at a cost that gave them an advantage over slave produced sugar. The colonies could sell only 57,000 out of their 80,000 metric tons of sugar in France. They were forced to find new export markets.

Cane sugar and beet sugar producers went to political war over the 'home' market. They both demanded special tax concessions. The debate called into question the very future of slavery, colonial production, and the importance of those enslaved to French economic development. The government sided with the enslavers and imposed a tax on beet sugar of 10 francs for 100 kilograms for 1839, and 15 francs, thereafter. But this did not stop the beet sugar producers from undermining and out-competing the enslavers.

In 1837-38, beet sugar production reached 50,000 metric tons, and 87,000 metric tons in 1838. This meant there was an over-production of beet sugar. The domestic sugar market was flooded and sugar prices fell sharply. In 1837 beet sugar cost 65 franc per 50 kilogram. In 1838 the price fell to 61 francs and in 1839 to 29 francs. This also meant that cane sugar producers in Martinique and Guadeloupe could not get their sugar out of the colonies and many went into bankruptcy. Cries of ruin were heard throughout the colonies. The decision by the metropolitan government to assist them merely helped to show how weak and irrelevant the colonies were to the new market economy.

Victor Schoelcher

It was within this context of the declining economic competitiveness of the enslavers sugar industry, and the division in French politics over which was the better path to emancipation that Victor Schoelcher, the anti-slavery advocate, had his finest hour. More than any other single person, he was the one who provided a solution to these debates, and secured the final passage of wide-ranging emancipation legislation in 1848. In 1848 he persuaded the minister of the Navy and Colonies to replace his plan for gradual emancipation with a law ordering immediate emancipation. Schoelcher also helped to implement the plan in his capacity as elected deputy for Martinique.

Fig 13.8 Victor Schoelcher

Schoelcher fought for African people's freedom all his adult life and was a public supporter of Toussaint L'Ouverture and the Haitian Revolution. He was a radical who believed in the principle of equality for all races and their equal right to liberty. He was always critical of those who thought that slavery could be reformed and made more acceptable. He was a campaigner for immediate freedom as a civil right for Africans in the Caribbean. He knew about the failure of the British Apprenticeship System in which the former enslavers were trying to re-invent slavery under a new name. Schoelcher believed that the principle of universal brotherhood and human rights should not be compromised.

The Revolution of 1848

The Revolution of 1848 brought to an abrupt end both the economic discussion between cane sugar and beet sugar producers. The Revolution of 1848 brought about the contest between those in favour of immediate emancipation and those who supported a gradual, ten-year exercise. The revolutionaries who took control of government backed Schoelcher. They promoted the ideology of *fraternalisme* (revolutionary brotherhood) and acted, as they did in 1794, by abolishing slavery with immediate effect in 1848. Schoelcher became the main spokesman for the emancipation process.

While it is true that it took the Revolution of 1848 to bring about general emancipation, it was the political work of Schoelcher and other abolitionists who created the consciousness within the country to make emancipation possible. While it is also true that the sugar colonies were no longer as important to French economic development as they were in the 18th century because the sugar planters were so uncompetitive, they strengthened the case of abolitionists and enabled the Revolutionaries of 1848 to claim that emancipation was in the national interest.

Schoelcher was greatly influenced by the failure of the British Apprenticeship system. He called for immediate freedom without any transitional arrangement. He also noted that the French enslavers at French Guiana, Martinique and Guadeloupe were making considerable profits in the period after the Haitian Revolution. He was disturbed by the agreement of 1825 which said that former enslavers of St Domingue were to receive compensation for the loss of property rights from the Haitian government to the sum of 150 million gold francs. He argued, as a result, that there should be no apprenticeship for the enslavers of Guadeloupe, French Guiana and Martinique and they should only receive a minimum token gesture of compensation. The level of compensation that was settled at emancipation in 1848 was 430 francs per slave at Martinique, 470 francs at Guadeloupe and 618 francs in French Guiana.

7 Emancipation in Danish and Dutch colonies

Emancipation in the Danish-colonised islands was triggered in 1848 by the rebellious actions of the enslaved themselves. In 1806, under pressure from the British, the Danish government abolished the trade in Africans to its colonies. In the 1820s it moved towards a policy of amelioration. With British emancipation in 1833, the

Danes also took steps to gradually phase in general emancipation. The government announced two policies:

a. As from 28 July 1847 all children born of enslaved mothers would be free. This became known as the 'Free Birth' policy

b. They would pass a law about general emancipation in 1859, giving enslavers time to reorganise production with free wage labourers, and Africans time to prepare for civil liberties.

However, the enslaved people had different plans. They rejected the Danish government's proposal for a drawn-out emancipation process. They noted that the enslaved people in neighbouring British colonies were already emancipated. They decided to act to bring about their own emancipation and establish their own time-frame for freedom.

The enslaved revolt

On the night of Sunday 2 July 1848, the enslaved people at St Croix revolted with the aim of securing their freedom. They lit signal fires on the sugar plantations on the western side of the island; they set off conch shells and estate bells to communicate the start of the rebellion. By the morning of Monday 3 July, Frederiksted Fort was the scene of a new political development. In front of it, over 8,000 Africans congregated, making speeches and pronouncing that they were declaring the end of slavery in the Danish colonies.

The Governor of the colony, General von Scholten, was away during the weekend on the neighbouring colony of St Thomas. He had arrived at Christiansted, the capital, only hours before enslaved people gathered at Fort Fredericksted. He was advised by his military counsel to send out troops and to bombard the crowd with artillery from the sea. He chose instead to address the crowd that day, and did so at 4 p.m.

General von Scholten

The enslaved people, however, were more concerned that the Governor heard their views on freedom. Before he could speak they informed him that it was their intention to work, but only for wages, and that they were no longer enslaved. Von Scholten listened and then he spoke. He told them, 'Now you are free; you are hereby emancipated'. In this short sentence, the Governor made the position of the enslaved legal, and formally abolished slavery in the Dutch island colonies. This was emancipation by a Governor's proclamation. It brought to an end the rebellion of enslaved people, by settling the matter of freedom for all.

Von Scholten was a shrewd political tactician. He knew that the emancipation target date of 1859 was only a guide, and not a policy to be defended by bloodshed. He knew that the British had also cut short the time originally set for full emancipation. They had abolished the Apprenticeship System in 1838 and not when they said they would, in 1840. By proclaiming emancipation in this way, Von Scholten diffused a potentially destructive condition, that could have led, as in Haiti, not only to the end of slavery, but also to the defeat of Danish rule in the Caribbean.

Also, with emancipation politics in the air, he did not want Denmark to be associated with the useless and bloody suppression of enslaved people, as was the case with the British in 1831 when the Jamaican emancipation war was brutally crushed two years before the Emancipation Act. It was much wiser, he thought, to ensure a smooth transition to the inevitable – general emancipation. The Governor's decision was unpopular with enslavers and with sections of Danish society; but it was soon approved of and sealed by royal proclamation.

In 1846 on the three Danish Virgin Islands there were 16,706 enslaved people at St Croix, 3, 494 at St Thomas, and 1,790 at St John. These colonies had experienced only one act of armed rebellion which took place at St John in 1733. It was crushed with the assistance of the French military. In 1759 a conspiracy at St Croix was nipped in the bud, though it had signalled the attempt of the enslaved people at self-liberation.

Rebellion

The morning after the Governor had proclaimed emancipation, a group of Africans were shot down outside of Christiansted. This led to a week of rebellion on the island. Von Scholten collapsed in illness, and the colony was put in a state of emergency. Mass rioting and looting followed. It was clear that Africans had organised strategies from the beginning. The alleged leader of the rebellion was Gotlieb Bordeaux, known as General Buddoe. He was an artisan from La Grange Estate, who according to one confession at the court martial, had said that the European man's days as enslavers were over.

Other leaders, like Martin King, and a large number of women were also identified as rebellion leaders. The court martial heard about the role of women in the struggle from Frederick von Scholten, the governor's brother:

> *Among the Black population, women played a role of great importance. They do the same work that the men do and their physical build and size renders them formidable adversaries in the rough and tumble of a fight. Throughout the disturbance they were more aggressive, vengeful and altogether more violent in their passion than the men."*

The court transcript mentioned Rogaine who spoke about burning the town as was done in Haiti, of Mathilda, Say, Sara, Martha, Penny, Rachel. These were all women who were destroying property, threatening enslavers and mobilising the general populace against slavery.

No turning back by the Danish

The Danish administration put down the rebellion within three days. But by then those enslaved had achieved emancipation and there was no turning back by the Danish government. The enslaved had spoken, and had succeeded in changing the emancipation timetable of the metropolitan government. The enslaved people argued that they wanted immediate freedom for themselves and their children, but they compromised on labour arrangements by accepting that adults would be tied to the estates of their homes until 1859.

The imperial government recognised that this was the best way forward in the situation. They agreed to approve the colonial proclamation and did so in September 1859. But at this stage a number of developments took place that tried to dampen the political enthusiasm of the self-liberated Africans. The imperial government agreed with the colonial government that it was important to let the Africans know that their bloodless mass revolt was no major achievement. They agreed to compensate enslavers for the loss of their property rights in human chattel to the value of 5 million francs. They established an elaborate system of social control that kept African people in an apprenticeship arrangement until 1878.

The Dutch

The Dutch (like the Spanish) were pioneers in the trade in African captives to the Caribbean. They were also among the last in the region to emancipate their enslaved captives by parliamentary legislation. The Dutch had established a Caribbean Empire that showed their two interests as merchants and as large-scale planters. They had built a regional commercial network by providing services to all European powers. Their interests were more in commerce than in colonial settlement. They did this by using the very small southern 'ABC' islands of Aruba, Bonaire and Curaçao, but also the northern islands of Saba, St Eustatius and St Maarten. On these islands the enslaved populations remained small and often there were more free than enslaved inhabitants. The Dutch large-scale sugar plantations were based at Suriname on the South American continent. There they established a slave regime that was typically Caribbean.

The Dutch in the early 19th century, unlike the British and French, did not take the emancipation of those enslaved seriously. The new kingdom of the Netherlands with William I as its first king abolished the Dutch African trade in 1814, but had neither the will nor interest to enforce this. The African trade continued illegally for another two decades into Suriname and the Caribbean colonies with considerable ease. It was in fact condoned.

At this time the Dutch were not even interested in the emancipation discussions of European societies. Enslavers were keen on maintaining the system of slavery, and there was no anti-slavery movement of any significance in the metropole. The 'friends of freedom – friends of Blacks', campaign had not taken root in Dutch domestic politics. Civil society seemed indifferent to the plight of those enslaved in their colonies. Even the so-called 'Reveil men' who were a group of influential Christians in the Netherlands campaigning for a new Calvinist revival, did not spread the view that slavery and Christianity were incompatible.

Anti-slavery movement in Holland

In the 1840s, however, there were significant changes. The impact of British Emancipation in 1834 was very important, as were the experiences of the French and Danish in 1848. Also of note was emancipation in Central America in 1823, Colombia in 1853, and Venezuela in 1854. In 1840, the 'Reveil' group took up the slavery matter, and linked it to sin, immorality, and crime against humanity. They established political links with the British anti-slavery society that led to the formation in 1842 of the 'Society for the Advancement of the Abolition'. The 'Reveil' group was at the forefront of the leadership of this new society. They wanted to abolish slavery as a step on the agenda of converting Africans to Christianity. The king, however, did not approve of the anti-slavery society.

Despite the fact that the king did not approve of the Society, in 1842 many members of government identified with the campaign to abolish slavery. In 1844, for example, the Minister of the Colonies, Band, in a report to the king called for an investigation into ways of preparing for abolition. The government took their lead from the king, and they remained indifferent to abolition. Nevertheless, the abolition movement gained in strength. They attracted larger crowds at public meetings, raised campaign funds, and secured the support of influential public figures.

An important sign of the growing mass support for abolition was the enormous amount of published anti-slavery materials at the time – letters, pamphlets, books, and speeches. The publication that captured the public imagination, and became the manifesto of the anti-slavery campaign was a book that came out in 1854. It was called *Enslaved and Free Men* and was written by Walter R. Baron van Hoëvell, a minister in the Dutch Reformed Church who became a politician. In parliament he led the anti-slavery campaign.

Parliamentary support

Van Hoëvell's book helped enormously to win the support of both the public and the parliament for emancipation. He succeeded in achieving his declared objective which was 'to rouse a general indignation against slavery'. Anti-slavery became a main topic in the government. It informed the thinking of the National Commission which was established in 1853 to inform the minister on colonial matters. In 1855 and 1856 a series of emancipation proposals were debated in Parliament. The issue of compensation for enslavers was critical. But all the proposals met with opposition from the enslavers, especially those in Suriname.

In July 1857 the Minister for Colonies submitted to Parliament a comprehensive emancipation plan for the Dutch Caribbean Empire. The Parliament rejected it on the grounds that the compensation package for enslavers was neither clear enough nor generous enough. There was not so much opposition in the Caribbean Islands but in Suriname sugar planters led an aggressive opposition.

The 'islands' had no sugar sector to defend. In addition many of their enslaved captives lived in towns and enjoyed social liberties that were unknown to plantation chattel in Suriname. The Dutch Parliament was sympathetic to enslavers in Suriname, and not completely swept along by political rhetoric about freedom or by religious claims by Calvinists. However, the Parliament could not ignore the economic fact that Dutch buyers could get cheaper sugar on the world market or from beet producers at home and in Europe.

It would have been unpatriotic for the Dutch Parliament to defend slavery in the light of there being a cheaper alternative supply of sugar at home. The question was: should we continue tolerating the suffering of those enslaved, the spiritual degradation of enslavers, and the increasingly hardening of cultural sensitivities at home, if the sugar produced by those enslaved was more expensive, and did not contribute much to Dutch economic development? Members of Parliament were under pressure from their electorate and so they saw emancipation as a logical response to the situation.

The Suriname enslavers were seen as cruel colonialists and they came to represent an old world that could no longer be defended morally or economically by the majority. A few political supporters remained firm and dedicated to their colonial culture.

Emancipation finally came to the Dutch colonies on 1 July 1863; a year after the Emancipation Act was passed. The Dutch government decided that emancipation should vary between the island colonies and especially at Suriname whose circumstances were so different. Compensation too would vary, as well as the post-slavery relations between employers and workers.

Compensation

The imperial government made 16 million florins in compensation available. This was to assure enslavers that their future role in maintaining Dutch rule in these colonies was still a priority. In Suriname enslavers were paid about 700 florins for each enslaved household worker. Sugar-producing enslaved persons were considered less valuable than domestics. It was argued that enslaved domestic workers had artisan skills, management training and that some were literate and proficient in more than one European language. However, enslaved sugar plantation workers were valued more than other agricultural workers. Cocoa farmers received compensation at about 325 florins per enslaved person, while those in the coffee industry received 330 florins per enslaved person.

Plantation owners received more compensation for each person enslaved than their urban colleagues on the small islands. The islanders received between 50 and 450 florins for each of their emancipated chattel. As was the case with the British, French and Danish, the enslaved people themselves received no compensation. Rather, the former enslaved persons were expected to pay into the public treasury a contribution to the 16 million florins for the loss of property. In addition they were placed under state authority to remain on the estate and offer their labour services as usual.

8 Emancipation in the Spanish colonies

The Spanish crept out of the slave system with legislation in much the same way that they had eased into it. They finally emancipated those they enslaved in 1886. This was nearly 100 years after the French Convention abolished slavery in St Dominigue, and Touissaint L'Ouverture in Spanish Santo Domingo (now the Dominican Republic). After British and French emancipation Cuba, which was the main Spanish colony, became the region's leading sugar producer. Enslavers and their official imperial supporters did not believe that emancipation had hurt the French and British. In their opinion, however, emancipation in Cuba at any earlier date would have shattered the economic potential of the colony that was perfectly placed to replace St Domingue/Haiti as the leading producer of cane sugar.

A recommitment to slavery

The Spanish expected to make great profits out of sugar production in Cuba at a time when the British colonies were in an economic decline and the French colonies were in confusion. In this time of emancipation, Cuban planters and the imperial government recommitted themselves to slavery so that they could take advantage of new market opportunities.

The British industrial and financial classes supported the Spanish in their determination to achieve an economic boom with sugar and slavery after the 1830s. They supplied them with money to modernise the sugar industry and enabled them to buy expensive railway systems and steam–powered sugar mills. This showed that British investors were prepared to ignore the British colonies that were making a low profit, and put their investment in a colony where the returns were highest.

The Cubans themselves expanded their slave system at a tremendous rate between 1830 and 1869, at a time of emancipation in the wider region. They were supplied with enslaved persons from American and European illegal slave traders. However in 1865, the American Civil War ended with victory for the northern anti-slavery forces over the Southern pro-slavery interest. Cuba now had no major supporter to help them expand their slave system. In addition, it did not help that in 1868, the Spanish Monarchy that had fully backed the trade in Africans was overthrown.

Anti-slavery leaders and movements

The new Spanish republican government had many anti-slavery leaders. They joined together against the enslavers in Cuba and Puerto Rico. Of equal importance was that the independence movement within the colonies was developing and adopting anti-slavery policies. The 'Grito de Yara' group in Cuba and the 'Grito de Lares' group in Puerto Rico were fighting a war of independence and had placed anti-slavery ideas at the centre of their policies for the new nations. They targeted slavery as an institution of colonialism and imperial domination. It had to go if independence was achieved.

Civil War

The decolonisation and independence movements in Cuba saw slavery as unattractive and undesirable. In 1870 Segismundo Moret was the Spanish imperial minister for colonies. As a reaction to the Civil War in Cuba, he received government approval to implement ameliorative reform to slavery. The legislation became known as the 'Moret Law'. It immediately emancipated all enslaved persons born after September 1868 and all those over the age of 60 years. This was only a first step. It was not general emancipation.

Moret indicated that the government wanted to review the situation once the Civil War was over. Many of those enslaved had joined the revolution on the promise of freedom and also because they wished to be part of an independent nation that would end Spanish colonialism in the Caribbean. Africans, free and enslaved, fought in the revolutionary army. They provided historic leadership in many battles with imperial soldiers. Antonio Maceo emerged as a heroic leader of the Cuban revolutionary movement and is now considered a founding father of independence.

Puerto Rican officials made a first move and abolished slavery on 22 March 1873. This was a reaction to the situation in which the enslaved and freed Africans were major participants in the political struggle. The officials made available 35 million pesetas in compensation. They also brought coercive measures into being to secure the labour of Africans.

The Civil War in Cuba from 1868 to 1878 is now known as the 'Ten Years War'. It weakened the viability of enslavers as well as the authority of Spain. Those enslaved did their best to ensure the downfall of slavery by supporting the independence struggle. They fought for their freedom and for the ending of slavery in the Caribbean world.

The end of slavery

The Spanish government had little choice but to bring the system of slavery to an end by law before the Spanish in the Caribbean were destroyed by war. Civil War together with slave rebellion and industrial technology had combined to threaten slavery as a social and economic institution. The sugar plantation sector responded to the new industrial technology by replacing enslaved labour with more scientifically trained workers in many areas of production. These processes questioned how relevant slavery was in the long-term. They also showed that slavery was not a modern labour system.

In 1880 the Spanish government was weakened by the financial demands of the Civil War it had fought to maintain control over the colonies. It passed a plan for the emancipation of the 210,000 enslaved men and women in Cuba. It chose a process of gradual emancipation, like others in the Caribbean. Within five years some 180,000 enslaved peoples were freed. On 7 October 1886 the Spanish government passed legislation to emancipate the remaining 30,000 enslaved persons. They did not pay any compensation to Cuban planters because they said that funds were not available. They also argued that the majority of Cubans themselves had been the architects of the emancipation process.

The process of emancipation in the Spanish Caribbean, like that in Brazil, was associated with the growing importance, within the slave system, of other forms of labour systems. Cuba imported about 125,000 Chinese indentured workers between 1847 and 1874. These contract workers laboured alongside enslaved workers on the sugar plantations. Also, thousands of 'free' wage earners were part of this labour market at the same time.

In Cuba there were three different systems of labour in use, each of which weakened the reliance upon slavery. There were free workers, contract workers and enslaved workers. Enslavers compared the three kinds of workers and could see that free labour was more reliable and productive in the sugar mill.

Also, enslavers discovered that enslaved labour was not the best labour to operate the new, modern sugar mills that required technical innovation and scientific management. Those enslaved, after all, were well-known for their resistance practices that included deliberate sabotage, malingering, unresponsiveness, occasional revolt and mass destruction of property. Even when slavery was expanding after the 1850s, enslavers generally preferred contract and free workers. Enslavers remained committed to using bonded labour but they were no longer interested in slavery to achieve this end.

9 Comparisons: emancipation in the USA

In the United States enslavers went to the battlefield to fight a major war to defend what they considered to be the slave-base of their culture. The USA had fought for their independence from Britain, which they achieved in 1776. From this time the relationship between freedom and slavery in the young nation-state was controversial. Not all social groups were comfortable with the decision to keep slavery as the main institution in the free nation. Between national Independence in 1776 and the 13th Amendment of the Constitution in 1865 that abolished slavery, Americans were deeply divided on the issue of slavery.

After 1776 many leaders of the American Independence Revolution expected that slavery would simply fade away into unimportance. But the opposite was to be the case. After 1776 the widespread importance of slavery grew. Slavery expanded in the post-independence years because of the development of the cotton industry in the southern states and the expansion of cotton textiles manufacturing in the northern states. Cotton production was given a new life when cotton textiles manufacturing in the northern states and in Britain grew. With this new life came a new demand for enslaved labour. In 1790 the enslaved population was 697,897; by 1860 it was 3,953,760. By this time slavery was the lifeline of some nine states.

Anti-slavery campaign

The American anti-slavery campaign after the 1830s used many of the arguments that the British had found effective in their anti-slavery campaign. Among the religious groups, the Quakers were vigorous in defining slavery as an irreligious and inhumane system. For them it was a cruel way to build economic prosperity and identity within the young nation. They received support from the Haitians and the British. The Haitians had shown an example of how to build a young nation without slavery. Even though the Haitian nation was so poor, the educated elite consisted of men and women of the finest quality within western culture. The British anti-slavery lobbies saw the some 700,000 enslaved persons freed in British colonies as essentially their handiwork. They were keen to assist their American brothers and sisters with funds, moral support and organisational links.

A booming economy in the South

The British anti-slavery movement had argued a solid case against Caribbean slavery on economic grounds. They had pointed to the financial decline of the plantations, the high cost of enslaved labour, the relative cost advantages of free labour and the benefits to the consumer of buying cheaper sugar from outside British sources of supply. However their American colleagues could not use these same arguments. Cotton production was expanding rapidly everywhere in the South because of slavery; and the southern economy was booming under the influence of cotton and slavery.

The abolitionists in the North saw the evidence of the expanding southern economic wealth. In these states anti-slavery lobbies could only use Christian morality to build their case. Enslavers projected slavery as more than a labour system, but as the very basis of a distinct American civilisation that was theirs to protect and defend. The southerners argued that slavery was the foundation of their way of life and any reforms to it would strike at the core of their identity.

As a result of this, in the North the anti-slavery movement took on the image of a crusade – a holy war against the evil, ungodliness of slavery. They joined forces with their English counterparts and created transatlantic anti-slavery sisterhoods and brotherhoods. In this movement Africans were prominent figures and great leaders. People like Harriet Tubman, Sojourner Truth and Frederick Douglas provided an authentic voice demanding freedom from within the enslaved community.

The southern enslavers considered their social and economic investment in slavery too large to abandon, with or without financial compensation. They maintained that it was not simply a case of money and property, but one of culture. The key to the southerner life-style was to keep Africans in a helpless position as a servant class, and the southerners were prepared to fight to defend this lifestyle. By the 1850s they threatened to leave the union if that was necessary to achieve their objectives. However, it was not good news for them when Abraham Lincoln was elected President in 1860. He was a known anti-slavery advocate who was hostile to the politics that White southerners stood for.

The Civil War and emancipation

In 1861 the South broke away from the Union. Lincoln was determined to preserve the Union and so he sent in soldiers and the Civil War began. Slavery was not the only issue in the war, but it provided the background against which all other matters were debated. At first Lincoln offered not to abolish slavery if the South came back into the Union.

In 1775, almost a century earlier during the War for Independence, General George Washington had been determined not to recruit Africans to fight what he called a 'white man's war'. He had issued a proclamation to this effect on 12 November 1775. It was the British Governor of Virginia, Lord Dunmore, who had recruited enslaved persons as soldiers. He had promised them freedom if they fought against the Independence movement. In response Washington reversed his policy, recruited enslaved persons, and offered them freedom for military service against the British imperialists. Thousands of enslaved persons fought for the Independence cause, and won battles that led to the rise of the American nation state. But slavery was retained as a national institution, and Africans had good cause to feel betrayed.

A century later, President Abraham Lincoln started on the same basis as George Washington. He did not want to recruit Africans to fight a 'white man's war'. He gave instructions in June 1861 that allowed enslavers to claim back their runaway enslaved who sought freedom within the Union army. But the enslaved saw the Civil War as their war, and volunteered to fight for general emancipation in their thousands. In July 1862 Congress authorised the use of African soldiers which was only followed up in January 1863 when the Emancipation Proclamation went into effect.

Enslaved Africans fought in the War for Independence but were not rewarded with freedom. Ironically, the first American to die in the revolution was an enslaved man, Crispus Attucks. He was a seaman who was killed by British troops in the Boston massacre of 5 March 1770. The Attucks incident highlighted the irony of the American condition; an enslaved person dying in a war waged by

British people for their constitutional freedom. Enslaved Africans went on to distinguish themselves as soldiers in the War of Independence. Salem Poor, for example, was honoured for his bravery in the famous Bunker Hill battle.

Fig 13.9 Abraham Lincoln

Lincoln's camp was anxious that they would lose the war and this is why he decided to use enslaved Afro-American troops in the Union army, and pass the Emancipation Proclamation. The Union army was faced with heavy desertion by European troops, fewer and fewer European enlistments and growing southern resistance. Lincoln had no choice but to call upon Afro-American and transform the war into a struggle to destroy slavery. Also, this way he could cause a mass resistance movement to grow among the enslaved in the southern states. African-American abolitionists like Frederick Douglas and Martin Delaney called upon all Africans to rise up and fight for their freedom.

Lincoln knew that this was the only way to win the war – destroying the slave system in the South with the help of the enslaved Africans themselves. Over 500,000 African-Americans, mostly enslaved, served in the Union army, half of them as soldiers, and the rest as labourers, servants and spies. Some 100,000 of these enslaved soldiers came from southern slave states. In addition, some 30,000 enslaved Africans served as Union seamen.

So African anti-slavery resistance was a key element in the Civil War that saw the defeat of enslavers and the declaration of general emancipation. As the war intensified, the North used the issue of slavery to mobilise public opinion at home and in Europe against the South. Those enslaved either fled to the Union cause or did not support the Confederates who wanted to maintain slavery.

Soon the position of the African-American was clear. They wanted freedom and the Union seemed their best ally.

In January 1863, the Union forces declared victory. African-Americans celebrated as President Lincoln issued the Emancipation Proclamation for all states. The 13th Amendment came in 1865 establishing the freedom of African-American as a constitutional right throughout the USA.

Fig 13.10 Slave Bell – Liberty Bell

To sum up

The slavery system that had cursed the sky with sounds of pain and grief and soaked the land in blood and tears was now torn away and removed so that freedom could reign. Nowhere did emancipation come about without conflict, war, tension, fears and anxieties. Economic systems were built with slave labour and enslavers and managers could not see how free labour would assist either production or profitability.

For them free labour meant economic decline, social ruin and political subversion. Only in Barbados, St Kitts, Antigua, Trinidad and Cuba did sugar producers increase their output with enslaved labour. But even in these places they continued to believe that slavery was the better system because it offered them socially unlimited power over African people in addition to economic control over their labour.

It is now estimated that over 120 million people of African ancestry now populate the Americas and diaspora communities in Europe. Their everyday experiences continue to be negatively affected by the legacies of slavery. One of the reasons is that emancipation was planned and implemented by colonial and imperial legislators to ensure the continuation of traditional economic, political and social domination.

Africans were to continue as social subordinates and second-class persons within society. Such inequality has not been totally eradicated even in societies where descendants of formerly enslaved persons now have political power. So, in many Caribbean societies, the popular 'up from slavery' concept in public life indicates that there is a strong opinion that the process of emancipation is not complete.

The descendents of the enslaved are now involved in movements to get rid of the legacies of slavery and honour the ancestors. Such movements include demands for reparation, declaring slavery a crime against humanity and seeking to build memorials for anti-slavery heroes and heroines.

Revision questions

'No metropolitan government willingly abolished slavery. Each was pushed to do so by a combination of political, economic, moral and cultural forces'.

1. a State three reasons why metropolitan governments would not 'willingly abolish slavery'.
    b State two political factors that pushed Britain to abolish slavery.
    a State two economic factors that pushed Spain to abolish slavery.
    b State three arguments used by the humanitarians to press for the end of slavery.
2. Why did slavery last longer in the Spanish than in the Dutch Caribbean?
3. Choose one of the following and describe how it came about:
    a emancipation in Haiti
    b emancipation in Santo Domingo
    c emancipation in the British Caribbean territories
    d emancipation in Martinique and Guadeloupe
    e emancipation in Cuba and Puerto Rico
    f emancipation in the Danish Caribbean territories.

Additional sources for teachers

Chapter 1

Cook, S and Borah, W, 'The Aboriginal Population of Hispaniola', *Essays in Population History* (Berkeley, 1971)

Crosby, A, *The Columbian Exchange* (Westport, 1972)

Denevan, W (ed.), *The Native Population of the Americas in 1492* (Madison, 1976)

Gardiner, G Harvey, *Naval Power in the Conquest of Mexico* (Austin, 1956)

Gonzalez, N, *Sojourners of the Caribbean: the Garifuna* (Urbana, 1988)

Hulme, P and Whitehead, N (eds.), *Wild Majesty: Encounters with Caribs from Columbus to the Present Day* (Oxford, 1992)

Keegan, W, *The People who Discovered Columbus: The Prehistory of the Bahamas* (Gainesville, 1992)

Knight, F, *The Caribbean: The Genesis of a Fragmented Nationalism* (New York, 1990)

Loven, S, *Origins of the Tainan Culture: West Indies* (Göteberg, Sweden, 1935)

Parry, J H, *The Spanish Seaborne Empire* (New York, 1966)

Sauer, C, *The Early Spanish Main* (Berkeley, 1966)

Shepherd, V and Beckles, H (eds.), *Caribbean Slavery in the Atlantic World: A Student Reader* (Kingston, 2000)

Thomas, H, *Conquest: Montezuma, Cortes, and the fall of Old Mexico* (New York, 1993)

Thomas, P, 'The Caribs of St. Vincent: A Study in Imperial Maladministration, 1763–73', *Journal of Caribbean History*, Vol. 18 No.2 (1984). pp. 60–73

Watts, D, *The West Indies: Patterns of Development, Culture and Environmental Change since 1492* (Cambridge, 1987)

Whitehead, N, *Lords of the Tiger Spirit: A History of the Caribs in Colonial Venezuela and Guyana, 1498-1820* (Dordrecht, 1988)

Wilson, S, *Hispaniola: The Chiefdoms of the Caribbean* (Tuscalosa, 1990)

Chapter 2

Andrews, K R and Canny, N (eds.), *The Westward Entrreprise: English Activities in Ireland, the Atlantic and America, 1480 – 1650* (Detroit, 1979)

Armesto, F, *The Canary Islands after the Conquest: The Making of a Colonial Society in the early 16th century* (Oxford, 1982)

Ball, J H, *Merchants and Merchandise: The Expansion of Trade in Europe, 1500–1630* (London, 1977)

Blackburn, R, *The Making of New World Slavery* (London, 1997)

Blake, J, *European Beginnings in West Africa, 1454–1578* (New York, 1969)

Boxer, C R, *The Portuguese Seaborne Empire, 1415 – 1825* (London, 1965)

Chiapelli, F (ed.), *First Images of America* (Berkeley, 1976)

Davies, K G, *The North Atlantic World in the 17th century* (Oxford, 1974)

Elliott, J H, *The Hispanic World, Civilization and Empire: Europe and the Americas* (London, 1991)

———————— *Imperial Spain, 1469 – 1716* (London, 1970)

Fernández-Armesto, F, *Before Columbus: Explorations and Colonisation* (Philadelphia, 1987)

Hyatt, V and Nettleford, R (eds.), *Race Discourse and the Origins of the Americas* (Washington, 1995)

McAlister, L, *Spain and Portugal in the New World, 1492–1700* (Oxford, 1984)

Pagden, A, *European Encounters with the New World* (New Haven, 1993)

Parry, J H, *Empire and the Wider World, 1415 – 1715* (London, 1949)

———————— *The Spanish Seaborne Empire* (New York, 1966)

Pike, R, *Enterprise and Adventure: The Genoese in Sevilla and the Opening of the New World* (Ithaca, 1966)

Scammel, G, *The First Imperial Age: European Overseas Expansion, 1415 – 1825* (London, 1989)

Shepherd, V and Beckles, H (eds.), *Caribbean Slavery in the Atlantic World* (Kingston, 2000)

Thornton, J, *Africa and The Making of the Atlantic World, 1400–1680* (Cambridge, 1992)

Van Sertima, I, *They came before Columbus: African Presence in Ancient America* (New York, 1977)

Verlinden, C, *The Beginnings of Modern Colonisation* (Ithaca, 1970)

Chapter 3

Boxer, C R, *The Dutch in Brazil, 1624–1654* (Oxford, 1957)

Bridenbaugh, C, *No Peace Beyond the Line: The English in the Caribbean, 1624–1690* (New York, 1972)

Broomert, A, 'The Arawaks of Trinidad and Coastal Guiana, 1500 – 1650', *Journal of Caribbean History*, Vol. 19, (1984)

Crouse, N, *French Pioneers in the West Indies* (New York, 1940)

Davies, R, *The Rise of the Atlantic Economies* (Ithaca, 1973)

Dunn, R, *Sugar and Slaves* (Chapel Hill, 1972)

Fortune, S, *Merchants and Jews: The Struggle for British West Indian Commerce* (Gainesville, 1984)

Hulme, P, *Colonial Encounters: Europe and the Native Caribbean, 1492 – 1797* (London, 1986)

Israel, J, *The Dutch Republic and the Hispanic World, 1606–1661* (Oxford, 1982)

Israel, J, *Dutch Primacy in World Trade, 1585–1740* (Oxford, 1984)

Jaenen, C, *Friend and Foe: Aspects of French Amerindian Cultural Contact in the 16th and 17th centuries* (New York, 1976)

Lewis, G K, *Main Currents in Caribbean Thought* (Kingston, 1983)

Newson, L, *Aboriginal and Spanish Colonial Trinidad: A Study in Culture Contact* (New York, 1976)

Price, R, *Maroon Societies* (New York, 1973)

Sauer, C, *The Early Spanish Main* (Berkeley, 1966)

Shepherd, V and Beckles, H (eds.), *Caribbean Slavery in the Atlantic World* (Kingston, 2000)

Tracey, J D, *The Rise of Merchant Empires* (Cambridge, 1990)

Walker, D, *Columbus and the Golden World of the Island Arawak* (Kingston, 1992)

Watts, D, *The West Indies: Patterns of Development since 1492* (Cambridge, 1987)

Williams, E, *Capitalism and Slavery* (Chapel Hill, 1944)

———— *Documents of West Indian History, 1492 – 1655* (Port of Spain, 1963)

———— *From Columbus to Castro: The History of the Caribbean, 1492–1969* (New York, 1970)

Chapter 4

Andrews, K, *The Spanish Caribbean: Trade and Plunder, 1530–1630* (New Haven, 1978)

———— *Trade, Plunder and Settlement: Maritime Enterprise and the Genesis of the British Empire, 1480–1630* (Cambridge, 1984)

Augier, R et al., *The Making of the West Indies* (London, 1960)

Beckles, H, *European Settlement and Rivalry in the Caribbean, 1492–1750* (London, 1983)

———— 'Kalinago Resistance to European Colonisation of the Caribbean', in Beckles, H and Shepherd, V (eds.), *Caribbean Slavery in the Atlantic World* (London, 2000)

Boxer, C R, *The Dutch Seaborne Empire, 1600 – 1800* (London, 1969)

Bridenbaugh, C, *No Peace Beyond the Line* (New York, 1972)

Craton, M, 'From Carib to Black Carib: The Amerindian Roots of Servile Resistance in the Caribbean', in Okihiro, G (ed.), *In Resistance: Studies in African, Caribbean and Afro-American History* (Amherst, 1986)

Dunn, R, *Sugar and Slaves* (Chapel Hill, 1972)

Elliott, J H, *Spain and its World* (New Haven, 1989)

Marshall, B, 'The Black Carib-Native Resistance to British Penetration in the Windward Side of St. Vincent, 1763 – 1773', *Caribbean Quarterly*, Vol. 19, (1973)

Pares, R, *Merchants and Planters* (Cambridge, 1960)

Parry, J and Sherlock, P, *A Short History of the West Indies* (London, 1956)

Sheridan, R, *Sugar and Slavery* (Bridgetown, 1974)

Sauer, C, *The Early Spanish Main* (Berkeley, 1966)

Watts, D, *The West Indies: Patterns of Development, Culture and Environmental Change since 1492* (Cambridge, 1987)

Chapter 5

Axtell, J, *Beyond 1492: Encounters in Colonial North America* (New York, 1992)

Beckles, H, *White Servitude and Black Slavery in Barbados* (Knoxville, 1989)

Bernal, M, *Black Athena* (New York, 1995)

Blackburn, R, *The Making of New World Slavery, 1492–1800* (London, 1997)

Cippolla, C, *Guns and sails in the Early Phase of European Expansion* (London, 1965)

Curtin, P, *Economic Change in Pre-colonial Africa* (Madison, 1975)

———— *The Rise and Fall of the Plantation Complex* (Cambridge, 1990)

Davies, R, *The Rise of the Atlantic Economies* (London, 1988)

Diop, C A, *Civilization or Barbarism* (New York, 1981) *Pre-Colonial Black Africa* (Trenton, 1987)

Eltis, D, *The Rise of African Slavery in the Americas* (Cambridge, 2000)

Fernandez-Armesto, F, *Before Columbus* (Philadelphia, 1987)

Hopkins, A G, *An Economic History of West Africa* (London, 1973)

Inikori, J, *Forced Migration: The Impact of the Export Slave Trade on African Societies* (London, 1982)

Klein, H, *The Middle Passage* (Princeton, 1978)

Klein, M and Robertson, C (eds.), *Women and Slavery in Africa* (Madison, 1983)

Kopytoff, I (ed.), *Slavery in Africa* (Madison, 1977)

Law, R, *The Slave Coast of West Africa* (Oxford, 1991)

Lovejoy, P, *Transformations in Slavery: A History of Slavery in Africa* (Cambridge, 1983)

Palmer, C, *Africa in the Making of the Caribbean* (London, 1981)

Shepherd, V and Beckles, H (eds.), *Caribbean Slavery in the Atlantic World* (Kingston, 2000)

Chapter 6

Bean, R, *The British Transatlantic Slave Trade* (New York, 1975)

Curtin, P, *The Atlantic Slave Trade: A Census* (Madison, 1969)

Eltis, D, *Economic Growth and the Ending of the Transatlantic Slave Trade* (New York, 1987)

Eltis, D and Walvin, J (eds.), *The Abolition of the Atlantic Slave Trade: Origins and Effects in Europe, Africa, and the Americas* (Madison, 1981)

Eltis, D, Richardson, D, et al., *The Transatlantic Slave Trade: A Database on CD-ROM* (Cambridge, 2000)

Eltis, D, *The Rise of African Slavery in the Americas* (Cambridge, 2000)

Galenson, D, *Traders, Planters, and Slaves: Market Behaviour in Early English America* (Cambridge, 1986)

Gemery, H and Hogendorn, J (eds.), *The Uncommon Market: Essays in the Economic History of the Transatlantic Slave Trade* (New York, 1979)

Inikori, J (ed.), *Forced Migration: The Support of the Export Slave Trade on African Societies* (London, 1982)

———————— *The Chaining of a Continent: Export Demand for Captives and the History of Africa South of the Sahara, 1450–1870* (Kingston, 1992)

Klein, H, *The Middle Passage* (Princeton, 1978) *African Slavery in Latin America and the Caribbean* (New York, 1986)

Lovejoy, P, 'The Volume of the Atlantic Slave Trade' in: *Journal of African History*, Vol. 23, (1980)

Law, R, *The Slave Coast of West Africa, 1550–1750* (Oxford, 1991)

——— *The Kingdom of Allada* (Leiden, 1997)

Manning, P, *Slavery and African Life* (Cambridge, 1990)

Miller, J, *Way of Death: Merchant Capitalism and the Angolan Slave Trade Statistics, 1698–1775* (Richmond, 1984)

Palmer, C, *Human Cargoes: The British Slave Trade to Spanish America* (Urbana, 1981)

Postma, J, *The Dutch in the Atlantic Slave Trade, 1660–1815* (Cambridge, 1990)

Shepherd, V and Beckles, H (eds.), *Caribbean Slavery in the Atlantic World*, (Kingston, 2000)

Solow, B and Engerman, S (eds.), *British Capitalism and Caribbean Slavery* (Cambridge, 1987)

Stein, R, *The French Slave Trade in the 18th century* (Madison, 1979)

Thomas, H, *The Slave Trade* (London, 1997)

Williams, E, *Capitalism and Slavery* (London 1944)

Chapter 7

Beckles, H, *Natural Rebels: A Social History of Enslaved Black Women in Barbados* (New Brunswick, 1990)

Bolland, N, 'Slave Labor and the Shaping of Slave Society: The Extraction of Timber in the Slave Society of Belize', in Bolland, N (ed.) *Struggles for Freedom in Belize* (Kingston, 1977)

Brereton, B, *A History of Modern Trinidad, 1783–1962* (London, 1981)

Dunn, R, *Sugar and Slaves* (Chapel Hill, 1972)

Fraginals, M et al (eds.), *Between Slavery and Free Labour: The Spanish-speaking Caribbean in the 19th century* (Baltimore, 1985)

Geggus, D, 'Indigo and Slavery in Saint Domingue' in *Plantation Society in The Americas* (Fall, 1998)

Goslinga, C, *The Dutch in the Caribbean and on the Wild Coast 1580–1680* (Gainesville, 1971)

Goveia, E, *Slave Society in the British Leeward Islands at the End of the 18th century* (New Haven, 1965)

Greene, J P, *Neither Slave nor Free: The Freedman of African Descent in the Slave Societies of the New World* (Baltimore, 1972)

Hall, G, *Social Control in Slave Plantation Societies* (Baltimore, 1971)

Higman, B W, *Slave Populations of the British Caribbean* (Baltimore, 1984)

Knight, F (ed), UNESCO, *General History of the Caribbean: Vol.3: The Slave Societies of the Caribbean* (Paris, 1997)

Knight, F, *Slave Society in Cuba during the 19th century* (Madison, 1970)

———— *The Slave Societies of the Caribbean* (London, 1997)

Saunders, G, 'Slavery and Cotton Culture in the Bahamas', in Shepherd, V (ed.), *Working Slavery: Pricing Freedom* (Kingston, 2002)

Shepherd, V and Beckles, H (eds.), *Caribbean Slavery in the Atlantic World* (Kingston, 2000)

Sheridan, R, *Sugar and Slavery: An Economic History of the British West Indies, 1626 – 1775* (Kingston, 1994)

Stein, R, *The French Sugar Business in the 18th century* (Baton Rouge, 1988)

Tomich, D, *Slavery in the Circuit of Sugar* (Baltimore, 1990)

Westergaard, W, *The Danish West Indies Under Company Rule, 1671–1754* (New York, 1917)

Chapter 8

Beckles, H, *White Servitude and Black Slavery in Barbados* (Knoxville, 1989)

Harper, L, *The English Navigation Laws* (New York, 1912)

McCusker, M, *The Rum Trade and the Balance of Payments of the Thirteen Continental Colonies, 1650–1775* (New York, 1991)

Mims, S, *Colbert's West Indian Policy* (New Haven, 1912)

Pares, R, Yankees and Creoles: *The Trade between North America and the West Indies before the American Revolution* (London, 1956)

———————— 'The London Sugar Markets , 1740 - 1769', *Economic History Review*, Vol. 4, (1956-7)

———————— *War and Trade in the West Indies* (London, 1963)

Scarano, A, *Sugar and Slavery in Puerto Rico, 1800–1850* (Madison, 1984)

Sheridan, R, 'The Plantation Revolution and the Industrial Revolution', *Caribbean Studies*, Vol. 9, (1969)

Sugar and slavery: An Economic History of the British West Indies, 1623–1775 (Bridgetown, 1974)

Stein, R, *The French Sugar Business in the 18th century* (Baton Rouge, 1988)

Walker, G, *Spanish Politics and Imperial Trade* (Bloomington, 1980)

Watts, D, *The West Indies: Patterns of Development since 1492* (Cambridge, 1987)

Williams, E, *Capitalism and Slavery* (Chapel Hill, 1944)

Chapter 9

Abraham, R and Szwed, J (eds.), *After Africa* (New Haven, 1983)

Bastide, R, *African Civilization in the New World* (London, 1971)

Beckles, H, *Natural Rebels: A Social History of Enslaved Black Women in Barbados* (London, 1989)

———— 'Crop over Fetes and Festivals in Barbados during Slavery', in A Thompson, (ed.), *In the Shadow of the Plantation* (Kingston, 2002)

———— *The Development of West Indies Cricket: Vol.1, The Age of Nationalism* (London, 1999)

Brathwaite, E, *The Development of Creole Society in Jamaica, 1770–1820* (Oxford, 1971)

Craton, M and Saunders, G 'Seeking a Life of Their Own: Aspects of Slave Resistance in the Bahamas", *Journal of Caribbean History*, Vol.24, (1991)

Craton, M, *Searching for the Invisible Man: Slaves and Plantation Life in Jamaica* (Massachusetts, 1978)

Debien, G, 'Les grandes cases de plantations à saint Domingue aux XVII et XVIIIe siècles' in *Annales des Antilles XV* (1970)

Dirks, R, *The Black Saturnalia: Conflict and its Ritual Expression on British West Indian Slave Plantations* (Gainesville, 1987)

Goveia, E, *Slave Societies in the British Leeward Islands* (New Haven, 1956)

Graham, M and Knight, F (eds.), *Africa and the Caribbean* (Baltimore, 1979)

Hall, N, 'Slaves' Use of their "Freetime" in the Danish Virgin Islands' *Journal of Caribbean History*, Vol.13. (1980)

Higman, B, 'The Slave Family and Households: The British West Indies' *Journal of Interdisciplinary History*, Vol.6, (1975).

———— *The Slave Populations of the British West Indies 1807–1834* (Baltimore, 1984)

Kiple, K, *The Caribbean Slave: A Biological History* (Cambridge, 1984)

Mintz, S and Price, R, *An Anthropological Approach to the Afro-American Past: A Caribbean perspective* (Philadelphia, 1976)

Nunley, J and Bettelheim, J, *Caribbean Festival Arts* (Seattle, 1998)

Patterson, O, *The Sociology of Slavery* (London, 1967)

Price, R, *First time, The Historical Vision of an Afro-American People* (Baltimore, 1983)

Shepherd, V and Beckles, H (eds.), *Caribbean Slavery in the Atlantic World* (Kingston, 2000)

Sheridan, R, *Doctors and Slaves, 1680–1834* (New York, 1985)

Simpson, G, *Religious Cults in the Caribbean* (Rio Piedras, 1970)

Chapter 10

Beckles, H, 'An Economic Life of Their Own: Slaves as Commodity Producers and Distributors in Barbados', *Slavery and Abolition, Vol.12, No.1*, (1991).

Berlin, I and Morgan, P (eds.), *The Slaves' Economy: Independent Production by Slaves in the Americas* (London, 1991)

Dickson, W, *Letters on Slavery (1789)*, (Westport, 1970)

Hall, N, 'Slaves Use of their 'Freetime' in the Danish Virgin Islands', in *Journal of Caribbean History*, (1980).

Higman, B, *Slave Population and Economy in Jamaica, 1807–1834* (New York, 1976)

——————— *Slave Populations of the British Caribbean, 1807 – 1834* (Baltimore, 1984)

Kiple, K, *The Caribbean Slave: A Biological History* (Cambridge, 1984)

Mintz, S and Hall, D, 'Origins of the Jamaican Internal Marketing System', in S Mintz (ed.), *Papers in Caribbean Anthropology, No.57* (New Haven,1970)

Shepherd, V and Beckles, H (eds.), *Caribbean Slavery in the Atlantic World*, (Kingston, 2000)

Sheridan, R, *Doctors and Slaves: A Medical and Demographic History of Slavery in the British Caribbean* (Cambridge, 1989)

Thome, J A and Kimball, H, *Emancipation in the West Indies: A Six Month's Tour in Antigua, Barbados and Jamaica in the Year 1837* (New York, 1838)

Tomich, Dale, *Slavery in the Circuit of Sugar: Martinque and the World Economy, 1830–1848* (Baltimore, 1990)

Turner, M (ed.), *From Chattel Slaves to Wage Slaves* (Kingston, 1994)

Chapter 11

Anderson, J, *Night of the Silent Drum: A Narrative of Slave Rebellion in the Virgin Islands* (New York, 1975)

Beckles, H, *Black Rebellion in Barbados: The Struggle against Slavery, 1627–1838* (Bridgetown, 1984)

——————— *Natural Rebels: A Social History of Enslaved Black Women in Barbados* (London, 1989)

Blackburn, R, *The Overthrow of Colonial Slavery 1776–1848* (London, 1988)

Campbell, M, *The Maroons of Jamaica, 1655 – 1796* (Massachusets, 1988)

Corzo, De La Rosa, 'Los Palenqves en Cuba: Elementos para su reconstruccion Historica', in *La Esclavitud en Cuba* (Havana, 1986)

Craton, M, *Testing the Chains: Resistance to Slavery in the British West Indies* (Ithaca, 1984)

De Groot, S, 'The Boni Maroon War, 1765–1793', *Boletin de Estudios Latinamericanos y del Caribe, Vol.18*, (1975).

Dirks, R, *The Black Saturnalia: Conflict and its Ritual Expression on British West Indian Slave Plantations* (Gainesville, 1987)

Gaspar, D, *Bondsmen and Rebels: A Study of Master-Slave Relations in Antigua* (Baltimore, 1985)

Geggus, D, 'On the Eve of the Haitian Revolution: Slave Runaways in Saint-Domingue in the year 1790' in *Slavery and Abolition, Vo.6*, (1982).

Genovese, E, *From Rebellion to Revolution: Afro-American Slave Revolts in the Making of the Modern World* (Baton Rouge, 1979)

Hart, R, *Slaves who Abolished Slavery* (London, 1978)

James, C L R, *Black Jacobins: Toussaint L'ouverture and the San Domingo Revolution* (New York, 1938)

Jones,H, *Mutiny on the Amistad: The Saga of a Slave Revolt and its Impact on American Abolition, Law and Diplomacy* (New York, 1987)

Okihiro, G (ed.), *In Resistance: Studies in African, Caribbean and Afro-American History* (Amherst, 1986)

Paquette, R, *Sugar is Made with Blood: The Conspiracy at La Escalera in Cuba* (Middletown, 1988)

Patterson, O, *The Sociology of Slavery: An Analysis of the Origins, Development and Structure of Negro Slave Society in Jamaica* (London, 1967)

Price, R (ed.), *Maroon Societies: Rebel Slave Communities in the Americas* (Baltimore, 1979)

Scott, R, *Slave Emancipation in Cuba: The Transition to Free Labor, 1869–1899* (Princeton, 1985)

Shepherd, V and Beckles, H (eds.), *Caribbean Slavery in the Atlantic World* (Kingston, 2000)

Shuler, M, 'Ethnic Slave Rebellions in the Caribbean and the Guianas', *Journal of Social History, Vol.3* (1970)

Thompson, A, *Brethern of the Bush: A Study of the Runaways and Bush Negroes in Guyana* (ISER, 1976)

Williams, E, *Capitalism and Slavery* (Chapel Hill, 1944)

Chapter 12

Beckles, H, *Black Rebellion in Barbados: The Struggle Against Slavery, 1627–1838* (Bridgetown, 1984)

——————— *Natural Rebels: A Social History of Enslaved Black Women in Barbados, 1627–1838* (London, 1989)

Blackburn, R, *The Overthrow of Colonial Slavery, 1776–1848* (London, 1988)

Brathwaite, E, *Wars of Respect: Nanny, Sam Sharpe and the Struggle for People's Liberation* (Kingston, 1977)
Bush, B, *Slave Women in the Caribbean during Slavery* (London, 1990)
Craton, M, *Testing the Chains: Resistance to Slavery in the British West Indies* (Ithaca, 1982)
Fick, C, *The Making of Haiti* (Knoxville, 1990)
Geggus, D, *Slavery, War and Revolution: The British Occupation of Saint Domingue, 1793–1798* (New York, 1982)
Goveia, E, *The West Indian Slave Laws of the 18th century* (Bridgetown, 1979)
Hart, R, *Slaves who Abolished Slavery* London, 1978)
James, C L R, *Black Jacobins: Toussaint L'Ouverture and the San Domingo Revolution* (New York, 1939)
Nicholls, D, *From Dessalines to Duvalier: Race, Colour and National Independence in Haiti* (Cambridge, 1995)
Ott, T, *The Haitian Revolution, 1789–1804* (Knoxville, 1971)
Shepherd, V and Beckles, H (eds.), *Caribbean Slavery in the Atlantic World* (Kingston, 2000)
Shepherd, V (ed.), *Women in Caribbean History* (Kingston, 1999)
Thompson, A, *Colonialism and Underdevelopment in Guyana, 1580–1803* (Bridgetown, 1987)

Chapter 13

Anstey, R, *The Atlantic Slave Trade and British Abolition, 1760 – 1810* (New Jersey, 1975)
Blackburn, R, *The Overthrow of Colonial Slavery, 1776 – 1848* (London, 1988)
Butler, M, *The Economics of Emancipation* (Chapel Hill, 1995)
Scott, R, *Slave Emancipation in Cuba: The Transition to Free Labor, 1860 – 1899* (Princeton, 1985)
Shepherd, V and Beckles, H, *Caribbean Slavery in the Atlantic World* (Kingston, 2000).
Williams, E, *Capitalism and Slavery* (Chapel Hill, 1944)

Supportive readings

Beckles, H and Shepherd, V, *Caribbean Freedom: Emancipation in the Caribbean* (Kingston, 2000)
Corwin, A, *Spain and the Abolition of Slavery in Cuba* (Austin, 1967)
Craton, M and Walvin, J, *Slavery, Abolition and Emancipation* (London, 1976)
Davis, D B, *The Problem of Slavery in the Age of Revolution, 1770–1823* (Ithaca, 1975)
Drescher, S, *Econocide: British Slavery in the Era of Abolition* (Pittsburg, 1977)
Eltis, D and Walvin, J, *The Abolition of the Atlantic Slave Trade* (Madison, 1981)
Eltis, D, *Economic Growth and the Ending of the Transatlantic Slave Trade* (Oxford, 1987)
Foner, E, *Reconstruction: America's Unfinished Revolution* (New York, 1988)
Fouchard, J, *The Haitian Maroons: Liberty or Death* (New York, 1981)
Green, W A, *British Slave Emancipation* (Oxford, 1976)
James, C L R, *The Black Jacobins* (London, 1938)
Klein, H, *African Slavery in the Caribbean and Latin America* (New York, 1986)
Higman, B W, *Slave Population of the Caribbean, 1807–1834* (Baltimore, 1984)
Levy, C, *Emancipation, Sugar, and Federalism: Barbados and the British West Indies, 1833–1876* (Gainesville, 1980)
Murray, D, *Odious Commerce: Britain, Spain and the Abolition of the Cuban Slave Trade* (Cambridge, 1980)
Nicholls, D, *From Dessalines to Duvalier: Race, Colour and National Independence in Haiti* (Cambridge, 1995)
Rice, D, *The Rise and Fall of Black Slavery* (London, 1975)
Scott, R, *Slave Emancipation in Cuba* (Princeton, 1985)
Turner, M, *Slaves and Missionaries: The Disintegration of Jamaican Slave Society* (Urbana, 1982)
Ward, J R, *British West Indian Slavery, 1750–1834* (Oxford, 1988)
Williams, E , *Capitalism and Slavery* (Chapel Hill, 1944)

Glossary

abolitionist	someone in favour of ending slavery and who engages in activism to end slavery
alienable property	property that can be transferred from one person to another
alliance	joined in a relation of co-operation
amelioration	the action of making something better; a plan to 'improve' slavery
amnesty	a general pardon
annex	to add a territory to one's existing possessions
appeal	a serious request, usually to the highest court or judicial body
archaeology	the study of human antiquities, usually by excavation
archipelago	a group of islands
aristocracy	government by, or political power of, a privileged class
arson	the deliberate setting on fire of someone's property
artisans	skilled workers, especially manual workers
barracoon	a place where enslaved people were kept, derived from the Spanish word for 'tent'
barter	to trade by exchange
beneficiary	a person who receives or is entitled to receive a favour or benefit
bonded labourers	workers in a state of a bondage, for example, enslaved people
bounty hunters	people who track and catch outlaws
buccaneers	pirates
capital	the money used for carrying on a business; accumulated wealth
capitulation	surrender
catechist	someone who teaches by question and answer, usually in the context of religious instruction
chattel enslaved	in law a chattel is a possession or a piece of property; thus a person owned as a piece of property; the legal recognition of a person as property
chronic	lasting a long time (usually said of a negative condition such as a disease)
civilisation	any developed organisation of human society
colonial/colonising	a colony is a state's overseas dependency, a territory that becomes dependent on another more powerful state and which is exploited economically by the more powerful entity; 'colonising' refers to the activity of acquiring colonies
commercialising	having to do with the buying and selling of goods and services
communal	shared or owned in common rather than individually
compromise	a settlement of differences by mutual agreement
concession	to concede is to yield or grant; a concession is a grant or the thing conceded
concubine	someone, usually a woman, who lives with another without being married
confederation	an association of more or less independent states; the United States of America is a confederation
conquistadors (or conquistadores)	the name given to the Spanish conquerors of Mexico and Peru
conscripted	soldiers who are conscripted are soldiers who are compelled to do military service
consignment	goods on consignment are goods that have been left in trust with someone who has agreed to sell them
conspiracy	a banding together for a purpose, often secret and illegal
contraband	goods that are prohibited or excluded by law
cosmology	the science of the universe as a whole
crop rotation	crops that are not all planted at the same time of the year but at different times during the year
deforestation	the destruction and loss of forested areas, very often as the result of human intervention
demographic	having to do with human population
depopulation	a reduction in the population of a given area or country

deported (or transported)	moved into exile, banished
diaspora	the scattering of a body of people outside their traditional homeland; used originally in the case of Jewish people
diplomacy	the management of international affairs by negotiation; a diplomat is the person who does the managing and an ambassador represents his or her country in another country
displaced	put out of place; displaced people are people who have been put out of the place that is familiar to them
divertissements	a French word meaning 'entertainments'
domesticated	tamed for human use
dynasty	a succession of kings of the same family, or of any powerful family or connected group
El Dorado	a legendary city of gold believed to be on the Amazon; any place which offers opportunities for getting rich quickly
elite	a chosen, or select, or favoured group
emancipation	the setting free from bondage
endemic crude rate of decline	a rate of decline that is habitually present in a certain area as a result of permanent local factors
Enlightenment	the spirit of the European philosophers of the 18th century, with a belief in reason and human progress and a questioning of authority
entrepôt	a commercial centre to which goods are brought for collection and distribution; a hub of economic activity
eurocentric	focused on Europe and european history and culture
expansionism	a policy of expanding a state's territory or sphere of influence
exploit	a deed or an achievement (not be confused with the verb of the same spelling)
free trade	an open and unrestricted trade
garrisoned soldiers	a group of soldiers kept in a fort or town for defensive puposes
genocide	the deliberate extermination of a race or other group
gibbeted	hanged
guerilla	a soldier (male or female) who fights, often unconventionally and in a small band, against a larger, conventional army
holocaust	a complete or large-scale destruction or sacrifice
huckstering	dealing in small articles
humanitarian	motivated by a concern for the well-being of one's fellow human beings
ideology	a body of ideas forming the basis of a political and economic policy
imperialism	the belief in the desirability of acquiring colonies and dependencies
indentured servants	servants bound to their managers by means of a contract; indentured servitude is the condition of being bound in this way
indigenes	native born or indigenous people
industrialising	a country whose economy is not predominantly agricultural but is significantly based on manufacturing and trade
infrastructural	having to do with basic systems and services that allow a society to function, e.g. in modern times: roads, sewerage, telecommunications
insubordination	the refusal to accept a subordinate or inferior or lower-ranking position
insurrection	an uprising or revolt
interloper	a ship or person engaged in unauthorised trading; a person who meddles in another's business
involuntary labour	labour not freely given
King's army	an army that takes its orders directly from the king or that has a special allegiance to the king
latitude	a place of specified angular distance from the equator
liberalise	make more free by removing restraints
lineage	direct line of descent

manifesto	a public declaration
marginalised	pushed to the edges of society
maritime	having to do with the sea and sea-trade
Maroon	a runaway slave
marronage	the act of running away and remaining in more or less permanent flight
martial law	arbitrary power exercised by the supreme authority during a time of emergency, e.g. during a war; derived from Mars, the Roman god of war
material culture	all those aspects of a culture that are material (buildings, clothes, crafts) as opposed to non-material (language, religious beliefs, ideas)
matriarch	a woman who dominates her family or society; a matriarchy is a government by a mother or mothers
matrilineal inheritance	inheritance through the mother or through females alone
mercantilism	a range of policies intended to regulate colonial trade in the interest of the mother country such that the colonies and the mother country form one economy from which foreigners are excluded
mercenary	a hired soldier
merchant class	those people in a society who make a living from trade
metropolitan	from 'metropolis' or 'mother city' pertaining to any large, important city
militia	a body of men trained as soldiers for home service
modernity	a way of life distinct from traditional patterns of living; a time characterised by rapid communications, choice between different lifestyles, complex and varied forms of employment and production
monarch	a sole hereditary head of state like a king or queen
monolithic	literally, a single stone; a state or organisation that is massive and immovable, and very often impersonal
monopoly	the exclusive possession or control of the supply or trade in a commodity or service
mulatto	the offspring of an African and a person of European descent
Neolithic period	the later Stone Age during which humans practised some agriculture, kept domestic animals and used boats, and bows and arrows
nomad	a member of a wandering community
non-conformist	a free-thinker, one who does not conform to a set way of thinking
oration	a formal speech; derived from the Latin word for prayer
pacification	peacemaking
papal bull	an order issued by the Pope
patronage	the support and protection given, for example, by the enslaver to the enslaved
peasant farmer	small rather than wealthy farmers who live on and work the land
perennial	a plant or crop that remains green throughout the year
pioneer	a founder of or an early worker in a particular field; also, an explorer, settler
privateer	a private ship sent to seize and plunder an enemy's ships
profligate	abandoned or given to reckless or wasteful living
propaganda	information, often incomplete or distorted, intended to persuade people to follow a particular course of action
psychic	having to do with the mind or spirit
puritan	a person who wishes to purify religious practice by rejecting unnecessary ritual and tradition and concentrating on scripture as the sole authority; any person who has very strict religious beliefs
racism	the belief that some races are superior to others; discriminatory practice based on this belief
ritual	an often repeated series of actions
royal charter	a formal deed by which a king or queen gives powers and privileges to his or her subjects
sacrificial	giving up or surrendering something of value for the sake of something else

sedition	an offence against the state
skirmish	a small or irregular fight between small parties
sophisticated	complex, refined, subtle; requiring special knowledge and skills
subject race	a race considered to be inferior by other races who wish to dominate it
subjection	the state of being dominated, controlled
subsistence economy	an economy where only what is required to live is produced
sumptuary laws	laws to limit the expenses of food and dress
transcript	a written or printed copy
tribunal	a body appointed to judge a particular matter
tribute	a payment made to another as a sign of dependence
tyranny	absolute power exercised cruelly and, often, illegally
viable	workable
voodoo	African cultural practice often associated with magico-religious elements
wet rot	a rot affecting plants with a high moisture content

Index

appendix | Index